ALCOHOLICS IN RECOVERY

SPIRITUAL AND CULTURAL REVITALIZATION

ALCOHOLICS IN RECOVERY

SPIRITUAL AND CULTURAL REVITALIZATION

Gail Carol

 HAZELDEN®

First published June 1991

ISBN: 0-89486-730-X

Library of Congress Catalog Card Number: 90-82766

Printed in the United States of America.

Editors note:
Hazelden Educational Materials offers a variety of information on chemical dependency and related areas. Our publications do not necessarily represent Hazelden's programs, nor do they officially speak for any Twelve Step organization.

Grateful acknowledgment is made for permission to reprint the following:

The Twelve Steps, Twelve Traditions and other excerpts from the A.A. literature are reprinted with permission of Alcoholics Anonymous World Services, Inc. Permission to reprint this material does not mean that A.A. has reviewed or approved the contents of this publication, nor that A.A. agrees with the views expressed herein.

Excerpts from the A.A. Grapevine are reprinted with permission of the Alcoholics Anonymous Grapevine, Inc. Permission to reprint this material does not mean that the Grapevine has reviewed or approved the contents of this publication, nor that it agrees with the views expressed herein.

Pat and Jack and Austin

Karen and Joe

All my Relations

How do you hold on to that which comes of letting go?
Passing it on is the only way I know.

Contents

PREFACE

This is a study of some of the spiritual ideas, practices and experiences of individuals who are recovering from alcoholism with the help of Alcoholics Anonymous. It is an exploration of their ways of being and seeing; an exploration of what William James describes as conversion—the religious reunifying of a discordant personality. It is a story told primarily by alcoholics in varying stages of recovery who during the initial phase of the research were either (1) residents of Hazelden Foundation's residential treatment program for adults or (2) guests at Hazelden's Renewal Center. It is a story told in prose, poetry, and pictographs.

There are two primary questions considered in this study: What evidence is there to indicate that Alcoholics Anonymous on an organic or organizational level serves as a revitalization movement as identified by cultural anthropologist Anthony Wallace, helping members create a more satisfying culture or way of life? What evidence is there to suggest that the alcoholics in recovery with Alcoholics Anonymous involved in this study experience a transition from a relatively discordant, dualistic way of being in the world to a more harmonious, unified one?

It is concluded that Alcoholics Anonymous serves as a revitalization movement congruent with the universal pattern identified by Wallace, and that participants in this study, as individual members of this movement, find in recovery a deepened awareness of the confluence of often opposed pairs: one aspect of the self and another, self and God or Higher Power, self and others, and self and the world as a whole.

A theoretical model of the nature of the recovery process for those relying on the program and community of Alcoholics Anonymous is set forth. This model is based upon prior direct experience and ideas, research in alcoholism and related fields, the literature and legacy of Alcoholics Anonymous, the stories of the twelve individuals interviewed for this study, and the responses of eighty-eight recovering alcoholics who completed a questionnaire designed to help identify some of the key issues in recovery. Similarities between the pattern that emerges for individuals in recovery from alcoholism and patterns of transformation identified within the larger community are explored.

This work was first published in its unabridged form in 1989 as the author's Ph.D. thesis "Practicing Peace in Recovery with A.A. (Alcoholics Anonymous)." Gail Carol is the author's pen name.

THANKS GIVING

So many have helped me cultivate the seed which has taken the form of the story told here. How do I thank them? Simply typing their names upon a page seems so stingy a way to tell of graciousness and generosity.

There are those at the University of Minnesota for whom I'm grateful. My advisor, David Born, who gently helped introduce backbone into a free-floating space of ideas, offered clear-minded counsel, and was invariably accessible and reliable. My thesis committee members, each of whom teach the presence of the sacred here and now: David Noble in his in vision of transcending time, Gayle Graham Yates in her ardent advocacy of original creative expression, Roland Delattre in his dedication to clarity and details, V. Lois Erickson in her trust of inner voice and vision, Indira Junghare in her unabashed authenticity, Mulford Sibley in his knowledge of the presence of and possibility for peace. Also at the University, Betty Agee, a staunch supporter of all American Studies students, who was always there to listen and to counsel and to guide; her husband Bill who let me solicit volunteers for my study in his American Studies classes; Dennis Coleman; Computer Lab Attendants, especially Brian, Doug, Matt, Joel, and Steve; Phil Furia; Health Ecology Staff; Jean Kilde; George Kliger, Dennis Lien; Russell Littlecreek; Fred Lukermann; the MacMillan Fund; Optimal Growth Team; Millie Richter; James Schaeffer; David Schrott; Margery Sibley; Mary Terpie; Gail Weinberg; John Wright.

There are those at Hazelden Foundation in Center City, Minnesota for whom I'm grateful. From Dr. Daniel J. Anderson, who teaches the joy of sharing mind-and-heart-opening ideas, I first learned of the work of Gregory Bateson, Morris Berman, and Thomas Kuhn. From him, as well as from each of the other officer/administrators with whom I've discussed this work, including Dr. Karen Elliott, Michele Fedderly, Dr. Gordon Grimm, and President Harold Swift, I have felt whole-hearted support throughout this entire process. Among others there who helped with this work in particular are Marilyn Beckman, Jeanne Berg, Betty, Kim Bluhm, Dave Brian, Phil Cavanaugh, Bonnie Cole, Bob Coombs, the Counselor Training People, John Curtiss, Judy Delaney, Jerry Dollard, Hal Durham, Jana Engdahl, Brad Engelbrekt, Wayne Forrest, Joan Frederickson, Joanne Fruth, Ann Gartman, Ted Giermyski, Kathleen Gilmore, Marie Gubbels, Kevin Hilde, Debra Hole, Fred Holmquist, Information Services, chef John, Brenda Johnson, Dave Johnson, Kevin Johnson, Shirley Jones, Nancy Karnes, Sue Keskinen, Judith Korf, Sandy Lachapelle, Michael Langin, Bruce Larson, Marie Larson, Agnes Lee, Tyrus Leffer, Elene Loecher, baker Lois, Dan M., Sister Mary Leo, Damian McElrath, Mike McKee, Lucille Moline, Maintenance Folks, Mike Mott, Marge Nelson, Martha Newman, Carrie Novalany, Lou Obst, Linda Palmer, Peggy Pepper, Art Perlman, the Professional Education Staff, Rehabilitation Staff, Marsha Reichenberger, Research and Evaluation, Research Committee Members, Barbara Reznicek, Rose Richter, Julie Riebe, Dee Riley, Sheri Rud, Lorraine Rue, Mary Ruyman, James Sager, Paula Sanderson, Eleen Schwann, Saul Selby, Ellsa Sorenson, Marie Sower, Rock Stack, Neil Stucky, Steve Susnik, Michelle Thompson, George Weller, Terence Williams, and Ed Yahle. Many more there are friends, and have helped with other projects in the past.

There are others who helped gather, enter, and review the materials in this dissertation. Robin Ciabattari and Deborah Leoni brought Joseph Campbell's work to my attention even before the series of interviews with David Moyers was aired. Ann Conrad, neighbor and legal secretary, just showed up at my cottage door one day and offered to help. She and I together transcribed the tapes from my interviews. Craig Curley commented on the connection between my study and the work of Julian Jaynes. Betty Feilzer helped edit this manuscript with a particularly sensitive eye and ear, as well as provided me with a Twin Cities home away from home. Kathy

Gilmore at Hazelden was an enthusiastic and patient project director. Debra Hole, also at Hazelden, helped shepherd the project, and offered guidance on issues of confidentiality. Julie Bach at Thompson & Company, Inc. helped tighten and clarify the text for publication. Brenda Johnson at the University of Minnesota followed up on the programming and data entry done by Hazelden Research and Evaluation people. Sue Keskinen at Hazelden created the computer program for data entry and analysis of the quantitative portion of this study and helped tremendously to bring order out of chaos. Joanne Kucharcyzk provided me with remarkably comprehensible material on statistical analysis. Joyce M. introduced me to the medicine wheel and Native American ways and works. Carrie Novalany entered much of the data from the quantitative portion of this study. Martha Newman kindly and competently helped administer and distribute the questionnaire designed for this study. Geri Perrault at the University of Minnesota helped edit the first summary of this project. Matt Walsh, also at the University of Minnesota, generously clarified my diagram design, shaded it, and translated it into the first computer graphic version of Illustration E. Matt also computer-scanned my hand-drawn cartoon which preceded the dissertation version of this book.

I am grateful too for those in the professional community who freely shared their time, ideas and experiences with me. Jean Shinoda Bolen, Stephanie Brown, Mark Byrne, John Carpenter, Michael Forman, Anthea Francine, George Gallup, Fran Hartigan, Nick Heyl (Norwich, VT attorney) William Hutchison, Julian Jaynes, Joanne Kucharcyzk, George Kohn, Ernie Kurtz, Lawrence Kohlberg, Greg Martin (pseud.), Frank Mauser, Andrea Mitchell, David Moberg, Martin Murdock, Jacob Needleman, Bill Pittman, Lewis Rambo, Edward Sellner, Steven Tipton, Charles Whitfield, Lois Wilson, Nell Wing are among them. For each of these individuals named there is at least one story of linking. For example, Ernie Kurtz, who was one of the first to encourage me to realize this dream, insisted that I meet with Karen Elliott at Hazelden, who subsequently became an "angel-in-my-life" mentor. Dr. Anderson and Joan Frederickson at Hazelden suggested I contact Bill Pittman, who introduced me to Nell Wing, a rich, reliable and delightful resource person. Nell, in turn, arranged my meetings with Lois Wilson, some of the most memorable experiences of my life. I am particularly grateful to those authors, publishers, and other individuals who generously allowed me to include ideas and passages from their own works, from seminars, and/or our conversations.

I am also grateful for the staff people and supporters of a number of public and private libraries, and for access to their collections. The Alcohol Resource Group Library in Berkeley, California is one such library; others are the College of St. Thomas Library in St. Paul, Minnesota; the Drug Information Services Library at the University of Minnesota; the Graduate Theological Union Library in Berkeley; the Hazelden Foundation Library in Center City, Minnesota; Rutgers' Center for Alcohol Studies Library in Piscataway, New Jersey; the San Francisco Theological Union Library in San Anselmo, California; Sonoma State University Library in Rohnert Park, California, and Baker Library at Dartmouth. I was also fortunate to use the archives of Alcoholics Anonymous in New York.

I am grateful for those at Sonoma State University in California and its Hutchins School of Liberal Studies, which I adopted as my academic home away from home. Les Adler, Francine Cummings, Michel Davidoff, Sally Jensen, Richard Karos, Barbara Koehler, Hector Lee, Dale McCarty, Warren Olsen, Pren Savito, Richard and Ann Zimmer (as well as their friends and children Jessica and Daniel), and Richard's class in Religious Consciousness are among those at Sonoma State who helped with this work.

I am grateful for those who offered personal support and guidance, food, rides and lodging. Amanda, Andrea, Ann, Ann, Annie, Ashley, Becky, Betty, Betty, Bill, Bill, Cal, Carol, Caroline, Carolytn, Casey, Clarice, Cliff, Corrie, Craig, Dana, Daniel, Deborah, Diane, Dorman, Doug,

Duncan, Ed, Edna, Elizabeth, Elizabeth, Ellie, Elsie, Ernie, Estelle, Eunice, Fran, Fran, Fred, Gayle, George, Gin, Hope Street People, Hal, Henry, Howie, Irving, Jack, Jan, Jeremy, Jim, Joe, John, Joy, Joyce, Judith Rose, Judy, Ken, Kevin, Kevin, Kit, Larry, Lisa, Marcie, Marie, Mark, Marlo, Martha, Maureen, Maureen, Maureen, Mike, Mita, Monk, Moses, Nancy, Nancy, Nancy, Normandale People, Northern Arizona Groups People, Paige, Pat, Pat, Pat, Paul, Paula, Peggy, Phoebe, Ralph, Renee, Robin, Salman, Samantha, Sandy, Sister Christine, Sister Mary Charlene, Sister Mary Lenore, Sean, Shawn, Susan, Susan, Syd, Ted, Terry, Tuffy, Twin State People, Vic, Visions People, Wendy, West Marin People, West Sonoma People, Willie, and Woody, are among them. Molly, Allen, and Bob provided me with a home-base in Northern Arizona, and generously offered their home, the use of their MacIntosh SE, companionship and unfailing enthusiastic support. Steve and Judy offered a similar base in South Central Arizona, as did Tess and Dave who tirelessly helped in so many ways. Another friend, Rahn, with his gentle, vibrant rhythm, is among those helping me greet the completion of this book with more joy than sorrow at a difficult passage into new form.

I am grateful too for those who helped transform my doctoral dissertation into this finished manuscript. The President's Fund Committee and donors to that fund helped make this production of my doctoral dissertation possible. Both Linda Peterson, Hazelden's Editor-in-Chief, and Brad Thompson, who was engaged to work on this manuscript, were beautifully open and sensitive advocates of this book and me. They allowed this text to remain true to my original dissertation. When I was feeling crunched with time and money worries, Brad repeatedly reminded me of the book's purpose; during the tedious and time-consuming task of obtaining permissions to use materials from other authors and publishers, he reminded me of the intent—to make explicit some of the connections between the ideas of one source and another. I am also grateful for the elves-behind-the-scenes at Dahl and Curry who worked with Brad to actually produce this text. They with Brad arranged for me to have office space in their building while I was in Minneapolis, thoughtfully went out of their way to help, and with their lively comraderie were a joy to be around.

There is my family of origin too, for whom I'm grateful—my grandmother Mary who was invariably true to herself, did what she felt she was to do, then let go; my first father who died a dreamer; my mother Mary and second father Bill who are and have been always there for me, even during a time of great pain. My aunts and uncles and cousins helped, too, especially Don and Tess and Dave and Betty and Neil and Joe and Steve and Judy who helped specifically with this work.

There are the mythic helpers, as well. Keepers of the watch.

Lastly, and indispensably, there are the recovering alcoholics who joined me in this work—all those in meeting rooms on the East Coast, West Coast, and in the Midwest; those who helped pilot the questionnaire; the eighty-eight who completed the questionnaire designed for this study; and the twelve individuals who let me listen to their hearts. In many ways their story is my own.

For each one who helped, I could tell at least one tale, and often many more, of kindness. How one person would bring me food and juice unasked during my marathon computer engagements at Hazelden, as another would supply me with healing hugs, and another would sing, another hum as they worked on their own tasks nearby. How someone else cut a talking sun out of paper and pasted it on my window-door when I felt dark and cold. How Kevin Johnson and the other dear computer people in Center City endured with me to the end. How Hal Durham and the Renewal folks simply opened their heart and home to me.

All of those mentioned here supported me and the idea of this work. They are representative of the seemingly inexhaustible supply of helpers who contributed to this work. I hereby exonerate them all from the outcome. Or implicate them. Maybe both, as they choose.

Early in my studies, Damian McElrath passed on to me the motto of Taizé, a monastic community in France. *Vivre en Provisoire,* he wrote. Live in the provisional. I still have his note. Maybe the greatest gift to me, which stemmed in large part from this study, is that I am coming to know my higher power as Divine Providence. Each of those listed helped me with this lesson. Each of them teaches abundance.

With some, I wondered out loud how I could ever thank all those who had helped. Thank your Higher Power, they said. Pass it on.

I hurry here
hurry there
worry about this
worry about that

and dreams when they come
visions when they come
myths and symbols
and synchronicities
when they emerge

are clearly havens—

timeless
fear free
gifts
offered
by a thoughtful Lover

seed-gifts
sown
in the ground
of my being

planted in
the field of a
time-worn
neophyte
gardener

one alternately anxious
expectant
digging seeds up
every second or so

or

neglectful
distracted

sometimes
despondent
discouraged
impatient with
their inviolable pace

well

seeds

they may grow

wild

untended

still

still

I can cultivate
the soil of myself
weed the weeds
with willingness

offer space
for seeds
and time

welcome
wind
and
sun
and
rain

then

when

flowers blossom
and there's fruit to spare

reap

and

share

and

sow

PROLOGUE

[A story is told] of a man who found himself at night slipping down the side of a precipice. At last he caught a branch which stopped his fall, and remained clinging to it in misery for hours. But finally his fingers had to loose their hold, and with a despairing farewell to life, he let himself drop. He fell just six inches. If he had given up the struggle earlier, his agony would have been spared. As the mother earth received him, so [we are told], will the everlasting arms receive us if we confide absolutely in them, and give up the hereditary habit of relying on our personal strength, with its precautions that cannot shelter and safeguards that never save.

William James in
Varieties of Religious Experience

There are those among us
who are learning to
live in peace
learning to
walk in peace
and breathe in peace.

They were
profoundly
dis-eased
discordant
destructive
and are learning
to live in peace.

There are those among us
who know
there is more to this world
than meets the eye—
than meets this body's eyes
(well more or less, I guess)

Those who have known
the misery of clinging
of futile attempts to control
by means of personal ego power
singular strength and will alone
those who have entered
through frustration
through exhaustion
through despair
into the way
of letting go

There are among us
those who lost themselves
a while
out there
now beginning to
turn within
now beginning
to learn from within

Those who turn inward
in less fear-filled isolation
than before
detaching now
from superficial sense impressions
learning of
confluence

and of coherence

conscious of
connections at the core

There are those who know
the freedom
the relief
of leaving
lengthy names
and
weighty worldly titles
worldly roles
at doors of meeting rooms

Discovering democracy

Those who have played
so many roles
their roles
have loosed their hold

There are those
who are beginning to
face their shadow-selves
like it or not
and finding their companions
in brighter light

Those
cut off
from family-family
at least a little while

finding
all
to be
Relations

being miles
away from home
and being home

Those for whom nothing
those for whom no one
was sacred
irreverently
finding all to be

xxi

There are those among us
who courted death
in quite uncourtly
fear-filled ways
invited death
to dance
then
stumble-danced away

die now
a daily death
to separate selves

shed sheaths

let go

till nothing's theirs

so all is theirs
to give

and
in the shedding
in the letting go
in emptiness
in openness
in willingness
feeling
light
at last

There are those among us
who know
there is more to this world
than fills the ear—
than fills this body's ears
(well, more or less I guess)

those who hear
and those who honor
soundless sound
in rhythms from the heart

Those learning
simply learning
how to balance
how to bridge
both
sound and sight
and body mind
self and others
self and world
self and Greater Power
God

how to balance
how to bridge
inside and out
past and future
life and death
sky and earth

how to balance
how to bridge
the active and receptive

and in the center
in the stillness
finding breath at last
finding height and depth at last
finding yes at last

Those
finding
peace
at last.

So many of these solitary souls now gather in groups. They are survivors of thwarted Herculean efforts to control one or another facet of their lives. They cluster together under different auspices, meet initially for seemingly divergent reasons. No matter. The fruit is the same: an expanding awareness of themselves in others; others in themselves; a higher greater power in all; a deeper understanding of the coincidence of interests; a dynamic experience of life-sustaining community.

There are many ways of reaching such a point, arriving at a willingness to let go of attempts to control the object world "out there" through the agency of a finite self. There are many ways of waking to the illusion of isolated individualism, separation, and control. There are many ways to discover the depth of our connections with others and with a power greater—infinitely greater—than our exclusive body selves. The way into recovery from addiction to mood-changing chemicals—alcohol and cocaine, marijuana and LSD, narcotics and barbiturates, and tranquilizers of every description—is one such way.

CHAPTER ONE

POLARIZATION
AND THE
IMBALANCE OF PAIRS APART

A STATEMENT OF THE PROBLEM

PART I
OVERVIEW: JUST FOLKS

This book is about a bunch of inveterate branchclingers, much like the one who stumbled off the cliff in the opening story from William James. It is about those who cling to beliefs that their very lives depended on their own unaided efforts. It is about those who let go only when they couldn't hold on any more. It is about those acting as though they are separate and distant from a rather unreliable Higher Power, separate and distant from earth, separate and distant from others in their lives, separate and distant from their very selves. It is a story about recovering alcoholics who, with the help of the Twelve Step program and society of Alcoholics Anonymous, are learning to close those distances through openness and are uncovering connections at the core of life.

It is a story based on the spiritual ideas, beliefs, practices, and experiences of a middle people, though hardly bland people. On a scale reflecting education, income and age, they would fall within a middle range. The participants in this research are all former clients of Hazelden Foundation in Center City, Minnesota. They each identify themselves as alcoholics[1] and report varying lengths of continuous daily abstinence from mood-changing chemicals (with the possible exceptions of caffeine, nicotine, and sugar). The research was done with individuals drawn from two groups. The first group was drawn from Hazelden's primary residential treatment program for chemical dependency; the second was drawn from guests at Hazelden's Renewal Center.[2]

Just as not every single alcoholic physically has a "bulbous enlarged nose, protruding abdomen, sallow or jaundiced skin with dilated capillaries, spider angiomas, scabbing, crusting papules, pustules,"[3] it is not suggested that every single alcoholic would identify with the spiritual portraits shared here. Some alcoholics are females. Some are males. Some are born in February. Some are born in April. Some are introverts, others extroverts, some in the middle. Some alcoholics are or were actively addicted to other drugs as well. Some alcoholics suffer from what are known as process addictions and all sorts of combinations thereof. Some alcoholics are also diagnosed schizophrenic, some manic depressive. Some alcoholics live or were raised in cultures other than mainstream contemporary America. So the stories told here are simply selections from individuals who are part of a much broader, much more heterogeneous worldwide population of individuals recovering from alcoholism with the help of Alcoholics Anonymous.[4]

It is not my intent to claim that Alcoholics Anonymous is the only way to recover from addictions to mood-altering chemicals. There are other ways, a position readily acknowledged by the founders of the movement. Nor is it claimed that everyone who has been introduced to A.A., who espouses a commitment to A.A., or who has attended A.A. meetings recovers—there are many who continue to suffer alone, many who are institutionalized, many who die. Nor do I advocate treatment in general or treatment at Hazelden in particular for all those who have lost control over their use of mood-changing chemicals. According to the most recent A.A. World Service Survey, fewer than half of its members have ever entered treatment. Nor is this in any way intended to speak either for Alcoholics Anonymous or for Hazelden Foundation as separate and distinct organizations.[5]

The spiritual experiences shared here were not shared lightly. Many spiritual experiences may well always remain a purely private matter, to be embraced reverently within. They may be passed on through changes in attitude, changes in behavior. It is possible also to become "hooked" on the experiences as an end in themselves and lose perspective. There is a danger,

3

too, of *comparing* spiritual experiences. Bill Wilson, a co-founder with Dr. Robert Smith of Alcoholics Anonymous, says, "I fail to see any great difference between the sudden experiences and the more gradual ones—they are certainly all of the same piece. And there is one sure test of them all: 'By their fruits, ye shall know them.' This is why I think we should question no one's transformation—whether it be sudden or gradual. Nor should we demand anyone's special type for ourselves, because our own experience suggests that we are apt to receive whatever may be the most useful for our needs."[6] That "God comes to one with a shout, another with a song, another with a whisper"[7] is an awareness beautifully acknowledged in the literature and legacy of A.A.

The experiences shared here are shared in part because, as anthropologist James Curtis notes, expectations play such an important role in perception. According to Curtis, "those who undergo . . . a *'gestalt* switch' . . . experience great tension, for they must find someone to whom they can communicate what they perceive."[8] It is hoped that these stories, as those shared in the A.A. literature, including the book *Came to Believe,* will serve as affirmation and help open the channels of communication if such a need is felt.

This project is not primarily devoted to an exploration of the pathology of active alcoholism but to the promise and experience of some peace in recovery for those who practice the program of Alcoholics Anonymous. This focus is chosen not because the pathology is insignificant (it is integral), but in part because much attention has already been paid to this subject. There are innumerable theories, too, about the etiology of alcoholism along with innumerable investigations as to the physiological aspects of the disease and accounts of various treatment modalities—more or less effective.[9] This entire study is rather exploratory, offered as a contribution to the community's attempt to identify themes which may be important for those in recovery from a frequently and always potentially fatal disease.

As Fritjof Capra notes in relationship to an exploration of a new paradigm (and I believe with cultural anthropologist Gregory Bateson that alcoholics recovering with the help of Alcoholics Anonymous are learning the ways of a new paradigm), we can only look at a limited number of relationships in limited ways. He says, "We *can* look at what seem to be the most important connections, the more potent ones"; we can look for the patterns, for the order; we can look for where "we cut the connections between the whole and the part."[10]

I have chosen to investigate what seem to me to be the most critical connections for alcoholics—the synapses between one facet of themselves and another; between themselves and a power greater than themselves, between themselves and others, and between themselves and the world as a whole. For drinking alcoholics, there are great distances between these apparently polar pairs. Recovery involves reconciliation with them all.

What follows is a story told in prose and poetry and pictographs. It is a story of changing ways of being and seeing and knowing, an exploration of what William James describes as conversion—the religious reunifying of a discordant personality.[11] It is about those who to one degree or another, at one time or another, let go, listened, and lived to tell the tale.

Their tale is worth telling not because they are unique or set apart as a chosen people but rather because their cases are often extreme ones. As Carl Jung noted, it is the extreme cases that can give "an almost exaggeratedly clear view of certain psychic phenomena which very often can only be dimly perceived with the limits of the normal. . . . [It is] the abnormal state [which] sometimes acts like a magnifying glass."[12]

William James, as well as Jung, looked to the "extremer examples as yielding the profounder information. To learn the secrets of any science, we go to expert specialists, even though they may be eccentric persons, and not to commonplace pupils."[13] And alcoholics may well be considered experts in attachment and attempts to control the world out there, experts in the experience of fractured selves, splitting time and space and power into pieces in their minds, and experts at imbalance. William Bateson, a pioneer in the field of genetics, found it was through an examination of "deviations, or morphological disruptions, that one could learn how the organism in question adapted, how it managed *not* to go to pieces."[14]

Their story is worth telling because the pattern which emerges in the lives of those recovering from alcoholism with the help of A.A. may simply be one variation on the familiar theme of mythic quest, as some suggest.[15] As such, it may offer some clues that help "unravel the pattern of modern mythology" which is, in historian David Noble's understanding, the original purpose of American culture studies. Insofar as the sense of separation experienced by alcoholics is likewise experienced by non-alcoholics in the main stream of American society, a study of changes in the culture or way of life of recovering alcoholics may provide insights into the "long-term viability" of the culture as a whole.[16]

PART II
MAZEWAY OF THE LARGER COMMUNITY

Man feels himself torn and separate. He often finds it difficult properly to explain to himself the nature of this separation, for sometimes he feels himself to be cut off from "something" powerful, "something" utterly other than himself, and at other times from an indefinable, timeless "state", of which he has no precise memory, but which he does however remember in the depths of his being: a primordial state which he enjoyed before Time, before History. This separation has taken the form of a fissure, both in himself and in the World. [17]
Mircea Eliade

The ancient Hebrew wisdom of the Kabbalah holds that we are split beings, living in a split world. It teaches that our task in life is to restore to wholeness as many fragments as we encounter along the path of our life. This is the art of being human. The Hebrew word shalom preserves this wisdom in a nutshell: it means not only "peace," but also "wholeness."[18]
György Doczi

These observations offered by cultural anthropologist Mircea Eliade and architect György Doczi speak of the universal nature of the experience of separation in the absence of attention to, acceptance of, and appreciation for the underlying unity. That this is a problem experienced by mainstream modern Americans becomes evident in the work of Robert Bellah, Richard Madsen, William Sullivan, Ann Swidler, and Steven Tipton. I will rely on their work to provide a cultural setting for the ideas and experiences of recovering alcoholics who participated in this study.

In their research and subsequent book *Habits of the Heart,* Bellah et al. inquire about the implications of individualism for American society and culture. They invite us to wonder with them whether our individualism has brought us to the point described by Matthew Arnold where we are

Wandering between two worlds, one dead,
The other powerless to be born.[19]

The authors of *Habits of the Heart* portray two spheres in their study. They refer to one as a culture of separation, the other as a culture of coherence. They are both here in America today.

Their shared citizens are too rarely aware of the intersection of these spheres as part of a still larger world experienced in different ways. They are too rarely comfortable with their dual citizenship and too rarely conversant in the language of coherence, the language of the heart.

CULTURE OF SEPARATION

The culture of separation portrayed in *Habits* is one in which the world "comes to us in pieces, in fragments, lacking any overall pattern. . . ." It is a world in which neither popular nor intellectual culture says anything about questions of meaning. It is a culture associated with *the world,* with *science,* and above all, with *individualism,* and "the modern world's instrumental control." [20]

They characterize the *world* as one of selfishness and immorality, rationality and competition; find that *science* itself is but "a collection of disciplines each having little to do with the others"; and say that the *individualism* is one unrestrained by either community or commitment. It is a culture in which "we are all—[men and women alike] supposed to be conscious primarily of our assertive selves." [21]

In the words of Alexis de Tocqueville, revived for contemporary Americans by the authors of *Habits of the Heart,* the citizens of this culture are "restless in the midst of prosperity . . . with minds which are more anxious and on edge" than the minds of those who live in traditional societies. The citizens of the culture of separation in America, from the perspective of this ninteenth-century French observer, "clutch everything and hold nothing fast." Each citizen is disposed "to isolate himself from the mass of his fellows. . . . They form the habit of thinking of themselves in isolation and imagine that their whole destiny is in their hands. They forget their ancestors," their descendents, and their contemporaries as well. [22] The authors of *Habits* believe de Tocqueville's remarks are an increasingly apt description of modern American society and culture.

CULTURE OF COHERENCE

The *home* or *family, religion* and *community,* associated with what the authors of *Habits* refer to as a culture of coherence, have traditionally been the sanctuary for and source of emotional bonds and all-of-a-piece acceptance. Bellah et al. note that "while science seemed to have dominated the explanatory schemas of the external world, morality and religion took refuge in human subjectivity, in feeling and sentiment." [23] As religion was located in the "affections" [24] according to Jonathan Edwards, so too were family and community.

Not only is there separation within the sphere historically associated with separation, but the values of separation and its cohort, individualism, are penetrating the culture of coherence as well. The *home,* which was once in Tocqueville's mind a "women's sphere" of "peace and concord, love and devotion" now contributes to its members' sense of separation from a public world and is often divided within itself. Those who participated in *Habit's* research expressed an inability "to think positively about family continuity," and in general spoke of a family which was "often not as reliable as they might hope." [25]

Nor was religious life exempt from the societal trend to an increased importance attributed to individualism and separation. Religion traditionally had the political function of supporting *mores* fundamental to democracy. [26] In particular, it had "the role of placing limits on utilitarian individualism, hedging in self-interest with a proper concern for others." [27] But as Bellah and his colleagues tell it, *by the early decades of the nineteenth century, the older communal and hierarchical society was rapidly giving way in the face of increasing economic and political competition, and religious change accompanied social change. Even in the longer-settled areas, ministers could no longer count on the deference due to them as part of a natural elite, while in the newer and rapidly growing western states no such hierarchical society had ever existed. With rapid increase in the numbers of Baptists and Methodists, religious diversity became more pronounced than ever. By the 1850s, a new pattern of religious life had emerged, significantly privatized relative to the colonial period, but still with important public functions.[28] [Increasingly, the] religious and secular realms that had appeared so closely intertwined in colonial America were now more sharply distinguished. Churches, no longer made up of the whole community but only of the like-minded, became not so much pillars of public order as "protected and withdrawn islands of piety."[29]*

Increased separation was occurring not only between the spheres of "the world" and religion, but also within the sphere of religion itself. The authors of *Habits of the Heart* note that religious individualism, which contributes to the separation within the domain of religion, is a familiar theme in American history. They say that

even in seventeenth-century Massachusetts, a personal experience of salvation was a prerequisite for acceptance as a church member. It is true that when Anne Hutchinson began to draw her own theological conclusions from her religious experiences and teach them to others, conclusions that differed from those of the established ministry, she was tried and banished from Massachusetts. But through the peculiarly American phenomenon of revivalism, the emphasis on personal experience would eventually override all efforts at church discipline. Already in the eighteenth century, it was possible for individuals to find the form of religion that best suited their inclinations. By the nineteenth century, religious bodies had to compete in a consumers' market.[30]

Bellah et al. observe as well that this trend to religious individualism, often associated with the alleged "hypocrisy" of institutional religion, has continued. They found mysticism to be a major form of religion in the twentieth century as well as the most common form of religion among those they interviewed.[31] They observed that "one person we interviewed has actually named her religion . . . after herself. This suggests the logical possibility of over 220 million American religions, one for each of us."[32]

The *community*, too, once seen as a haven from a culture of separation, is now, in the assessment of the authors of *Habits of the Heart*, increasingly under its influence. Traditionally the function of *community* was, in the words of John Winthrop, to "knit individuals together in mutual support." This type of community was based on "a universal obligation of love and concern for others that could be generalized beyond, and even take precedence over, actual kinship obligations."[33] The authors of *Habits of the Heart* concluded that today those who do join communities often do so motivated by self-interested individualism. They describe this as a "giving-getting" model which they feel prevails in contemporary American culture.[34]

Bellah et al. do assure their readers that not *all* of those who participated in their study were unable and unwilling to live beyond their own self-interests. They "even talked to some for whom the word *soul* has not been entirely displaced by the word *self* . . . those for whom the self apart from history and community makes no sense at all." They found, however, that these folks were "often on the defensive,"[35] struggling to express themselves, "bereft of a language to transcend."[36]

IMBALANCE BETWEEN CULTURES OF SEPARATION AND COHERENCE

Habits' authors are careful to emphasize that individualism in itself is not the problem. In fact, they believe that individualism lies at the core of American culture, and "a return to traditional forms would be to return to intolerable discrimination and oppression."[37] The problem is rather a problem of imbalance. The authors leave little doubt that here in mainstream modern America, what they call the culture of separation prevails.

The problem is one of imbalance between two extremes within the sphere of religion—mysticism, a form of religious individualism, on one end and cult membership on the other.[38] The problem with mysticism is the lack of community, the lack of a shared context in which to practice and share beliefs.[39] The other extreme within the sphere of religion, cult membership, can be problematic insofar as the individual members are subordinated to group doctrine and practices, and also insofar as cult members set themselves off from others.

The problem is imbalance within the sphere of the family, with all members considering themselves to be the most important member, negligent of their responsibilities to their parents or children and negligent of their responsibilities to siblings.

The problem is imbalance within the sphere of community, with each individual at best seeking to maximize his or her own profits in a contractual relationship with another person, which the authors of *Habits of the Heart* term "therapeutic contractualism." The relationship is one based on expectation of return and considered legitimately terminated if those expectations are not met.

The problem is imbalance between individualism and community. Whether the problem is an imbalance toward community at the expense of individualism, as in Puritan communities in seventeenth-century America, or individualism absent an association with a stable community as among European settlers in seventeenth-century Virginia,[40] the problem is the dichotomy, the either/or. The problem is one of a society which values the two halves of a whole unequally, preferring one and failing to honor the other. The problem is the inability or unwillingness to balance and hold the two equally and simultaneously.

The portrait offered by Bellah et al. of our society today is one characterized not only by a domination of the culture of separation but also an undervaluing and undermining of the culture of coherence, creating an overall imbalance in the culture at large.[41] They feel this trend seems to be "producing a way of life that is neither individually nor socially viable."[42] If it continues in this form, they feel that individualism may "eventually isolate Americans one from another and thereby undermine the conditions of freedom."

OTHER FORMS OF SEPARATION

The express intent of *Habits of the Heart* was to examine the implications of individualism in American society. The authors portray Americans today as individualistic, isolated from meaningful community. In addition to being isolated from community, individuals in modern America isolate themselves and are isolated in other ways as well. Some of the other forms this separation takes are mentioned in *Habits,* while necessarily developed less fully than is the central theme.[43]

Citizens of a culture of separation also experience separation between active and receptive ways of experiencing the world (spoken of in *Habits* as control versus acceptance), separation between themselves and a power greater than themselves, separation between their inner world and outer world, and separation between themselves and time. Other researchers have investigated these different facets of the society of separation described by Bellah, Sullivan, Swidler, Madsen, and Tipton. Representative insights will be included in Chapter 4, as they contribute to the theoretical findings of this study.

Imagine, if you will, how it might feel to live in a state of separation.

A COMMUNITY SPLITTING
SPACE AND TIME AND POWER-CAUSE

Consider if you will
two cultures, side by side

one the place of the intellect
the other affections
one a place of rationality
the other emotionality
one the public world
the other home and family
one the sphere of science
the other religion
one revolving around the individual
the other around community
one a place of competition
the other cooperation
one a place of control
the other acceptance

Imagine
how it might feel
if the culture of
intellect
and rationality
and science
and individualism
and competition
and control
was encroaching on the other

Permeating the other culture
of affection
and emotions
and religion
community
cooperation
and acceptance

Call one a culture of separation
one a culture of coherence
as do the authors of Habits of the Heart

Imagine these two spheres
growing further and further apart
with one expanding
infiltrating
the other seemingly shrinking
in significance

Imagine how it would feel if the values
of self-interested individualism and science
and control
became heavy with self-importance
and the values of community and religion and
acceptance
seemed to fade into air

Imagine a mainstream culture
which began with the Puritans in Northeast
imbalanced toward community
at the expense of individuals
like Anne Hutchinson

an "ethnocentric godly utopia"
in the words of David Noble
a society claiming exclusive rights to God

becoming
imbalanced towards individuals
at expense of community

diversity and more freedom found
community lost

a culture caught in the terrible twos
swinging from one to the other
unwittingly
each with their own form of imbalance
sharing the superficial
imbalance of two over one

Imagine what it would feel like
to live in a place
where males and females alike
were to be conscious primarily
of their assertive selves
as Bellah and friends have found
Even females
who it is said
used to think
of relations
more than separate selves

Imagine how it would feel
if such a culture
scientific and individualistic and rational and
    intellectual
was to influence all others
Leak over into the home and family
religious life and community

Imagine both cultures
separation and coherence
most mindful of assertive selves

With even ancient organs of coherence
less devoted to relations than
to separate selves

Imagine imbalance
in the realm of religion
with the individualism of mystics on one hand
collectivities of cult members on the other
the first cut off from community
the second cut off from culture as whole

Imagine imbalance in community
with individuals bonding in self-seeking ways
contractual relationships
this for that
that for this
harboring merchant mentalities
as Meister Eckhart would say

Imagine imbalance in family
so that
the do-er
the worker
the earner
is more important
than the Elders
than the Children

Imagine a culture
caught
in twos

the dual way of science

dismissing spirit's one

collective expression of science way
male and modern
collective expression of spirit way
female traditional

Imagine what it would feel like to be in a place
    where
male principle prevails

Male way
taking over
as it does

Imagine
how it might feel
if just one culture

modern
male
industrial

were to
dominate
the Earth

• • •

Imagine
a People
upon this land

Imagine them
tipped
out of balance

leaning left
leaning right
tilted forward or aft

with heads thrust upward
or slumped over

A People
wide or deep
domineering or dependent
thin or fat
heavy with the past
or with the future

one minute to the next

a lopsided people
red-and-yellow-and-black-and-brown-
    and-white-skinned whites
male-and-female males

a people out of balance

attached to one half of a pair

rebounding
unwittingly
to the other

Imagine
a People
strangers to
one half of themselves
or the other
feeling vaguely incomplete

those
with minds and bodies racing
in the absence of inner stillness
or sedentary
with inner sparks
sputtering

living hard
with no room for rest
living lazy
void of zest

A People
so constricted
or so loose

from one minute to the next

SPACE

Imagine a People
who favor Sky
to Earth
a people flying
always flying
away

a folk un-rooted
like addicts
always somewhere else
never where they are

always
moving
on

a People
who deny the sanctity of female
defile the sanctuary of their bodies
of their Body
Earth

• • •

Imagine
a people
who value
"I" over "we"
individual
above community

so will not
value family
large or small
young or old

TIME

Imagine
a people who act as if
life and death are split
decades apart

Those who
refuse to grow old

11

refuse to hold
their elders
loathing decay
hide them away

those who clutch youth
to themselves
refuse to grow up
and offer clean space
for their children

A People
who do not honor death
to separate selves
so die of
Egotism
Pride

POWER

Imagine
a place
where
mechanical
is preferred to the
mystical[44]

a
place
where
the linear
the rational
the sequential
the predictable
is valued
and
control
by separate selves
is King

a place
full of people
not yet free
of cause and effect
predictability

unfree of mastery
by separate selves

those who
lose mystery
maybe
and miracles

•   •   •

Imagine
a
main stream People
stuck in
scientific twos
at the apparent expense
of the cyclical
a-rational
a-causal
spirit-one

A People
acting as if
the ancient flow
between
the two of
Science
and
Spirit's one
is constricted

A main stream People
who live loud
with no space for silence
the ground of sound

A People who
devalue night and darkness
the ground of sight

birthplace of dreams

Imagine
a People
who do not honor
female spirit way:

Receptive.

In such a state of separation and imbalance, in the presence of what sociologist Theodore Roszak calls "crazy-making dichotomies," experiences of unity may be relatively rare. Gerald May discusses this possibility in *Will and Spirit*. He observes that while what he refers to as "unitive experiences" apparently occur

> *quite naturally within the lives of human beings regardless of age, culture, personality type, or historical era, [a] good deal of hoopla has been made about them recently due to the renewed interest in spirituality in Western culture. Some hypotheses maintain that so-called primitive cultures are more accessible to unitive experience and that our modern western preoccupations with willful thinking, planning, and doing make us less available or open to such moments. Whatever the reason, unitive experiences seem quite special in our culture, while in others they may be seen as far more ordinary.* [45]

Still, from time to time in the life of a community—whether relatively traditional or modern—when it is inescapably clear that the way of separation, the way of dualism, the way of imbalance, the way of self-will divorced from the greater good, has broken down; when stress and distortion are endemic; when and where experiences of unity have become relatively rare, a community will be open to a new way. The seed of an idea will be planted in the open mind and heart of one or many, and a movement will arise which helps members become reconciled to themselves, their community, and a power greater than themselves and the world as a whole.

Anthropologist Anthony Wallace has studied such cultural-system innovations and refers to them as revitalization movements. He describes such movements as "a deliberate, organized, conscious effort by members of a society to construct a more satisfying culture."[46] He distinguishes such movements from cultural change through "evolution, drift, diffusion, historical change, acculturation" by characterizing the former with deliberate intent and an abrupt shift into a new *Gestalt*.

He says that individuals in what he feels to be "society-as-organism" each maintain a mental image, or mazeway, of their body and its behavioral regularities as well as a mental image of their society and its culture. The mazeway's purpose is to help the individual function in ways that will reduce stress on all levels. Wallace found that a precondition for revitalization is the repeated failure of a mazeway to allow an individual to continue to tolerate his or her stress, along with that person's decision to change the mazeway.

Wallace identifies five basic stages of the revitalization process. The first is what he calls the steady state, in which chronic stress remains within tolerable limits; the second is a period of increased individual stress; the third is the period of cultural distortion during which some persons may turn to "psychodynamically regressive innovations" such as alcoholism, depression, and self-reproach and in which disillusionment with the mazeway and apathy toward the problems of adaptation set in. He describes the fourth phase, the period of revitalization, at length. He notes that this phase is hardly inevitable, and if death resulting from deterioration is to be avoided or postponed, the revitalization movement needs to perform at least six tasks. These tasks of the fourth phase of revitalization include (1) mazeway reformulation and subsequent (2) communication, (3) organization, (4) adaptation, (5) cultural transformation, and (6) routinization. If this stage proves viable, it will be followed by a fifth stage, which he calls a "New Steady State."

One such movement which Wallace tells about occurred in the northeastern part of this continent among the Seneca with the prophecy of Handsome Lake. Handsome Lake's first vision was in 1799, during a period in the life of the Seneca that witnessed the convergence of their traditional culture with a more modern one. Alcohol, previously introduced into the native culture by non-natives, had become a disintegrative force in their community. Many were experiencing "ruinous" consequences associated with its use. Through his vision, Handsome Lake understood that he and his people were to abstain totally from the use of alcohol.[47] As a result of this movement, which is presently known as the *Gaiwiio* or Longhouse Religion,[48] it became possible for members to abstain from alcohol and become reconciled with themselves, with a power greater than themselves, and with the community and the world as a whole.

A similar spiritual solution was offered over a century later to a more heterogeneous and widely dispersed community—a community of other individuals who were experiencing equally ruinous consequences of their alcohol consumption. It evolved into the principles and program, practices and people of Alcoholics Anonymous.

PART III
MAZEWAY OF THE ALCOHOLIC

When an alcoholic applies the Twelve Steps of our recovery program to his personal life, his disintegration stops and his unification begins.[49]

Come then the Twelve Steps of recovery, bringing to him a personality change. The shattered prospect feels reassembled; he now says he seems all one piece. We understand exactly what he means, for he describes the state of being at oneness; he is talking about personal unity. We know he must work to maintain it and that he can't stay alive without it.[50]

We now humbly gaze upon 80,000 miracles of personal recovery [at this convention]. We see that each of us has been enabled by God's grace to achieve the impossible. In each life, unity has risen far above former chaos.[51]

Bill Wilson

Many have written on the problem of separation in the lives of alcoholics. Ernest Kurtz, a historian and student and teacher of American civilization who has thoroughly studied Alcoholics Anonymous, feels that "the most common diagnosis of the source of modern malaise describes that cause as 'alienation' and *anomie*—the feeling of separation and the despairing loneliness of a deeply sensed isolation which, because there are no norms, denies the very possibility of meaning."[52] He feels that this is the malaise of the alcoholic as well as of society as a whole. He observes that a major contribution of Alcoholics Anonymous is that it understands that the alienation comes "from modernity's claim and attempt to separate three aspects of human life and experience that are in reality essentially conjoined—the physical, the mental and the spiritual. The A.A. insight insists first that body, mind, and spirit are so intimately related within each individual that what affects one influences the others." He says that

> *modern individuals seem divided into the distinct categories of those who think but can't feel, those who feel but don't think, and those who act and so have time for neither thinking nor feeling . . . [In the absence of] sensitivity to each of these three components in both self and others . . . alienation occurs—a felt-separation the pangs of which are both two-sided and twofold as they mutually reinforce each other. This destructive mutuality arises because feeling divided within oneself both results in and is intensified by feeling separated from others, while at the same time the felt-separation from others both reinforces and is furthered by deliberate dissection of the self. Feeling "messed up" leads to distance from others, as others' distance encourages "feeling messed up." . . . False separation within the self and destructive separation between selves are mutually related.*

Kurtz finds that "A.A. teaches that the physical, mental, and spiritual components of each alcoholic's individual life are mutually connected. To injure one is to harm the others, and to treat one healthfully is to promote the well-being of all three and so of the whole organism."[53]

Harry Tiebout, a psychiatrist specializing in the treatment of alcoholics, devoted his life to understanding the problem of separation in the lives of alcoholics as well as to the study of what he considers to be the solution of surrender.[54] In the assessment of Ernest Kurtz, Tiebout "published a series of perceptive analyses of alcoholism and of the therapeutic dynamic inherent in the program of Alcoholics Anonymous," which he came to know through his role as personal psychiatrist to Bill Wilson. This dynamic is the dynamic of conversion.

Like Bellah, Madsen, Sullivan, Swidler, and Tipton, Tiebout talks of two worlds. The worlds he describes exist in time as "before" and "after" states in the lives of alcoholics in recovery with the help of A.A. The "before" state described by Tiebout is the one characterized by active alcoholism; the "after" state is the state of recovery.

The first state is one of separation and imbalance. Tiebout says that alcoholics are always at war with themselves and the world around them. He describes the drinking alcoholic as one who develops a personality pattern with a characteristic negative, hostile coloring. This includes a tendency to be "(1) tense and depressed; (2) aggressive, or at least quietly stubborn; (3) oppressed with a sense of inferiority, at the same time secretly harboring feelings of superior worth; (4) perfectionistic and rigidly idealistic; (5) weighed down by an overpowering sense of loneliness and isolation; (6) egocentric and all that implies in the way of a basically self-centered orientation; (7) defiant, either consciously or unconsciously; and (8) walled off and dwelling, to a large extent, in a world apart from others."[55]

Tiebout places particular emphasis on the last of his list of characteristics of the drinking alcoholic. He cites from the case of one of his female alcoholic patients to illustrate this walled-in or walled-off feeling:

> *"Do you know what I was able to do with my mind when I was at the X hospital? I suffered intensely. I did not know why I was there. At night there do you know how I was able to push things aside? I was able absolutely to push things out of my mind. I trained myself and now when anything comes up that I don't like I am going to think about it. I don't want it to get buried. . . ."*

Tiebout compares this process of hers with the burying that is the hardening process in criminals. He notes that later in their relationship this same client volunteered additional information:

> *"I liked things nice in people and nice in myself. I used to want life all sunshine. Now I know it is neither all good nor all bad. I could not make sense about drinking and my bad self so I built up a wall . . . I was proud of walling myself off from any hurt . . . I was a wall within a wall . . . I can't tell you this release of feeling. Before I was disjointed, suspended in mid-air. Now my voice is expressive and I use gestures."*[56]

The imbalance here is an imbalance in which the individual is separated from an unwanted aspect of himself or herself, separated from the community, separated from a power greater than himself or herself and from the world as a whole. The dynamic of this imbalance is a constant swing between attempts at mastery and feelings of total powerlessness.

In terms of the alcoholic's relationship with the self, Tiebout notes an imbalance toward the activity of control and resistance over receptivity and acceptance. He says the drinking alcoholic "brooks no control from man or God. He, the alcoholic, is and must be master of his destiny.

He will fight to the end to preserve that position."[57] What Tiebout found in recovery was a "striking alteration in the prevailing feeling tone." He quotes one of his alcoholic patients as saying "in words that were reminiscent of (Bill) Wilson's in his spiritual experience, . . . 'I feel wonderful but not like I do when I've been drinking. It's very different from that; I feel quiet, not excited and wanting to rush around. I'm more content to stay put, and I don't think I'm going to worry so much. I'm relaxed, yet I feel better able to cope with life now than I ever did."[58] In recovery, aggression, either "active or passive," diminishes. For example, one of his patients said she was less inclined to demand that things be "thus and so."[59] Another patient says "will-power to dominate has left. That seemed to be part of my structural make-up."[60] Tiebout notes the related presence of a perfectionistic attitude in the drinking alcoholic. He says that "one of the most striking and at the same time most illuminating changes brought about by the conversion experience is the loss of perfectionistic and idealistic strivings and with their departure, the disappearance of the problem of guilt." He refers to one of his patient's statements to explain this phenomenon: "Before I always knew what I did right and wrong. I would always be trying to live up to ideals. . . . Now I know I have been doing right and wrong all my life but I don't have to be virtuous about being good or guilty about being bad."[61] Tiebout says his patients in recovery have a "live and let live" attitude toward themselves. "They no longer drive themselves so vigorously nor criticize themselves so harshly, which results in the disappearance of the perfectionistic tendency with its idealistic overtones. They not only become gentler with the world but gentler with themselves."[62] While drinking, there was a battle between one aspect of the self and another, which in recovery gives way to greater peace.

In terms of the imbalance toward the individual and away from a Higher Power, Tiebout says that "religion by its demand that the individual acknowledge the presence of a God challenges the very nature of the alcoholic. . . . *If* the alcoholic can *truly accept* the presence of Power greater than himself, he, by that very step, modifies at least temporarily and possibly permanently his deepest inner structure and when he does so without resentment or struggle, then he is no longer typically alcoholic."[63] He provides an explanation given by one of his patients: "I have a different feeling about God. I don't mind the idea of Some One up there running things now that I don't want to run them myself. In fact, I'm kind of glad that I can feel there is a Supreme Being who can keep things going right. I guess maybe this is something like that spiritual feeling which they talk about. Whatever it is, I hope it stays, because I've never felt so peaceful in all my life."[64] During drinking, there is a battle with and/or denial of any greater power, which in recovery gives way to acceptance of a power source greater than the finite self and consequently to greater peace.

In terms of the imbalance toward a greater valuing of the self, and a relative devaluing of others, Tiebout again provides examples from his patients which he feels are representative of alcoholics in general. He says one patient was "literally unaware that other souls existed except insofar as they affected him. That they, too, might have separate existences, similar yet different from his, just never had taken on the aspect of reality." One of his patients said that she always expected other people in her life to "take *me* into consideration. I wanted complete understanding. . . . I was critical, not understanding."[65] Tiebout says of one of his recovering alcoholic patients, "New insights illuminated his previous relationships with people. He remarked,'Do you know, I'm beginning to feel closer to people. I can think of *them* sometimes. And I feel easier with them, too. Maybe that's because I don't think they're fighting me, since I don't feel I'm fighting them.' "[66] Tiebout feels alcoholics in recovery can see themselves in relation to the world and have "no further need to dominate and to fight to maintain that domination. [They] could relax and take things easy."[67] According to Tiebout, "the problems of inferiority and superiority drop out and in their stead patients think and feel in terms of 'live and let live,' a state of mind which permits them to accept the difference of their fellows from them."[68] In recovery, "they can really like people and be tolerant of them, even if they know much about them which once would have kindled strongly hostile attitudes."[69] While drinking, the alcoholic found his or her own interests in conflict with others; in recovery, there is an increased appreciation of complementarity.

In terms of their relationship with the world as a whole, Tiebout says defiance is the dominant feeling-tone of the alcoholic: "Defiance and the projections which produce and maintain it are to be found in case after case. The sequence typically seems to be inner hostility which becomes, when projected, outer hostility against which the wall of defense is erected. Then since the hostility has become placed in the outside world, the patient defies that world to do its worst. It is the defiance of the world with its array of fact, order, law, and reason which makes the alcoholic display such peculiar logic. He is forever creating straw men in his environment and then getting defiant and being abused by their existence."[70] In recovery, "the disappearance of this inner barrier to effective relationship with the outer world" gives way to "increased self-reliance, self confidence, a real willingness to trust one's own feelings." This breakthrough results, in the words of one of Tiebout's patients, in a feeling that "now I can function in this world, being a part of it."[71] This increased feeling of being a part of the world rather than apart from it is evidenced in the following patient's comment about time: "About working—it is amazing. I am doing sewing, not painstaking like it used to be. I am making kimonos for Agatha (her grandchild). It's just part of work. I start something and find myself very much occupied doing it. I don't feel it is a chore."[72] Tiebout believes that the central effect of Alcoholics Anonymous "is to develop in the person a spiritual state which will serve as a direct neutralizing force upon the egocentric elements in the character of the alcoholic." Instead of defiant individuality, the person can live "in peace and harmony with and in his world, sharing and participating freely." He says Bill Wilson called his spiritual experience "a great synthesizing experience in which everything for the first time became clear to me."[73] The conflictual relationship with the world during active addiction to alcohol gives way to a relatively complementary and peace-filled one in recovery.

•

From time to time in the life of an individual, when it has become unavoidably clear that the way of separation, the way of self-will divorced from the greater good will no longer work, there may be an instant of openness to a new way. Just as Wallace described such occurrences in the life of a community, Tiebout describes such times in the lives of individuals recovering from alcoholism with the help of Alcoholics Anonymous.

Whether for communities or individuals within those communities, this point of exhaustion when it is clear that the old mazeways have failed is what Gene Wise refers to as a pivotal moment. It may be followed by still further deterioration and death, or may become a transformative experience. In Tiebout's opinion, the subsequent direction is contingent upon a willingness to surrender. For alcoholics, surrender means they "gave up the battle and surrendered to the need for help . . . [entering] a new state of mind."[74]

Tiebout describes a "fundamental psychic occurrence" that takes place when an alcoholic responds favorably to the society of Alcoholics Anonymous. He calls such an occurrence *conversion*. As a result of this change, he says, the person loses "his tense, aggressive, demanding, conscience-ridden self which feels isolated and at odds with the world, and has become, instead, a relaxed, natural, more realistic individual who can dwell in the world on a 'live and let live basis.' "[75] Tiebout says that the most striking change may be in the loss of isolation and loneliness:

> The alcoholic patient does not feel merely isolated and alone; he feels that he actually exists in a world apart from other people and that something almost tangible keeps him from any deep human contact. Variously he calls this almost tangible something a wall, a shell, a barrier. One patient dreamed of it as a moat between himself and the world.[76]

He goes on to say that

> the breaking through of the wall by the patient does something more than bring the patient closer to life. It actually makes him feel freer to meet life. More than the patient has ever realized, the wall has acted to give him a sense of being confined and restricted.

> When the wall suddenly melts as in a sweeping personality turnabout there develops a peculiar phenomenon which people conversant with religion refer to as "a release of power." By "release of power" they are trying to describe a sensation of freedom and inner strength which comes when people find themselves liberated or released from the confines of their psychological wall. This state of ecstasy, for that is what it is, represents, therefore, a time when the individual is at least momentarily able utterly and without reservation to identify himself with his environment, to unite himself totally and without hostility to all that goes on about him. Conflict, tension, doubt, anxiety, hostility, all dissolve as though they were nothing and the individual discovers himself on an exalted plane where he feels he is in communion with God, man, and all the creative forces of the universe.[77]

Tiebout believes that "the ecstatic type of conversion does not fall to many people. The more common conversion experience comes about gradually." In either case, it is accompanied by "the disappearance of this inner barrier to effective relationship with the outer world."[78]

Imagine that the natural world is at peace. It is we who are afflicted, conflicted, doing battle with ourselves in a thousand guises. Imagine, if you will, what it may be like to be an alcoholic.

ALCOHOLICS SPLITTING
SPACE AND TIME AND POWER-CAUSE

Imagine
for an instant

from the safety
of your sacred self

Imagine
with your mind
in your heart

Imagine
yourself
out of balance
off center

swinging
from the way of the one
to the way of the two

sliding

back and forth
in endless figure eights
from one loop to the other

feeling bewildered

Distrusting
dismissing
one side of the swing
clinging to the other

rebounding unwittingly
as homeostasis is threatened

On the surface
the one in twos
the polar pairs

down under
gut level
the whole

Wonder
if you will
about
this primal pair

way of the two
way of the one[79]
appearing legions and light years apart
the distance of
space and time and power apart

a distance
apparently
unbridgeable

the distance
of differences
apart
the distance
of inequality
apart

Imagine
longing for the one
wondering
how that fits with
what you see
what you hear
what you do

Unable to hold the two
both two and one

with
two and one
the polar pairs
in conflict

unreconciled

Imagine
the pain
of separation

Imagine
the depth
of the longing
for peace

Try if you will
to imagine
finding
a temporary truce:
alcohol. Maybe other drugs as well.

Seemingly solvents

masculine way to the feminine

Seeking return
to that moment
those precious moments
that resting place
when boundaries dissolved
and you belonged

A part of all and
all a part of you

Finding instead
greater conflict

Imagine
trying to recapture that time
those precious times
you were out of it—
out of time
the world of the two

trying to
recapture the time
you manipulated it

slowed time down
or sped it up
until it stayed still
dissolved
and
distance collapsed

Imagine
the suffering
of rebound

a return to
the two

the splits

the splinters
the separations
of sober states
with each time
rifts
wider
deeper
longer

One piece here
another there
one piece now
another then

Knowing gut deep
we are one

Imagine
what it's like
when you act
as if
space
and time
and power-cause
is split

•   •   •

SPACE AND TIME AND POWER SPLIT: SELF FROM SELF

Imagine acting as if
space
and time
and power's split
into pieces
of you
and them
and world
and maybe god

Imagine
some of the ways
you are divided
within yourself

SPACE SPLIT: SELF FROM SELF

Imagine
being
out of balance

acting as if
the place inside of you is split
into head and body
brain and heart

favoring one
distrusting the other

Imagine
the denial
the deceit
involved in
the separation

Imagine the
destruction
that follows from
acting as if
your body is an object
apart from you

believing somehow
that if
you kill your body
you can free your mind

Imagine
pouring poisons
in you

punishing
your creature body self
with its ceaseless demands
insatiable appetites

seeking
release
from
the pain of
pretense

relief from belief
in the bondage of

body's barriers

yearning to fly

Determined
to die
to separation

afraid
of loosing
yourself

afraid
of losing
yourself

Imagine
living
in your head
with body
heart
and feelings
dead
or dying

in their wake
only
some vague sense
of being unreachable

acting unteachable

believing one way inside
behaving another out there

Imagine
acting
split in space.

Imagine
splitting space.

Imagine
blaming
yourself.

TIME SPLIT: SELF FROM SELF

Imagine
acting as if
time
is split
apart from you
and split
inside
itself

living in an
impotent
"if only"
or maybe
in the future
with tomorrow
soon enough
for change

knowing
only
an absent present

past and future
tyrants
with
no rest
no equilibrium
in the clear space
of present center

generational
here and now

losing the moment

Imagine
space
and time
and power's split
into life and death divorced

the distance of years and years and years apart

with birth the beginning of past

death the end of future

plunging into both

withdrawing

afraid
to take
a chance

Knowing nothing of
daily death
to separate selves

Imagine
acting
trapped
in
time.

Imagine
blaming
yourself.

POWER SPLIT: SELF FROM SELF

Imagine
acting as if
power is split
within you

there is good you
and bad
acceptable and not

Imagine
fearing
that to be loved
you've got to be
all good
really gooey

distancing
yourself
from bad
burying it in the body

yours or ours or someone's

tying it in knots

tightly

containing it in
constricted spots

Imagine
driving and driving
pushing and pushing
trying
to make
things
happen

your way

Quick

Leaving
no room
for receptivity

no space for slow

Imagine
acting as if
there is only one way

the way of
power
force
control
by isolated selves
knowing nothing of the
grace of powerlessness

only the pain

Imagine
acting as if
power is split
within you.

Imagine
splitting

22

power

Imagine
blaming
yourself.

SPACE AND TIME AND POWER SPLIT: SELF FROM OTHERS

Imagine
acting as if
space
and time
and power's
split
into
you
and them
and they
are split within.

SPACE SPLIT: SELF FROM OTHERS

Imagine
acting as if
there is no you in them
or them in you

they are there
and you are here

alone

knowing that you are unique
sure that no one else is

Imagine
feeling
set apart
in space

acting aloof

Imagine
blaming
Them.

TME SPLIT: SELF FROM OTHERS

Imagine
resentment
and expectation
controlling
how you are
with Others

so past and future
decree
the way it always was
will be

Imagine
blaming
Them.

POWER SPLIT: SELF FROM OTHERS

Imagine
acting as if
power's split
between me and them
and they are split
in good and bad
friends and foes

Imagine
power's split
into good and bad
distancing yourself from bad
being afraid
to find it
within

driving it out
along with beauty

unrevealed

leaving a void

seeing both
reflected in
your sisters
and your brothers
fathers or mothers
sons and daughters

shoving them or
blaming them
or running away
when you glimpse
your defects

chasing after
clutching them
devouring them
when you glimpse
your beauty

one way or another
empty still

Aching
to be filled
aching
to be filled

hungry to be held

Incessantly
demanding
more

receiving nothing

Imagine believing
power's split
into you and them
so that
they cause you
or you cause them

you are
master
you are
servant

aggressor
victim

swinging
from one
to the other
and back again

unbeknownst to you

with
no rest
in the free space
in the equilibrium
of equality

Imagine
acting as if
you have male traits
without female
or female
without male
and
males do this
females do that

without rest
in the equilibrium
in the free space
of androgyny

Imagine
blaming
Them.

SPACE AND TIME AND POWER SPLIT:
SELF FROM HIGHER POWER GOD

Imagine
acting as if
space and time and power-cause
is split
between you and a Higher Power God
and God is split within.

SPACE SPLIT: SELF FROM HIGHER POWER GOD

Imagine
wishing
you could believe
there is a god
on earth

being greedy for god
making your own
in multiples

hoarding them

then
with you
as God-maker
mistaking
your separate self
for God

Taking up the slack
until you're sure
that you alone
are powerful

no need
at all
for a greater power
God

Imagine
acting as if
God
is
there not here
or here not there
here in beliefs but not there in behavior
here in my way not there in theirs

Imagine
blaming
God.

TIME SPLIT: SELF FROM HIGHER POWER GOD

Imagine
acting as if
God is then
not now

At birth
maybe
or death
but rarely
maybe
never
inbetween

possibly
at baptisms
or funerals

Sunday morning
after the newspaper
during church
but not in the supermarket for sure
or at the bank.

Imagine
acting as if
God is either
creative or destructive
male or female
up or down.

Imagine
blaming
God.

POWER SPLIT: SELF FROM HIGHER POWER GOD

Well
if there is a God
right here and now
unlikely as it seems

this God'd have power
or you would
God'd make you do that
or you'd make God
with threats and bribes
embroidered entreaties
for this favor or that

Wills at war
without the peace
of tuning
small self will
with Spirit's

Imagine
blaming
God.

Imagine
acting as if
God is split

Imagine
splitting God

Imagine
feeling apart
from God.

Imaging
blaming
Higher Power God.

SPACE AND TIME AND POWER SPLIT:
SELF FROM WORLD

Imagine how it might feel
if you split yourself
from the world
and split the world
in space and time and power cause.

SPACE SPLIT: SELF FROM WORLD

Imagine
acting as if
there's a world out there
apart from you
a world full
of that which you lack
and you crave
that which you lack and you fear

Feeling pulled toward your cravings
repulsed by your fears
from one minute to the next

Imagine
trying to hold
the things you want
together

hold
every item
in place
with you
at center

askew

Trying to hold off
all the things you fear

singlehandedly

Being
caught
in the attachment of
attraction and
aversion

Imagine
the burden
of it all.

Imagine
blaming
the World.

TIME SPLIT: SELF FROM WORLD

Imagine
acting as if
time is split
apart from you
and split inside itself

Time is
somewhere in the world out there
spliced
into seconds
minutes
hours
days and
weeks
and months
and years and years

Imagine
time out there
stretched out
in space
in rigid rows
of past at left
to future right

Imagine
feeling
tense with hurry
tight with worry

Imagine
living
in taut time

with power
power packed in the past
with the habitual—
profane ritual

power packed in future
with the predictable—
the future trapped in past

Imagine trying
to manage time
out there

to slow it down
or speed it up
until it stops

Imagine
living in
digital time
kronos time
line time

knowing nothing of
timelessness in the round
except a tantalizing taste or two
in drugged states
or endless days and nights

an inauthentic now

Knowing nothing
of the central space
of kairos
pregnant moments

child of
timelessness and time

Imagine
blaming
the World.

POWER SPLIT: SELF FROM WORLD

Imagine
acting as if
the world
is split
in good events
and bad

Imagine power's split
so that
circumstance
causes
you
or you

cause circumstance

cause is here
effect is there

never in fullness
of union

believing that
if any change is to be made
it has to be made
out there

Imagine
being
caught
in
control

Imagine
blaming
the World.

SPACE AND TIME AND POWER SPLIT
IN SELF AND OTHERS, GOD AND
WORLD

Imagine believing
space and time and power's split in
bad and beautiful you
and them and you and
god and you and world

They make you
or you make them
God makes you
or you make God
the world makes you
or you make it

experiencing the
see-saw
of wills
at war

Imagine
trying to make things happen

failing
trying to make people do what you want
failing
trying to blot out awareness or sharpen it
failing
longing to love
feeling unable
longing to be loved
feeling unfilled

Trying to free yourself
unaided
from patterns of the past
and fears of future

Imagine
the
burden
of it all

Imagine
being
so tired
from
endless effort

not
even
caring
any
more

• • •

Imagine
what it's like to
be an alcoholic

living in your head
untrue to your heart

Imagine
finding
a program
a people
a way of life

which help you balance
your assets with your defects
yourself and others

your self and Higher Power God
yourself and the world as a whole

Imagine
finding
a way
to help you
balance

power on with power off
the form with formless
now with then
and space and time and power cause

finding
a program
a people
a way of life
which help
you
unclog
the pathway

discover
connections

between

one and another

Finding

a program
which helps
you discover
the power of wholeness
the joy of fullness

Finding
the place
where
space
and time
and cause
converge

a place where
sacred is here
and there
and now
and then

again

Imagine
being
actively alcoholic

Finding
A.A.

PART IV
QUESTIONS TO BE CONSIDERED

The world consists of darkness and light. I can master their polarity only by freeing myself from them by contemplating both, and so reaching a middle position. Only there am I no longer at the mercy of the opposites.[80]

Carl G. Jung

To integrate, unify, make whole, in a word to abolish the contraries and reunite the parts, is in India the royal Way of the Spirit.[81]

Mircea Eliade

It is the intent of this study to identify some of the polarities, or opposing pairs, experienced by alcoholics in this study and to discover whether or not these opposing pairs become relatively reconciled for them in recovery with the help of Alcoholics Anonymous. The primary questions addressed are these:

(1) What, if any, evidence is there to indicate that Alcoholics Anonymous serves as a revitalization movement as described by cultural anthropologist Anthony Wallace, helping members create and accept a more satisfying culture or way of life?

(2) What evidence, if any, is there to indicate that the recovering alcoholics/addicts who participated in this study report a less dualistic, discordant culture or way of life in recovery than they did while actively drinking?

PART V
CLARIFICATION OF TERMS

For our purposes here, culture will be considered simply as the way of life of a people. Kai Erikson in his study of a flood and its effect on a community in Appalachia explains this clearly. He says that

> when one talks about the "way of life," or "ethos," of Appalachia or Norway or any other place on earth where people seem to share a distinctive style of life and thought, one is talking about culture. The term itself has come to mean so many things to so many people that it is hard to supply a crisp working definition, but it is used through the social sciences to refer to those modes of thinking and knowing and doing that a people learn to regard as natural, those beliefs and attitudes that help shape a people's way of looking at themselves and the rest of the universe, those ideas and symbols that a people employ to make sense of their own everyday experiences as members of a society. On the face of it, at least, one would think this definition broad enough to handle almost any conceptual emergency, since all it really means is "the way a people live."[82]

The people who compose the community considered in this study are alcoholics who at least have in common what Dr. Daniel J. Anderson refers to as a "repetitive, maladaptive, stereotypical pattern of behavior"[83] associated with their use of alcohol.

In this work, I use the phrase "the way of the two." By this I mean a dualistic or scientific way characterized by (1) dichotomous thought patterns and related splitting of subjects from objects, (2) perceived need for change, (3) resistance, and (4) the way of control.

I also use the phrase "the way of the one." By this I mean a unified or spiritual way characterized by (1) awareness of unity beneath surface variety, (2) belief that all is well, (3) acceptance and receptivity, and (4) the way of letting go.[84]

The way of the two will be considered as a state of separation which is inherently discordant; it lacks attention to, acceptance of, and appreciation for the unity. This state of separation, which characterizes a scientific way of relating to the world *in the absence of attention to, acknowledgment of, and appreciation for the underlying unity,* is inherently an imbalanced state. A discordant world environment will be considered as one in which an individual perceives his or her world as consisting of apparently unrelated events or processes, a world fragmented by conceptual splits in space, time, and power or causation. The dualistic way includes the dualism between the one and the two; the unification includes reconciliation of the one and the two, and the ability to hold either or both as appropriate. An inclusive, unified environment will be considered as one in which apparent dualities, dichotomies, binarisms and/or paradoxes come to be seen as what Ralph Waldo Emerson called a "bipolar Unity." Each pair may overlap or interconnect with others.

A yogi explains the distinctions between the way of the one and the way of the two:

> *Science looks from the point of view of emptiness and imperfection. Spirituality looks at things from the point of view of perfection and fullness. When you look at things from imperfection, only then can they be improved. Science provides the bed; spirit provides with sound sleep. Science deals with an attitude that depends on duality. Spirituality looks at things from the point of view of unity. Separation is a must for scientific growth and understanding. Unification is a must for real mystical experience. The core of science is in non-acceptance. Resistance is the core of science. The core of spirituality is acceptance. There needs to be a balance—a very subtle balance is required. Science cannot function without a doer. In spirituality, you lose the doer and become the seer. Without science, mankind is lame. Without spirituality, mankind is blind.[85]*

The terms "active" and "receptive" are used throughout in association with the way of science and the way of spirit respectively. Active is here meant not necessarily as physically active, but rather as activation of self-will, mental activity, or rumination. Receptive is not meant as simply passive, but rather as open, willing, accepting. While activity is considered here in association with the male principle and receptivity with female principle, it is not intended to imply that these are the exclusive characteristics of these principles.

For our purposes, the relative cohesiveness of a respondent's world view will be indicated by their self-reports in (1) responses to interview questions intended to explore the reconciliation of perceived splits and (2) responses to a primarily quantitative questionnaire designed for this study.

The term "religion" will be used in three ways. One way is as small "r" religion. As such it will be considered as Steven Tipton used the term in his book *Getting Saved from the Sixties*—religion "in the literal sense that [it] binds together heretofore disparate elements."[86] Vine Deloria describes well what I mean by this when he says that religion "is a force in itself and it calls for the integration of lands and peoples in harmonious unity."[87] Tiebout describes religion as an "emotional force."[88] He says "too often religion has been identified with its dogma and not with its essence of spirituality. It is not the form which religion takes, it is its function in achieving a frame of mind which is significant."[89] The second way I will use the term "religion" is as a state of being associated with the affections, emotions or feelings. According to Bellah et al., Jonathan Edwards reportedly saw religion as "located in the 'affections.' "[90] The third and least frequent reference will be to capital "R" religion, by which I mean organized, institutional religion associated with particular dogmas and rituals.

Throughout, it will be assumed that active addiction in general is (1) an extreme form of attachment to that which is perceived of as desirable and lacking, coexistent with (2) an extreme form of detachment or alienation from that which is considered undesirable. Both are simply different forms of attachment—the first form attraction, the second form aversion. Both are based on subject–object splits, or dichotomous thought in the absence of attention to the underlying unity.

Alcoholism in particular will further be considered, as a storyteller in *Alcoholics Anonymous*, fondly known as The Big Book, describes it, "as a state of being in which the emotions have failed to grow to the stature of the intellect."[91] Emotions will be associated with the realm of religion, intellect the province of science. An alcoholic will be considered as one "who cannot predict with accuracy what will happen when he [or she] takes a drink."[92]

PART VI
PREMISES

The distance between one aspect of self and another—as the distance between self and Higher Power, self and others, self and the world—is an eminently collapsible one. We create it, we can dissolve it, we can create it once again, according to the need or circumstance. We can do this. Separate selves can not. As separate selves we are incomplete; therefore we search for what we feel we don't have but want and are attached through attraction, and we find what we fear to be and are attached through avoidance. Attached states are dependent ones. Matthew Fox notes that the German word that fourteenth century mystic Meister Eckhart uses for attachment means ownership. In an attached condition we own or are owned one minute to the next. As Jung says, "As long as we are still attached, we are still possessed." As long as there is other, there is a fear that we may *not get* what we want and we may *get* what we don't want. We barter to get one and avoid the other. Our relationships are invested with what Eckhart calls a "merchant mentality" and all such relationships are unfree.

As long as we are in time, there is a purpose for each of us. There is a universal blue print. It is extraordinary. Each being has its place. We have distinct tasks as separate selves and as peoples and as nations. And we have shared tasks as well—to love, to listen, and to tell our truth.

There is a story told by Houston Smith in *Religions of Man*. He says that "In Toaist perspective even good and evil lose their absolute character. The West, encouraged in the last few centuries by puritanism, has tended to draw categorical distinctions between the two. Toaists are seldom this positive. They buttress their reticence with the story about a farmer whose horse ran away. His neighbor commiserated only to be told,

> *"Who knows what's good or bad?" It was true. The next day the horse returned, bringing with it a drove of wild horses it had befriended in its wanderings. The neighbor came over again, this time to congratulate the farmer on his windfall. He was met with the same observation: "Who knows what is good or bad?" True this time too: the next day the farmer's son tried to mount one of the wild horses and fell off breaking his leg. Back came the neighbor, this time with more commiserations, only to encounter for the third time the same response, "Who knows what is good or bad?" And once again the farmer's point was well taken, for the following day soldiers came by commandeering for the army and because of his injury the son was not drafted.[93]*

So this is a story about members of a particular community, separated perhaps in time and space, recovering from active addictions together, with the help of a unique and universal movement. It is about one community making the transition from a way of being in the world based on a belief in separation, to a way of being in the world based on an awareness of an underlying coherence. It is about a community learning to balance the way of scientific twos with spirit's one. It is about a community of people who are finding their old world to be dead, their new world born in powerlessness. This study is devoted to this community and their new way.

This is not a study, as was William James' seed work on religious experiences, of those who are necessarily widely known, who are necessarily "most accomplished in the religious life and best able to give an intelligible account of their ideas and motives," as modern writers or authors of materials that have become religious classics.[94] It is rather about our neighbors, our aunts or uncles, brothers or sisters, grandmothers or grandfathers, mothers or fathers. Maybe you are one of them. Maybe we are they. Just folks.

Chapter Two

Stories From Scholarly Sources

A Review of Literature and Description of Procedures

PART I
STUDIES ON ADDICTIONS IN GENERAL

Many have written before me on the problem of separation in general and in the lives of addicted individuals in particular. Many have written on ways in which that problem may be resolved.

William James lectured and wrote at the turn of the century about the process of conversion, during which, he said, discordant world views become unified. His book *The Varieties of Religious Experience,* based on a series of lectures he gave in Edinburgh, played an important part in the transformative spiritual experience of Bill Wilson, co-founder with Dr. Bob Smith of Alcoholics Anonymous. According to Ernest Kurtz, a historian who thoroughly studied Alcoholics Anonymous, the early members of Alcoholics Anonymous "launched their claim to intellectual respectability from their real relationship with the thought of William James." He says that "the Harvard philosopher-psychologist's book *The Varieties of Religious Experience* had in fact influenced Wilson at a critical moment, and early members of Alcoholics Anonymous habitually recommended this book to any who complained of difficulty with'the spiritual side' of their program."[1]

Throughout his book, James looks at a variety of ways individuals separate themselves from the whole.

While he and his work predate A.A., James includes in his examples the stories of a number of alcoholics who were relieved of the compulsion to drink through surrender experiences. One explanation he gives of the attraction to alcohol of some individuals is that the "drunken consciousness is one bit of the mystic consciousness."[2] It dissolves boundaries that keep people feeling alone. He comments that "the sway of alcohol over mankind is unquestionably due to its power to stimulate the mystical faculties of human nature, usually crushed to earth by the cold facts and dry criticisms of the sober hour. Sobriety diminishes, discriminates, and says no; drunkenness expands, unites and says yes."[3] According to James, this unification, this saying yes, this acceptance is the heart of conversion for alcoholics and non-alcoholics alike. "The keynote . . . is invariably a reconciliation."[4]

James addresses the split between the individual and a power greater than the finite self and speaks of conversion as a reconciliation between the two. He cites one of his correspondent's beliefs that "the first underlying cause of all sickness, weakness, or depression is the *human sense of separateness* from that Divine Energy which we call God."[5] With a healing of this split, James concludes "it is as if the opposites of the world, whose contradictoriness and conflict make all our difficulties and troubles, were melted into unity. Not only do they, as contrasted species, belong to one and the same genus, but *one of the species,* the noble and better one, *is itself the genus, and so soaks up and absorbs its opposite into itself.*"[6]

James deals not only with the nature of the split and reconciliation between ourselves and a Higher Power, but also discusses a means of reconciliation. He says the healing is made possible through surrender, which James unabashedly advocates. He enjoins readers to "fling [themselves] on God's providence." He tells them: "Give up the feeling of responsibility, let go your hold, resign the care of your destiny to higher powers and be indifferent as to what becomes of it all, and you . . . gain . . . inward relief. . . ." What is given up is "the tension of . . . personal will."[7] James says that the core of our religious problem is simply this: "Help help!"[8] He supports this position with source material from Edwin Starbuck, who similarly found that "relief persistently refuses to come until the person ceases to resist, or to make an effort in the direction he desires to go."[9]

James finds that regardless of the variety of conversion experience, there is a similar pattern in which there is "a firmness, stability and equilibrium succeeding a period of storm and stress and inconsistency."[10] As a result of conversion, a "will to assert ourselves and hold our own has been displaced by a willingness to close our mouths and be as nothing."[11]

In addition to his advocacy of surrender, another major contribution James makes to facilitate this reconciliation is to offer any struggling individuals among his readers the language and permission to conceive of a Higher Power in his or her own way. Acknowledging the variety of ways we imagine Divine Energy or Providence or God, James in essence gave permission to his readers to simply conceive of God using his or her own term, and in a way acceptable to him or her. The only essential was a basic willingness to acknowledge that "beyond each man and in a fashion continuous with him there exists a larger power which is friendly to him and his ideals. . . . Anything larger will do if only it be large enough to trust for the next step."[12] Alcoholics Anonymous subsequently adopted this notion. In its literature and meeting rooms there are repeated references to the inclusive term "Higher Power" and the phrase "God as you understand God."[13]

James also addresses the split between the intellect and the feelings, or emotions. He associates emotions with religious feeling, saying that "feeling is the deeper sense of religion." While he notes that while "feeling [is] valid only for the individual," and reason is "valid universally,"[14] the truth of religious feelings in conversion may become evident through its fruit or effect.

James identifies the split between the ideal self and the self acting in the world. He quotes Saint Paul's lament, a familiar song to alcoholics: "What I would, that do I not; but what I hate, that I do."[15] He identifies this split as one which may be healed following conversion.

James, through his reliance on the findings of Principal Caird, addresses the reconciliation of the modern reverence for progress with the traditional reverence for cyclical change. Caird found that religious life is progressive but the "progress is not progress *towards,* but progress *within* the sphere of the Infinite. It is not the vain attempt by endless finite additions or increments to become possessed of infinite wealth, but it is the endeavor, by the constant exercise of spiritual activity, to appropriate that infinite inheritance of which we are already in possession."[16] Likewise addressed is the reconciliation of limits with limitlessness. Caird felt that "to acknowledge your limits is in essence to be beyond them."[17]

James speaks of reconciliation of the individual with nature. He comments that "when we come to study the phenomenon of conversion or religious regeneration, we shall see that a not infrequent consequence of the change operated in the subject is a transfiguration of the face of nature in his eyes. A new heaven seems to shine upon a new earth."[18]

He, like Harry Tiebout writing after him, finds conversion to be a shift from a dualistic way of being in the world to a way of being based on acceptance. He believes that, finally and fundamentally, "the whole concern of both morality and religion is with the manner of our acceptance of the universe."[19]

Like William James, Gerald May, writing and conducting seminars today, also addresses himself to the primary split between an individual and a power greater than himself or herself. Like James, he advises that the healing of this split occurs with a shift from attempts at control or mastery to a willingness to be open and let go of habitual behaviors which he feels close us off to grace.[20]

May observes that in a condition of addiction, individuals are "fully at war with [them]selves." He equates addiction with control[21] and says major addiction is the "sacred disease of our time."[22] Addictions, he believes, are what we make more important than God. He believes that addiction is good insofar as it "brings us to our kness" in powerlessness. He discusses the falsity of the belief that addictions may be overcome through willpower. He says one of the toughest tasks for our society is to be willing to accept that uncontrollability. The objects of our addictions become our false gods, our idols.[23] He says that we would even make an idol of God through fixed images, and expresses the belief that God refuses to be an object of our addictions. This is so, he says, because true love can only exist in freedom, and can only give freedom. Freedom for May is a condition of non-attachment.

May is aware of the dynamics of addiction, the swings between one extreme and the other which characterize addicted states. Equilibrium or balance is one of his central themes. He describes it most graphically at the physiological level. He states that the brain itself works on an addiction model. He says everything in the body wants to maintain equilibrium. He describes the way the body becomes addicted to substances: "The substance alters a balance of natural body chemicals; the body adjusts to this alteration by trying to reestablish the proper balance. In so doing, the body becomes dependent upon the external supply of the substance."[24] There is invariably a rebound in which the person experiences symptoms that are the exact opposite of those caused by the addictive behavior.[25]

Gerald May says that there is a tendency, when struggling with one addiction, to "plug a less troublesome addiction into the space the old one occupied." He asks if we can bear to leave the space empty. He says that faith is what makes that possible. "Faith is always saying there is another risk to take. [It is asking] can you risk yet again? a little deeper? a little more? In a way it doesn't let you rest. It is always asking beyond what we are secure in." It is this risk-taking which helps heal the split between ourselves and God or Higher Power.

For Gerald May, the dialectic is between our attachment to "normality," which is predictable, and the possibility of grace. He says we long for unitive experiences, deep intimate connecting experiences *and* we keep holding back from them. He says faith comes from a "mysterious coinherence of grace and will. Grace is always a present possibility for individuals, but its flow comes to fullness through community."[26]

So for Gerald May, we stay in separation as long as our lives are filled with attachments and attempts to control, as long as we are unwilling to leave space for grace.

Marion Woodman concerns herself with the same theme, expressed in the language of Jungian psychology. In her book *The Pregnant Virgin* and her article "Worshipping Illusions," she identifies many of the ways in which we split ourselves and our world.

While she speaks in terms of the male/female polarity and how the individual distances himself or herself from one or the other half of this polarity, the question is clearly not simply one of gender but rather one of male and female principles. Woodman, as well as others such as June Singer and David Bakan, associates the female principle with receptivity and the male with activity.[27] Woodman is among those who feel that the feminine principle "for centuries has been denied in our culture."

Woodman says we split head from body. "It seems a lot of people are cut off at the neck, so that they talk from the head. Meanwhile, something completely different can be going on below the neck. There's a real split inside."[28] When this happens, the soul is left empty, and the "real food of the soul is metaphor."[29]

She says we split the ideal from behavior. Involved in this is the notion of perfection and the idea of love based on performance. She says that for her, "perfection is a patriarchal word that splits everything into contraries: black or white. You are then living in constant conflict, and integration is not possible."[30]

She offers some ideas that help readers with reconciliation of the separation between beliefs and behavior. She says some people despair of ever changing and believe themselves to be going around the same circle. "Closer discernment, however, helps them to realize they are not in the same place, but on a new rung of a spiral. Perhaps they are not so identified with the despair as they were last time—nor the fear, nor the pain, nor the abandonment. Perhaps they are more objective, allowing the grief and rage to flow through them without being swept away by either . . . .Certainly there is a death going on, a sacrifice, which must be perceived as sacrifice and treated as such or it can turn into annihilation."[31]

Woodman speaks of the split between the individual and the community. She believes many in our society are attempting to undergo transformation alone, "without any ritual container and without any group to support the influx of transcendent power."[32]

As William James looks to surrender for resolution of separation, and Gerald May looks to a letting go of the normality of attachments for openness and grace, Woodman talks of the healing power of ritual and symbol. She says it is through the symbolic image that opposites are brought together.[33] She says that the function of images is to mediate so that we are not possessed either by spirit or by matter. They allow us to dwell in an intermediate world which is the world of soul-making, the domain of ritual.[34] She says we simply "must have access to that symbolic realm, because we are not animals only, and we are not gods, only. Somehow there has to be a bridge between the animal and the divine within, and that is the symbol."[35]

Anne Wilson Schaef also addresses the theme developed by James, May, and Woodman—the theme of control and letting go. Schaef like Woodman associates the male principle with control and activity and the female principle with letting go and receptivity. She writes about the phenomenon of addiction as it manifests itself on the societal level. She equates the white male system with the addictive system and says repeatedly that the need for control is at the core.[36] She asserts, as others have asserted, that American society is an addicted society and describes those features she feels characterize this addicted society. She describes the myths (in this case associating the term with falsehoods) of white male systems. Among them are belief in control, belief in superiority, belief that it is possible to know and understand everything, belief that it is possible to be totally "logical, rational and objective" (in the process frequently dismissing experience), belief that "it is possible to be God as defined by the system." Schaef says an addictive system places great emphasis on cause and effect, "which . . . is closely related to the illusion of control."[37] She believes we need to "admit that our society is based on the illusion of control and recognize that the system in which we live is an Addictive System."[38]

Roland Delattre believes that the dominant American culture at least nourishes addiction.[39] He notes Lawrence Hatterer's assertion that "addictive behavior has invaded every aspect of American life today."[40] Delattre talks of two types of addictions, one that he calls activity addictions, the other substance addictions.[41]

Delattre looks at the way we split ourselves off from the world. He describes our culture as one in which individuals seek satisfaction from a variety of external sources. He describes a culture dedicated to procurement, a culture on the take. He finds "ordinary people engaged in the ceaseless pursuit of the good life while being constantly reminded of their powerlessness."

Delattre discerns the separation inherent in a state of attachment in which there is lack of awareness of underlying unity, a state such as that described by the authors of *Habits of the Heart*. He describes the dynamics of such a state: swings between one extreme and the other. He finds that one of the primary polarities in the lives of alcoholics is a problem for those in the larger community as well—the fundamental division between power and powerlessness. He says an important feature of addictive behavior is a "kind of all-or-nothing disposition that swings between grandiosity and a sense of one's own insignificance, between a sense of near omnicompetence and complete incompetence. One extreme makes for dangerous flights of over-reaching ambition; the other makes for resignation, submission, and passivity."[42]

While both extremes involve subject–object splits, the first involves an individual seeking to act on an objectified environment, the second involves a feeling that an objectified environment is acting on the self. There is ceaseless swinging between these states, which results in a greater sense of separation.[43]

PART II
STUDIES ON ADDICTIONS AND ALCOHOLICS ANONYMOUS

Each of the following works is specifically concerned with alcoholism and specifically explores the role of Alcoholics Anonymous in recovery. I have clustered them into three groups. The first are those written from a cultural perspective; the second are those written from the vantage point of psychology; and the third are those written from the perspective of religion.

CULTURE

Gregory Bateson examined what he called "schismogenesis," or "growing splits in the structures of ideas" in the lives of alcoholics and described the effect of the Twelve Steps of A.A. on the healing of these splits. He talks in terms of systems theory.

Bateson's cybernetics and systems theory as it applies to recovery from alcoholism for those using the program and fellowship of A.A. is probably most succinctly expressed in his article "The Cybernetics of Self, A Theory of Alcoholism." In that article he observes that the addicted alcoholic is operating, when sober, in terms of a dualistic epistemology that is "conventional in Occidental culture" but not in accord with systems theory in which all elements are considered connected. He believes that intoxication provides "a partial and subjective short cut to a more correct state of mind." He believes that A.A. provides the sober alcoholic with an epistemology that coincides with systems theory in an acknowledgement of connections between the parts and the whole.

He discusses the A.A. member's reconciliation with the community, with God, and with the universe as a whole. He says that "the religious conversion of the alcoholic when saved by A.A. can be described as a dramatic shift from [a] symmetrical habit, or epistemology, to an almost purely complementary view of his relationship to others and to the universe or God."[44]

Bateson makes a number of observations as to the split and subsequent reconciliation between the alcoholic and others. He suggests that alcohol allegedly makes the individual feel and act as a part of the group—it enables a feeling of complementarity. He asserts that anonymity is a "profound statement of the systemic relation. . . . The variable to be maximized is a complementarity and is of the nature of 'service' rather than dominance."[45] As to the split and subsequent reconciliation between the individual and the world as a whole, Bateson believes the purpose of A.A. is in the creation of a "non-competitive relationship to the larger world."[46]

"Elpenor" [pseud.] traces "A Drunkard's Progress" with the help of Alcoholics Anonymous.

He explains some of the basic tenets and practices of A.A. in poetic prose. He describes the drunkard's progress in terms of mythic quest.

He talks of the reconciliation between self and other that happens in A.A. He says that he finds a spiritual discipline in meetings: "to attend to what's being said, to keep one's mind open to the spark of recognition, to wait in mounting tension for the moment when one will be called on, then finally to hazard a link between one's own story and another's."[47]

Elpenor speaks of the reconciliation between the dream clouds of alcoholics and the earth. He says the fellowship exists to "ground the drunk's ladder on solid earth" instead of floating on water.[48] Meetings, he mentions, are almost always held in basements, "close to the world's center of gravity."[49]

He speaks of the reconciliation of talking and listening. "A.A. drama is oral, preliterate. In fact, the whole culture of A.A. is oral, a tribal culture which gets passed on by means of stories and maxims." Elpenor speaks of the coincidence of heroes and monsters. He says the stories are ones of "cynicism and trust, despair and hope, death and life, death and love. . . . ."[50] They are channelled "along the lines of a quest story." He says "we end up in a barroom, say, screaming a challenge to take on any man in the place."[51] In meetings, we speak of the "cruelty that human beings bring to the task of destroying themselves." In recovery, they "like nine tenths of their fellow Americans . . . believe in God"[52] and tell stories about how God as they understand God is doing for them what they could not do for themselves.

He talks of control and letting go. "Voices reach us" at the bottom, "urgent voices. One, heroic in timbre (though strangely demonic), cries out, 'Hold on!' Another, so close to the bottom we're lying on that it might be coming from there, speaks in a croak. 'Let go,' it says, 'let go.' "[53]

He speaks of the reconciliation between one religion and another. He notes that although there is "no question that the Higher Power most A.A. people have in mind is the Judeo-Christian one, . . . no one in A.A. has ever attempted to 'help' me by pointing the way to his notion of God." He goes on to add that "never, for example, have I heard anyone in A.A. refer to Jesus Christ. This is astonishing, for most A.A. people are Christian (like most Americans)."[54]

PSYCHOLOGY

George Kohn is attentive to the fundamental split and imbalance in alcoholics between active and receptive ways of experiencing the world. He calls for the development of a spiritual model of recovery from alcoholism that is based on bimodal consciousness, as described by Arthur Deikman. He concurs with Deikman's assertion that there are two basic modes of consciousness—the action mode and the receptive mode. Deikman associates the action mode with manipulation of the environment, object-based logic, heightened boundary perception, and striving to achieve personal goals.[55] In contrast, the receptive mode is associated with intake of the environment, and with *decreased* boundary perception. Relying on these distinctions, Kohn proposes "the development of a spiritual program that increases right-hemisphere experience while integrating it into an organized left-hemisphere system for interaction with the objective world."[56]

George Kohn proposes a model of spirituality based "on achieving a balance between hemisphere functions and modes of consciousness [which] could provide a non-chemical alternative to the use of alcohol." He says it is the "integration of modes that distinguishes the adept from the psychotic and defines [spiritual] experiences as fruitful rather than delusional."[57] Kohn connects Deikman's theories and recent research in the differentiation of functioning between left and right hemispheres of the brain. Kohn recommends the use of hemispheric dominance as a way of talking about the place of spirituality in recovery. In his article, Kohn cites other research which may indicate a greater incidence of "right-hemisphere-dominant individuals among a group of alcohol abusers than in general population control groups." He suggests that "the development of a spiritual program that pays attention to hemispheric imbalance could provide an answer to many of the problems previously seen in psychosocial models as 'causes' of alcohol abuse."[58] He notes that such a model of spirituality would also have relevance for "sociocultural definitions of alcoholism and alcohol abuse." Connecting the receptive mode with characteristics that are stereotypically considered "feminine," he says that "the denigration of feminine function in society is thus related to the disregard of spirituality. A revaluing of spirituality could go hand in hand with a revaluing of women's roles in the culture." He notes too that "the special incidences of alcoholism among various ethnic groups could be the result of genetic differences in left/right hemisphere dominance, different cultural evaluation of such balance differences, or a difference in hemisphere valuation between a subculture and a dominant culture."

Most valuable here, it seems, are his suggestions about the differing *valuations*, and his belief in a need for the revaluing of the feminine in American culture.

Stephanie Brown's contemporary work in the area of recovery from alcoholism serves as a fine text and emphasizes the importance of the concept of powerlessness. Her book *Treating the Alcoholic, A Developmental Model of Recovery* draws on many original findings from her dissertation project and is addressed primarily to therapists working with alcoholics. She explains the epistemological shift that occurs at the juncture of drinking and recovery with reference to Gregory Bateson's work in this area. She states A.A.'s and Tiebout's premises succinctly and memorably in terms of "before and after": "I am not an alcoholic. I am in control" giving way to "I am an alcoholic. I am not in control." One of the most valuable contributions of her work is her emphasis on the fact that "the person maintaining abstinence has acknowledged a lack of control and is not striving to regain it. A helper who has not experienced a similar internal struggle with an acceptance of loss of control may focus the treatment on the exact opposite, still holding onto the basic belief that self-control is the ideal goal."[59]

Brown proposes four stages of alcoholism and recovery: (1) drinking, (2) transition, (3) early recovery, and (4) ongoing recovery. She suggests that acceptance of loss of control and the identity as an alcoholic form the core of the continuum of recovery. In stage one, Brown says, the primary issues are power versus powerlessness and the separation between the individual and the world as a whole. In this drinking stage, she reports, many other writers have reported "increasing isolation, constriction, and a narrowing of the individual's world to an overwhelming focus on alcohol and the struggle for control."[60] She states that alcoholics who are reaching the bottom are "often paranoid and view the world as their enemy."[61] She states that in the transition phase, phase 2, the issues are power versus powerlessness and the split between intellect and emotion. In this phase, the individual is characterized by an absence of or narrow range of affect. She also notes that this period is often "characterized concretely by a split in identity with a sense of one foot in and one foot out"—in control or not.[62] She describes a task of stage three as identification with others and increase of affect. A task of stage four (ongoing recovery) is identified as increasing involvement with, valuation of, and interpretation of self and others. She believes that in recovery there is a shift from a passive to an active stance accompanied by the assertion of autonomy.[63]

Brown describes the critical role of receptivity in recovery. In her case studies she notes that as one man progressed in recovery, he more carefully examined the "important symbolism of alcohol. He and his friend had shared the belief that drinking was part of their masculine, even macho, identity. They enjoyed 'men's' drinking lunches that reinforced their sense of power; 'hard drinking men are strong.' "[64]

Brown's dissertation was entitled *Defining a Continuum of Recovery in Alcoholism*. In this she rejected what she described as the linear models of Jellinek and Bacon on the progression of active addiction for extension into an understanding of recovery. She suggests instead a new non-linear continuum with an ongoing, interactive presence of "two major axes." One, she says, is a continuing though sometimes underlying or symbolic focus on alcohol. This "axis" represents the central organizing principle in recovery. The other axis she conceptualized as an expanding spiral around the main alcohol line, representing concerns besides alcohol that emerge following abstinence. (See Chapter Six for a diagram of her model of recovery.)

Brown found 82 percent of her respondents accented external support without reciprocation in noting the kinds of support they valued "at first." She goes on to say that there are then "indications of increasing reliance on interpersonal support and the beginnings of a subtle shift from external to internal support. People report increasing self-reliance, internal spiritual support, and action in the form of '12-Step' work."[65] She says the changes during abstinence may be characterized "psychologically or dynamically as movement from isolation to involvement, from dependency to independence, and from a passive, recipient posture to one of active involvement and reciprocation."[66]

The primary polarity with which Brown concerns herself is the one between power and powerlessness. The before recovery state for an alcoholic is identified with assertions of control; the initial stage of recovery is a passive state; the denial of feelings and tentative exploration of feelings is associated with early recovery; and ongoing recovery is, in her view, characterized by reciprocity and an active, internally supported stance.

Margery Jackson studied the "Actualization of Alcoholics Anonymous Members." She states that her purpose is to determine whether, "in addition to achieving abstinence, Alcoholics Anonymous members are moving toward a state of full humanness." She says her study addresses itself to the "wellness theory" and the position that some people have taken "that having been an alcoholic and having achieved sobriety through the Alcoholics Anonymous program contributes positively to a person's life, spontaneity, wisdom, understanding and creativity."[67] She theorizes that this would be discoverable in "comparative measures of self-actualization between those who have not had the alcoholic experience, those who have had and have achieved sobriety for a substantial period of time, and those who are just trying to achieve sobriety."[68]

Jackson administered two tests to these three groups. One was the Personal Orientation Inventory (Shostrom 1963), the other the Hartlage-Hale Self Concept Scale, which uses a semantic differential instrument (Hartlage and Hale 1968).[69]

The Hartlage-Hale Self Concept Scale findings showed no significant differences between the three sample groups. On the Personal Orientation Inventory, A.A. members who had been sober three to eight years had POI scores one to one and a half standard deviations above the newcomers, which according to Jackson "would indicate that these Alcoholics Anonymous members in addition to achieving sobriety, have been growing toward full humanness." She notes that although "there is some discussion in the literature that Alcoholics Anonymous works by creating dependency relationships, that the organization is limiting and constrictive, and is, in effect, a society of compulsive non-drinkers," her research demonstrates that the Alcoholics Anonymous experience "was for this population an expansion of self rather than a drawing in to self."

Jackson also notes that for the A.A. members tested, sobriety was accompanied by improved time competence and scores that indicated better self-worth and self-acceptance. An individual who had been sober for three to eight years would typically "perceive man in a positive way and has a high capacity for intimate contact. He has the ability to accept his feelings of anger and aggressiveness and sees opposites as meaningfully related. He has, in short, become quite similar in his attitudes and attributes to a group of persons clinically selected as representative of society's best."[70]

Sandra Schnall in her dissertation study, "An Interpersonal Approach to Alcoholism: The Transformation of Self through Alcoholics Anonymous," says her approach to the problem of alcoholism is through understanding the nature of self.[71] She hypothesizes that the recovering alcoholic needs to incorporate "a positive introject" and that this may be done only through an undermining of the negative introject which she sees as the "bad mother."[72]

In her study she observes that what is lacking in the various explanations of how participating in A.A. effects change "is a theoretical framework pertaining to what change is, how it occurs, and what types of change the alcoholic needs to make."[73] Another interesting comment she makes in discussing the "symbolic interactionist approach" is that persons susceptible to alcoholism have a constant need to shut off inner, failure-predicting messages.[74] She says "the act of drinking is initially seen as the blotting out of inner-voices—punitive, failure-predicting messages . . . blotting out the inner audience leads to a loss of control and to the erosion of the Self."[75] She believes that alcoholics' "vulnerability to other persons' evaluations and their tenuous sense of themselves . . . coped with by a forced autonomy . . . helps to insulate [them] from others."[76]

In her discussion of H. S. Sullivan's work, Schnall states that it is hypothesized that in the alcoholic, "the psyche becomes truly split; passive, dependent, child-like,'feminine' traits are repudiated by forced autonomy, activity,'masculinity,' and rigid control." She speculates that this is due to the "alcoholic person's attempt to free themselves of the [negative] parenting figure by denying their need for tenderness and support."[77] She presents alcoholism as a coping mechanism and suggests that the alcoholic totally repudiates the inner world. "It is this inner split," she says, "between a repudiated inner world and a truncated outer Self which the recourse to alcohol appears to maintain."[78] She delineated a "series of six phases which outline how the Self is transformed."[79]

Harry M. Tiebout's work provided the foundation for the identification of the problem of separation in the lives of alcoholics in chapter 1. Several additional comments are relevant.

Tiebout's work with alcoholics led him to believe that conversion involves "a deep shift in the patient's emotional tone, not consciously willed but arising from changes in the unconscious psychodynamics, which caused the disappearance of one set of feelings and the emergence of another and very different set."[80] He says that without this change, a recovering alcoholic's chances of remaining sober were minimal. He says that the alcoholic must "hit bottom" before he or she can be helped. This involves an inner conviction that one cannot continue as one has been going. The alcoholic must also "develop and maintain humility." He says the treatment implications of these two elements in recovery are the need for surrender and the need for ego reduction. He says the word "surrender" is in "good favor in A.A. circles." He says also that the "existentialists, when they advocate being oneself, advise one to let go and be. They view surrender as a letting go of control, and presume that such dropping of the reins will permit greater spontaneity and naturalness and a greater sense of being a person." Tiebout identifies despair, or the feeling " 'I cannot go on, . . . I am licked' " as the source of surrender.[81] He says that the very seeking of help is an act of surrender. He described one of his patients after surrender: "[T]he aggression subsided materially, the feeling of being at odds with the world disappeared, and with it vanished the tendency to suspect the motives and attitudes of others. A sense of peace and calm ensued with real lessening of inner tension; and the lines of her face softened and became gentler and more kindly." Tiebout quotes Bill Wilson as saying that "the success of the group with any alcoholic depends upon the degree to which the individual goes through a conversion or spiritual activation."[82] He goes on to say that a religious or spiritual awakening is the act of giving up one's reliance on one's omnipotence. The defiant individual no longer defies but accepts help, guidance, and control from the outside. Tiebout says that the result of a conversion is a new and different "life pattern and outlook." He quotes Bill Wilson as saying that 10 percent of A.A. members have a rapid awakening, while the other 90 percent attain the same result more gradually.

Tiebout believes that the central effect of Alcoholics Anonymous "is to develop in the person a spiritual state which will serve as a direct neutralizing force upon the egocentric elements in the character of the alcoholic."[83]

Volpe and Rooney's work in exploring androgyny for individuals recovering from alcoholism offers some interesting findings. They studied separation in terms of male and female qualities. Their study was a longitudinal one done with women in a halfway house. Although in the summary of their work they do not specifically state whether the halfway house program was based on the philosophy of A.A., it seems implied by their comparison—for extension of their longitudinal time frame—of the women in the halfway house with women who had been in recovery with the help of A.A. and had several years of abstinence. They report finding that there is a greater balance between qualities associated with the masculine and qualities traditionally associated with the feminine for those recovering from addiction. They used the Bem inventory to measure the relative presence of these qualities. The comparison study with those who had longer-term sobriety indicated *fewer* androgynous characteristics than in those who had just completed the halfway house program.[84]

Charles Whitfield, too, has studied the relationship between alcoholism, a sense of separation, and imbalance. Whitfield's work is an insightful exposition on how the program and fellowship of Alcoholics Anonymous fits primarily with the field of transpersonal psychology. He agrees with Brown and others that control, or lack of it, is the most important issue in early recovery. He says another word for control is attachment.[85] He says recovery is physical, mental, and spiritual.[86] Whitfield discusses the importance of story telling in recovery.[87] He mentions methods of unifying science and spirituality.[88] He offers several charts, one for example comparing the schemas of Carl Jung, Ram Dass, and others. He offers a binary model of recovery, comparing the Mind with the Self, associating the former with the left hemisphere of the brain and the latter with the right hemisphere. He discusses the role of paradox in recovery.[89] He offers many ideas for further exploration. His comparison of recovery in A.A. with the monomyth of Joseph Campbell is noted in chapter 5 of this work.

RELIGION

Homer Alexander Hall studied "The Role of Faith in the Process of Recovery from Alcoholism." He was concerned primarily with the rupture between the individual and a power greater than himself or herself. In a discussion of Roessler's work, Hall notes that alcoholics "recognize [their] spiritual disconnectedness because of an intense longing to feel connected." He concludes that "alcoholism can be combated by developing in the alcoholic a sense of contact with God." He identified his purposes as identifying spiritual resources beneficial to the recovery of alcoholics, developing a program model to be used, and providing ministers with "viable techniques on the utilization of faith resources" in the recovery process.[90] Hall designed a religious attitudes inventory for use in his exploration. In his study he presents a variety of definitions for spirituality and for religion. He suggests that the A.A. approach assumes "not only that faith, not belief, is the essential element for spiritual growth, but more strongly, that an emphasis on belief can retard religious development."[91]

Greg Martin (pseud.) examines the relationship between Christianity and Alcoholics Anonymous in his dissertation "The Gospel of Christ and The Gospel of Alcoholics Anonymous: Divergent Paths of Human Liberation." Martin looks at the "spiritual dynamics" of the Twelve Steps of A.A. and compares the Biblical story of Lazarus to the experiences of alcoholics recovering in A.A. He notes that Lazarus wins by losing, and lives by dying. And, Martin suggests, "the alcoholic in A.A. has learned precisely the same lesson. We are positively 'un-American.' We topple all the old ideas and values. We call into question the basic goals of our society . . . not because we want to, or set out to do it; but because we were killing ourselves trying to do it the other way!" He suggests that the spiritual experience of A.A. and the liberation theologian have a "common source in the faith of the mystic."[92] He concludes that A.A. is compatible with Christianity and questions the claims of some Christians to an exclusive gospel of salvation.

S. James Roessler designed a program to "raise spiritual consciousness" in individuals at a 28-day treatment facility for alcoholism in Olney, Maryland. Participants were given a questionnaire prior to treatment and upon completion of treatment four weeks later. He noted that results verified his hypothesis that "structured planning of spiritual aspects into the treatment of alcoholics increases their chances of maintaining sobriety in the first three months."[93] The general topics of the spiritual consciousness-raising group which was part of his program were (1) Faith in God (2) Prayer and Meditation (3) Who/What is God? (4) Faith and Recovery from Alcoholism and (5) Spiritual Consciousness. This program was apparently used in conjunction with the Alcoholics Anonymous program. His primary focus was on the split between the alcoholic and a power greater than him or herself.

Edward Sellner describes his dissertation as a pastoral theological study of eight people's lives: "four alcoholics who participated in A.A.'s Fifth Step and four Roman Catholic parishioners who participated in the revised rites of the sacrament of penance." The four alcoholics who participated were clients of Hazelden Foundation in Minnesota. He hoped that by a comparison of the two types of confessional encounters the Catholic Church could learn something about the ministry and liturgy of reconciliation. He also expressed a hope that A.A. would learn something about the ministry associated with the Fifth Step.

Sellner's focus was on the Fifth Step as an "event of self-revelation" and the influence those he interviewed said it had on their lives. He summarizes Tiebout's work on conversion and suggests that without specifically systemizing his thoughts, Tiebout describes four phases of the conversion process: (1) the crisis, (2) hitting bottom, (3) the conversion experience, and (4) harmony and peace. Sellner's study is most helpful in that he too examines the change from an isolated, fragmented self to one that in the words of Tiebout, is "in communion with God, man, and all the creative forces of the universe."[94]

C. Roy Woodruff's study is confined to what he refers to as Christian conversions. He identifies four main categories: psychosocial conversion, restrictive Christian conversion, limited Christian conversion, and comprehensive Christian conversion.[95] He makes reference to Kazimierz Dabrowski's personality development concept called "theory of positive disintegration." Woodruff finds that Dabrowski's greatest contribution to an understanding of the relationship between alcoholism and conversion is Dabrowski's view that the personality "develops through the loosening of its cohesiveness," that the "developmental instinct . . . by destroying the existing structure of personality allows the possibility of reconstruction at a higher level."[96]

Each of these works addresses one or more ways in which the individual splits him or herself from the whole. Most suggest one or more ways in which a reconciliation of these pieces or pairs may occur.

Like many of my predecessors, I believe that alcoholism involves both a splitting off from the whole, a sense of separation, and imbalance. Like many of them, I believe the principles and program and community of Alcoholics Anonymous serve as one way for alcoholics to repair the ruptures.

PART III
RESEARCH DESIGN

I will briefly describe how I went about exploring these ideas, the manner in which the findings will be presented, and some of the limitations of the study.

The research design of this dissertation draws upon a combination of commonly recognized forms. It is "qualitative-descriptive" in that it primarily involves a subjective description of the research topic—spiritual renewal in recovery from alcoholism with the help of Alcoholics Anonymous. The individuals involved are compared primarily to themselves, by means of self-report. The design is "quantitative-descriptive" in that it uses numbers not to test but to describe the worldview of members of respondent groups.

The quantitative component of this study was an original questionnaire administered to 88 individuals in recovery from alcoholism.

The purpose of the questionnaire was (1) to help identify some of the most fertile areas for further inquiry; (2) to get some sense of the representativeness of the stories told by those who would later be personally interviewed; (3) to provide some indication of the prevalence of particular spiritual beliefs, experiences, or practices within a larger population for those areas that were not explored in personal interviews, and (4) to provide some indication of the process, movement, or direction of recovery in general.

The questionnaire I designed was divided into four basic content areas. The first content area was designed to elicit background information; the second set of questions was to determine depth of involvement in and commitment to A.A.; the third to indicate the distance respondents felt between each of the above-mentioned pairs, e.g. self and Higher Power, self and others, male and female; and the fourth was to find out how strongly respondents agreed or disagreed with statements about themselves, a Higher Power, other people, and the world as a whole.

I designed a questionnaire intended to ascertain whether the individual respondents experienced themselves-with-environment as a coherent whole.[97] One part of the question-naire utilizes a semantic differential technique which presents a series of key concepts along with frequently paired words. The second component of the questionnaire uses Likert scale (strongly agree–strongly disagree items on a scale from 1 to 7) and short answer questions to elicit information. For most Likert items, respondents were asked to indicate where they were in relation to the question on a seven-point scale from strongly agree to strongly disagree. In other Likert items, respondents were asked to indicate where they were in relation to the question on a seven-point scale in terms of frequency, with one representing "never"and seven representing "all the time."

The centerpiece of this study was qualitative, consisting of in-depth interviews with 12 individuals who completed the questionnaire. These people were and are in the process of recovery, and generously agreed to share their insights and experiences. Each of the 12 identified himself or herself as a recovering alcoholic. Four were living on the East Coast, two on the West Coast, and the remainder were living in the Midwest. Six are females, six are males. They ranged in age from 21 to 56. Of these, two were between the ages 21 through 30, seven were between the age of 31 and 50, and three were age 51 or older.

Seven of the interviewees said they were initially admitted for treatment for problems with alcohol alone, four indicated problems with both alcohol and other drugs, and one said she or he was initially admitted to treatment for problems with drugs other than alcohol.

At the time they completed the written questionnaire, they ranged in sobriety from two weeks to 21 years. In the cluster of those who had from two weeks to one year of sobriety are Bob, Paul, and Jane (although Jane had previously had five years in A.A. before drinking again). In the middle group with between one year and five years sober are Jean, Jim, Ann, Jennifer, Roger and Carol. Those clustered in the third group with five or more years of cumulative daily abstinence are Joyce, John, and Donald.

In terms of their occupations at the time of the interviews, two were professionals, one was a student, four were technical workers or semi-professionals, one was retired, one was a business owner, one was a skilled or semi-skilled worker, one was a service worker, and one was a clerical worker. Five were single, two were divorced, four were married, and one was living as married. Four of the 12 have children. In terms of education, one completed vocational school, four were high school graduates with some college, two were college graduates, and five were postgraduates.[98]

The format for the interviews was conversational. I provided some structure by asking specific questions, but there was no attempt to limit respondents as they spoke freely about their spiritual ideas, beliefs, practices, and experiences in recovery.

Since I was reluctant to pattern and confine responses to verbal communication, each person interviewed was invited to submit a creative work expressive of their worldview, or alternatively to identify any creative works already extant which they felt would express their ideas and experiences. For the same reason I included a section on the questionnaire where respondents were asked to draw a diagram or picture representing the relationship between themselves, others, their Higher Power, and the universe.

PART IV
GATHERING DATA

In the formulation of the theory for this study and in an attempt to gain some understanding of the cultural context of these ideas, I relied on traditionally modern research techniques —personal searches of relevant topics such as conversion, transformation, and renewal as well as computer-assisted searches of these same topics. However, far more valuable to me, I believe, was the material that found *me*—possibly during some temporary lapses into receptivity. The process which results is beautifully described in one account by Dr. Hilty cited in William James's *Varieties Of Religious Experience:*

> *. . . books and words (and sometimes people) come to one's cognizance just at the very moment in which one needs them; . . . when the time has come for something, one suddenly receives a courage that formerly failed, or perceives the root of a matter that until then was concealed, or discovers thoughts, talents, yea, even pieces of knowledge and insight, in one's self, of which it is impossible to say whence they come; finally, that persons help us or decline to help us, favor us or refuse us, as if they had to do so against their will, so that often those indifferent or even unfriendly to us yield us the greatest service and furtherance. . . . Often, too, persons are sent to us at the right time, to offer or ask for what is needed, and what we should never have had the courage or resolution to undertake of our own accord.*[99]

I will give you just a couple of examples from my own experience while working on this story.

I had determined to interview only a few individuals from the groups that had already taken the questionnaire. I met Donald *after* that phase of the research had been concluded. When I told him what I was doing, he began (uninvitedly and enthusiastically) to tell me of his experiences in recovery. While my initial silent plea was "no, don't tell me, that doesn't fit in with my research design," I succumbed. The next day while I was staying at Hazelden's Renewal Center I woke up early, found John all alone in the dining room, heard this inaudible voice pipe up—"ask him"—and I did. So much for plans.

PART V
LIMITATIONS AND CIRCUMSCRIPTION OF THE STUDY IN GENERAL

A quotation from a particular source, whether that source is one of those specifically interviewed for this study, or whether the source has been used as background material, does not necessarily imply agreement or endorsement. As is repeated in many A.A. meetings, the opinions given here are strictly those of the person giving them. They are *not* intended in any way to represent an official position of Alcoholics Anonymous; *not* intended in any way to represent a position of Hazelden Foundation; and not intended necessarily to represent my personal view.

I made no effort to verify the accounts of my respondents. In my opinion, subjects felt a responsibility to themselves to be as truthful as possible.

The ideas offered here are not at all intended to suggest that separation and imbalance is the exclusive cause, or exclusive cause and effect, of alcoholism.

The discussion here is primarily in terms of American society and culture for two primary reasons. One is simply to establish some parameters. The other is because I believe that as alcoholics are extreme examples of self-centeredness and control and attachment, America itself is an extreme example of national self-consciousness, control, and attachment to material satisfactions. Paradoxically, many alcoholics have expressed a longing for a life in which the sacred and profane are unified, and this longing has also been an integral part of our American identity, from the respective communities of Native Americans through the Puritans in New England and continuing throughout our history. As the alcoholic may be representative of all who suffer from addictions, America may be representative in that we have living here people and descendents from all over the world. As Emerson says, America is a "huge composite."[100] Because of the diversity and complexity we have a great capacity for both cacophony and symphony. Insofar as the dilemmas of America are representative, it is as fine a laboratory as any for the study of separation and imbalance; recovery as well. While the instrument and task of America are likely unique, as are the tasks of other nations, the nature of each is the same. What is said about America and American society and culture is *not* meant to be *exclusive* to America and those living within the political boundaries of the United States.

I did *not* consider here what others have referred to as lack of boundaries in the recovering alcoholic. I believe that the primary need for garden variety alcoholics in recovery is to balance a dualistic way with a unified one and then to make distinctions between self and others as appropriate. I may be wrong. As I understand it, while the need to draw boundaries is an ongoing differentiation that needs to be made, for example, from the family of origin,[101] I believe that often what is referred to as "boundarilessness" is actually simply a reference to boundaries viewed from the posture of victim rather than aggressor (that is, "*They* are doing this to me instead of me to *Them*"). In such instances, the individual would remain acting as if helpless, unfree, attached. As Jungian psychologist Helen Luke says, "You have to separate in order to unite, because uniting means two unique things that meet. Not two fuzzy things—that merge!"[102] Jay Lifton says there is one overall issue, "the breakdown and re-creation of the boundaries of our existence."[103] What is needed is the freedom which allows us to draw and withdraw boundaries appropriately. It is to each to know the nature of our own imbalance.

I have included a number of stories and teachings from Native American sources. I do not mean to imply that the diverse Native American nations, tribes, clans, or individuals would necessarily agree with or practice these teachings. I have included them in part because these teachings have found a place in my own heart, and I believe they are helpful and in concert with the principles and program of Alcoholics Anonymous.

I have drawn a line of demarcation between a scientific way of experiencing the world, and a spiritual way. I do not mean to imply either that scientists are not spiritual, or that religious persons are not scientific. Julian Jaynes, for example, mentions how during World War II "British physicists used to say that they no longer made their discoveries in the laboratory; they had their three B's where their discoveries were made— the bath, the bed, and the bus."[104] Many scientists and mystics meet in the middle. I believe we need to know both ways of being.

I have explored a counter-clockwise movement in recovery, and have omitted any discussion of a complementary sun-wise motion.

In this study I have somewhat arbitrarily split the Space/Time/Causation continuum, with the intent of clarifying the nature of the problem.

The bulk of the editing of interviews concerned the dissection and assignment of responses to the categories I designated. Most of the other editing was done through omission of those responses that did not bear directly on the questions. As far as possible, in cases where responses are included, they have been recorded as they were originally spoken. My fear is that in my categorizing of responses into Self/Self, Self/ Higher Power, Self/Other, Self/Nature, and so forth, I have muted or distorted the person's true voice. I'm sorry if I did that. I wish you could be with them and listen to them as I did. I fell in love with them. I didn't plan to. I just did.

Part VI
Findings: Sharing Stories

The findings of this research project will be presented in two chapters. The first, Chapter 3, entitled "Principles and Program for Practicing Peace," is in response to one of the two primary questions of this research project: What, if any, evidence is there to indicate that Alcoholics Anonymous serves as a revitalization movement as described by Anthony Wallace, helping members create and accept a more satisfying way of life or culture? Chapter 3 will be devoted to Alcoholics Anonymous as a movement that helps members close the distance between splits within themselves, splits between themselves and a power greater than their separate selves, splits between themselves and others, and splits between themselves and the world as a whole.

Chapter 4, entitled "People Practicing Peace," is in response to the second primary question: What, if any, evidence is there to indicate that the twelve recovering alcoholic/addicts who participated in this study report a less dualistic, discordant culture or way of life in recovery than they did while actively addicted? While the questions addressed in Chapters 3 and 4 are related and of equal importance, this story is devoted primarily to the latter—the people who participated in this study and their reports of ideas and experiences of confluence in recovery with A.A. Chapter 4 is devoted to some of the ideas and experiences of the recovering alcoholics who participated in this study. It begins with an introductory section consisting of excerpts from both the questionnaire designed for this study and excerpts from the interviews of twelve recovering alcoholics regarding their views about and relationship with Alcoholics Anonymous.

In the questionnaire designed for this study, I organized items around what I imagine to be significant splits experienced by addicted individuals: the splits between (1) active and receptive ways, (2) male and female, (3) self and higher power, (4) self and others, (5) sacred and profane, (6) inner and outer, (7) past and future, (8) life and death, and (9) self and nature. For the purpose of presentation I clustered these pairs into four more inclusive categories. The first category, which addresses the self in relationship with the self, is entitled "Practicing Peace with Themselves" and is identified as Part I of Chapter 4. It includes splits 1 and 2 which I combined into one section entitled "Active/Receptive," (Section A) as well as a third inclusive split which I call "Acceptable/Unacceptable Self" (Section B). The second part (II), which centers upon the self in relationship with God or Higher Power, is entitled "Practicing Peace with God or Higher Power." It includes item 3, "self and Higher Power" which I have further divided into these four sections: "God Is There, Not Here?" (Section A), "God Is Here, Not There?" (Section B), "God Is Not Deaf, but Mute?" (Section C), and "God Is Like This, Not Like That?" (Section D). The third part (III), concerned with the self in relationship with others, is entitled "Practicing Peace with Others." It includes item 4, "self and others," which is the only section to this part. The fourth part (IV), concentrates on the self in relationship with the world as a whole and is entitled "Practicing Peace with the World." This part includes splits 5, 6, 7, 8, and 9. It is divided into four sections: Inner and Outer Worlds (Section A); Past and Future (Section B); Life and Death (Section C); and Self and Nature (Section D). (Please refer to the Table of Contents for help in following this method of presentation.)

Chapter Three

Principles and a Program for Practicing Peace

Findings: I

INTRODUCTORY

There is at least one community, more than one and a half million strong, that is learning to make the transition from separation to communion, from the dualistic way characteristic of science to the unitive way of spirit. It is a community composed of young people who are old in sobriety, old people young in sobriety, and recovering extremists of middle age. It embraces people from all economic classes and all religious backgrounds. Its members come from and live in lands all over the world.[1] They share at least one common bond by which they identify themselves as members. That bond is their stereotypical, repetitive, mal- or un-adaptive patterns of behavior in connection with their use of alcohol and other mood-altering chemicals.[2] This chapter is about a program and its principles and practices that help members of that community balance the dualistic, scientific way with a spiritual one. The program followed by this community is the program of Alcoholics Anonymous.

A.A. is described in its own literature as

a fellowship of men and women who share their experience, strength and hope with each other that they may solve their common problem and help others to recover from alcoholism.

The only requirement for membership is a desire to stop drinking. There are no dues or fees for A.A. membership; we are self-supporting through our own contributions. A.A. is not allied with any sect, denomination, politics, organization or institution; does not wish to engage in any controversy, neither endorses nor opposes any causes. Our primary purpose is to stay sober and help other alcoholics achieve sobriety.[3]

A.A. began in 1935 in the town of Akron, Ohio, with one drunk, William Griffith Wilson, helping and being helped equally by another, Dr. Robert Smith. Two people. Within fifty years, there were approximately 85,000 groups throughout the world. The basic principles and practices of these Alcoholics Anonymous groups are codified in its Twelve Steps and Twelve Traditions. [Please refer to Appendixes 1 and 2.]

Alcoholics Anonymous was born in the mid-1930s, in the midst of an intemperate America. From the perspective of Ernest Kurtz, the first historian who thoroughly studied and reported on Alcoholics Anonymous in the United States,

the 1930s were the "Depression Decade." As some of its alcoholics at decade's depth reached their realization of personal "bottom," the culture reckoned its own deflation "Great," both as Crash and Depression. At their bottom of Crash and Depression, Americans struggled to understand these phenomena in order to rise from them. In their understanding of how their plight had occurred, many arrived at insights similar to those of their alcoholic compatriots. They looked back on the decade of the twenties as a false and artificial "high," deeming that their downfall had come about because of high-flying speculation. . . . The people of the thirties also revolted against the 1920s as a decade of privacies. Some harkened readily to leaders who offered them a sense of unity, if only against so largely mythical a common enemy as "Wall Street." Others sought new bases for more practical unions in enthusiasms as diverse as the C.I.O. and the Civilian Conservation Corps, the bonus march and Townsend Clubs.

The America of the thirties looked backwards in disillusionment on the twenties, which were themselves disillusioned with the Progressives who in their turn had been disillusioned with yet earlier absolutes. The America of the thirties was the America of failed Prohibition and the Great Depression. The America of the thirties itself evolved into as disheartening decades: the forties' horrors of World War II, the fifties' anxiety over Communism, and thereafter ever increasing fears of loss of control. In that America, all sense of temperance in its classic meaning had been lost . . . the temperance of balance, of the middle between extremes.[4]

53

While the decade began with the Progressive Era and "a self conscious quickening of hope in the possibilities of extending rationalization and control in service to human happiness and fulfillment,"[5] and "identifying 'doing' and 'making' with *being*," by 1934 the times were such that there was in the field of religion a group that felt relying on human strength was not enough. Ernest Kurtz says 1934 was known in the history of American religion as

> annus mirabilis, *"that wondrous year." It marked the blossoming in the United States of the age of neo-orthodoxy. This "new-old" theology strongly reasserted the omnipotence and otherness of a sovereign God. It merged a deep aversion to all emphasis on human strengths with a profound objection to any stress upon merely human sufficiency, and so expressed "protest against the prevailing tendency to glorify man and all his works." Neo-orthodox thinkers were diverse. Their essential consensus lay not in specific doctrines, but "in a sense of urgency and a demand for moral and intellectual humility." The "finitude of all things human must not be ignored," they said; "the tragic sense of life must be apprehended." Neo-orthodoxy's sense of hope "rested on faith in the God who was beyond, beneath, and above all human possibilities."*[6]

In 1934 it was becoming increasingly evident that the old ways were no longer working, neither for society nor for one man working on Wall Street, William Griffith Wilson, who became, with Dr. Robert Smith, one of the co-founders of Alcoholics Anonymous.[7]

Imagine
how it might have been for Bill

Proud veteran of WWI
a securities investigator
a financial finagler
a decisive man
a willful one

drinking beyond control

A man
stealing
spare change
from his wife's purse
writing promises to her
in the family Bible
that he would
never drink again

breaking the promises
over
and
over

his mind and body
battling

Bill trying

will power
again and again

failing

Hearing his doctor
tell Bill's wife Lois
her husband would likely spend
his life locked up

thinking of suicide
as the only way out

•   •   •

Imagine in the pain
and the confusion
a schoolmate friend
and former drinking buddy
Ebby
coming to visit
to tell of how with others
how with a higher power
he had been able to stop

how he had met another drunk
Rowland

who had been told by Carl Jung
that therapy had failed

Only some sense of spirit
could help

Bill being able to listen
a little at least

then getting drunk again
with still another drying out
another hospital room

November 1934
being in despair

crying out

asking for help

Being in light
feeling the air of spirit

finally
knowing
grace

Feeling he was to
pass it on

• • •

Imagine the zeal
the fervor
of wanting everyone
to have this too

Trying to make them have it
sell it to them
finding no takers

In spring
traveling to a distant city
staying in a hotel

feeling alone
discouraged
despondent
after a business-deal collapse

feeling a pull
to the bar
down the hall
on one side

feeling guided
to the church directory
on the other

Calling clergy

Asking for help

asking for directions
to another drunk like himself

Imagine
Bill
being led to Henrietta
who had been praying for help
for Dr. Bob

Henrietta
calling Anne, Bob's wife,
who had been praying for help for Bob
a drinking doctor
who had been smuggling liquor home
hiding it in the coal bin
the clothes chute
over door jams
over beams in the cellar and in
cracks in the cellar tile
a doctor in debt
working to get enough money for alcohol

The two of them
Bill and Bob
getting together
on Mother's Day
1935

Bill finally knowing
gut deep
he needed Bob
equally
as he was needed himself

• • •

Imagine in that knowing

freedom from the compulsion	*in that insight*
allergy of the body and	
obsession of the mind	*the beginning of a program*
	that could not be birthed
Imagine	*of one alone*
in that sharing	
in that reaching out	

In the 1920s, Bill Wilson was wheeling and dealing on Wall Street and living in style with his wife Lois in New York. By the mid-1930s, Bill had been hospitalized repeatedly for his drinking, and his very life was in jeopardy. He had gone from one extreme to another. Then, Bill with Dr. Bob and the rest helped to find another way. One of balance. One of balance and reconciliation between one aspect of themselves and another, their own needs and interests with those of others; themselves and a higher power and with the world as a whole. As such, the new way serves the community of alcoholics as that type of cultural system innovation described by Anthony Wallace as a revitalization movement.

PART I
ORIGIN AND NATURE OF REVITALIZATION MOVEMENTS

A revitalization movement as defined by Wallace is "a deliberate, organized, conscious effort by members of a society to construct a more satisfying culture."[8]

Alcoholics Anonymous began as the result of the dissatisfaction of Bill Wilson, Dr. Robert Smith, and other active alcoholics with their experience of society and the inability of their constructed mazeways or mental images and understandings to help them deal effectively with stress. According to Bob's son, Smitty, Bob had "almost no practice left. He would be in hiding, or home and indisposed. Mother lied to his patients" as did his office help. "Mother always tried to frisk him when he came in. She wanted to see if she could possibly keep him in good shape for the next morning. But Dad had ways of getting around it."[9] Bill was no longer able to earn a living.[10] He had as his constant companions "terror, self-hatred, and suicidal thoughts. . . . In a state of such continual torture, physical and emotional, Bill was insane with alcoholism. Death seemed to him the only escape from his agony."[11] Surely the steady state for this community of two drunks was long gone, replaced first by stress and then distortion. Why else would they be willing to make radical changes in their way of life? As Bill Wilson later wrote, "the dying can become remarkably openminded."[12] "Who wishes to be rigorously honest and tolerant? Who wants to confess his faults to another and make restitution for harm done? Who cares anything about a Higher Power, let alone meditation and prayer? Who wants to sacrifice time and energy in trying to carry A.A.'s message to the next sufferer? No, the average alcoholic, self-centered in the extreme, doesn't care for this prospect—unless he has to do these things in order to stay alive himself."[13]

Revitalization movements have their origin in vision-trance types of transformation which are often preceded by physical stress and exhaustion.[14]

By the time of Bill's vision, he was exhausted. According to Robert Thomsen, Bill Wilson's biographer, in the preceding year, to the best of Bill's recollection, he had begun panhandling for drinks, and taking their household goods to pawn shops.[15] Bill's physical health was deteriorating—he was "eating little or nothing on his two and three day binges, having days of black-out drunkenness, and showing signs of brain damage. He was also suffering from periods of *delirium tremens*, . . . depression, interpersonal isolation and [had] episodes of being incontinent."[16] His doctor, Dr. Silkworth, had told Lois that Bill would have to be confined. "You will . . . have to lock him up somewhere if he would remain sane, or even alive. He can't go on this way another year, possibly."[17]

On the day he reported having his vision, he was a patient at Charles Towns Hospital in New York where he had been placed on a withdrawal regimen from alcohol.[18]

A revitalization movement is characterized by "personality transformation dreams or visions."[19]

According to Wallace, with few exceptions, "every religious revitalization movement . . . has been originally conceived in one or several hallucinatory visions by a single individual. . . . Generally they show evidence of a radical inner change in personality soon after the vision experience: a remission of old and chronic physical complaints, a more active and purposeful way of life, greater confidence in interpersonal relations, the dropping of deep-seated habits like alcoholism."[20]

Bill's remembrance of his transformative dream or vision is re-told in A.A. literature. As Bill tells it, prior to his vision he had been visited in the hospital by a former drinking buddy, Ebby T., who had "found religion" and had been able to stay sober.

> *So Ebby finally took his leave. Now the jaws of the dilemma really crushed. I hit an all-time block. I can only suppose that any particle of belief that there was a single thing I could do for myself alone was for the moment rubbed out.*
>
> *My depression deepened unbearably and finally it seemed to me as though I were at the very bottom of the pit. I still gagged badly on the notion of a Power greater than myself, but finally, just for the moment, the last vestige of my proud obstinancy was crushed. And I found myself as a child, utterly alone in complete darkness. And I cried out as a child, expecting little—indeed, expecting nothing. I simply said, "If there is a God, will he show himself?"*
>
> *Suddenly, my room blazed with an indescribably white light. I was seized with an ecstasy beyond description. Every joy I had known was pale by comparison. The light, the ecstasy—I was conscious of nothing else for a time.*
>
> *Then, seen in the mind's eye, there was a mountain. I stood upon its summit, where a great wind blew. A wind, not of air, but of spirit. In great, clean strength, it blew right through me. Then came the blazing thought "You are a free man. . . . This is the God of the Scriptures." I know not at all how long I remained in this state, but finally the light and the ecstasy subsided. I again saw the wall of my room. As I became more quiet, a great peace stole over me, and this was accompanied by a sensation difficult to describe. I became acutely aware of a Presence which seemed like a veritable sea of living spirit. I lay on the shores of a new world. "This," I thought, "must be the great reality."*
>
> *Savoring my new world, I remained in this state for a long time. I seemed to be possessed by the absolute, and the curious conviction deepened that no matter how wrong things seemed to be, there could be no question of the ultimate rightness of God's universe. For the first time, I felt that I really belonged. I knew that I was loved and could love in return. I thanked my God, who had given me a glimpse of His absolute self. Even though a pilgrim upon an uncertain highway, I need be concerned no more, for I had glimpsed the great beyond.*[21]

Wilson goes on to say that then "reason returned, my modern education took over. Obviously I had gone crazy. I became terribly frightened. Dr. Silkworth came in to hear my trembling account of the phenomenon. He assured me I was not mad; that I had perhaps undergone an experience which might solve my problem. Skeptical man of science he then was; this was most kind and astute. If he had said 'hallucination' I might now be dead."[22] Bill later said, "These gifts of grace, whether they came in a rush or very gradually, were all founded on a basis of hopelessness. The recipients were people who in some controlling area of life found themselves in a situation that could not be gotten over, around, or under. Their defeat had been absolute, and so was mine."[23]

Nell Wing, long-time associate of Bill and Lois Wilson and also A.A.'s first archivist, said that Bill sensed he was to pass on this experience. "Whether he 'heard' that he was to do this depends on what you mean by hearing. To try to describe that—it's uncanny. It's not always in words. You hear in non-verbal terms. During what he called his 'hot flash' he got the impression he was to work with other people as he was being helped by his friend Ebby and Doctor Silkworth."[24]

Lois Wilson, Bill's wife and the co-founder of Al-Anon, said that Bill explained " 'If I had a spiritual experience, so could other people,' and that's what he tried to do—he tried to set the background so new A.A.s could have a spiritual awakening."[25] He knew he needed to change his way of life.

Part II
Six Tasks of Revitalization Movements

The first task of revitalization movements, according to Wallace, is that of mazeway reformulation.

Wallace defines a mazeway as a mental image of "nature, society, culture, personality, and body image, as seen by one person."[26] Revitalizations reorient their members in relationship with themselves, with others, with God or Higher Power and with the world as a whole.

PEACE WITH THEMSELVES

"Changing the mazeway involves changing the total Gestalt of [this] image of self."[27]

For members of Alcoholics Anonymous, this means reconciling an *active* way of being in the world with a *receptive* one. This means a change from an exclusively dualistic way of experiencing the world with attempts to control and consequent swings from power to powerlessness, to one in which acceptance, receptivity, and unity are acknowledged and appreciated.

For Bill Wilson and other members of A.A., the old Gestalt was the way of self-reliance which failed.[28] In the words of A.A. literature, "There was an insistent yearning to enjoy life as we once did and a heartbreaking obsession that some new miracle of control would enable us to do it. There was always one more attempt—and one more failure."[29] One of the essentials for recovery in A.A. is that members "be convinced that any life run on self-will can hardly be a success."

> On that basis [of self-will] we are almost always in collision with something or somebody, even though our motives are good. Most people try to live by self-propulsion. Each person is like an actor who wants to run the whole show; is forever trying to arrange the lights, the ballet, the scenery and the rest of the players in his own way. If his arrangements would only stay put, if only people would do as he wished, the show would be great. . . .

What usually happens? The show doesn't come off very well. . . . He decides to exert himself more. He becomes, on the next occasion, still more demanding or gracious, as the case may be. . . . Admitting he may be somewhat at fault, he is sure that other people are more to blame. He becomes angry, indignant, self-pitying. . . . Is he not a victim of the delusion that he can wrest satisfaction and happiness out of this world if he only manages well? Is he not, even in his best moments, a producer of confusion rather than harmony? [30]

The new *Gestalt* for members is one in which they move from "self-will run riot"[31] to reliance on a power greater than themselves. Members learn that "defeat, rightly accepted, need be no disaster. We now know that we do not have to run away, nor ought we again try to overcome adversity by still another bulldozing power drive that can only push up obstacles before us faster than they can be taken down."[32] In his first letter to Dr. Carl Jung, Bill Wilson wrote that the common denominator of conversion experiences was that of "ego collapse" at depth.[33] Bill Wilson believed with Harry Tiebout that a spiritual experience is *"the act of giving up reliance on one's own omnipotence."*[34]

The basic text of Alcoholics Anonymous, officially titled *Alcoholics Anonymous* and affectionately referred to by members as the Big Book, was published in 1939 with one purpose in mind: to enable readers to "find a Power greater than yourself which will solve your problem. . . . lack of power, that was our dilemma. We had to find a power by which we could live, and it had to be a *Power greater than ourselves.*"[35] Bill promises that members will be

> *restored to sanity, provided we condition ourselves for the gift of restoration—or, to put it in religious terms, to the inflow of God's grace which results in the expulsion of the obsession. Nor does it seem to matter how we define God's grace. We can still claim if we like that we have tapped a hidden or unused inner resource. We don't need to actually define just where that came from. Or we can believe, as most of us finally do, that we have tapped the resources of God as he exists in us and in the cosmos generally. None of us can presume to know exactly how this is. . . .*[36] *Our new way of staying sober is literally founded upon the proposition that "Of ourselves, we are nothing, the Father doeth the works."*[37]

For members of Alcoholics Anonymous, changing the Gestalt of the image of self involves reconciling those aspects of the self previously found *acceptable* with those aspects of the self previously found *unacceptable*.

Finding a power greater than the separate self, even if it was simply the A.A. group as a whole, helped provide the courage necessary to take a personal inventory. The old way was living a life of deception, of presenting a "stage character" to the world—the one "he likes his fellows to see . . . but knows in his heart he doesn't deserve."[38] The new way was to be one of "rigorous honesty." Members are to go "far beyond those things which were superficially wrong with us to see those flaws which were basic, flaws which sometimes were responsible for the whole pattern of our lives."[39] One of the key spiritual axioms of A.A. is that "every time we're disturbed, no matter what the cause, there is something wrong *with us*."[40] Some of the ways recovering alcoholics had available to deal with what was wrong included taking "searching and fearless" moral inventories which included enumerating assets as well as admitting defects of character, asking God (as understood by the individual member) to remove character defects, making amends to people harmed, praying for knowledge of God's will and the power to carry it out, helping others, and trusting the principles of recovery in all areas of life.[41]

"Changing the mazeway involves changing the total Gestalt of this image of . . . nature and body."[42]

For members of Alcoholics Anonymous, recovery from alcoholism involves reconciling the body and the mind. The peace of this reconciliation and recovery itself is felt by A.A. members to be contingent upon daily total abstinence from alcohol. Dr. Silkworth, first Bill's doctor and then an ardent advocate of A.A., early on defined alcoholism in terms of the conflict between mind and body. Bill says he described it as "a sickness of the emotions, coupled with a sickness of the body, which he loosely described as an allergy."[43]

Bill draws on Dr. Silkworth's explanation to describe the battle that was waged within him while he was drinking. He describes an "obsession that condemns you to drink against your will and true interests, even unto destruction, and the bodily sensitivity that guarantees madness and death if you drink at all." Bill adds that he understood from Dr. Carl Jung through Jung's alcoholic patient Rowland and Rowland's alcoholic friend Ebby that there was "no way out known to the doctors." Bill concluded that "my God, science, the only God I had then, had declared me hopeless."[44]

For recovering alcoholics in A.A., the foundation for a new life is abstinence from alcohol one day at a time. This is the basic principle of non-harm applied to one's own body.[45] Stephanie Brown makes this point clearly as she describes the continuing axis in recovery as abstinence from alcohol. The gifts of sobriety are contingent on abstinence. And while as far as I know there is no specific reference in A.A. literature to a changing view of nature, in practical terms, abstinence from alcohol relieves not only the body of the abstinent alcoholic, but greatly relieves the collective body Earth as well.[46]

PEACE WITH GOD OR HIGHER POWER

In revitalization movements " . . . interest shifts to a god. . . ."[47]

Bill Wilson, writing in A.A.'s Big Book, says that *"It was only a matter of being willing to believe in a Power greater than myself. Nothing more was required of me to make my beginning."* Although previously he acknowledged that "the word God . . . aroused a certain antipathy" in him, he seized upon the notion of choosing a god of his own conception, and thereafter "placed [himself] unreservedly under His care and direction."[48] In a chapter of A.A.'s Big Book, which was intended to reach those suffering alcoholics who could not be reached personally, Bill specifically addressed agnostics, and declared that "as soon as we were able to lay aside prejudice and express even a willingness to believe in a Power greater than ourselves, we commenced to get results, even though it was impossible for any of us to fully define or comprehend that Power, which is God. . . . As soon as we admitted the possible existence of a Creative Intelligence, a Spirit of the Universe underlying the totality of things, we began to be possessed of a new sense of power and direction."[49]

Bill is careful to explain that "Alcoholics Anonymous is not a religious organization; there is no dogma. The one theological proposition is a 'Power greater than one's self.' Even this concept is forced on no one. The newcomer merely immerses himself in our society and tries the program as best he can. Left alone, he will surely report the gradual onset of a transforming experience, call it what he may. Observers once thought A.A. could appeal only to the religiously susceptible. Yet our membership includes a former member of the American Atheist Society and about 20,000 [this in 1949] almost as tough. . . . Of course we speak little of conversion nowadays because so many people really dread being God-bitten. But conversion, as broadly described by [William] James, does seem to be our basic process; all other devices are but the foundations. When one alcoholic works with another, he but consolidates and sustains that essential experience."[50] Bill says that in recovery, members of Alcoholics Anonymous "want nothing else but God's will for us, and his grace for our fellows."[51]

PEACE WITH OTHERS

In revitalization movements, " . . . interest shifts to . . . the community. . . ." [52]

In the Big Book, members and potential members are promised that in recovery they "will lose interest in selfish things and gain interest in [their] fellows. Self-seeking will slip away."[53]

The A.A. basic text describes selfishness or self-centeredness as the root of an alcoholic's troubles. It says that alcoholics are "driven by a hundred forms of fear, self-delusion, self-seeking, and self-pity" and that "our troubles, we think, are basically of our own making. They arise out of ourselves, and the alcoholic is an extreme example of self-will run riot, though he usually doesn't think so. Above everything, we alcoholics must be rid of this selfishness. We must, or it kills us! God makes that possible."[54]

Recovery depends to a large degree on the individual's willingness and ability to sense his or her connection with others—to gain, often for the first time, a true sense of community and shared interests. Members learn that they "can do together what [they] can't do in separation."[55] They are advised to "identify, not compare" with those who share their personal stories of recovery. The Big Book counsels that the task of members in recovery is to be "of maximum helpfulness to others."[56]

Members begin to find connections between themselves and others through what Kurtz calls the dynamic of the "shared honesty of mutual vulnerability openly acknowledged."[57] Both the willingness to be vulnerable and the ability to relate to others as equals are facilitated by such practices as rotation of service positions and the sharing of stories freely.

Nell Wing, who was a long-time worker at what was first called the Alcoholic Foundation, then Alcoholics Anonymous General Service Office in New York, says she believes anonymity is the greatest principle of A.A. "When you come in to A.A. you can be a celebrity and you can be a titled person. But you come in as a peer of the guy off the street and this is what makes A.A. work. It would not work if it was not for that humility which being on the peer level brings. Which is spirituality—the humility which [comes with that equality]. Without that, it couldn't be done. This person who is very important in the world at large is 'only a drunk,' as Bill would say.[58] The person who may be well-known needs the same kind of loving attention and the same peer quality the guy from skid row needs. The same as the youngster or the woman or the nun or the priest or whoever. So that there is this anonymity, this togetherness, all-in-the- same-boat kind of thing that affects A.A. wherever you find it."[59]

Changing the mazeway involves changing the total Gestalt of this image of . . . society.

While Wallace found that it may also be necessary for revitalization movements to "make changes in the 'real' system in order to bring mazeway and 'reality' into congruence,"[60] in the Twelve Step movement of A.A., the attention is on effecting changes in the mazeway, rather than attempting to change the "real " system directly. Those changes involve finding an appropriate balance between the needs of the individual and the needs of the community. The first of Twelve A.A. Traditions (which are guides to how A.A. relates among itself and to society as a whole) reads: "Each member of Alcoholics Anonymous is but a small part of a great whole. A.A. must continue to live or most of us will surely die. Hence our common welfare comes first. But individual welfare follows close afterward. Most individuals cannot recover unless there is a group. Realization dawns that he is but a small part of a great whole. . . . It becomes plain that the group must survive or the individual will not."[61] At the same time, the text goes on to say surely there is no other society which "more jealously guards the individual's right to think, talk, and act as he wishes. No A.A. can compel another to do anything; nobody can be punished or expelled. Our Twelve Steps to recovery are suggestions; the Twelve Traditions which guarantee

A.A.'s unity contain not a single 'Don't.' They repeatedly say 'We ought' . . . but never 'You must!' " [62] Bill Wilson says there is also "a recognition, common in all forms of society," that "the individual must sometimes place the welfare of his fellows ahead of his own uncontrolled desires. Were the individual to yield nothing to the common welfare there could be no society at all—only self-will run riot; anarchy in the worst sense of that word."[63] This balancing of needs and responsibilities are among the contributions which the principles and program of Alcoholics Anonymous make to a new way.

Members come to realize that their own interests are coincident with those of others, that as they help others they simultaneously help themselves. Lois Wilson expressed the awareness of the communion with others which is discovered by members of Alcoholics Anonymous in recovery when she said that "it wasn't a question of getting on with Dr. Bob and Anne Smith. They were *part* of you."[64]

Not only does the A.A. program help members connect with the society of other alcoholics, it helps them re-connect with the rest of society as well. One of the primary objectives of the Twelve Steps is to help members "develop the best possible relations with every human being we know" and to live in the "greatest peace, partnership, and brotherhood with all men and women, of whatever description."[65] Members are advised that they may "come into harmony with practically anyone" if they act with "courtesy, kindness, justice and love," and ask themselves if they are doing to others as they would have them do unto themselves.[66]

PEACE WITH THE WORLD AS A WHOLE

In revitalization movements, "interest shifts to . . . a new way."

The new way for members of Alcoholics Anonymous involves balance where before there were extremes, bonding where before there was separation, and boundaries where before boundaries were unacknowledged.

As already noted, the new way involves aligning *personal will with surrender,* in other words the active way with the receptive, and power with powerlessness. It involves reconciling *body and mind*. It involves a reconciliation of *acceptable and unacceptable* aspects of the self. It involves bonding and balancing between *self and other*—A.A. could not begin until there were *two equals* Bill Wilson and Dr. Bob—both giving, both receiving. It involves balancing and bonding between the *individual and the community as a whole*. It involves bridging *personal limits with an unlimited Higher Power*. This is exemplified by the often-repeated saying, "God is doing for us what we could not do for ourselves."[67] Here the recovering alcoholic becomes aware that the ego-deflating idea of their individual selves as "not-God"[68] is balanced by the concept of an unlimited Higher Power.

The new way also and relatedly involves balancing *the visual with the oral*. Elpenor, whose article was reviewed in chapter 2, says that in A.A. "no one is under any compulsion to speak. On the contrary, old-timers tell you again and again that one of the great virtues they discovered in the program is the capacity to listen: truly to listen, without making assumptions or jumping to conclusions, without analyzing, categorizing, glossing, or comparing . . . but with appetite, imagination and sympathy."[69] He says that "A.A. drama is oral, preliterate. In fact, the whole culture of A.A. is oral, a tribal culture which gets passed on by means of stories and maxims. There's an A.A. maxim for every contingency: *Count your blessings, One day at a time, Easy does it, Live and let live, First things first.*"[70]

The new way also involves bridging *history and myth, monster and hero*. In telling the story of recovery within the framework of "what it was like, what happened, and what it's like now," each member's personal history—that is, his or her accounts of resistance and conflict—is transformed into what Elpenor describes as a hero's quest—the stuff of myth. Elpenor says that at an A.A. meeting, "the newcomer learns to channel the maelstrom of his experience along the lines of a quest story."[71] During the telling of the historical portion, the story teller invariably sounds suspiciously like Holdfast, one of the mythic monsters described by Joseph Campbell. During the telling of the recovery part of the story, the storyteller begins to sound like a dragon-slayer, practicing the steps of A.A., each of which is ego-deflating.[72]

The new way involves reconciling *what is and what might be*. This is evident in the A.A. claim for "spiritual progress rather than spiritual perfection," a deliberate modification of the call for "Absolute Honesty, Absolute Purity, Absolute Unselfishness, and Absolute Love" by the Oxford Group to which many early A.A. members belonged.

It involves reconciling *one idea with its apparent opposite*. An example of this may be found in the sayings frequently repeated in A.A. circles, such as "winning through losing, keeping it by giving it away."

The new way involves reconciling *works with grace*. Bill Wilson says that the A.A. member knows that "once the miracle of sobriety has been received, that Providence expects all of us to work and to grow—to do our part in maintaining our blessings in full force. A perpetual miracle—with no effort or responsibility on our part—simply isn't in the cards. We all understand that the price of both personal and group survival is willingness and sacrifice, vigilance and work."[73]

It involves reconciling *past and future*. While to most new members the idea of not drinking for the rest of their lives seems absolutely impossible, the program emphasizes the importance of living one day at a time. At the bedside of the man who was to become the third member of A.A., Bill and Dr. Bob emphasized the importance of limiting the future to the next twenty-four hours. As told by this subsequent member, Bill and Bob asked, "'You can quit [drinking for] twenty-four hours, can't you?' I said, 'Sure, yes, anybody can do that, for twenty-four hours.' They said 'That's what we're talking about. Just twenty-four hours at a time.' That sure did take a load off my mind."[74]

The idea of living in terms of daily cycles came to apply to more than abstinence. Through the Big Book early members offered members guidelines for an entire day.

On awakening let us think about the twenty-four hours ahead. We consider our plans for the day. Before we begin, we ask God to direct our thinking, especially asking that it be divorced from self-pity, dishonest or self-seeking motives. Under these conditions we can employ our mental faculties with assurance, for after all God gave us brains to use. Our thought-life will be placed on a much higher plane when our thinking is cleared of wrong motives.

In thinking about our day we may face indecision. We may not be able to determine which course to take. Here we ask God for inspiration, an intuitive thought or a decision. We relax and take it easy. We don't struggle. We are often surprised how the right answers come after we have tried this for a while. What used to be the hunch or the occasional inspiration gradually becomes a working part of the mind. Being still inexperienced and having just made conscious contact with God, it is not probable that we are going to be inspired at all times. We might pay for this presumption in all sorts of absurd actions and ideas. Nevertheless, we find that our thinking will, as time passes, be more and more on the plane of inspiration. We come to rely upon it.

We usually conclude the period of meditation with a prayer that we be shown all through the day what our next step is to be, that we be given whatever we need to take care of such problems. We ask especially for freedom from self-will, and are careful to make no request for ourselves only. We may ask for ourselves, however, if others will be helped. We are careful never to pray for our own selfish ends. Many of us have wasted a lot of time doing that and it doesn't work. You can easily see why.

If circumstances warrant, we ask our wives or friends to join us in morning meditation. If we belong to a religious denomination which requires a definite morning devotion, we attend to that also. If not members of religious bodies, we sometimes select and memorize a few set prayers which emphasize the principles we have been discussing. There are many helpful books also. Suggestions about these may be obtained from one's priest, minister, or rabbi. Be quick to see where religious people are right. Make use of what they offer.

As we go through the day we pause, when agitated or doubtful, and ask for the right thought or action. We constantly remind ourselves we are no longer running the show, humbly saying to ourselves many times each day "Thy will be done." We are then in much less danger of excitement, fear, anger, worry, self-pity, or foolish decisions. We become much more efficient. We do not tire so easily, for we are not burning up energy foolishly as we did when we were trying to arrange life to suit ourselves.[75]

The new way of life envisioned by Bill Wilson, Dr. Bob Smith, and other early A.A.s is perhaps described most succinctly in what have come to be know as the A.A. promises, which include the assurance that members' "whole attitude and outlook on life will change" and that they will find a power greater than themselves doing for them what they could not do for themselves.[76]

As a result of practicing the recovery program, members are promised they will undergo "a profound alteration in [their] reaction to life," and that "with few exceptions, our members find that they have tapped an unsuspected inner resource which they presently identify with their own conception of a Power greater than themselves."[77]

The second task of revitalization movements is communication.

After engaging in mazeway reformulation, i.e., shifting from one *Gestalt* to another, Wallace states that communication becomes and remains one of the primary activities of revitalization movements. He says that "frequently, within a few years, the new plan is [communicated and] put into effect by the participants in the movement."[78]

Within four years of its founding in 1935, when Bill Wilson and Dr. Bob Smith met in Akron and helped each other stay sober, members had published the movement's key text, which they called *Alcoholics Anonymous*. In March 1941, an article written by Jack Alexander and published in the *Saturday Evening Post* resulted in free national publicity and a subsequent jump in membership. Both A.A.'s basic text and the Alexander article described the philosophy of A.A. and recounted personal stories of members who were successfully practicing the program.

The geometric progression of A.A. membership during those first years is reported in one of the appendices of *A.A. Comes of Age* (p. 310):

5 recovered at the end of the first year.
15 recovered at the end of the second year.
40 recovered at the end of the third year.
100 recovered at the end of the fourth year.
400 recovered at the end of the fifth year.
2000 recovered at the end of the sixth year.
8000 recovered at the end of the seventh year.

According to Wallace, with revitalization movements in general there are two fundamental motifs to be communicated: "that the convert will come under the care and protection of certain supernatural beings; and that both he and his society will benefit materially from an identification with some definable new cultural system."[79]

These messages were part of A.A. communications. In the Big Book members are advised that "without help it is too much for us. But there is One who has all power—that One is God. . . . Half measures availed us nothing. We stood at the turning point. We asked His protection and care with complete abandon."[80] The A.A. literature does allude to material benefits of membership; however, throughout A.A. literature the emphasis is on the spiritual gains that will ensue as a result of following the suggested program. In A.A., what is communicated is that "*fear* of economic insecurity will leave us." [Italics are mine.] In cases where money has once been a master, it will become a servant,[81] and will cease to be among the alcoholic's unacknowledged pantheon of gods.[82]

The third task of revitalization is organization.

Wallace quotes Max Weber as saying that the "routinization" of charisma is a critical issue in movement organization, since "unless this 'power' is distributed to other personnel in a stable institutional structure, the movement itself is liable to die with the death or failure of individual prophet, king, or war lord."[83]

The Twelve Traditions were developed to guide the A.A. community in organizational matters. Bill Wilson says that "the Twelve Points of Tradition are little else than a specific application of the spirit of the Twelve Steps of recovery to our group life and to our relations with society in general. The recovery steps would make each individual AA whole and one with God; the Twelve Points of Tradition would make us one with each other and whole with the world about us. Unity is our aim."[84]

One of A.A.'s Twelve Traditions, Tradition Two, is that "For our group purpose there is but one ultimate authority—a loving God as He may express Himself in our group conscience. Our leaders are but trusted servants; they do not govern."[85] And again, "Leaders do not rule by mandate—they lead by example."[86] There is an absence of hierarchy and entrenched bureaucracy. As Nell Wing has observed, throughout nearly the entire course of A.A. growth, "the leadership of A.A. comes from the people, comes from the members. It's the people who make the whole thing work and have the ultimate say. That's a unique thing right there."[87] Bill comments that "An A.A. group need not be coerced by any human government over and above its own members."[88] "We reason that we must hang together or die."[89]

Bill explains the organization—or relative lack of organization—of Alcoholics Anonymous at length. He acknowledges that

> *naturally, the explosive potential of our rather neurotic fellowship is enormous. [Still,] our deep kinship, the urgency of our mission, the need to abate our neurosis for contented survival; all these, together with love for God and man, have contained us in surprising unity.*[90]

> *Many people are coming to think that Alcoholics Anonymous is, to some extent, a new form of human society. In our discussion of the First Tradition, it was emphasized that we have, in A.A. no coercive human authority. . . . With respect to its own affairs, the collective conscience of the group will, given time, almost surely demonstrate its perfect dependability. The group conscience will, in the end, prove a far more infallible guide for group affairs than the decision of any individual member, however good or wise he may be. This is a striking and almost unbelievable fact about Alcoholics Anonymous . . . .We need not depend*

overmuch on inspired leaders. Because our active leadership of service can be truly rotating, we enjoy a kind of democracy rarely possible elsewhere. . . . Therefore we of Alcoholics Anonymous are certain that there is but one ultimate authority, "a loving God as he may express himself in our group conscience."[91]

Bill observes that "the least possible organization, that's our universal ideal. No fees, no dues, no rules imposed on anybody, one alcoholic bringing recovery to the next;—that's the substance of what we most desire, isn't it?"[92]

The organization itself has been called anarchistic. Bill responded to such criticism with the observation that "when the anarchy of the alcoholic faces his tyrant [alcohol], that alcoholic must become a social animal or perish. Perforce, our society has settled for the purest kind of democracy."[93]

Although Bill Wilson and some of the other early A.A. members were said by contemporaries to be charismatic leaders, leadership in A.A. is generally more prosaic in nature. Those in A.A. who exemplify the program in practice are A.A. sponsors. In A.A. literature, a sponsor is described as someone "who has made some progress in the recovery program" and "who shares that experience on a continuous, individual basis with another alcoholic who is attempting to attain or maintain sobriety through A.A."[94] Through the process of sponsorship, new members are afforded individual attention and guidance.

The fourth task of revitalization movements is that of adaptation.

Wallace describes revitalization movements in general as revolutionary organizations and believes they will almost "inevitably . . . encounter some resistance."[95]

That A.A. has encountered so little resistance may be attributed to a number of factors.

One reason that A.A. has encountered so little resistance is likely due to the nature of its traditions. As a whole, the traditions work to ensure that A.A. maintains an internal focus and does not become involved on the organizational level in trying to change situations in the larger community.

Tradition Five, for example, states that "each group has but one primary purpose—to carry its message to the alcoholic who still suffers." Tradition Six states that "an A.A. group ought never endorse, finance, or lend the A.A. name to any related facility or outside enterprise, lest problems of money, property, and prestige divert us from our primary purpose." Tradition Seven is that "every A.A. group ought to be fully self-supporting, declining outside contributions." Tradition Ten states that "A.A. has no opinion on outside issues; hence the A.A. name ought never be drawn into public controversy." Tradition Eleven is that "Our public relations policy is based on attraction rather than promotion; we need always maintain personal anonymity at the level of press, radio and films."

Another reason that Alcoholics Anonymous has likely encountered little resistance is that in A.A. members learn to accept personal responsibility and practice the principles of recovery in all areas of their lives. As in what Steven Tipton describes as alternative religious movements such as Zen in contemporary America,

> *[members] pay their creditors, satisfy their employers, keep their personal promises, and make their business appointments. In short, they fit in better as functionally related components of a complex society, but they do so more by virtue of their ethical convictions than their technical skills.*[96]

In the chapter to employers in the Big Book, it is stated that a recovering alcoholic will work hard and "thank you to his dying day."[97] The author of this passage says that he himself has two recovering alcoholic employees, who produce as much as five normal salesmen. "But why not? They have a new attitude, and they have been saved from a living death."[98] Accepting responsibility for oneself is one of the fundamental components of the Twelve Step recovery programs.

Alcoholics Anonymous has likely merged with its larger cultural environment harmoniously because, as with those movements studied by Tipton, "experiencing and accepting the world instead of trying to control it remains a central theme."[99] Bill Wilson, writing in the A.A. magazine *Grapevine* in March 1962, states that

> *our very first problem is to accept our present circumstances as they are, ourselves as we are, and the people about us as they are. This is to adopt a realistic humility without which no genuine advance can even begin. . . .*

> *Provided we strenuously avoid turning these realistic surveys of the facts of life into unrealistic alibis for apathy or defeatism, they can be the sure foundation upon which increased emotional health and therefore spiritual progress can be built.*[100]

The A.A. position of experiencing the world is expressed in one protracted sentence:

> *Service, gladly rendered, obligations squarely met, troubles well accepted or solved with God's help, the knowledge that at home or in the world outside we are partners in a common effort, the well-understood fact that in God's sight all human beings are important, the proof that love freely given brings a full return, the certainty that we are no longer isolated and alone in self-constructed prisons, the surety that we . . . can fit and belong in God's scheme of things—these are the . . . satisfactions of right living for which no amount of pomp and circumstance, no heap of material possessions, could possibly be substitutes.*[101]

The importance of acceptance for those recovering from alcoholism is also well-stated in some of the personal stories included in the Big Book by one writing as "Doctor, Alcoholic, Addict": "I must keep my magic magnifying mind *on* my acceptance and *off* my expectations, for my serenity is directly proportional to my level of acceptance."[102]

One of the most basic reasons that A.A. has encountered so little resistance is that A.A. has not overturned tradition and replaced it with something entirely new. Rather

> *[it] has drawn out strands from traditional moralities and re-woven them into a fabric that ties into American culture as a whole yet differs in pattern from any one of its traditions. . . .*

> *I[t] is religious in the literal sense that [it] binds together heretofore disparate elements within a pluralistic culture, revitalizing tradition as [it] changes it. . . .*[103]

I have identified here just some of the "strands" woven through American history and consciously or unconsciously now part of the fabric of A.A. These are some of the ideas and practices of Alcoholics Anonymous which preceded it in time. I could not include them all.

Key practices and ideas that were later reflected in A.A. emerged during the period of American history that historian of religion William McLoughlin describes as the first of America's four great religious awakenings which he dates from 1730–1760. From this period came the idea of itinerants delivering the "message of salvation" in a "new medium—the spoken word of the common man," and the "democratization of religion, the breaking down of colony and class lines, denominational and regional differences."[104]

The Seneca among the Iroquois Nation were among those affected by the increased exposure to other belief systems that occurred during this period. Anthony Wallace believes such a conflux of cultures contributed to the revitalization movement which began among them with the vision of Handsome Lake in 1799.[105] It becomes evident through the work of Anthony Wallace that there are many similarities between the ideas and practices of revitalization among the Seneca and the program of Alcoholics Anonymous. I will give some examples.

Since the Seneca had been suffering from harmful consequences of drinking, one of the key changes called for was total abstinence from alcohol.[106] *Recovery from alcoholism with the Twelve Step program of Alcoholics Anonymous is contingent upon total abstinence.* When Handsome Lake's followers were asked why they were unable to leave their drunken habits before, since the "ruinous" consequences were clear, the reply was that " 'when the Great Spirit forbid such conduct by their prophet, he gave them the power to comply with their request.' "[107] *It is said in Alcoholics Anonymous that "God is doing for us what we could not do for ourselves."* Handsome Lake did not debate over whether alcohol was good or bad in itself. They were not to judge if others outside of their community drank alcohol.[108] *In Alcoholics Anonymous, no position whatever is taken on the drinking practices or abstinence of non-members.* Handsome Lake's vision evolved into a code. *Bill Wilson's vision evolved into the Twelve Steps and Twelve Traditions of Alcoholics Anonymous.* Along with abstinence was the key ritual change of introducing confession as a major sacrament. Handsome Lake believed that "if all men would but repent, 'the earth would become as new again.' "[109] *The practice of A.A.'s Fourth, Fifth, Eighth, Ninth and Tenth Steps pertain specifically to acknowledgment and admission of harm-doing.* Another similarity between the revitalization of the Seneca and Alcoholics Anonymous lies in the fact that the Seneca, according to Wallace, "were not accustomed to thinking in terms of exclusive church 'membership.' "[110] Handsome Lake did not believe he was offering a new religion, simply reviving the old. *Bill Wilson acknowledged that the principles of A.A. came from ancient sources.* Handsome Lake "apparently was willing for Indian converts to Christianity to remain with their new faith," and remain a follower of his as well.[111] *This pre-dates the attempt in Alcoholics Anonymous to be as inclusive as possible when it came to welcoming members from diverse religious backgrounds.* Handsome Lake advised his people to " 'live in peace and love one another and all mankind, white people as well as Indians" and Cornplanter, a successor to Handsome Lake, also expressed his wish "to be at peace with all men."[112] *This is similar to the suggestion in the literature of Alcoholics Anonymous that members seek to live in greatest peace with with everyone.* Cornplanter said in an address before he died that he wished to be reconciled with anyone to whom he had done any wrong or in any way had given offense.[113] *This reconciliation occurs for A.A. members as they practice the Eighth, Ninth, and Tenth Steps of A.A.'s Twelve Step program.* Handsome Lake said that if his followers were to be doomed, it would be brought on them by their own "sins."[114] *This is somewhat similar to A.A.'s notion that "our troubles, we think, are basically of our own making."* Handsome Lake adapted what he liked from the Quakers in particular and modern societies in general, and left the rest.[115] *A frequent recommendation heard at meetings of Alcoholics Anonymous is that all members "take what they like, and leave the rest."* While the A.A. movement is able to balance the modern with the traditional from the perspective of the modern, Handsome Lake's revitalization movement joined the modern with the traditional from the perspective of the traditional.[116]

During the same period that gave birth to the *Gaiwiio* ("The Good Word") passed on through Handsome Lake, McLoughlin said white Euro-American society was experiencing a Second Great Awakening (1800–1830). From this period some of the ideas and practices that later found a place in Alcoholics Anonymous included the emphasis on self-help and the idea that "that government is best which governs least" which McLoughlin feels characterized this awakening.[117] Also from this period came the appearance of new benevolent associations and voluntary reform societies.[118] Making their appearance on the scene as well were converts to a new way of life wanting to "share their experience of liberation and bring the joy of salvation to others."[119]

The close of the nineteenth century brought the "human religiousness"[120] of William James, particularly as expressed in *The Varieties of Religious Experience,* along with his appreciation for pragmatism and pluralism in the field of religion. Ernest Kurtz said that Alcoholics Anonymous made great use of these insights of James'; that A.A.'s "largest link with his philosophy lay precisely in their application of pragmatic pluralism to religious insight."[121] Nell Wing says Bill and Dr. Bob were both "pragmatic, William James people. . . . They were concerned with what works."[122]

From the Third Great Awakening, which McLoughlin dates from 1890–1920, came the legacy of Charles Grandison Finney's stages of a revival—" 'conviction of sin, . . . a deep repentance, a breaking down of the heart, [and] reformation.' "[123] There were also his interdenominational meetings, and his emphasis on evening meetings when clerks, shopgirls, and mechanics would be free to attend.[124] Another of his beliefs which later found a fundamental place in the community of A.A. was the idea that once "reformed," an individual "should set out with a determination to aim at being useful in the highest degree possible."[125] Finney's beliefs were also compatible with A.A. in that he felt drinking alcohol was a problem "to be eradicated by conversion, not by temperance pledges or prohibition laws."[126]

The ideas and practices of the Oxford Group in America of the 1920s and 1930s played a major and direct role in the founding of A.A. Many founders of A.A. were associated with the Oxford Group, including Bill W., Dr. Bob, and their respective wives, Lois and Anne. From this group were directly learned the principles of self-examination, acknowledgment of character defects, restitution for harm done, and working with others.[127] Also learned were the benefits of remaining non-denominational; the benefits of meditation or what was known in the Oxford Group and subsequently in some A.A. circles as "Quiet Time" during which time members asked for guidance from a power greater than themselves and practiced listening within; the efficacy of decision-making through the taking of a group conscience;[128] the use of the Lord's Prayer in meetings; the idea of meetings held outside of churches, often in the homes of individual members—a practice which continues today in AA; the idea of each member having a higher power of his of her own conception; the practice of holding meetings when it was possible for working members to attend; and the sharing of personal experience, which was called "witnessing." According to Ernest Kurtz, the five procedures of the Oxford Group which later found a place in A.A. were (1) give in to God; (2) listen to God's direction; (3) check guidance; (4) make restitution and (5) share.[129] The two other practices present in the Oxford Group and subsequently vital to A.A. were to "never be paid for . . . aiding others to attain the 'changed life'; and an emphasis on the obligation to engage in personal work with others in order to change the *helpers'* lives."[130]

This list is hardly exhaustive, nor are the ideas attributed to a particular source necessarily unique to or original with that source. This section is merely intended to indicate that the movement of A.A. is well in keeping with American spiritual, religious and philosophical tradition, both Native and Euro-American, and is essentially inclusive in nature. This is a reality acknowledged by Bill Wilson in his statement that members need "humbly reflect that each of A.A.'s principles, *every one of them,* has been borrowed from ancient sources,"[131] which find expression in America and elsewhere.

The fifth task of revitalization movements is cultural transformation.

A.A. facilitates cultural transformation not only for members of the immediate community, but within the larger culture as well, as members "practice these principles in all [their] affairs."

One of the key collective contributions of A.A. not only to members but to the society as a whole is in its bridging and balancing of what were considered, culturally, opposing pairs.

Alcoholics Anonymous balances science and religion. Bill says, "We like to think Alcoholics Anonymous a middle ground between medicine and religion, the missing catalyst of a new synthesis."[132] He says that it was important to emphasize that "A.A. *was a way of life* that conflicted with no one's religious belief. . . . At all times, religion would be the province of clergymen, and the practice of medicine would be for doctors. As laymen, we were only supplying a much-needed missing link."[133] Bill was careful to educate and enlist in support of the movement those whom Marshall calls the "high priests" of applied science—the doctors—as well as members of the clergy.[134]

It reconciles evolution with involution with revolution, serving as a cultural system innovation and continuation. A.A. embraces the emphasis of science on evolution with its notion of progress and improvement, especially in the sense that it combines many themes of great awakenings in American history as, for example, identified by William McLoughlin. Balanced with this is the A.A. emphasis on involution, which involves an interior progress.[135]

It is revolutionary in the modern world in its advocacy of letting go— the mode in which one accesses the spiritual realm. It is revolutionary in the sense that not only does it emphasize helping others, but it also places these offers of help in the context of helping self as others are helped in non-contractual relationships. All of the steps of the program are ego-deflating,[136] as is the great fundamental principle of anonymity.

It is revolutionary in its balancing of the scientific mode with the spiritual, the active with the receptive, and asking for guidance from a higher power in determining which mode to use. This request finds expression in one of the "staple" prayers of A.A., attributed to Rienhold Niebuhr: "God grant me the serenity to accept the things I cannot change, the courage to change the things I can, and the wisdom to know the difference."[137] It emphasizes spiritual progress rather than spiritual perfection, thus avoiding the dichotomies created by insistence on perfection which Woodman, Schaef, and others feel is characteristic of the main stream American system.

It embraces both differences and similarities. One of the tasks for A.A. was to accept and embrace diversity within its own membership. Nell Wing describes how this worked. "A.A. in the beginning—face it—was sort of a gentlemen's club. It was white male middle-class or upper middle-class guys who didn't necessarily want to see a lot of women around. The very early women members, the very early black members, the early young people had to start their own groups. That has changed. There were special groups—there was a priest group, there were nuns, there was an international doctors' group, and international lawyers'. There was a Wall Street Group, and I remember the first Madison Avenue Group. Then in the '40s, there were a lot of groups in jails and prisons, and after the war there were groups in the Veterans' Administration hospitals and so there were all kinds of people being helped by this fellowship. Not just straight office workers." The similarities are emphasized at every meeting, where members are invited to identify with speakers rather than to compare.

It is an expression of both historical and mythic themes. Its place in history has been thoroughly examined by scholars, most notably, I believe, by Ernest Kurtz, with his pioneering work in A.A. history, and more recently by Robert Thomsen and others, in addition to the historical accounts made available through A.A. and Al-Anon literature. Some of the mythic themes expressed in the experience of alcoholism and in recovery are some of the themes identified by

John Bierhorst as themes he finds common to most Native American traditions—one such theme he calls "fair and foul," another "crossing the threshold."[138] The similarities between what Joseph Campbell describes as the nuclear unit of the monomyth and recovery in A.A. will be discussed in chapter 4.

A.A. embraces values associated with modern cultures as well as values associated with traditional ones. A.A. embraces the diversity and specialization associated with modern industrial cultures. Its founding members took great care that none who wanted to join and had a desire to stop drinking would be excluded. In A.A.'s terms, "you are a member when *you* say you are a member." It was the express intent from the start to provide a structure and philosophy that would accommodate any person from any religious tradition who desired to stop drinking. Ernest Kurtz calls this tendency in A.A. "joyous pluralism." Starting out as almost exclusively male and middle-class, it has subsequently opened to women, young people, and other minorities; it has accepted change. It facilitates and acknowledges change and values progress.

It has also retained core beliefs and symbols and myths valued in traditional societies as well. For example, as in many Eastern religions, it has as a basic and underlying theme the suffering associated with attachment. The principles and program of Alcoholics Anonymous, as do the major philosophical and religious systems of the East, place great importance on the principle and practice of non-violence, *ahimsa.* Its importance is evident in A.A. through such practices as making amends with all those harmed and its emphasis on treating respectfully the views of others without seeking to impose one's own truths. An example of the values shared with American Indians as well as East Indians is the value placed on community and extended family. This is evidenced in A.A., for example, in the respect shown to newcomers and elders as well.[139] Likewise of major importance in all Native American and East Indian philosophical systems is centrality of storytelling, which many feel to be the main dynamic of Alcoholics Anonymous.

The sixth task of revitalization is that of routinization.

The next section will explore how the principles and practices of Alcoholics Anonymous have been incorporated into the lives of those who participated in this study.

The principles and program of Alcoholics Anonymous have also become routinized in the larger cultural environment.

Not only do A.A. members find the program helpful, but non-alcoholics do as well. Nell Wing says that "the good will, the interest, excitement on the part of non-alcoholics always amazed me." She tells these stories:

> I was the receptionist in the office [of what was then called the Alcoholic Foundation] from 1947–1954. I can remember sitting in the reception office and people would occasionally come in off the street wanting to know about the program. These were not alcoholics. They had read about the program and they said they would like to use the program themselves.
>
> Just a couple of years ago I went to have my annual medical exam. This nice young medical assistant asked me what I did before I retired. I said oh. . . . (and I told her about my work with Alcoholics Anonymous). She said "I use the program too." I said, "What group do you belong to?" thinking she's a member. "Oh, I'm not a member. I just use the program because it helps me. I live by the steps." I said, "Well, gee, so do I."[140]

Nell adds that she believes there's "hardly any family today of any size that's not touched in one way or the other" by the program. There are presently over 40,000 groups meeting in the United States alone and over 85,000 groups worldwide.[141] Also in evidence are bumper stickers counseling "One Day at a Time," "Easy Does It," and "Keep It Simple."

The very proliferation of Twelve-Step movements based on A.A. offers evidence as to the routinization of its principles and program. Alcoholics Anonymous' General Service Office in New York lists twenty groups that are similar to or modeled after Alcoholics Anonymous. I believe that is a conservative figure.

So A.A.'s beauty is in its balancing and bridging and bounding and bonding. The balancing in each area is accomplished through such practices as sharing personal stories, practicing the Twelve Steps, reading A.A. literature, and repeating A.A. slogans. It is facilitated by attending meetings and based on abstaining from the use of alcohol one day at a time.

CHAPTER FOUR

PEOPLE PRACTICING PEACE

FINDINGS: II

This chapter is a report of selected responses to one primary question: "What, if any, evidence is there to indicate that the twelve recovering alcoholics/addicts who participated in this study report a less dualistic, discordant culture or way of life in recovery than they did while actively addicted?"

It is preceded by an introductory section that provides background information on the respondents to this study in regard to their commitment to and feelings about Alcoholics Anonymous. Following this introductory section, material is presented in four primary groupings: Practicing Peace with Themselves, Practicing Peace with God or Higher Power, Practicing Peace with Others, and Practicing Peace with the World. With the exception of Practicing Peace with Others, each of the primary groupings or parts is divided into sections, and each section is divided into three sub-sections. In the third subsection, Illustrative Excerpts from Questionnaires and Interviews, there are a number of statements taken from the questionnaire, followed by the percentages of those in treatment and those in recovery who agreed or disagreed. Those in *treatment* refers to those who were newly sober in Hazelden's Residential Treatment program for adults and who voluntarily completed the questionnaire; those in *recovery* were those who were at least nine months sober. Both groups are in recovery, simply at different stages.

In both the Introductory section, Respondents and Alcoholics Anonymous, and in each of the four primary parts of this chapter, illustrative excerpts from the interviews are presented in the order of the daily cumulative abstinence of those interviewed. The respondents and their comments are divided into three groups. Bob, Paul, and Jane, each with less than a year of sobriety when they completed the questionnaire, make up the first group. Jean, Jim, Ann, Jennifer, Roger, and Carol had from one year to five years of consecutive daily abstinence, and make up the second group. Joyce, John, and Donald each had five or more years of cumulative daily abstinence and will be considered the third group of respondents.

Introductory
Respondents and Alcoholics Anonymous

Illustrative Excerpts from
Questionnaires and Interviews

On a scale from one to seven, with one (1) being the lowest possible commitment and seven (7) being the greatest, how committed would you say you are to the program and fellowship of Alcoholics Anonymous?

>*68% of those in treatment responded with a "6" or "7."*
>*75% of those in recovery responded with a "6" or "7."*

I practice each of the Twelve Steps of A.A., including the Twelfth Step, on a regular basis.

>*14% of those in treatment agreed.*
>*55% of those in recovery agreed.*

How committed do you feel you were to a spiritual way of life in the period *before* you became associated with A.A.?

>*9% of those in treatment responded with a "6" or "7," with 7 being "deeply committed."*
>*12% of those in recovery responded with a "6" or "7," with 7 being "deeply committed."*

On a scale from one to seven, with one (1) being the lowest possible commitment and seven (7) being the greatest possible commitment, how committed would you say you are to a spiritual way of life?

> *50% of those in treatment responded with a "6" or "7."*
> *75% of those in recovery responded with a "6" or "7."*

The program and fellowship of A.A. is or was important in bringing about my awareness and acceptance of a power greater than my finite, personal self.

> *50% of those in treatment agreed.*
> *91% of those in recovery agreed.*

A.A. was or is instrumental in bringing about my commitment to a spiritual way of life.

> *34% of those in treatment agreed.*
> *79% of those in recovery agreed.*

FIRST GROUP OF RESPONDENTS (LESS THAN ONE YEAR SOBRIETY)

Bob

My connections with A.A. are not real strong now. I have just now found an A.A. group I'm comfortable with.

Paul

It's my first year A.A. birthday[1] at the end of the month. It's so bizarre I just can't believe it. A whole year has gone by. Fifty-four weeks ago I would not have believed I would be able to not have a drink or drug for a year. I don't know. I read the literature, I listen to people, and they say that's how it works, and I say, "Oh, yeah, I'll follow that. It's working."

I *love* [A.A.] meetings. I go to two a day. I go to places that have two or three in a row. I like them. My rationale is that I used to spend all my time in bars drinking—as a public nuisance. That was my public rationale. When people would ask me how many [meetings] I go to, I would say at least two a day. I would say, "Well, I [used to be] out in the bars all night." Actually, I *love* the meetings. I *love* the stories.

Jane

I had never been that involved with Alcoholics Anonymous before I started drinking again. I find I want to be involved more now. I do Twelfth Step work, [carrying the message of Alcoholics Anonymous]. I speak at women's prisons. I was the secretary of a meeting. I did it because I felt I had to give more. I knew I would also get it back. If anyone told me I would feel this good, I'd say forget it. I can see others in the program stuck like I was, going through the motions and nothing happening—it's frustrating. I had to be willing to *trust*. Taking risks is what makes the difference.

SECOND GROUP OF RESPONDENTS (ONE TO FIVE YEARS OF SOBRIETY)

Jean

The philosophy of A.A. is so universal. No spiritual path, no religion, could possibly disagree with it. It's a framework that anything can fit in with—be honest, accept yourself, try to repay what you've done wrong, accept that there is a God beyond your self, and try to maintain contact with that God. Try to move beyond yourself to make contact with other people.

A.A. is definitely helping to change me from being a completely miserable person trying to control everything herself to someone who can let go to something outside of herself. I tend to think the chances are real good that if I hadn't gone to A.A., I might have ended up dead. I really think that the futility and pain of trying to manage everything myself would have eventually been overwhelming, and I don't know where I would have gone with it.

A.A. is vitally important to me because I need to stay sober, and A.A. is how I do that, but I'm much more than just a recovering alcoholic. My spirituality is larger than that. A recovering alcoholic is a facet of me that is vital, but not all-encompassing. I need it. I'd just as soon *not* be an alcoholic, but given where I am now compared to where I was five years ago after I had left my spiritual path. . . . A.A. is not like religion. I think for a lot of people, it *is* their religion—I sound like I draw more lines than I do. A.A. is part of my spirituality just like everything is. I *am* a grateful alcoholic. I'm grateful I went through all that and got where I am now. I could easily have gone along three score years trying to scratch my way through life.

I think whether we're an alcoholic or addicted at all to anything, people get to these breaking points where something has to give. I'm glad I got there at 27 or 28.

Jim

The A.A. group is to me a support group. I think that's what they're supposed to be. You go there and you hear other people's problems. God, I'm glad I ain't there no more. I'm through that. I can remember back when I used to drink. There are a few things in my life that are pretty dramatic yet. My brother said he cannot believe the changes that have happened to me. He just didn't believe it would happen. This past Christmas party, everyone in the office said I was so relaxed they couldn't believe it. In fact the [people in the office] say the change is incredible over the last year.

Ann

I will be sober two and half years in February 1988. I am an A.A. sponsor and I have an A.A. sponsor. During my first year of sobriety I was always out doing all these things and never slowed down. I did a lot of Twelve Step work. I spend a lot more time alone now, not feeling like something's wrong—it's okay.

Jennifer

My whole life changed because of the A.A. program. Everything that I'm talking about couldn't have happened unless I got sober and into recovery. So all of what I say [now] is directly a result of being sober and going to meetings. And if life gets too difficult and my spirituality seems to be lost, I go to a meeting, a beginner's meeting,[2] and I get my priorities straightened out. If I get lost along the way, I always hear what I need to.

I went to Overeaters Anonymous before I went to A.A. I'm not going to O.A. now. I guess I'm not willing to give up [the compulsive use of] food completely. I've been free of drugs for two and a half years.

The A.A. program brought me to a certain level of spirituality. It opened the door. A workshop I went to on spirituality provided another door opening. My life and my husband's life changed at that point; our spirituality changed. It was a turning point and now my husband's illness (Aids Related Complex) is in remission. I'm involved with people who are healing themselves of AIDS.[3]

Roger

What A.A. does is help me with fear. It allows me to develop a feeling of being safe. I had a fear that people in A.A. would reject me, so when they offered me a place where that fear didn't become real, I learned they weren't going to do that. The fellowship of A.A. gives me a place to disprove my own fears. It still does that.

I view recovery as the three essentials—honesty, open-mindedness, willingness—even more than the [Twelve] Steps. Honesty and open-mindedness are definitely values of mine. Without those you don't do the Steps anyway. Willingness and open mindedness come from the bottom. You don't do them very easily unless you surrender. It all kind of comes from getting beat up.

Carol

A.A. has been the most important thing that's ever happened to me. I'm learning to be clear. Without the booze and the drugs I am a very frightened person. It's taken four and a half years of sobriety for me to find courage within myself. It has to do with a power greater than myself that I rely on. I didn't believe in God when I got sober. I didn't like God so much all over the place [in A.A.], and that was part of my rebellion. It took a while for me to get that it could be a God of my own understanding. The Big Book and the chapter on the agnostics is very good for me to read. It talks about creative intelligence. I had not been creative or intelligent for a number of years.

THIRD GROUP OF RESPONDENTS (FIVE OR MORE YEARS OF SOBRIETY)

Joyce

My whole life changed with A.A. No doubt about it. I go to more meetings than I used to. I go to two or three a week. I used to go once a week. I sponsor several people.

John

I knew I was in deep trouble, so I started to go to meetings. I am grateful for Alcoholics Anonymous. I had never had a sense of belonging before. I was so happy about being an alcoholic, right from the start. I go to an A.A. meeting and hear just what's needed so many times. Recently in recovery, though, I worry that I go to Alcoholics Anonymous meetings and feel like something's expected of you. Over the years I've sponsored so many people in a small community. I feel I have a certain responsibility. I've been around so long. I don't want to share by rote. I've been getting a little phony and that's partly why I'm here at the Renewal Center. I'll feel better now when I go back.

Donald

I try to live A.A. in everything, not just weekends, but to live it. In everything. I take an inventory of myself during the day to see how I'm doing with that. The A.A. program is the center, the core. I keep that center going. You ask what is the center of the center—that's where almighty God is. "Relieve me of the bondage of self."[4] You see, I suppose that's a core, that's what the Twelve Steps teach us—the submission of our will to God's will. Then we come close. We live according to His will and everything else flows from that.

[Aldous Huxley] said Bill Wilson will go down as the greatest social architect, and I believe it. Look at the program. Of course it wasn't original with him—there was the Oxford group, the Washingtonian movement, and so forth, but he had the ability to put it together, to put it all together. Be guided by God and he gives the power . . . that tremendous power of . . . one drunk helping another. That doesn't come from me. That's too simple, you see?

PART I
PRACTICING PEACE WITH THEMSELVES

SECTION A
ACTIVE AND RECEPTIVE

1.
Statements Illustrating the Nature of the Problem

Addicts are fully at war with themselves.[1]

> *Gerald May*

Our materialist society and science tries to locate the problem in a thing, in a "bad value," in "drink," in "weakness," or in "dependence." . . . We use linear yardsticks of virtue that make strength "good" and weakness "bad" and we split-off this badness from us. But suppose "weakness" or "security," are not in themselves pathological but that the pathology lies in the severance of their relationships with their complementary values, "strength" exclusive of "weakness" or "risk" exclusive of "security." . . . [Gregory] Bateson calls this process of splitting schismogenesis, *literally a growing split in the structure of ideas.*[2]

> *Charles Hampden-Turner*

In both the tantric system and the yogic system of Patanjali, which is based on Sankhya philosophy and psychology, a developmental process is described in which the individual becomes aware of and resolves the splits within himself. At [earlier] stages of development, a person identifies with one side of a polarity and discards the other, participating in a dance and drama with the discarded other. In the process of personal evolution, one gradually learns to assimilate his discarded half and to attain a more encompassing perspective that embraces both. When this is achieved with respect to each and every polarity, the individual has completed the developmental process. He has realized that there is only one unity in all apparent diversity . . . . ..Yoga psychology . . . seeks to dissolve all polarities in the sense that they have no hold or determining influence on the individual. This does not mean that the polarity is necessarily destroyed, rather, its domination over the person is ended as he achieves an equilibrium with respect to that polarity.[3]

Swami Ajaya

[We] plunge ahead in a compulsive style of drivenness in the "ways of the world."[4]

Ernest Becker

> *. . . I felt myself a man carrying a loose tottering bundle*
> *along a narrow scaffold: if I could carry it*
> *fast enough I could hold it together to the end.*[5]

Wendell Berry

[In Paul's First Epistle to the Corinthians, two kinds of wisdom are noted,] . . . one which consists in the knowledge of words and statements, a rational, dialectical wisdom, and another which is at once a matter or paradox and of experience, and goes beyond the reach of reason."[6]

Thomas Merton
citing Paul, First Epistle
to the Corinthians

[In the Vedantic tradition native to India, it is said that] knowledge and truth are of two kinds: the lower and phenomenal and the higher and supraphenomenal. The first kind of knowledge and truth is the product of senses and intellect; name and form are the warp and woof of such knowledge and truth. . . . On the other hand, the higher knowledge and truth are . . . not the product of sense and intellect but of primordial intuitive insight into the nature of existence. . . . Such knowledge and truth surpass all distinctions and oppositions. More importantly, unlike the lower knowledge and truth, the higher knowledge and truth . . . bring about a total transformation of him who attains them.[7]

Puligandla

Continual activity kept up by power and energy very often results in disaster. Every activity should be balanced by passivity. One should be active when it is the time to be active, and become passive when the conditions ask for passivity. It is in this manner that success in life is attained and that happiness, which is the quest of every soul, is gained.[8]

Hazrat Inayat Khan

[Society too long has been lopsided in the direction of] intellect or thought, an important but over-valued faculty that doubts and inquires, that recognizes time and space and the material limitations, that slowly systemizes, that works by small increments and cumulations, that formulates, that concentrates, works, reworks and reviews; that goes slowly, deliberately; that makes very firm and sure and eventually arrives at a science of logical statements that shall shape and define the scheme that is to underlie, penetrate and support the form of an art. . . .

The average man does not let himself alone. He is constantly interfering with the free working of his own powers. He is forever absurdly suppressing and repressing them. Hence, he does not grow solidly in imaginative strength . . . does not let his faculties grow and unfold and thus beget an activity and strength, which hunger for work.

Modern man is a traitor to himself in suppressing one-half of himself.

[We have been untrue to man's oneness.] It has happened too often that the man who could see with the outer eye could not see with the inner eye; because the other man, rhapsodizing with the clear insight of faith, had no thought of the other. Neither has inferred from the presence of the other, the necessary existence of a balancing but hidden power.[9]

Louis Sullivan

What I see in a broader sense is that the feminine principle, which for centuries has been so denied in our culture, is forcing its way, her way, back in again. If you're an addict, you have got to come to terms with the feminine principle. You've got to feel that slow rhythm—the rhythm of the earth is slow—you have to feel that slowing down, you have to quiet the soul, and you have to surrender, because eventually you have to face the fact that you are not God and you cannot control your life.

[What has to be surrendered] is power.

I see the repression of the feminine principle as the biggest problem on the planet, and since the planet has become a global village, power alone just isn't going to work any more. We will destroy ourselves. The feminine . . . changes lives, and it could change the whole culture.

Feminine consciousness rises out of the mother, and you have to be grounded in that, because without it you'd just be blown away by spirit. Feminine consciousness . . . has to do with love, with receiving—most of us in this culture are terrified of receiving. . . . We are talking a masculine principle and a feminine principle—we are not talking about gender. . . .

Women are trapped in this power principle just as much as men.[10]

Marion Woodman

The principle that we shall find no enduring strength until we first admit complete defeat is the main taproot from which our whole Society has sprung and flowered.[11]

Alcoholics Anonymous

2.
Story Illustrating the Unity

"The human being is the earthly symbol of the sacred tree in animal form. This tree is called the Tree of The Shaman And Shamaness, or the Animal Tree.

"The Animal Tree represents human growth and learning. There is as much tree above the ground as there is below. The tree we see above the ground is called the Sun Lodge Tree. It represents the half of the mind we understand as being awake. The tree below the ground, which we know as the roots, is called the Moon Lodge Tree. This represents the half of the mind we experience when we are dreaming, our sleep dreams and also our daydreams."

Estchimah listened raptly. Sweet Medicine continued . . . "The Sun Lodge Tree is our conscious mind, and the Moon Lodge Tree is our subconscious mind—the shadow mind.

"The Medicine People tell us we are the principal person in each of these two lodges. However, one of us is male and the other is female. These twins are one principal person but have two minds.

81

"In the beginning, the chiefs tell us, when we are seedlings, we are completely dependent upon the roots of the sacred tree. All of our power comes from the roots. The roots are the eyes, ears, voice, and mind of the young seedling. But when the tree is adult this is reversed, and the roots are completely dependent upon that part of the tree within the sunlight.

"That portion of the tree that is below ground remembers all. Its memory goes beyond itself, its roots, into the total of the earth. But that portion of the tree that is above ground remembers only those things it needs to grow.

"If the roots do not nourish and provide for the tree above ground, the tree will die. And if the tree above the ground does not nourish and provide for its roots, again the tree will die.[12]

Hyemeyohsts Storm

3.
Illustrative Excerpts from Questionnaires and Interviews

I experience direct, intuitive insights.
20% of those in treatment agreed.
36% of those in recovery agreed.

I do or have done spiritually inspired work—for example,
a poem, painting or musical composition.
25% of those in treatment agreed.
39% of those in recovery agreed.

Strength comes out of weakness.
43% of those in treatment agreed.
73% of those in recovery agreed.

"Letting go" is the same thing as being passive.
82% of those in treatment DISAGREED.
86% of those in recovery DISAGREED.

I can only keep what I give away.
35% of those in treatment agreed.
82% of those in recovery agreed.

I welcome the idea of being relieved of "the bondage of self," that is, my finite, personal
self.
66% of those in treatment agreed.
73% of those in recovery agreed.

I can live exclusively by personal individual strength and intelligence.
86% of those in treatment DISAGREED.
84% of those in recovery DISAGREED.

I am centered—or still—within myself, even when I am physically active.
18% of those in treatment agreed.
41% of those in recovery agreed.

I rely on the help of a power greater than my finite, personal self.
32% of those in treatment agreed.
64% of those in recovery agreed.

I try to follow guidance from a power greater than my finite, personal self.
34% of those in treatment agreed.
73% of those in recovery agreed.

There is both a "male" and a "female" part of me.
25% of those in treatment agreed with this.
57% of those in on-going recovery agreed.

There are times when I feel I am neither male nor female.
14% of those in treatment agreed with this.
30% of those in on-going recovery agreed.

Paul

I know I'm more receptive now than I was when I was drinking and using other drugs. I am more receptive in that I'm less judgmental, less harsh on other people. Remarkably, I'm less harsh on myself. I seem to be willing to roll with a few more punches with better reasons than before. I connect listening with being receptive. The [A.A.] program helps with that inadvertently. I think it's one of those plusses in that you have to learn to listen at the meetings, otherwise you're going to spend the entire time comparing with the external event kind of thing. If we don't learn to listen, we won't get what we need. We'd keep walking out saying "Can you believe those ridiculous [stories]?" To me it's more important to understand part of the feelings [like the feeling of] worthlessness that informed that behavior [than to compare the people, places, and things in my life with the external things in someone else's life].

I have learned to be receptive. It seems once I said "yes," I'd go to detox, I haven't been faced with any major difficulties. I might have also learned in the past year [of sobriety] to just let go of the things I can't do anything about. Maybe that's happened and I'm not fully aware of it. Before, that would have been difficult. I never really ever had to work for anything and I get nervous about my recovery. I don't want to take it for granted. I had a certain kind of education, and a certain amount of intelligence and willingness, and I'm bright, essentially. School came very easily to me, all those SATs and GREs. In that kind of testing I would go off the scoreboard. But I remember the kinds of things they were asking—they don't mean anything, all those measurements. Recovery also has been easy for me. Maybe I just choose to look at it that way, not to remember the pain during treatment and the anger that was always there. It worked out real well. I didn't have difficulty putting ninety days together. I don't feel I had to work for it. I feel it was sort of given to me.

What does the phrase "letting go" mean to me? One of the phrases I didn't quite get? Letting go of my anger, letting go of my pain. It's hard letting go of my pain, because I don't know what's going to replace it. Even your worst pain—at least you know it! I don't think I'm very good [at letting go] yet. I don't think of letting go as passive, I think it's very active! I don't think it's passive at all.

I'm not sure whether it's because I'm gay, or if it has to do with being gay, that attributes that are generally perceived as female—like being soft, compassionate—are things about myself that I think are true. I'm fairly intuitive, also. To me that word means—essentially—reality. Intuition is always a decision based on previous observations. [They're there,] they just don't come to the fore. All my past experiences that were sort of like that are why I think it's this way. That's really what I think intuition is. I'm willing to feel things, I'm willing to act on feelings, not decisions based on facts. That in the past has been ascribed to female personalities. I still have times when I feel I am neither male nor female. I'm not a Freudian. I don't believe the whole world operates out of a sexual behavior pattern all the time. I'm really intrigued by androgyny and gender bending—that's a purposeful shock event— purposeful in the ability to weave in and out. People like Boy George[13] would be a gender bender. It's not something I myself in particular choose to pursue, but it doesn't bother me with other people. Another part of androgyny is the attempt to create a new kind of personality that can draw on both male and female more readily, I think with better results. I would like to be more androgynous. I think it would be great. I like the idea that that kind of choice opens up things. It opens up possibilities or experiences or whatever, as opposed to a blocked-up, heavily masculine man or an excessively feminine woman, because they get locked into behavior. As you move closer to the center, you can do both and experience more.

Jane

The Third Step [in the A.A. program] is the key to open the door—willingness. A lot has happened without me trying to make it happen. I can't take credit for it. I've just been willing to put myself in a position where it can happen. I have to let myself be vulnerable, open, receptive, honest, willing, be open to what others have to offer. When I came into Alcoholics Anonymous, I figured I had all the answers.

In letting go, you realize you don't have the answers. You let your Higher Power direct you. You have all the answers for life inside you. The subconscious or spirit inside knows what makes you happy. When you let go and get out of the way, your Higher Power has a chance to come through. Then let it happen. It can be painful. If you can get through it, if frees you up.

I ask for guidance. One time I was packed up to move to another state. I was praying for some guidance. A little voice said "Why don't you stay?" I liked it where I was, it was a different mind-set than other places. It seems more relaxed, easier, more open than other places I've been. I stayed.

Jean

Being receptive is kind of like my theology. Being receptive, being open, surrendering is a very conscious thing. It takes risk; it takes effort and practice and real commitment. It means being open to God's will and to other people and being open to moments of wonder, to the intuitive side of myself, being open to both my masculine tendencies and my feminine tendencies, not making value judgments. Being receptive— maybe it's just a word, maybe someone else would use a different word like being loving, or being faithful—I don't know what. Being receptive to me—that is how I'm spiritual. Opening up some free space in me. Letting other good things in, not always having to have answers. I think A.A. helps people to be receptive. The whole program is geared to being receptive, or at least it's geared to an idea of a power greater than yourself. So you have all these slogans: "Let Go, Let God," "Easy Does It." The whole program is about being receptive—accepting, re-learning. You cannot manage life by yourself. It's also about being accepting of other people. It's also about unity with other people. There's an enormous cross section of people in A.A. There is enormous trust of other people in A.A.— bound together in the common human condition of being spiritually hungry. The whole program's about that. I do equate listening with being receptive. A lot. Because it's listening in an intuitive way. It's more than just listening—it's hearing, it's empathy. The program helps with just your basic "letting go." Every newcomer hears "Bring the body and the mind and heart will follow." "Just show up," that's one of the phrases that's heard all the time in A.A.—that's a way of being receptive. The phenomenal lack of structure in A.A. as a whole—is related to its changing and growing and being receptive to new demands.

Feeling in the presence of God is always a matter of me being open to it. I always believe I'm in the presence of God. That's a fundamental belief. That's why I meditate. I have to make space to be *aware* that I'm in the presence of God. I think everybody has moments of awe or wonder or vignettes that they remember . . . seeing a crocus in the snow . . . seeing things that make them aware there is goodness in the universe. To me it's not enough to just go haphazardly through life waiting for rare moments of insight. I think those moments come because we are open to them. So meditating is a way to practice holding myself open. It's an exercise. If you've ever tried to relax your body you find out how very *unrelaxed* you *are*. How you tense back up and you don't realize it and you think, how could I tense up and not know it? It's like the principle of being in the presence of God. Meditating for forty-five minutes is a sort of practice so when I'm sitting in rush hour traffic I'm not just tensing up and losing my mind. I can relax my thoughts and my feelings and look at the clouds or think about something constructive. It's just practice. So I feel in the presence of God any time when I can relax enough, and some days that's easier than others. I do have those moments, I've written them down before, but I really think that they're just run-of-the-mill type things.

I started to meditate about a year ago because I felt suffocated, or I felt like I couldn't breathe, I was not feeling calm. A women in inpatient treatment worked with me while I was there. She was a resident. I've done real minimal work with yoga. The way I meditate is a modification, or a simplification, of Transcendental Meditation. There's a book that describes it—*The Relaxation Response*. It's real simple. Deep breathing.

In recovery, I am trying to make some sense of what happened to me (I was raped several years ago) . . . [pause] . . . I want to do something constructive for other people. At this point, I'm trying to decide what I may be called to do. I believe there is some good that I can do. If I'm receptive, that will be shown. In the mean time, I'll just put one foot in front of the other and listen.

[I agree that there are both male and female parts of me.] I'm at this point working more with the female—the negative mother and the good mother. I am still struggling with the female aspect. I guess in a lot of ways that ties back in with surrender and vulnerability and rape issues. I'm still struggling with that. I'm aware that that's a vital part of myself I've tried to ignore. I'm definitely trying to integrate the female. It's much safer to attempt masculine-type endeavors—to be assertive and aggressive—instead of being receptive. I used to equate the feminine and passivity. You could have put a gun to my head and asked "Do you equate feminine with passive?" and I would have said "No," but I did. I no longer feel that way. I think it takes more strength and energy to respect the feminine side of myself.

Jennifer

The A.A. program helps me be receptive. I go to a meeting and I always hear what I need to hear. The inner voice I hear is intuition, that's what it is. It's my higher self and God's will. My intuition is not guesswork. Intuition is a voice of my higher self which is the God within me. I [don't hear that as well if I'm blocked.] Eating sugar for me blocks it. Stuffing, stuffing with food blocks it. Certain foods with sugar block it and anger blocks it. Also being judgmental. I can get caught up into being too busy, too. I usually hear when I keep quiet and I can listen. Sometimes I hear judging voices taking inventory. I catch that and I turn those off and then I can listen again. The minute I start judging people and taking their inventories, I'm not listening.

I meditate. I like to do guided meditations with a tape or someone leading. Right now, that's the easiest for me to do. Sometimes [A.A.] meetings are meditative. It's the time that I'm quiet and I'm able to listen. Just to be able to sit and listen! I've come a long way. There was a time when I couldn't sit through a meeting. The A.A. program helps me listen. I mean, just the slogan that you hear in meetings: "Take the cotton out of your ears and put it in your mouth." There are many times I want to share and I raise my hand. A voice says, "Jennifer, just forget wanting to be heard. Just sit there and listen." I get that voice pretty often, more and more lately. I get it when I'm with my mother, too. There are things I want to say, to just talk about myself and all of a sudden I say "Now, wait a second. You don't have to say that. Just listen. Just be there. Your being there is important." I learned a little bit of *Shiatsu*, too, and that was a good part of the class, just being there. *Shiatsu* is a form of massage based on energy meridians. It's based on releasing the blocks along the meridians to get the balance of energy flow.

I think we're all male and female—fifty/fifty. It's up to us how much of ourselves we allow to be male or allow to be female.

Roger

Letting go—I hesitate to use these expressions. I come up with my own expressions for the same thing. I'm very much a believer in listening to intuition. The year that was so great for me was all intuitive. That's all it was. Has intuition *ever* not been there? *Ever*? Just think of one time. I have all day. [The year I felt everything was intuition], mostly I didn't stop to entertain fear. Intuition is my immediate response or reaction to stuff—a sixth sense. I think mostly I was in the "now." If something came up, I would just react to it, and fear didn't come into it—I call that intuition, because I didn't plan the response. I lived in real time. I think I am going toward the same goal in a much more rich fashion, much more solid, secure. I also believe that a lot of what I should do is right in front of me. For the sake of conversation, call it God's will—the stuff that's right in front of me. There were also times when my intuition would say "no." I don't want to imply that I think "yes" is always the response. In fact, I have a problem saying "no," a real severe problem saying no. How do I know God's will for me? I just follow what is put in front of me. I seem to be much more creative. I guess removal of fear helped a lot . That's a biggie—fear seems to thwart intuition and creativity and spontaneity and all those things that are the beautiful side of a human being. If I had to describe intuition, I would say I think of intuition as a slight tug in a certain direction that you just go along with, go with the flow. Like a magnet drawing a little bit. I make the decision to go with it—that's how intuition seems to be. It's a feel, a leaning, it's subtle and yet so important. It has to do with receptivity and listening. [Long pause.] When I said go with the flow, that is a receptive state for me. Receptive state means stuff from other places comes into me and I let it come in. When I'm not receptive, I'm in the driver's seat and I am somehow determining through my mind what to do next and sometimes my mind is out to kill me it seems. It seems to give erroneous information.

I didn't use to let much in. I was a coke [cocaine] addict besides being an alcoholic. I used to pride myself on how many days I could go without sleep. I'd stay up. I was into dope [heroin]. I would talk and talk. I'd talked for so many years before I came into recovery that nothing new could come into my life. I wasn't receptive. When I first started talking it was okay and people did like to listen because it was relatively fresh stuff. I think I was dying from not letting new stuff come in. As the irony of life would have it, one of the terrors I had in A.A. kept me from speaking. It probably served quite well. I basically sat there and listened in meetings for two and a half years. I think it was a really good thing for me. It may not be good for another person, but for me it was a good antidote. For someone who talked incessantly, I've been practicing how to listen. I had developed a habit of cutting people off. I'm just becoming aware of it. Sometimes I'll just stop and let someone else go ahead. It's hard.

I am more relaxed now in recovery than I used to be. I used to make the table move, I was so shaky. What I really seek is to feel okay while doing nothing. I want to be able to not do anything and feel all right with myself. I always hope to be peaceful. I want to die sober. The worst thing would be to be on my deathbed and have regrets about all the times I balked. When I get desperate, I have to leap now and trust more as a part of life, because it worked at critical moments.

Carol

I knew it all. I knew it all since I was six years old and I spent the rest of my life trying to convince everyone I knew it all. In recovery, I stopped trying to be an intellectual. I found a lack in my education. We were always analyzing other people's work. Most ridiculous. I wanted to know something about myself. I decided I was going to intuit. I guess intuition is just the process of facing yourself and knowing yourself.

Once I reached adolescence, I allowed myself to become a channel and I used to work myself up in those states, you know, sometimes with the booze and the drugs. Three years before I got sober, I found that I could no longer do that. I was pretty terrified because by that time, when I opened myself up to be a channel, most of the things that came through me were just terrifying. I was totally out of control and there was no joy in it. Basically [in opening yourself up to be a channel] you transcend yourself. You get out of your own skin and your own way and preconceived ideas. For me, you know, that dream state in sleep—total unconsciousness— can bring you up to it. So can working late hours in your studio in full concentration.

[I am most receptive] when things are quiet and I'm alone. Often that's in the early morning, or twilight when I've been working all day. More often that not [I'm] in my studio by myself. For me, the creative act itself is to look to be inspired by something greater than myself. [To be more receptive, you] get rid of the negative, your negative energy, get rid of your conscious state, get rid of your assumptions and presumptions. You sit and wait. You can be preparing the dirt and getting your hands dirty and making the plaster right and I guess that's prayer. You say, make me a channel. It can be done with joy or it can be done with suffering. There are many ways to transcend yourself. Sometimes you just have to start working with a mundane idea that is not fixed. Sometimes it works and [you are] in the middle of doing [something] that you can get lost in. Sometimes you have to throw away the piece you're working on because it's just no good, you can't get out of yourself. I admit it sounds kind of crazy that you can make yourself a medium and it can just occur any time and therefore a masterpiece is always at your fingertips. It doesn't happen that way. Some of the stuff is more successful than others. But it's certainly not just you doing it. You know that. I mean, I used to weld or grate pieces of steel together. I didn't know how they got done sometimes. I managed to do things that I never thought I could do. You're talking to somebody that didn't change a light bulb until she was 21. I mean I never worked with my hands before. Never considered it—it didn't run in my family. At 21, I started to work with my hands and that was a great experience. In my studio I have to prepare the dirt and the earth and the plaster and that's all part of it. I have been a vegetarian for years at a time. I have gone through periods of doing yoga, and I've done meditations and things like that. I've never been able to get the same feeling that I have with the creative act. All of a sudden you're beyond criticism, you're doing something that nobody else is doing. You're finding your own voice. You're taking responsibility for things that have never been created before. It's a great feeling. You take all the risks and make all the judgments and, you know, you fall flat on your face. So you know you're taking your life in your hands. But it's art— you're doing something no one else has ever done. The risk is greater.

When I agreed that you can only keep what you give away, I was probably thinking of generosity of spirit. I said on the questionnaire that I feel there is both a male and female part of me. I know the Chinese have the yin and the yang and it's a balance of yourself. I know the saints combine this right before Nirvana or before you reach God. Before I got sober I didn't know what I was—I'd lost it by that time. [Laughter.]

Joyce

I listen more now. It isn't that I didn't used to listen to people, but I think probably my mind wasn't with them. I was probably already going on to what I wanted to say next, and I still do that. I'm better at *not* doing that now, though. Before at [A.A.] meetings, I would be thinking about what I was going to say rather than listening. But now, maybe because I've been in the program longer, I know I'm going to have something to say, and I have real empathy with people who are speaking. I can feel for them, with everything that is going on. I usually find most things that most people say interesting.

I took a personal growth class once. One of the speakers had a horrible voice and no personality whatever. Our facilitator asked the next time, "How did you like the speaker?" and nobody liked him. It was terrible. "Well, what lesson did you learn?" We said we didn't learn a lesson, we couldn't figure out a thing that we should have learned. "Well, was the information he gave you of value?" It was. But we were discounting the information because we didn't like the way it was presented. That turned out to be a valuable lesson to me. I try to remember it whenever I hear people speak now and look beyond whatever else is going on with them to what they're saying. I listen for the principles, like they tell newcomers in A.A., rather than pay attention to personalities.

I equate being open with listening. I'll tell you about one experience I had with that recently. I was not at a good place, I was unhappy, and I didn't know what I needed. I had not gone to meetings for a while at that point. I was down to the [A.A.] club a lot working, but I was not attending meetings. This one Sunday morning I thought, I've got to go to the Big Book [A.A.] meeting. Afterwards I started talking to three men there that I know. I was having doubt with my faith, I didn't think God was living up to his side of the bargain, and I went to a meeting and these three men talked to me from noon until 2:30. Well, see, that's a miracle. I could accept all they said with love, where if somebody else had told me that, I might have been hurt or resentful. To be talking with three men in the first place! To open myself up like that was pretty unreal.

I guess I can be open without being receptive. Receptive means for me that I'm going to get the information because I want to make a change at that point. Open means more that I'm willing to listen to it, but I'm not necessarily going to change. It's more like something will have to be proven. I feel A.A. definitely helps people be open. It definitely helps people be honest, open, and willing. It does that through sharing experiences or stories in A.A.

I can get too analytical and I don't let go of things and let them happen enough. Where I'm at with therapy is sort of letting go of things, but I still feel the need to do things and I don't know if that will change or if it would be better or not. I see letting go as being very passive and submissive, and I'm better at it now than I was. When I first got in the program I felt it was turning the other cheek and I wasn't in a place to do that. At that time I had too much anger in me. I guess there's some things that I can let go of. If I think I can't do anything more, I let go. But then I keep trying to do things. I can't look at something right away and turn it over. It takes a lot of work for me to do that. I am more likely to let go when I just can't do anymore. I would pretty well exhaust all avenues.

I'm on a real spiritual quest right now and it just came to me because I've been doing a lot of journaling and everything and because of the therapy I've been taking. I'm working on turning within. I think I should let go of a particular problem, let God handle it, and I won't think about it anymore. But no, I've got to go out and buy books and take classes and all that kind of stuff. What happens when I do let go? The problem goes away. I've never had any problem with the alcoholism since I quit and I quit smoking three years ago. I was smoking three packs a day at that time. That was something that I feel God can play in. I can pretty much let go of my caretaking of other people now. I've improved a lot.

I like the idea [that came from the last Vatican Council]. You grow up, you decide within you who God is and what he wants of you. You listen, you study (that's what I feel I do), and listen to wise people. But you make the choice of what God wants for you, and that's using your inner self. I had never heard that before. It made a lot of sense. The only thing I ask for is his will. In making decisions, I ask for God's help to do what is right. I'm trying to become more attuned to listen to my body, to listen to what it says.

I strongly believe that I can only keep what I give away. I think I feel that way because of the A.A. program. The more active I become [in working with others], the stronger my recovery program is for me.

John

[The A.A. program teaches receptivity by teaching] acceptance; accept that it's all a gift—I mean the whole thing. And then what's been so important to me—and I think that's one of the things that I've been real lucky about (that's not to say it's been practiced perfectly ever since) was receiving the gift when I first went into recovery and not questioning it anymore. It just was, well, I don't deserve it, but I've got it! I've got it! [He says this with wonder.] I've never, ever doubted that. There have sure been degrees of losing the gratitude just a little bit—not wanting to do my day's work or whatever dissatisfaction with where I was at—but never for one minute doubting the gift of sobriety. I think maybe it was also recognizing that there's going to be some dark clouds. It's spoiled of me to think that every day will be glorious, wonderful— that's—maybe why not either? Maybe if my attitude was perfect, maybe they would be! God, I wish I could explain how the program helps someone to be receptive! Put that down in black and white and make people understand it. Make! I'm saying make—like you can make anybody do anything! When you think of new people coming in or people who are having trouble with the program, it could be so easy if they could understand the importance of acceptance. But then I can't think of what to say. I wish I could.

I would say there is definitely a male and female part of us. For me, the female part would be the vulnerability and the sensitivity that I have but spent most of my life trying to cover most of that up. I didn't use to be comfortable with that female part. Sometimes I'm not now. It is much better. It helps me to know that maybe it's to some degree present in everybody. As I described it, one time I had to be totally one hundred percent masculine. Be tough and cool.

Donald

I think I tend to be a cerebral-type person. I think the program helped me put the focus on listening more. To make it more a part of my day. It helped me be disciplined. I feel listening and being receptive are similar. To communicate with God, I just be still and listen. I don't have any difficulty. It just seems to happen. I can be in deep reverie. I can just let go. I don't know that I used to do that while I was drinking. Prior to sobriety there sure were times when I felt estranged or alienated from other people and God. I couldn't figure out why I was right and the rest of the world was wrong.

I've had lots of inspiration. It happens when I'm making walking sticks, in business, it happens when I read. I'm an idea person. I'm very creative that way. So when the light bulb goes on . . . there it is. Whatever it happens to be. I see things where other people don't see things. I see possibilities, see wholes where other people see parts. I see an opportunity to make something. I have an ability to see the solution to a problem. It's just there. I intuitively see. When I'm working with people, I know I've said words and afterwards said "Gee, that was great, I'll have to remember that so I can use it again in another situation" and five minutes later I have no recollection of what I said. I think it has to do with imagination. I've been that way all my life.

SECTION B
ACCEPTABLE AND UNACCEPTABLE SELVES

There are other ways alcoholics imagine themselves split beings. For example, a great deal has been written on the way people split their minds from their bodies, their intellect from their emotions, and their beliefs from their behavior. Here, I categorize these splits generally as the split between "Acceptable and Unacceptable Selves" and provide just a few examples of how these splits are healed in recovery.

1.
Statements Illustrating the Nature of the Problem

The displacement upward of the personality, where the ego and breath are forced up toward the head, is the typical problem in our culture. We are split between the head and the body. We construct magnificent monuments to that split, such as medical centers where psychiatrists and physicians work separately on the illness of body and mind. It is not surprising. All of western culture has been split in body and mind since the time of Descartes.[14]

Sam Keens

I doubt there has been such a hostile breakdown of communications between head and body . . . as in our [culture].[15]

Theodore Roszak

[An alcoholic is one whose] emotions have failed to grow to the stature of the intellect.[16]

story-teller in Alcoholics Anonymous

In the end, all the dividing emotions—self-pity, pride, resentments, and so on—become servants of the disease of alcoholism. Like political palliatives, they siphon off healing energy and allow the sickening agent to stay in power. Their tone and mood are part of the voice of booze.[17]

Lewis Hyde

We belong to a generation which has paid for outer mastery with psychological disorientation and infantility. . . . Consciousness has split open the world and the soul, has polarized them and involved them in . . . civil war. . . . With the rise of ego-consciousness the opposites are cleft asunder, one pulling one way and one the other.[18]

Eleanor Bertine

2.
Teachings Illustrating the Unity

"See," Ochwiay Biano said, "how cruel the whites look. Their lips are thin, their noses sharp, their faces furrowed and distorted by folds. Their eyes have a staring expression; they are always seeking something. What are they seeking? The whites always want something; they are always uneasy and restless. We do not know what they want. We do not understand them. We think that they are mad."

I asked him why he thought the whites were all mad.

"They say that they think with their heads," he replied.

"Why of course. What do you think with?" I asked him in surprise.

"We think here," he said, indicating his heart.

I fell into a long meditation. For the first time in my life, so it seemed to me, someone had drawn for me a picture of the real white man. It was as though until now I had seen nothing but sentimental, prettified color prints. This Indian had struck our vulnerable spot, unveiled a truth to which we are blind.[19]

*Told to Carl G. Jung
by Ochwiay Biano*

"Do not judge yourself," Crazy Dog said. "You hardly know yourself."[20]

3.
Illustrative Excerpts from Questionnaires and Interviews

I feel grateful.
46% of those in treatment agreed with this.
70% of those in recovery agreed with this.

I am satisfied with the way I function in the world.
2% of those in treatment agreed.
30% of those in recovery agreed.

Bob

I had a period of severe depression while I was drinking. I was seeing a psychiatrist for it. He said it was clinical depression. He was aware of my drinking. The depression was really scary. I was single and living alone when it happened. I was 42. I would go through traumatic mood changes. It would happen in a matter of minutes. I could feel it coming on. It felt like someone had thrown [over me] a dark, heavy substance I could see through, but barely. It was dark and heavy, really scary.

Since I stopped drinking, I am more at peace with myself. I've thought frequently that if I were to go through this period of my life with alcohol it would really be chaotic. I'm more comfortable with myself now. The biggest change is that I'm less critical of myself. One of the biggest changes is my ability to ask for help. I'm more open and able to express my feelings. I'm not perfect at it. It has been hard to express my feelings. It had been very, very difficult for most of my life. A.A. is a big piece of it. Going through treatment was the first time in my life that I took that amount of time to look at myself, my values, what is important to me, what I am doing to myself. I don't think people take the time to look at that. What is important to me is finding inner peace. Having a rewarding relationship with people I care about is important to me. Having time to smell the roses is important. Those are key things. Love and caring for each other is the most important aspect of our lives and everything else—like circumstances, events—is peripheral. Love and caring is the glue that binds and is the most important thing. That's the ideal I'm getting closer to today.

Paul

I'm not as dreadfully hard on myself as I used to be. I still want to be perfect, but I don't climb the walls about it by letting myself not be perfect. I'm letting other people make their mistakes. I don't climb the walls immediately. I'd always expect fifteen out of twenty of them, but then I'd expect twenty out of ten from myself. If I want them to be perfect, I have to be twice as perfect. I feel a little more connected now, but I still feel outside of it. I was talking to my A.A. sponsor last night about that. I think that for some of us, our patterns were worked out even before drinking and drugging, and we do tend to get better or hopefully we do, but many of us are coming out of left field for a variety of other reasons. I think I might just be one of those people.

My sponsor was telling me about people who have stayed sober for fifteen or eighteen years who become really weird and it's because they are themselves more so than other people ever will be. They don't have the inclination or patience to conform. In my life, many rewards came because I didn't conform. I chose a career that is the most radical cutting edge in that area. I think for people in A.A., for us to get better—for me to get better—requires attention to myself. If they've been sober fifteen or twenty years they know a great deal about themselves. They've made decisions about what is important for themselves, and what is important for the collective unconscious.

Jean

[In recovery], I don't think I'm going to make a complete shambles of the universe anymore. I've gotten to the point where I don't care if I'm right or not. I don't care if it makes sense or it doesn't. If I'm wrong, fine. As long as I'm open, it will be rectified.

I had experiences of [timeless time, connection of inner and outer worlds and joining of self and other] before recovery, but I did not experience these things while I was drinking. Not from the time I was 21 until in the last year. It's like there is an eight-year block of my life that was a void. It was awful. I tried to fill it with all kinds of things—eating and drinking and frantic activity and when none of that worked, just shutting down and becoming clinically depressed. Recovery has been a process. First I had to quit drinking and then I had to do what I'm still doing— practice trying to be open. Be open to God and to all the parts of myself—the good and the bad—and to other options of change, and I think that's basically what my recovery has been about.

Roger

Before I got into recovery, I used my head for everything, and a head trip makes it real difficult to get close to God. Before, everything had to be quantifiable. I saw everything as black or white. I'm just now learning that gray is where it's rich.

I always used to wear brown and live in basements and be a mole. Sometimes I would crawl in bed in the fetal position. I have now started buying clothes. I bought colorful shirts, one a beautiful green. It helped. I lost 70 to 100 pounds in Overeaters Anonymous.

In recovery, I'm learning to accept myself more. I love to dance. I'll just click and I'll go out there all by myself and just dance all by myself for three hours. I don't care. The freest I ever get is on the dance floor. I learned a lot about freedom. There could be no one out on that floor and I'd go out there and dance. Dancing is the height of my freedom of expression. Dancing is a form of spontaneity.

I've been so imprisoned all my life. We appreciate the joy of freedom when we haven't had it. That's a sure thing about us human beings. We take it for granted if we've always had it. With the all the destruction in my life, I took so much for granted. I lost it—the values, habits, ethics I was raised with. I took them for granted until I lost them. Then you have to reacquaint yourself with them. The good side is that I walk around feeling grateful a lot more than I would a while ago.

Joyce

The greatest change in the way I experienced my life before and the way I experience it now is that before I experienced it with fear and I don't have that now. There might be some areas, you know, it's never one hundred percent, but I'm aware of them and willing to do some work on changes. The program [of Alcoholics Anonymous] gave me the freedom to do that. It gave me the freedom. Before I would feel guilty if I took time for myself and the program gave me the freedom to change that.

When I drank I was always hopeless and my dream figures were always like spirits, ghosty-like, floating around, and I was always looking down and never able to talk. The first thing I noticed after I quit drinking was that the people in my dreams became solid.

John

There is a great contrast in my life between before recovery and after. Knowing what it was like once. That's a dimension that I feel so many people don't have in their life—a before and after. But because of my illness and the pain it caused, there's a definite before and after. I really know what the dark side is like. [He laughs.] Real well. There wasn't a gray area. It was real black and there was a line drawn between them. I can compare the two and the memory of the dark is always kept real close to the surface memory because of our [A.A.] program. What stands out most for me from the dark was the despair. The phoniness and no communion with anybody, the loneliness.

Before and after—it's such a distinct feeling. The despair was gone, of course. My musical taste changed from Chopin to Mozart. I don't know why, but Mozart was so cheerful. I still love Chopin, but he has a tinge of melancholy, always that melancholy.

Donald

I started a journal shortly after the spiritual experience I had in Boston. I use that as a catharsis. For years it's been a record of my life—what's true for me. The content began to change as I settled down. In recovery I need balance. I need rest, I need meals, I need my spiritual life, my marriage, sociability, reading, study, worship, exercise. I make walking sticks out of old dead branches, like a shillelagh—an Irish walking stick. They're full of knots.

You say Edwin Starbuck asked the question what would you now do and be if you realized your ideals of the higher life. Well, that would be just what I'm doing. I've been practicing this [program of recovery] for almost twenty two years. I'm not getting good at it, but I am learning those things that I don't want. Henry David Thoreau says "Simplify, simplify, simplify." If I were to offer advice to anyone I would say "Simplify, simplify, simplify." And discipline. For me, I believe that without a great deal of self-discipline, my problems would be right back. I'd be a surface sober person, and that's not good enough for me. I want the thing I yearned for before—the spiritual awakening. I attribute that to A.A.

Carol

[When I arrived early for my interview with Carol, she was bent over her typewriter. She looked up briefly, asked if I could come back in a little while. When I returned, she was still engaged. She settled me in at an adjoining table and continued to work. After a few minutes, she pulled the sheet of paper from the typewriter. She had written the account which follows. It is a passage indicative of a healing of all of the splits mentioned above, and more. I have mercifully left it intact.]

A Spiritual Education
by Carol

In Webster's Seventh I ran across a definition of the word "miracle": "a divinely natural occurrence that must be learned humanly." I thought it an appropriate definition that accurately describes my life. It's been a seeming jungle of contradictions for as long as I can remember, and for just that long I have been unraveling the mystery of it all to the best of my ability. Trying to separate the spiritual part of my life is going to be a little like trying to tell you which part of the Atlantic Ocean is wet.

I remember first seeing Hiroshima when I was about five years old in 1952, nothing was as it should be, nothing grew, the earth was dead. Behind our house lived a Japanese family who worked for us, a nephew of theirs was permanently scared [sic] from the radiation of that bomb. He was a very angry boy and enjoyed torturing me because I was an American. In a way he held me responsible, in a way I understood. I was very touched by this experience and feel it was the beginning of my journey. To understand that man was cruel and finite was a great gift, to know that I was capable of the former but could make a decision to resist, to know that I was powerless over the latter became for me significant knowledge and remains so for me today.

You mentioned William James, whom I know less intimately than his brother, Henry, but admire him nevertheless. As the originator of the doctrine of Pragmatism he has been of significant influence in my life; more so since I have been a member in the fellowship of Alcoholics Anonymous these last four and a half years. Of course I agree that all human undertakings are viewed as attempts to solve problems in the world of action. I tried to solve problems, my own and the world's in many ways for many years, I ended up very frustrated, very frightened and very alone without the ability to take any action. I did not understand that to perceive a problem was not to take an action to solve that problem, it was however, an attempt at something—poetically the collapse of the spiral of illusion and delusion was occurring—it has taken time and suffering before I had the courage to face myself. It has become a daily commitment, softened by a love based on actions not simply ideals. Good for William for being much more articulate than I feel at the moment and good for me that I have learned to listen.

To be aware of cruelty in man and nature and to be in wonder at the beauty of it all were planted in my childhood heart and though overgrown they have not been uprooted. When I am in harmony with man and nature they reside equally and lightly without resentments. I have surrendered to a power greater than myself. I have at times in my sobriety wished that I would be struck efficient but I seem to go in spurts and splashes with prayer and meditation. I can tell you that I have become more kind to people in my actions and less sentimental. My sculpture has begun to have a voice all its own as I have acquired slowly, my own voice as well. It has everything to do with the unification of my spirit, the reconciliation of my ideals (hopes and dreams) with my actions and experiences. It has become an adventure that is looked upon with hope more often than not. I still have very little faith but my world view is no longer a frightened and negative perception where I am the ineffectual center of the universe protecting myself from the "slings and arrows" so to speak.

I have undergone a conversion, it has brought me a freedom I have never known before.

SUMMARY: PRACTICING PEACE WITH THEMSELVES

There is evidence to indicate a healing of the imbalance between an active and a receptive way of experiencing the world. This type of healing is indicated by reports of an active, dualistic, control-based orientation while drinking (the activity includes mental activity) in which the individual felt she or he was to rely on personal efforts alone, followed by admission of need for help from a power greater than the finite self, asking for guidance from a power greater than the personal self, increased importance attached to meditation, and increased appreciation for listening and being open.

All of the respondents spoke of the importance of receptivity in their recovery. Respondents talked of receptivity variously in terms of listening, openness, and acceptance. To hear them tell it, their initial decision to let go of the active way of attempts to control was hardly a noble one.

Paul speaks of surrender born of despair. "I was desperate. Part of me was so desperate that I kept saying yes to whatever was suggested . . . I listen to people. They say that's how it works and I say 'oh, I'll follow that. It's working.' " Paul said that he can't recall ever surrendering to anything before he became involved with A.A. in recovery. "I [always] got what I wanted." He says he feels he has surrendered to his powerlessness over alcohol, that he has surrendered to the people in meeting rooms. Paul associates surrender with death, and says he does not believe in an afterlife. At the time of our conversation, Paul and Bob believed their surrenders to be only limited ones, a surrender to powerlessness over alcohol, although Paul clearly has also surrendered to his sponsor and people in A.A. meeting rooms.[21]

Bob said that a willingness to ask for help is part of his spiritual awakening. While he says he would like to be more like his wife and more able to trust the universe, at this point in his recovery, he seems doubtful that this will happen, associating male ways with rationality and female ways with emotion.

Jane says that she was completely miserable while trying to manage everything herself, and remembers the futility and the pain of this period of her life. She says that she went from being someone who constantly tried to be in control to someone who can let go to a power greater than her finite self.

Jean is willing to help others and is open to guidance from her Higher Power as to the direction this service will take. She is willing to re-evaluate her choices as to both her marriage and her career in an effort to be sensitive to the will of her Higher Power. Jean frequently mentioned the importance of receptivity and openness in her life. She says she does not consider a state of receptivity to be a passive one, and speaks of *making a decision* to be receptive. Jean commented that "the whole [A.A.] program is about being receptive." Jean says that recovery is a process in which she first had to stop drinking, then do what she does all day—practice trying to be open.

Roger is another for whom surrender was born of despair. He says "It wasn't virtue that got me to surrender. What did I have to lose?"

Carol reports that she has always been sensitive to the importance of being receptive. She says that during the period of her active addiction, offering to be a "channel" for a power greater than her finite self became a frightening thing, and that in recovery it is once again an important part of her life.

Joyce speaks of surrendering when "all other avenues had been exhausted."

John says he was beyond caring one way or another when he surrendered.

Donald says he sees surrender as the biggest difference in his life between before recovery and in recovery. "That's when the force enters."

Jennifer and *Roger* explicitly associate intuition with their inner voice and their Higher Power.

While I did not specifically inquire in the interviews as to the healing of the split between good and bad within the self, or about the split between body and mind, or the split between intellect and emotion, many of the respondents noted a greater acceptance of both good *and* bad, body *and* mind, intellect *and* emotion when I asked about the main difference for them between active alcoholism and recovery. I noted just a few examples of each simply by way of acknowledging other splits and healing which may have been explored as part of this study.

Jean, for example, reports being open now to both "good and bad" parts of herself. She reports a spiritual experience of peace related to a deep feeling of acceptance.[22] after she took her first Fifth Step in the program of Alcoholics Anonymous.

Roger made repeated references to freedom of expression through dancing, and not worrying about what people think of him dancing alone.

Carol says her life is much more balanced now than it used to be. She says she is aware of both good and evil, and in recovery is able to choose.

So there is evidence of reconciliation of some of the opposing pairs within the self. A mending of these rifts is indicated by reports of awareness and a least some acceptance of what are referred to in the Twelve Steps of A.A. as "shortcomings" and "defects of character" as well as by reports of a less perfectionistic, more self-accepting attitude and awareness of assets than the participants previously experienced.

PART II
PRACTICING PEACE WITH GOD OR HIGHER POWER

SECTION A
GOD IS HERE, NOT THERE?

1.
Statements Illustrating the Nature of the Problem

Religious differences have caused endless wars and disasters for the human race. The reason of this is that the spirit of unity has not been recognized . . . .

What is needed is religious awakening; the awakening of that religion which is of every soul, not of a particular sect or faith. If the spirit of democracy is born, it will only be born in hearts awakened to spiritual life. Every faith and belief has its principles, right or wrong, good or bad. Some follow these, others do not. They are given to humanity for a particular time, when a message is given for that period for a certain race. Whenever a spiritual wave has come to the world, in the time of the prophets and great teachers of humanity, it has always been a great spiritual ideal to awaken democracy. In the scriptures of Zarathushtra, in the Bible, in the Qur'an, in the Kabala, it is always the same voice teaching the equality of man and love for one's brethren.

If only we would recognize the inner voice, we would see that the different scriptures all contain words spoken by one and the same voice.[1]

Hazrat Inayat Khan

What Western man misses is the rather logical implication of the unity of life. If all living things share a creator and a creation, is it not logical to suppose that all have the ability to relate to every part of the creation?[2]

Vine Deloria, Jr.

2.
Teachings Illustrating the Unity

Man divides, God unites, humanity. Man takes pleasure in thinking and feeling, "I am different from you; you are different from me in nationality, race, creed, or religion." In animals this feeling is still more pronounced. But as man evolves, this tendency is to unite, to become one. Did Jesus Christ come to form an exclusive community called Christian, or Buddha to found a creed called Buddhism? Or was it Mohammed's ideal to form a community called Mohammedan? On the contrary the Prophet warned his disciples that they should not attach his name to his message, but that it should be called Islam, the Message of Peace. Not one of the masters came with the thought of forming an exclusive community, or to give a certain religion. They came with the same message from one and the same God. Whether the message was in Sanskrit, Hebrew, Zen, or Arabic, it had one and the same meaning. The difference between religions is external; their inner meaning is one.[3]

Hazrat Inayat Khan

All nations he has created from a common origin, to dwell all over the earth . . . meaning them to seek for God on the chance of finding him in their groping for him. Though indeed he is close to each one of us, for it is in him that we live and move and exist . . .[4]

Acts 17: 26-29.

Deep ecumenism is the movement that will unleash the wisdom of all world religions— Hinduism and Buddhism, Islam and Judaism, Taoism and Shintoism, Christianity in all its forms, and native religions and goddess religions throughout the world. This unleashing of wisdom holds the last hope for the survival of the planet we call home. For there is no such thing as a Lutheran sun and a Toaist moon and Jewish ocean and a Roman Catholic forest. When humanity learns this we will have learned a way out of our anthropocentric dilemma that is boring our young, killing our souls, trivializing our worship, and exterminating the planet.[5]

Matthew Fox

3.
Illustrative Excerpts from Questionnaires and Interviews

I was given a spiritual or religious education as I was growing up.
59% of those in treatment agreed.
47% of those in recovery agreed.

My experience with organized, institutional religion in the period before my involvement with A.A. was a positive one.
18% of those in treatment agreed.
7% of those in recovery agreed.

I am a member of a religious organization.
48% of those in treatment said "Yes."
55% of those in recovery said "Yes."

In order to grow spiritually, it is necessary to belong to a particular religious organization.
82% of those in treatment DISAGREED with this statement
86% of those in recovery DISAGREED with this statement.

Bob

I had little early religious education. My father was a disenchanted Roman Catholic with little use for the Roman Catholic church. My mother went to a Lutheran church. It was not a very important thing in our family. I did go, but rarely.

Paul

My uncle just came to visit. He said, "Everybody says you're much better. What's the matter with you?" I said "Oh. . . . " He said, "I thought you drank a little." I said if I drank a *little* I wouldn't have this problem, and he said, "Luckily you always kept your faith." I said, "I never had any faith to begin with." I just didn't have it. I wasn't enraptured by the ritual [of the Catholic Church] when I was a little kid at all, and I just walked away in respect to God. I just don't believe in God.

I had twelve years of Catholic grammar school. In one way, they dropped talking to me about God in about sixth grade. It was there—it was sort of floating around me. Whether or not I catch it is another thing.

Jean

I had a very strict church upbringing. It was Presbyterian, fairly liberal. I had a born-again mother. She was very unhappy. She couldn't decide what color socks to wear in the morning without divine guidance. I saw that as a dreadful, debilitating dependency. I didn't believe that that's what God intended people to do with their life. It's sort of like growing up as the child of an alcoholic. I thought, it's never going to happen to me. I'm never going to be a religious fanatic. My dependency came out in a chemical way instead of a religious way. I had some really good experiences with my church. I was very active, served as a deacon. I'm not active now, though.

From the time I was about five until the time I was nine, I really felt in the presence of God. It was a terrible time for my family. I remember consciously praying during that time, but I felt safe. Then once the hardest time was passed, it was like I don't need this anymore and life went back to being difficult. Throughout high school I felt real comfortable with what I believed. It wasn't what my mother believed. I did believe in God. I did at that time ask for guidance for things in my life consciously. I sought that. My mother completely abdicated responsibility for any earthly concerns. I thought that was terribly irresponsible and a horrendous waste because she was miserable. It would have been one thing if she was wonderfully happy, but to zone out and be miserable. . . .

I do a lot of spiritual reading each day. I read John Powell devotional books. I read *Seasons of the Heart*—it's excerpts from all books. [One] of the devotional books I read is the *Daily Word* from Unity. There's a lot I like in the Catholic church. I like the idea of confession. I like the idea of God within us in the Eucharist. Presbyterians only do that periodically. I've never gone to Unity. I've gone to Unitarian churches. I subscribe to Unity because a friend subscribes to it. I read the *Course in Miracles* straight through one year. It was real comforting to me at the time. Now I pretty much just read *A Gift of Peace,* which is excerpts from the *Course in Miracles*. I wasn't ready to buy into the fundamentalist, evangelical Christianity that was my mother's [way], but the *Course* speaks of Christ in universal terms, so having those references was helpful to me to put it into a new context. That was a bridge back to the best things of God. I've been reading different types of theology, most of which is Christian. Thomas Merton, Buber, à Kempis, Kierkegaard. I also read Alan Watts—all of Alan Watts—several books by Henry Nouwen, Hegel. Pretty much everything because of the things I don't know.

I believe there are as many ways to talk to and listen to and worship a Higher Power as there are people. I don't believe there is any one true or only way. Although my form is Christianity, it has to do with my upbringing and socializing and living in this century and this country as it does with the truth of this. That's what I'm comfortable with.

Roger

I was raised Catholic. A lot of stuff was taught to me. It really makes sense, but I didn't see it or understand it. Or I [had problems with] the way it was presented to me. I'm not religious. The difference for me is that I think religions arise when man wants to try and conquer God. If you can define it and get all the rules down. Religions are based on someone having a bunch of definitions trying to make it concrete in a sense. The way I look at it, whenever I want to know something, it's because I want to own it, control it, and if I could just get enough theology down, I would have God down. Something someone said in a meeting that I liked is if God were small enough for me to understand, He wouldn't be big enough to help me. That's where the *Course in Miracles* came in for me. It seems to have allowed me a place to talk about things that are spiritual and to share spiritual experiences and feel safe and okay about it. In February, I started the *Course in Miracles*. It's helping me shape a different picture, cultivate a loving God. It gave me a place where I could talk about spiritual stuff.

Jim

I was raised Catholic. I guess you'd call our family middle-of-the-road Catholics. I had a really bad experience in Catholic grade school. When I got out I was in trouble with the law, in trouble with a lot of stuff. When I got to Catholic high school they really got me on the straight track. I wound up at the top of the class. I got married young and my wife was a very strong Catholic. I'm not in any organized religion now. I've got some problems with what I was taught. I've really gone with the belief that God is inside of me, that I can find the answers in myself. I don't doubt someday I'll go back to my original religion . . . but I've really found that I can get the answers within me.

My grandfather always ate meat on Friday—thirty years ago you used to hear that if you ate meat on Friday you go to hell—and I remember a priest one time telling my grandmother, "Don't worry about it. The man's a good man. If that's all he does is eat meat on Friday, you don't have to worry about it." If I am living a whole life, if I'm living a spiritual life, you know, it does not have to be within the confines of a defined religion. Again, maybe someday I'll wind up there. Who knows?

Although I was raised Catholic, I have not gone with the life in the Catholic religion. I've really gone on with the life that God is inside of me, that I can find the answers in myself. I don't doubt someday I'll get back to my original religion. I've found a nice service at Christmas time and I go [to that] but I've really found that I can get the answers from within me. I think you've got the basic rights and wrongs within you. You know what's right and wrong. I'm not saying I don't believe in God. I do, definitely do believe in God. I have a hard time believing if you steal a quarter you're going to hell. I can tell if I'm doing right or wrong. I can seek out the answers myself. I guess it's a matter of letting go.

Ann

I've had strong religious training and have never gotten back to that. I used to go to religious school four days a week, Saturday school, Sunday school, *bat mitsvah,* everything. Five days a week for at least ten years. And summer camp. I went to a Jewish summer camp for five years.

Before, I equated religion with spirituality and it's not the same thing. In spirituality, there aren't any procedures. In religion there are rituals and things that are done certain ways and there isn't that with spirituality, I think. When you get to that point where you find that piece of the [Alcoholics Anonymous] program where you don't have to struggle any more, that's when you could start going into spirituality.

Joyce

I was raised Catholic. My husband and I were divorced for about three or four years. During that time I was doing a lot of searching, going to different churches. I am still a Catholic. I am also now studying the Course in Miracles.

I feel I'm a strong person spiritually, but there are a lot of doubts coming up. Suddenly I'm questioning my long-held beliefs. I'm reading this book by two nuns. It seems it's a natural thing to start doubting your values. Where what you had was all right growing up, now you start turning inward, you know. A lot of the things they were saying . . . made a lot of sense because I am Catholic, and a fairly strong Catholic, but since being in the program my spirituality has changed. The program is not religious, you know, it's more spiritual. I mean, where before the program I would not have missed mass if my life depended on it, now that doesn't bother me because I feel I'm closer to God than I was before. I'm working with a series [of cassette tapes] by Ernie Larsen[6] called *"Recovering Catholics."* I have not thrown out my religion, but at the same time I don't buy everything I did when I was younger. I mean, I believe in Jesus Christ. I've got no problem with that, but I see too many people who don't believe in Jesus and you can't take and condemn all these people because of that.

John

I was not brought up in any particular religion. Yet we did go to Sunday school. We went to a variety of different churches. We went to a Methodist Church for a while and then we went to a Unitarian Church until I was about thirteen. I still don't know what Unitarianism was except that it was kind of liberalizing. I grew up with the strongest bias against Catholicism. My mother talked about how dogmatic it was. She didn't care for it. So I guess I grew up not caring for organized religion as such. I would say I sure grew up loving the out-of-doors. Nature, plants, animals. I was really interested in wildlife, but I didn't think in terms of God or religion. Later, during my drinking, I had feelings of some ordaining nature, but as a kid I didn't think in terms the way I do now of a Higher Power having a lot to do with everything. As a kid, I didn't think that deeply about it. I thought it was real beautiful, I was real appreciative of nature, beauty. In one way, you might think I had been deprived of a religious upbringing, but it left me open. [In recovery], I didn't have any preconceived ideas at all. I hadn't tried something that hadn't worked. That's something I hear about a lot in A.A. I was sort of a God hater—God as far as church religion is concerned anyway. I sure had some sad feelings in my later drinking, drug-using times that I was really wishing, wishing there was something, yearning for something. There were so many miracles. I could see so many things in nature, like certain kinds of butterflies imitated other ones, and yet I couldn't figure out how that could have evolved. It would have had to have been made, created. It was later in my drinking when things were pretty bad that I started experiencing the spiritual longing.

In treatment one of the things I did was decide to do everything different in my life. *That's* a big change. I wanted to do everything totally the opposite—I tried church. While in treatment, I went to a different one every week. I went to the Methodist one, I went to the Catholic one. When I came back to my neighborhood, I just went to the one closest to me. I did not have a driver's license—it had long since been revoked—so I went to the one I could walk to—it happened to be Episcopalian. I went every Sunday and it was okay. I let it all happen. I let myself be baptized—I had never been baptized. I also read the whole Bible from start to finish right after leaving treatment. I was just trying to see if I could find some Higher Power.

I also read the *Bhagavad Gita* and some other books on the religions of the world. I found myself liking them all. I found myself thinking Jesus is fine, too, someone to talk to [he laughs]. My [A.A.] sponsor's "born again." He had these meetings about that. I could never buy all that. I felt like that happened [in Alcoholics Anonymous] anyway. There wasn't any word that had to be put on my Higher Power, no name, either. I've sure tried it all, as hard as I could. I went to those prayer meetings with my sponsor and lots of other A.A. people who were doing that in my area and it was okay. I could sure see how the early Christianity was really the A.A.

program and how it was wonderful. But my feeling was that all the other religions basically had the same thing, too, and that God revealed Himself in different ways to everybody and the name didn't make any difference *at all* and Jesus didn't intend for it to become the way it became. He was maybe just a man that was really lit up with truth—I don't know. I sure love everything I've ever read about him and everything that he said, but I don't like the rest of the New Testament. I don't like Paul.

Paul started getting sort of preachy, saying you have to do this, you have to do that. Jesus wasn't that way at all. He just said love each other, it seems to me. I like that. Maybe I'm wrong, I'm not a scholar. I do think of Jesus a lot because I'm a Westerner and that's my Western tradition and I'm going to accept that. Why should I try to be so different? I don't like the kind of Christianity that says if you don't believe Jesus is the Son of God, you've got to be saved. In other words, my mother doesn't go to church, she doesn't pray, she doesn't have any thing like that and yet all her life she's been doing nice things for everybody and she's a happy lady. She's got it, whatever it is, and she doesn't need saving, is my feeling. I know lots of people like that. Whatever they've got is fine. They have a Higher Power of some sort. I needed to put a word on it because I was so unstructured in my life. I needed a name. Jesus or something. But language or words can mess everything up. Jesus could have been all kinds of different things to all kinds of different people. Sometimes people say this is the way it is, it's rigidly defined, with words. You have to believe in a certain dogma. If you don't believe in it exactly the way I say, you need saving. I don't like that. [He laughs.] I don't think of myself as a Christian and yet I sure like Jesus [he laughs]. Maybe Jesus is just a word I use, because I'm human. I have to think of a word to focus on, because something showed me or told me or made me feel that. Jesus, sure. There's something there that I felt. I can visualize something if I say that, but I can't so much in saying he's God. I need to put it into human terms, that's just for me. It sort of means truth to me. Gandhi is a hero of mine. I became a vegetarian for two to three years—I'm a lapsed vegetarian, now. [He laughs.] I love it. I wouldn't become a Hindu, but I love it. That's there, but I'm here. Maybe that's the way it's supposed to be—to be presented to me in the framework where I came from.

Donald

I went to church and Sunday School. I was confirmed in the Lutheran Church. I think the Sunday after confirmation I probably stopped going to church. Confirmation was a couple of times a week and Saturday morning. You don't take away Saturday morning from a kid. That was essentially the end of my education as far as religion was concerned. I kept reading about it. I left what I consider to be a rigid religious type of thing and I was going to do it on my own. By the time I was 16, I was pretty much calling my own shots.

I think I believed quite strongly in God in childhood. As a youngster I came close to drowning when I fell through the ice. How I got out of there is a miracle to me, but I did. I remember praying to God to get me out of there. Yes, I do remember that. I believe I prayed all through my life until the time I started drinking. I did stop towards the end because I lost all faith. That's when I became an athe-gnostic—that's a cross between an atheist and an agnostic. I think I prayed to God with the "gimme" prayers, but never got any help so I turned my back on Him. I became quite vocal in the sense that I argued against the existence of God with anyone who wanted to talk about it. That was all through my drinking, from the time I lost control about ten years after I started.

SECTION B
GOD IS THERE, NOT HERE?

1.
Statements Illustrating the Nature of the Problem

Euro-Americans . . . tended to see the world in more divided ways. The sacred world of divine power was separated from the profane one of ordinary existence. God had caused the world to be, and his law governed its movements: in that sense, he could be said to dwell within it. Yet he also far transcended it, and meanwhile his human creatures had increased the separation between God and the world by the fall in the garden of Eden. Sin had entered the world, and it had affected not just human beings but all of nature. For Euro-Americans, the world had become . . . a three-level affair. God tried to control human beings, and human beings tried to control nature. If there was rebellion in both cases, it only emphasized the fact that the seamless garment of one creation had been, in the Euro-American view, pulled apart.

While Euro-Americans tended to separate material from spiritual realities and in their religions exalt the spiritual, Native Americans expressed in many ways their sense of the sacredness of matter. The distinction between a natural and a supernatural realm, an easy shorthand for describing Euro-American religions, was forced and strained when applied to the religions of Native Americans.[7]

Catherine Albanese

This tendency to split reality into material and spiritual spheres, a characteristic of modern thought in general, constituted an important difference between European culture and the premodern Cosmologies of the Native Americans and Africans.[8]

Carroll and Noble

2.
Stories Illustrating the Unity

The multitude of beings is a terrible affliction.—The vision of the Presence has released me from it.

Through contact with an Object so specially loved, something entered, like a ray of light, into the dark cloud.—A crystal drop spread through the powdery opacity.—And everything became not only warm and diaphanous but radiantly transparent. Everything was transformed into a single limpid whole, in which the separateness of things could no longer be seen. Brightness reigned throughout.

And at the same time that transparence reached me in my turn. It penetrated me. It made its way down into the very depths of my being—to where I thought nothing could still be found. Passing through me, it washed away in its mysterious waters the plurality and the dark places of my being. And I knew an unbelievable solace in feeling that there was indeed an Other; and that through that Other I was one with all things.[9]

Teilhard de Chardin

. . . he who receives whomever I send receives Me; and he who receives Me receives Him who sent me.[10]

John 13:20

103

3.
Illustrative Excerpts from Questionnaires and Interviews

I have had a spiritual awakening or change in outlook which has developed gradually.
48% of those in treatment agreed with this statement
75% of those in recovery agreed with this statement

I have had a spiritual awakening or change in outlook which was sudden and/or spectacular.
27% of those in treatment agreed with this statement
24% of those in recovery with A.A. agreed with this

There has been at least one time when I have felt in the presence of God as I understand God.
66% of those in treatment agreed with this statement.
82% of those in recovery with A.A. agreed with this.

Bob

I would like to have a stronger belief in God. I wish my beliefs would solidify. It's comforting to believe God is all-powerful and directing our lives. That would be a comfortable way to be, but I'm not ready for that. That will take care of itself. I don't think there's anything I can do to make that come faster. If it happens, I think it will be a gradual process. I would like to move more in the direction of my wife [who has a lot of faith]. The ways in which women think and men think are different. Men are more logic-based thinkers; women are more feeling-based. Men tend to want to look at facts. A counselor that I'm seeing made the observation that I tend to be very solution-oriented. My wife is in feelings, and I'm off trying to solve problems. I'm not sure I'll overcome a logic base. I'm not sure I want to. That would mean reliance on blind faith and denial of what's in front of us—the facts—the facts are what we perceive to be.

I think I am much more aware of my own spirituality [in recovery]. I'm much more open today than I ever have been. I recognize that there are influences on our lives and there are places to go for help and comfort. I am more aware of those things than ever before. I'm more able to ask for help. I definitely, very definitely, think that's spiritual. I think the fact that my wife and I realize that we're starting to have a problem and sought help early on is evidence of that. The fact that I'm going to a counselor is, too. It was also suggested that I get a goal partner for my job search. Before I would have considered that hogwash, but now I've done that. My ability to ask for help and my comfortability in asking is enhanced. I equate that with a spiritual awakening. Awareness and ability to ask for help. That's quite a change. I was a person who just about never asked.

I haven't had a sudden spiritual awakening. I don't expect that. I am becoming more forgiving of myself. I used to beat myself up when I didn't do things perfectly, now I don't do that so much. I think that is part of a spiritual awakening. I think I am being aware and more realistic now than I ever have been.

Paul

I don't think that there were ever any times I felt I surrendered before treatment. I was full of rage, and that rage kept me fighting everything. I guess that's part of the reason I know I was an alcoholic. I knew that years ago, I just didn't know there was any way to *not* be—to not be active. I know that I have turned that over—I haven't turned over the responsibility for my life, but . . . When I was in treatment and I was told I didn't have to drink, I was dumbfounded, completely dumbfounded. That First Step,[11] I've turned *that* over. I cannot drink. I can drink, I just don't want to die, that's all. I spent my life reading Leconte, and couldn't get a handle on *myself*. This program makes a great deal of sense. The simplicity. We complicate things in such a weird fashion that if they [the founders of A.A.] had anything beyond a simple declarative sentence it would be all over for everyone. If there was room for interpretation there would be really hard times. I think it's very clear to me that I cannot have a drink. Other people can have *a* drink. I could never have a drink. I could never understand what that was all about. I know I believe them when they say what will happen to me if I choose to have a drink. I *believe* them. Because I know how horrible it was for me. And it can get worse. That's a frightening thing for me. I don't want it. I don't like that part. I'm making the choice not to have a drink but it's based on the recognition that I'm *powerless* over alcohol. I'm *powerless* over that. I fear what the results would be and it's much easier to surrender myself in the [A.A.] rooms. I love my meetings.

I think my spiritual life is very much wrapped up with my feelings on art. That's where I get some of my spiritual stuff, my nurturing. I'm so happy, I can look at art again. There are certain responses that I have to art that are purely emotional. I'm coming back to that attempt to make universal that which is personal—that is what art is to me. It is the most incredible affirmation of human aspiration. An artist is really a generous individual, offering up themselves to a world which to a large extent doesn't care or understand, and the artist continues to do it. Some artists affect the way everybody looks at everything. Art helps me get out of myself.

Jane

When I first went into A.A., I hadn't been arrested or anything. I decided I would take the time to go to treatment. I realized I had to ask for help and realized other people could help me. In treatment, I first accepted I was powerless. It was a process of surrendering. I looked at myself. I knew I was powerless. The feeling just came up through my gut up through my chest. There was joy and warmth and tears in my eyes. It was really powerful, seeing myself with new eyes. It made me feel I surrendered for the first time. It was so intense, wave after wave. I did a Fifth Step [of Alcoholics Anonymous][12] there in treatment. There was an incredible feeling of freedom. I can still remember that coming, radiating up through my face, warm and tingly. Before, I always felt ashamed about being an alcoholic. After, I started to feel that was okay. I didn't have to fight anymore. I saw acceptance. I was okay. I was fighting it before. I told my family I had been around A.A. Before I never told my family. After my Fifth Step, I felt I didn't have to hide anymore. I feel I surrendered in treatment about alcohol, but not with drugs. I did prescription drugs after that.

I had a dream five or six months sober. I was praying for some kind of help. Is there a God out there or somewhere? I was really tense, and developed a head cold, bronchitis. There was a real noisy guy in the apartment above me. I was really stressed out in school. I finally got to sleep. I would wake up with a knot in my stomach. I felt drained, like someone wrung me out. I didn't know if I could go on. Every time I would breathe, I just couldn't take it anymore. It got so I said, "If there's anything out there, please show me." I was semiconscious, or in a trance, half asleep. I could see the room through cracks in my eyes. Then I sensed the presence of a golden light every time I breathed. A light so vast I couldn't take it all in. I could breathe it in. It was so vast, so much all around me. I could feel warmth in my chest, a warm glowing light around me, then I lost it. I only had it again intermittently. I felt something there with me looking after me.

I think I'm getting a spiritual awakening. It's been fragile. These past few weeks I've been able to grow a lot. At times it's been really painful. I've taken a big step. I have slow periods, then

105

a big jump. Ever since I went to an A.A. meeting overseas, I never went back [to the old way]. It's slow. I had a hard time letting go. I had a spurt in treatment. I was still stuck with old ideas. I would go along, get a jump. It's like I can only handle so much at a time. I was feeling so good, but also feeling too much. It was all I could take. I reach a plateau, then go through spurts.

I've had to develop a relationship with a Higher Power. I've been getting a lot closer. Hopefully, that will keep getting better.

Jean

I had something of a [spiritual] breakthrough. I finally talked about the fact that I was raped. The person I did my Fifth Step with was a Catholic priest, and he urged me to let my anger be a prayer, to not push it down. In a sense that was a spiritual awakening—realizing that whatever I felt was acceptable and could be a legitimate form of prayer. Whatever I am feeling, whoever I am is acceptable to God. Assuming there are things that are not acceptable to God puts limits on God. It's extremely presumptuous [to think that] God can't understand. I think that is one of the most fundamental spiritual needs—unconditional love. The way you get it is by believing in a God. Certainly no human is capable of that.

Jennifer

Yes, I've felt in the presence of my Higher Power, sometimes more than others. The day of my wedding was one time. It happens a lot, sometimes at meetings. It's just an overwhelming feeling of love. That is something I've never felt before in my life. I felt it my first sober Christmas and New Year's. I was giving service, standing behind a table serving food and sodas [at an A.A. function] and that Higher Power was so present. My mouth got tired from smiling. How much joy and love I was feeling. There are times that I'm feeling direct connection with my Higher Power, very close and very connected. I would really strive to be that way, but sometimes I just let it happen. All of a sudden I get a flash at a meeting and I feel that feeling. It's not mysterious like this awesome lightening bolt—a man speaking from the clouds—it's not like that.

I keep talking about how the feeling of love and my spiritual awakening has to do with the feeling of love. The first time I ever felt it, that was definitely a spiritual awakening for me. The first time I felt love was in an A.A. meeting. I don't know exactly, there are degrees, starting with holding hands, starting by people coming over and hugging you and caring about you. That was a spiritual awakening. It was a process after that. It was getting familiar with the feeling, allowing it. It was starting to allow myself to nurture that feeling, help it grow, learn how to achieve that feeling, [keep it] in different situations and different interactions. It was starting to understand when the feeling left and when the feeling came. It just started with a feeling of love. I never felt that ever before in my life. I can't say that I feel it fifty times a day or three times a week. It goes in and out of my life at different times. I know that I have to be open to it. Open and willing to the experience.

Ann

I felt in the presence of a power greater than me at *Rosh Hashanah* services. I felt so peaceful. I just felt like I loved what they were talking about. I really got a message from this and it was a great high I felt. That lasted quite a few days, too. I felt really there's a message there for me and it's about God and what everything means in the world. On that holiday they start with the story of Abraham taking Isaac up on the mountain and getting ready to sacrifice him and trusting that much in God that he was doing the right thing. I felt I finally understood some of those things. All the Biblical stories, all the poems, the prayers. I felt peaceful, felt serenity. I can have that kind of feeling more, I just have to be a little more open and trusting.

Spirituality is more that peace that comes from accepting a Higher Power and then accepting other things. Things just happen in life and, you know, it's not really worth struggling so hard against things that are just going to happen anyway. That doesn't mean being passive to me, it means not being so angry. Surrender is just giving up that struggle to be able to do what I wanted all the time. Because things were so bad— everything was so bad—in my life that when I got to the point where I could just say fine, I'll do whatever you want me to, it was so much easier. There's still a lot of things to do, but it wasn't that struggle. I don't always do that, but I do it more than I used to.

Jim

I was a lot more at peace after I took time for a spiritual retreat. I was really starting to let go of stuff. I started to get a firm grip on where I wanted to be, where I wanted to go. I was pretty messed up when I got there. It's almost like somebody hit me on the head while I was there and said, "Hey, now you're going to follow me. You're going to snap out of this crap. Clean up your act and find out where you want to go. Straighten your life out and go on from all that garbage and all that confusion. God is here, Christ is within. You've had enough hurting in your life. It's time to pull your mind together and get moving, and I'm going to help you." It's hard to explain. It's hard to explain the feeling. It's just that God is here and God's here to help me, and I'm going to do it. It was all of a sudden. I came to the Renewal Center where there are nice buildings, a nice place to sleep, nice scenery. I'm thinking of building a townhouse out there [by the lake in this place of nature], and all of a sudden God is around you. The presence is here. All of a sudden He's in my life, He's here. He is within me. I can get the answers from Him. I didn't have that before. I mean I haven't had that. I don't think I've ever had that. Well, I didn't go to church that much, but even when I did go it was kneel down, stand up, sing—you know, it's so structured. I'm not saying that's wrong. It goes far, far beyond that. Christ is within you. He's there. I think I am following God's will. It's exactly what I'm doing. I started getting some real direct answers after that. I went over to the aftercare unit and started dealing with the loss of my wife, I started dealing with childhood issues, I started dealing with the sexual issues. I cleaned up a lot and worked through them and they don't bother me anymore. It was kind of a turning point. Well, it was a real turning point. From chaos to "here's a God who wants to help me." Here's a God, He's here, He's going to help you, and now let's go on.

Roger

I surrendered in October 1984. It will sound like a small thing. I got up in the middle of the night and ate seashells. I ate *seashells*. It wasn't virtue [that got me to surrender]. It was what do I have to lose? That was a precious, precious moment—the cornerstone of my recovery. I got on my knees. "I give up." From that moment on, my life changed. After the surrender, there wasn't any dramatic release. But I cried. I felt better, but it was not a dramatic change.

I had two spiritual awakenings. My first experience was a dramatic spiritual one—where everything changed just like that—overnight. It was more the sudden spiritual experience. It was the burning bush. When all that energy got down to reality, I didn't hang in there. That was in 1971 or 1972. I was about thirty. I fell in love. I'd never been in love before. I didn't know what love was. I didn't know what that strong passion—love attraction—was. It didn't last. I fell in love with this woman and it didn't last. Within a week she was back with this guy [she had been with before]. I didn't feel much pain, but what I felt was I wanted to hold on, I wanted to be able to live. It had just felt like I was alive and I got so angry and so desperate and I thought I either wanted to die . . . [his voice trailed off]. I remember yelling out to a god I didn't believe in. I said "Screw you, God!" That was really gross. I said "I don't care. I'm just going to do the best I can and if that ain't good enough for you, you made a screwed-up world. Tough . . . ! That's all I got to give." And I don't know where that came from, but it was real . . . I yelled it out. From that moment on, everything changed. I lost all fear, not all fear, but most of my fear. I lost my compulsion to use and drink. I'd end up going to bars, have a beer, and be so interested in people I'd forget the beer. I became very involved in this co-op [cooperative store]—it was rather new. I got totally involved. I stopped dealing drugs. I lived just a couple blocks from there. I put all my time in it. I did do acid [use the drug LSD] sometimes, but I finally felt useful, I finally had a purpose. I didn't believe in a god the way I have a god today, but I did believe in a cosmos—Mother Nature.

Talk about coincidences. Things happened to me that I couldn't believe right after that. For someone who had no love life, no sexual life, no nothing I ended up having relationships with three people in the house. People would wander into my life and be intimate with me—just really bizarre. I was out in the yard and a neighbor said, "I'll see you tonight," and she showed up in my room that night. Stuff like that happened. You know that that happens . . . just like there's this magnetism going on. People detect you're alive. I was so alive that I was attracting other people that were alive. It seemed like everything was sped up. All the interaction between human beings went into a real fast mode. You could connect and be talking person to person real quick. It was the most alive I've ever been. I thought I'd found something. And the answer was just do the best you can—that's all you're supposed to do. In a way, it's like turning it over, right? But I kind of got preachy about it and couldn't figure out why other people didn't understand and I tried to share it with people and I was overpowering, overbearing, maybe . . . I was never so happy. I had a sexual life, I had relationships, a working life. I had work, fun, and play, I had all three of them going. I had no idea what life was like until then. I recovered so well physically that time. I worked for twelve hours a day and played handball for five hours a night. You know all that self-will stuff that gives you apparent results. You look good, people compliment you, but it's not the same—it never helps— because as soon as I got injured and couldn't play handball, as soon as something threw that thing off, I was back into a relapse, and I'd take two weeks out and do a bunch of cocaine or something. I hit it more heavily. You know, looking back on it, I needed all those convincers before I was going to give up.

Shortly after this first awakening, this woman that I had met [in the yard] behind the house had come to my room that night and we made love and it was just this beautiful experience. I got together with this same woman after I got back to the drugs, and I remember being in this room and turning to her and her saying "You're sick." She was saying that because I could no longer relate to her as a human being. She knew it. That just killed me, because I knew she was right. I was totally baffled. I gave up. That's when I knew . . . I said there ain't no hope for this cookie. It was one of the most single powerful experiences of my life.

I was so shaken that I could give up all that. Just blew me away. I mean, I could understand me doing drugs and alcohol when life was miserable—to kill the pain, but when things were going pretty good, when things got tough, just a little, when I felt some pain somewhere along the line, I still chose the drugs and alcohol.

I got away from that state, came to the one where I'm living now, and stopped shooting up heroin. The process of awakening this second time has been much slower. I'd have to say for myself *fast don't last*. There was nothing wrong with the first experience. It was the best year of my life, the best year of my life. It just doesn't seem like I learned what I needed to learn.

The first spiritual experience I had, I had no community. Today I have A.A. That implies an acceptance of limits and knowing something else has to do the rest. I treasure A.A. All these experiences. The first experience lasted a long time, but I had no one to share it with. I had no family, no fellowship. Today I hold on to this experience a lot. I know I can feel great and go off on my own and lose it. I would just repeat what happened that time. All the stuff I have today I feel very secure with, and yet it's so fragile—it's so darn fragile. Every so often I see the fragility of it and it's just that I'm doing the best I can do. [Roger interrupts himself here] Phew! My editor just turned on—I feel that I'm preaching. [He resumes.] That's pretty much the basis of my sobriety. When I surrendered that [first] time, that was the *best* I could do. Even the second time, after [I ate] the seashells, I remembered what happened the first time I had a spiritual awakening. I knew that when I just did the best I could and just did what was in front of me, everything was just great. But I never had the strength to do that again. I could think about it mentally. I don't know why I could do it that one day. I think that's the mystery. The basis of my sobriety today is still that—I do the best I can and that's all there is—there ain't no more. Now lots of people think that that's a cop-out, they think it's a rationalization. You know all these things that I say are based on self-honesty. If you don't have self-honesty. . . . Show me anybody out there who can do better than the best they can do. Then the perfectionist comes out. I get in trouble when I do that. That's been a real hard one for me to hold onto [doing the best I can]. That's self-acceptance and forgiveness and being gentle on myself. That's where my little kid [inside me] helps.

Carol

I have had spiritual dreams or visions. I remember waking myself up elevating horizontally in clouds, kind of elongated, stretched out on clouds, light blue, gold, that kind of thing. It's recurring. It's great. I get dreams for sculpturing, even mathematical equations. This has been since I've been sober. I've just started having this recently within the last year. It's most pleasant when you wake up. I wake up stretched out. It seems as if I'm waking up rising in the clouds. It's a nice way to enter the world again, as if protected. My body goes up as I go up.

It seems as if it first happened in the springtime. I was invited to a retreat. I was doing a lot of things at the time and I just wanted to go and sleep. I was exhausted, physically and mentally. It crushed my will. I just collapsed. Surrendered is a good word. I just had to take it as it came. For the first time in my life I felt taken care of. I felt the ability to float free and no harm would come. At the retreat, they served me breakfast and gave me a studio. They took care of the food, my room. My experience affected my relationship with the other thirty or so people there for six weeks. To be able to wake up in the morning and eat breakfast with them, have conversations, eat dinners with them. I was a citizen. I enjoyed conversations. I could bring something to the breakfast table. I had great affection for these people I lived with. When I was drinking and drugging, there were big secrets to be kept—that's no longer there. I was happy to be open and vulnerable. That stayed with me while I was there. Many people didn't like me, that was okay too. I enjoyed their company. It was great to be able to give people the right not to like me. Before when I was drinking I had to convince you that you were wrong or I had to turn into somebody else for you to like. I walked away enhanced from the whole thing, and I feel like I enhanced other people's lives as well. I felt my experience was a private thing. It's not so interesting to talk about those kinds of things. It's kind of self-centered and a one-way conversation. There are a couple friends of mine—one is a writer and one is an artist—and we do talk about our dreams and it's kind of a regular conversation.

I've had this particular dream a number of times. The few times it's occurred lately it's wonderful because I've been angry. I fell in love with this man. He decided he didn't love me anymore and I got very angry and resentful. A couple of days would go by and I would have this dream and it would be okay. I'm grateful for that. Anger can exhaust me. It's the worst thing, the worst thing I've had to live with. I'm so very sensitive to my anger. I'm a very angry person. I had to be awfully high or drunk to act out on it. It springs from being cold and demanding and wanting to be loved and to love.

Joyce

I was in therapy with depression. I had known for a length of time that I wasn't happy. In the Catholic Church there's a portion in the mass where you say prayers for this one and that one and you ask for your own intention. I can remember always asking God to help me with my problem. I didn't tell Him what it was. But I was in denial at that point and didn't really think I had a problem. I mean, if I would have been faced with it I could have said yes, but I chose to ignore the whole thing. I feel God played a role in what happened after, although I wasn't particularly interested in Him doing that.

I was so depressed and unhappy that I decided to go in for therapy. When I was in therapy on the third or fourth visit, my therapist asked me, what would be the worst thing to ever happen to me. I said, "That I'd be an alcoholic." When I said that, that's when things started to happen. We did an analysis[13] and that's when I went for treatment. The first night I went to the outpatient program they gave us some reading materials and one was the Big Book of Alcoholics Anonymous. I'm a compulsive reader and I didn't know anything about A.A. I started to read. As a matter of fact, I read the whole book that night but for the stories. And I read Step Three, about making a decision to turn my will over to the care of God. I looked at that and I thought, You know, I just can't. I couldn't ask God for any help, you know. And so then I thought, I felt, I need a form of penance. The next morning as I was driving to work—I had left an hour earlier and I don't know why—there were some people going into one of the neighborhood churches—in my neighborhood you have a Catholic church on every corner. And so I went in. I thought, well I'm going to go to mass and I went in there, and at the end of the mass the priest said starting the next morning they were going to have like a novena,[14] but it would be mass every day for a week. And I thought, that's it. That's what I'll do. And that was really beneficial, because then I felt like God was more on my side and everything. What happened is . . . I sat way in the back because I had to get in and out for work. The very last day, at the end of mass, the priest said now after mass we're going to have the blessing of the sick and of course that used to be the rites for the dying which you couldn't receive unless you were on death's bed. He was going to have a special blessing and he said, "Anybody can come up here. If you don't feel good, you have a cold, or you're an alcoholic." I thought "Oh, my God, he can see me back here." I always say that was my spiritual awakening.

In recovery, there have been other times when I felt close to God and others. Although there have been things I didn't think I could forgive to begin with, I think the thing that turned that around for me was saying the Lord's Prayer in a meeting one night. We say it every single night, you know. I mean, I've said it millions of times. Suddenly the phrase "forgive others, as I forgive you" started clicking for some reason. I think God talks through people. We were holding hands in a circle; we always do. I'd had problems and the people who were there knew that. I had gotten advice to just pray for the willingness, and that's what I was doing, I was praying for the willingness. They'd suggested I write a letter to God about that and I had done that, and then I don't know, it was just saying the Lord's Prayer. It just hit me, you know, I'm asking for his forgiveness but yet I'm not able to forgive. So I was able to let go of whatever that was that I was holding on to, which I can't even remember any more. That happens quite often in meetings. Somebody's going to say something that you can hear a thousand times and for some reason they'll say it and it'll be like *oh yeah,* you know, *yeah.* [Standing there saying the Lord's prayer], it felt like a burden lifted, lightheartedness.

The other thing that happened one time—it was the same type of thing—was that I was probably three months into recovery and I didn't know anything about A.A. and I'm going to these meetings, everybody's slipping [drinking again] and I'm thinking, God, does this have to happen to me? I was really getting nervous and scared. I was in a meeting and it was on the Fourth Step[15] and one of the fellas said that when he did his inventory he had pages of liabilities and the only thing he had on the asset column was that he had the ability to change. And that was just like a wind or something coming. I thought, *yeah,* I've got that. I knew I had that if nothing else and I thought, I'm going to make it. It was just as clear as anything. And I've never doubted it since that time. I never doubted that I would drink again and granted, we go one day at a time, but I feel real strong that I wouldn't. There's only been one time that I was in the place where normally I would drink—with being depressed and self-pity and that type of thing, you know, a feeling of real hopelessness. And that's when I started therapy again. [I was feeling I was six years in the A.A.] program, so why didn't I have that serenity that everybody else did? It was still that empty feeling inside. It's lessened and it's changing, but it's not there yet. I still feel that I'm missing a certain part.

John

[My connection with a Higher Power] came about in treatment very suddenly and it's a very hard one to describe. I don't share it very often, either—hardly ever— because as I hear myself talking about it, it sounds fishy.

I was so ashamed of myself before. I didn't even like anybody to look at me. I just felt dirty and awful and scummy and I didn't come here [to treatment at Hazelden] because I wanted to get well at all. I was sent here, sort of brought here. I didn't care where I went. I thought I would be locked up or something when I got here, and I thought that was right and proper. I had no idea of what I was going to find here, but all I knew is that I deserved something awful and instead it was real beautiful. Then just coming out of the fog in this environment was just so beautiful and being able to understand that was a gift. I think just really seeing that I was like so many other people. It was wonderful.

So about a Higher Power—it just was like part of the program. I think my feelings were I was just so *grateful* [he sounds amazed]. The first prayers that I ever did were just thanks. I never asked for help—ever in words—even here. I never said "Please help me get this program" or anything. Just thanks for giving me this and that's the way it's sort of been most of the time since, which is really weird.

I remember walking out on the lake by the treatment center—it was frozen cold—it was January. It was dusk kind of like last night only it was really cold—20 below zero probably [he laughs] and just looking at this cluster of buildings—it was only a small cluster in 1970—and they were all lit up just like . . . I don't know what it was just like . . . and that was an experience I'll never forget. It was sure an experience of knowing that I was totally confident that I was going to be fine and that I would not have to use drugs or chemicals or alcohol again. It was sudden. I was relieved. What struck me? Just that . . . this is where God lives . . . here . . . whatever God was . . . it really was true. [He had put his hand to his heart.] In my heart. And again, how can I explain that? It was just an overwhelming feeling of everything is okay. And will continue to be okay. There wasn't any question left. This was right. I finally belonged somewhere. [pause] Maybe in the world . . . there was a community to which I belonged. I was sure I was going to be well and fine. It was Higher Power for sure. It was a deep inner knowing. I don't understand it. I feel so very, very lucky it happened that way. I don't know why . . . [the last in a whisper].

I'm almost . . . sometimes I'm almost ashamed of it. I feel guilty about it and so that's why I don't speak about it at a meeting. I never speak about the suddenness of that. I sort of gloss over it if I have to talk about it, you know, when we're at a step meeting talking about the Steps, the Third Step or the Eleventh and Twelfth Step spiritual awakenings. I don't want to talk about it because it's so sudden and it doesn't seem like . . . it wasn't the kind of thing I would have ever believed. I was so skeptical about the possibility of that happening, but it did. It took a real down-and-out-drunk, a bum, a 24-hour around-the-clock drinker and drug user for years and years and years. I never drank or used again, never felt *any* desire to. There is a definite before and after in my life right from the moment on the lake. Absolutely. It's another life totally. Another me or whatever that I don't even feel like was me. Although there were parts of the present me there. In saying, that [I realize] it's not entirely true. I'm glad everything happened, too. Well, the surrender very much so happened before I came to treatment. Now in looking back I know that that's what happened. The surrender was really important to me, too. What happened on the lake was definitely a spiritual experience. I'd say definitely it was sudden because it was right here. I think mine was like Bill's [Bill Wilson's]. I know Bill's story very well and I really identify with it. That's another reason I don't share it because I don't want to compare myself with Bill in any way. He also had said that can sure happen. But still, it was definitely sudden.

No! I don't believe it was anything I did or didn't do that led to the moment on the lake. It wasn't anything I did for sure. Absolutely not. Because one of the overwhelming feelings I've always had was that I was totally undeserving of this and I was also, I should add—because it's very important to me—I was a free bed patient and for the first time there was nothing in it for the people here. They were giving so much and I was getting this for free. It was a gift. Talk about a gift. There was total acceptance and love and caring for somebody who had done nothing ever to deserve it. I've been feeling it this week again here. I've been just walking around holding back tears. This place is so beautiful—I know it's just a physical reminder of that miracle of having the compulsion lifted. That's simplifying it, I guess. It was more than that . . . well obviously . . . well that's so much . . . it's . . . being given your life . . . again. [Silence.] Words . . .

Donald

The first deeply spiritual experience I had was a few months before an even more profound one which happened in Boston. I don't trust my memory, but I believe it was relatively a few months before. One Sunday I was sitting in the living room and I had this feeling in my head. This was the same feeling I was to have during my second experience in Boston. It was almost like a practice session to prepare me, not quite as deep but with many of the same things. The feeling of being at peace. Deeply spiritual. I don't remember the specifics of the circumstances. I do know I was struggling with a number of things. I was struggling with business. I was struggling with sobriety. I would guess I had been sober twelve to fourteen months at that time. I don't recall a feeling of surrender. I had been trying hard to understand the program but there were so many things to be understood. It was like I was treading water and I had to keep treading faster all the time. It was a struggle. I'm going to guess that I might have hit a little plateau where the struggle wasn't too bad, and maybe that's when I realized and got out of the picture a little bit. Maybe the Almighty stepped in and said, here, I'll give you a little shot of what you can expect. Yes, I do connect relaxing and getting out of the picture with the spiritual experience. Absolutely. No question. Absolutely, and I think the reason for it is in such a profound way you can't explain it. I think if I could explain it then I could say it's psychological. I've never wondered, questioned or sought, never asked anyone what happened. I couldn't explain it. I knew this is beyond that. It feels like a secret—well maybe not a secret, because it is at that point when you start to give the program away with sincerity. I have a feeling that the first experience was slight and momentary. It was almost like God was saying, "Don't give up, here's a little hope," and that's about what it taught me. That experience intensified my desire, my yearning to go on. I experienced the yearning a lot. All the time. I think I've always wanted what I have now, and am getting now, but it was always out of reach. What I have now and am getting now is some contentment and serenity. I had the yearning while I was drinking too. There were times when it was pretty strong. I couldn't say what I wanted. I think that's all tied up with guilt, because I think we know we're better people. We don't like what we're doing so we have a yearning to be better, if that yearning is for nothing more than to be sober and sane. I think I've always had an intuitive feeling that there's something there that I wasn't reaching and I think that feeling would come on at times. At times when I was perhaps filled with more despair than normal, if that's normal. I had this yearning to be complete.

When my second spiritual experience happened, I was at a convention in Boston. I had been sober for eighteen months. I used to go to these conventions a lot. [I had been at a show.] I went back to my room, showered, shaved. I lay down on my bed and I had been lying there. I have no recollection of what I was thinking about. Suddenly this force began sort of to encase me. I was enclosed in this aqua-colored air or case. I just felt so light. I felt I was raised off the bed and I never had such a close, intense, soft, loving feeling and then it just slowly . . . and I said, "This is God's grace." I thought I said it out loud and suddenly I was normal in the sense that . . . it was such a long time ago . . . It's been twenty years now. But anyway from that point on my struggles with sobriety, all those questions that I had were answered. It just felt as though I had had a block there. From then on, I carried a feeling in my belly. An omni station. It seemed like an omni station. Pilots fly from one omni station to another—there's a tower and then there's a radio, a beacon. When I say I listen for it, I stop. If you're busy, there's lots of confusion, so I stop to tune in. I would tune in to it. That feeling seemed to be unintelligible. I felt I was lifted from the bed. If I had to explain that or tell someone about it, it felt I was lifted, the aqua glow was all around me. It didn't go from here to here. I felt it all around me. I was like laying in an iron lung. Aqua color, that's how I had the impression, the vision that I had been lifted up. It seemed like a long time, but maybe it was in our meaning of time only a minute or two. For four or five years I didn't talk about it. I was reluctant to share with someone who wouldn't understand. It was a dividing line, and from that point on, before and after, the grace of God. For eighteen months, I hadn't surrendered. At the moment of surrender I was encased, lifted right off the bed. So this is it. I think it had to do with the load one carried. I had a deep resentment. I had resistance. I was somewhere between an atheist and an agnostic, so I called myself an athe-gnostic. From the time I was encased in light, from that time on, I never had any doubt or questions, predicated in my surrendering. That's it. I can't handle it. When you get to that point, the gift is given. I took everything after that really automatic. Words were all there. I didn't have to wonder or struggle. The gifts were laid at our feet and we had but to pick them up.

My old earth passed away. My old concept of heaven and earth prior to my spiritual experience all passed away. It's fun now. Before there was a lot of wonderment, doubt, anxiousness perhaps, and now I don't feel that so much. At least about God and about faith, and love. [The new heaven and earth] I suppose are more pure . . . here again it's difficult to explain. Before, I suppose, there was fear. I don't conceive of heaven. All I know is it's going to be all right. It is all beyond my comprehension. Then I have to accept the fact of [God's] benevolence and that I am a mere little child, no matter what my age and experience. So its natural that I make mistakes. I'd rather not look at them as sins but simply as rather unpleasant learning experiences or consequences. It takes the guilt out of it. I choose to say that words like sin are too heavy. I have unpleasant learning experiences in growing up. God's going to send me to hell for this? That's the old God, the old heaven, the old earth. I don't need any of that. I think that as children that's the way we're taught. Sure, I was taught that. The fear of God. Yes, I felt one with my Higher Power during this experience I had in Boston. Yes.

Do you know how many times God is mentioned in the first 164 pages of the Big Book? One hundred and thirty times in the first 164 pages. Four times in the Steps. One hundred forty-two times in the Twelve Steps and Twelve Traditions. The word G-O-D. Once in the Serenity Prayer. That's 277 times the word God appears in our literature. So what's this business about higher powers? [He laughs.]

There was a clear line between my life before the spiritual experience in Boston and afterwards. The main difference is difficult to sum up in a few words. It's just the old life, the new life. Life without an understanding or acceptance of God and all that that means and life filled with God. I would have to say that in that process there is a surrender. At that moment that surrender happens, the spiritual force, power, enters my heart, my soul. That's the main difference between after and before. I feel surrender was certainly involved.

SECTION C
GOD IS NOT DEAF, BUT MUTE?

1.
Statements Illustrating the Nature of the Problem

My god has forsaken me and disappeared,
My goddess has failed me and keeps at a distance
The good angel who walked beside me has departed.

One who has no God, as he walks along the street,
Headache envelops him like a garment.[16]

> Cuneiform Tablets from
> the Second Millenium B.C.
> cited in Julian Jaynes

2.
Stories and Teachings Illustrating the Unity

The chief function of the . . . gods was . . . that of fitting people and functions into these societies. . . . Perhaps in ancient peoples—to put it in a popular fashion—the right hemisphere [of the brain] was 'talking' to the left, and this was the bicameral mind. [The bicameral mind] produced answers to problems and decisions . . . . After the hallucinated voices no longer told people what to do, there seem to have developed various other ways of discerning messages from the gods to make decisions. We call these methods divination.[17]

> Julian Jaynes

Nanny sent Janie along with a stern mien, but she swindled all the rest of the day as she worked. And when she gained the privacy of her own little shack she stayed on her knees so long she forgot she was there herself. There is a basin in the mind where words float around on thought and thought on sound and sight. Then there is a depth of thought untouched by words, and deeper still a gulf of formless feelings untouched by thought. Nanny entered this infinity of conscious pain again on her old knees. Towards morning she muttered, "Lawd, you know mah heart. Ah done de best Ah could do. De rest is left to you."[18]

Zora Neale Hurston

Grandfather Francisco taught me how to pray to Umna'ah, our Creator. He told me to go alone into the mountains, to find a quiet beautiful place and to pray. He said I should talk out everything, say whatever I felt or needed, and then listen for an answer. That's the secret: to listen. You have to say everything that's in your mind, cry until you're empty. Then listen. He will speak to you.[19]

Ruby Modesto and Guy Mount

Indians . . . value silence, and recommend it in stories and pointed sayings . . . "Listen, or your tongue will make you deaf," "No flies come into a closed mouth," and a clause in an Indian prayer, "Oh my Grandfather, may I lose no good opportunity to hold my tongue."[20]

Evelyn Eaton

God's invitations may be dramatic and strong or still and small, but anything more than invitation will not protect our freedom and potential for love.[21]

Gerald May

3.
Illustrative Excerpts from Questionnaires and Interviews

I pray.
30% of those in treatment said they pray all the time or nearly all the time.
57% of those in recovery said they pray all the time or nearly all the time.

I meditate.
16% of those in treatment said they meditate all the time or nearly all the time.
32% of those in recovery said they meditate all the time or nearly all the time.

In the period *before* I used alcohol and/or other drugs abusively, I prayed.
25% of those in treatment said that they prayed all the time or nearly all the time.
7% of those in recovery said that they prayed all the time or nearly all the time.

In the period *before* I used alcohol and/or other drugs abusively, I meditated.
5% of those in treatment said they meditated all the time or nearly all the time.
0% of those in recovery said that they meditated all the time or nearly all the time.

While actively abusing alcohol and/or other drugs, I prayed.
9% of those in treatment said they prayed all the time or nearly all the time.
5% of those in recovery said they prayed all the time or nearly all the time.

While actively abusing alcohol and/or other drugs, I meditated.
5% of those in treatment said that they meditated all the time or nearly all the time.
0% of those in recovery said that they meditated all the time or nearly all the time.

My relationship with God as I understand God is a direct, personal one.
56% of those in treatment agreed with this statement.
77% of those in recovery agreed with this statement.

It is important for me to know God's (as I understand God) will for me.
48% of those in treatment agreed with this.
61% of those in recovery agreed with this.

Bob

I communicate with God through prayer. I do some asking. I don't ask much for myself, I ask more for peace and happiness for the people I care about and myself too. I don't recall asking for tangible things. I did practice meditation while I lived in Europe. I went through the Transcendental Meditation course. It definitely works. It absolutely works. It's restful. I got out of the habit of practicing. I want to get back to that. I have a mantra. I had a discussion with a Roman Catholic priest. He said priests have been meditating a long time, and use chants and some prayer similar to mantra and achieve the same effect. What gets in the way of me doing it is that it requires practice—you don't achieve it easily. Also not finding the time to do it. When I'm having some success with meditation, things that are otherwise stressful become less important.

I do some kind of reading in the morning. I ask for guidance from God. [He smiles.] I ask for strength and wisdom more than anything else. I don't ask to be led through the day. I just ask for strength, courage, wisdom. I'm not sure at all it's given. I eat, go to work. I don't pray during the day. I will sometimes spend time reflecting on what's going on, slow myself down a little. Sometimes I consciously choose to alter my breathing. It definitely helps to change from shallow to deep.

Jean

I do daily readings in the morning. The reason I do them then is because I'm nearly comatose then and trying to meditate in the morning doesn't work. I'm just not there. But I pray during the day. That doesn't mean I kneel and light candles. It means I say "I'm really losing my mind and I need to calm down" and that's a prayer. Or "this sunshine is great" and that's a prayer or "isn't she a controlling person" and that's a prayer. All of my legitimate feelings are acknowledged. That's prayer. Also in the evening usually right after I come home from work, I meditate a while. I do deep breathing and focus on a thought of God and being still and then at night before I go to sleep I just sort of summarize and go over what is still bothering me about the day or what was really good about it and talk that through, then fall asleep. There are three separate times I do an actual thing. My spirituality isn't limited to those three times. If I missed my meditation or orientation meeting with God in the morning, I have to somehow work something like that into my schedule or I realize the day is going really awful. I read nine devotional books. I do. And I underline them. It takes about half an hour or forty-five minutes. Some mornings there will be something that really speaks to me in all of them. It's sort of insurance—there *will* be something there that will help.

Jennifer

I guess I was willing to be open to a Higher Power. What really helped me at the beginning was that this guy John who I got sober with asked me if I ever prayed. We had this really big fight one Jewish holiday and he asked me if I prayed. I said no, or maybe I said sometimes. He asked how I pray. I said, if I prayed, I'd pray from the inside out. He said "Why don't you try praying from the outside in?" Today I know it's a combination of those two, even though he insisted that I pray from the outside in. That was the spark that helped me. Because I guess I was the center of my own universe at the beginning and it helped me. When I started praying from the outside in and pretending that I had this outside force, this power greater than myself, [it helped]. I just started praying as if there was one, and that helped me a lot. I think that started awareness a little bit. I always thought people were talking about a Being in the sky, and even though I didn't believe that, I said well, I guess I'm going to pray to a Being. I don't know what it is, but it's greater than me, outside of me. My [inner] self was a negative self. I'm so negative and destructive. I don't know what I was doing, I just know that this makes sense to me so much that I decided to listen to him and to try his way. That's when the [A.A.] meeting rooms became my Higher Power. Right after that came the feeling [from] everyone holding hands at the close of a meeting and that was a feeling outside myself. And so things just happened.

Jim

[I started to do this visualization that someone suggested in which I imagine myself as a statue that someone else has carved of me.] You have to take a look at the statue first to see if the statue's happy or sad. It would give me an impression of how I felt, because theoretically, someone carved the statue of what they think you look like. So you see what maybe somebody else is thinking you're looking like, feeling like. You talk to the statue a little bit and then you get in and you ask the Higher Power to come in and you ask your Higher Power some question—to me it's a picture of Christ. You get the answers back. You can get some answers out of that. At least I do. They were confusing, but they're getting clearer. It's really getting into your inner self. I think it's more of a feeling. I don't think there's any question Christ is within me. I don't think there is any question Christ is within all of us. It's that spiritual part of us. I guess that's why I believe I can get the answers, because he is part of me.

Joyce

I pray every morning or talk to God when I wake up. It's an automatic thing now. That hasn't always been with me, but the first thing I think of now in the morning is God. I've done some meditation, but see, my perfectionism comes in there and I think, "Oh well, I'm not doing this right," you know, "Oh well, I don't have an hour to do it so I can't do it today." The first thing in the morning I think of God, thank Him for the night—wake up and say "hi." I had a good night or I had a lousy night. What I'm praying for is on a day-to-day basis. I try not to think of work at that point, I can get real quick into work. I try to make it more thinking of the good things. I ask for His will to help me. I always do that at that point, but I do more thinking about the fact that I'm not lying there freezing in the bedroom but I'm warm and cozy under the covers and "gee isn't this nice" and that type of thing. I'm just grateful for all the little things right at that time. I'm working on getting into meditation more than I do. I'm trying to meditate on a regular basis, I am praying about that, but it hasn't gotten good yet. I haven't worked that into my routine the way I would like to. When I do try to meditate, I spend most of my time trying to keep my mind from wandering. I suppose that's why it's so hard for me to get into it. I think the only reason that I do it is that I know the rewards are there. I think you will get a lot of peace and it's supposed to be the time that God talks to you, you know, and you're listening. There are times when I've meditated when after, not necessarily when the meditations come on, but after, I feel real at peace and real serene. I think that happens probably in different ways, I don't know, but that's what I'm looking for. I'm not balanced. I don't lead a balanced life. I go from one extreme to another, and I think meditation would bring the balance into my life that I'm trying to find.

I go to extremes. I tend to be real compulsive. That's where I'm trying to get some balance. If something doesn't turn out the way I want or if my life is unhappy, I have a tendency to want to run, and that's internal, too. I shut myself off, shut myself off from God. I never pray when I'm in trouble. I pray when things are good. I've a real hard time asking. That has a lot to do with my upbringing, I'm sure, but that always amazed me because you go to meetings and basically people are praying when they have problems and it seems to me that that's when I feel, Oh well, I've got to do this by myself. I can't ask for help. And that's what I'm trying to bring into balance.

I don't want to be so materialistic and I'm not too much that way, but I'm enough. I have fears as far as security when I get old and things like that. I don't want that, I want that to go. I think that will only come from finding more what God's will is. And it has to be, I feel the ability to be able for me to ask God for things. I think that's all right, but I can't do that, you know, and definitely not on a material thing. There are some people who say that you shouldn't, but I've heard other people say yeah that's okay. I do believe that you can ask for material things if that's your desire. If you know what it is you want.

I was at the [Hazelden Renewal Center] in a group and the facilitator asked us to write a letter to God. Let's see how it was. It wasn't a letter, it was sort of a dialogue like God was talking. Anyhow, I thought the whole thing was stupid. I was having a real tough time with it and the facilitator said why don't you start writing about what you're doing here. What came out of that is that God was talking to me. It was like he said "Joyce, you still fear me." And I thought, well, that's not so. See, I don't want to say that, because that's what I felt. I almost didn't want to look at it, almost like if I don't read it, then I won't know that I wrote it, because you shouldn't fear God. There's a lot of "shouldn'ts" in there. It felt like it was God writing it but that I was bad, if I have to put an emotion on it, bad to think that. I shouldn't have that fear, even though He was telling me. I definitely felt He was the one telling me that, and it wasn't said in an unkind way. My feeling is that it was said in a more understanding and gentle way, but I couldn't quite accept that. I think that's where the conflict comes, or why I started therapy. There is conflict in there with feeling things that I thought I shouldn't feel.

Maybe I back away from that, because there still is a level of fear and so I don't get too close to that. I have an issue with trust and with fear. I can put God as just my bosom buddy and we're doing all this talking in the morning, or else, when I go to church, he's up there on the altar with a big distance between us.

Donald

My prayers to God are very, very simple. In totality, they are listed in the Eleventh Step.[22] Praying to know God's will for me and having the power to carry it out. It's so simple, so beautiful. I won't have to ask for a thing, because He's already given me everything I need, except that knowledge of His will and the power to carry it out. It takes me out of the problem. It is taking the inflammation out of the boil. Usually if I relieve that pressure, the answer is there. Pretty obvious. Let's say I'm confronted with a problem situation. My first response can be reverting to my old habits, and suddenly I'll realize when I'm taking that inventory at that moment in time and place, I say "Hey, this is the wrong thing to do." I turn it over to Him, to guide me. If He wants me to go this way or have this thing or whatever, it works. If it doesn't work, why worry about it? If I'm comfortable inside me, no nervousness or anxiousness, it's right for me. The nervousness or anxiousness is *my* will, *my* desire, *my* hunger, *my* appetites wanting to be filled, and the fear they're not going to be fulfilled. So if I'm comfortable, that's God's will for me. As to major decisions, I guess I don't see anything as life and death anymore, as a crisis. I take a long time sometimes to make decisions. I let them happen, let them evolve. I don't get in the way so much. Obviously there are times when you have to make a quick decision.

The Third Step Prayer[23] goes through my mind frequently. I have a set of prayers and I just sort of do it all at once. The Serenity Prayer, the Lord's Prayer, the Third Step Prayer, a couple of Lutheran prayers—I call them Luther prayers, little prayers I learned as a child. I have to start at the beginning and say the whole thing before I could tell you what I say. *Relieve me of the bondage of self.* You see, I suppose that's a core, that's what the Twelve Steps teach us. Submitting our will, the submission of our will to God's will. Then we come closer. We live according to His will and everything else flows from that. Be guided by God and he gives the power. That tremendous power of one drunk helping another. The greatness in one helping another. That doesn't come from me. That's too simple, you see? The important things, the profound things are simple! It's really quite amazing.

Section D
God is Like This, not Like That?

1.
Statements Illustrating the Nature of the Problem

The pervasive use of masculine language for the divine . . . has tended to link the male with the numinous and exclude the female. . . . God pictured in wholly masculine images is not conducive to an understanding of the feminine as participating in the divine. . . .[24]

Mary Farrell Bednarowski

All Hindu deities, female as well as male, demonstrate a symbolism of the coincidence of opposites. . . . [This] . . . seems to be very weak in current Western religious imagery.[25]

Rita M. Gross

2.
Stories Illustrating the Unity

She say, My first step from [God as] the old white man was trees. Then air. Then birds. Then other people. But one day when I was sitting quiet and feeling like a motherless child, which I was, it come to me: that feeling of being part of everything, not separate at all. I knew that if I cut a tree, my arm would bleed. And I laughed and I cried and I run all around the house.[26]

Alice Walker

I believe in the absolute oneness of God and, therefore, of humanity. What though we have many bodies? We have but one soul. The rays of the sun are many though refraction. But they have the same source.[27]

Mahatma Gandhi

119

3.
Illustrative Excerpts from Questionnaires and Interviews

My idea of a higher power is more encompassing—or larger—
now than it was before I became familiar with A.A.
65% of throse in treatment agreed.
89% of those in recovery agreed.

I find God (Higher Power) within myself.
41% of those in treatment agreed with this.
73% of those in recovery agreed with this.

I can see God (HP) within others.
59% of those in treatment agreed.
82% of those in recovery agreed.

God is or is in nature.
77% of those in treatment agreed.
86% of those in recovery agreed.

Bob

I think I am getting closer to God. I do believe in God, but I'm not sure that he's willing or able to influence our daily lives. In my view, God's probably a he, but may not be either a he or a she. I question whether he influences our daily lives or has a plan when I see so much hardship and strife. I question if he's able to influence it, if he's caring at all. I see God as external.

Jane

I'm re-defining what my Higher Power is like. Before, it was like my parents. I projected an image of my parent on my Higher Power. I was a lost child. I thought a God up there . . . maybe he had time for me, or maybe not. It might help me out, maybe not. If yes, maybe he would throw some old crumbs. I felt no one cares about me.

Now I feel I have a sense more of having a Higher Power within me and surrounding me. I have a warmth in my chest, almost a pressure. The fact there have been more people in my life [is evidence of a Higher Power]. My Higher Power is sort of like a light around me, in me. I don't feel so separate from God or different, more like we're in it together. I feel pressure in my chest most of the time lately. Sometimes it's a great feeling. I close my eyes and visualize the light.

Jean

I believe there is an intelligent and caring power in the universe far beyond myself and my comprehension. I believe that people are ultimately good, and that all things can work together for good. I believe that there is a God that does care for me and everyone else, all evidence to the contrary. It's a real practical decision— the decision to believe in God. You either decide to believe or not to believe. For me, believing gives me strength to deal with uncertainty. I guess the difference I see between my faith and my mother's is that I don't expect all the answers from my faith—she does. My faith, my God, gives me a place to be with my questions and feel loved and accepted even with the questioning. I can't conceive of a God who wouldn't understand that people are just rebellious, frightened.

Jim

I have as God a picture of Christ. I mean, if I'm going to reflect on specific things as being God it would be a picture of Christ. However, God is everywhere. His presence is everywhere. If there's three in one, Father, Son and Holy Ghost, fine. It's still God.

I believe the Lord is an all-loving Lord, an all-forgiving Lord. Then again, what do you have to be forgiven for maybe? I mean, certainly I know if I go out and shoot somebody, I have done something wrong and I'm going to have to pay for that. However, I don't think he can forgive you until you've forgiven yourself. I have to realize the wrong mistakes I've done and be sorry for them before he's going to forgive me. I think that's where I believe God is within you and is part of you. This is hard, I don't know how to say it. . . . He's there. He's within me. I know where I am. I know where I want to go. I know where I've come from and what I'm waiting for. I think he's helping me.

Ann

Those times when I've felt really great, that serenity feeling, I feel my Higher Power is a part of me. I don't ever think of a Higher Power looking like something. I guess I would say it's not something I could draw.

It took me a while to really accept a power greater than myself. A.A. helped me with that. Before, I felt that I had to do it myself. I felt that I was the only person who was going to help me out of anything. Whatever happened, it was my responsibility, I had to take care of it. In the last year or two years that I was using drugs, I would feel so alone, and when things got really crazy, really bad, I would think, I am just alone, nobody knows how bad this is, nobody knows how horrible my life is. I can't get up every day. I would go some place, I would think, they must know by looking at me. I can barely get out of bed. That was about a year ago. It started to get that way this fall, too. I thought, the bottom's falling out and nobody sees that. I need to know that I'm powerless and that I'm not alone.[28]

Jennifer

My Higher Power is all over the place. It's in everything. *Everything.* And it's even in the toilet bowl. Louise Hay has a morning meditation. It took me a little while to understand this, but in this meditation you thank the bed you slept in, you thank the chair, you thank the furniture, and you even thank the john for taking the sewage and the waste material and transporting them away. When I listen to this, "thank the toilet," but yeah, because energy is in every single thing. In the sixties when they had those posters "God is Love," I never really understood what that was all about. I had no idea what they were talking about. When I got sober and I felt love for the first time, all of a sudden it came so naturally. It was natural for me to say God is love.

Roger

It's always hard to talk about God. It's a very personal experience. It's kind of like I want to but. . . . There are lots of times when I *feel* God. On this journey, especially in early sobriety, God is a friend, God is a mother, God is father. God is a *lover.* [He says this with wonder in his voice, with awe.] He really was all these things to me, and I mean feeling-wise. The prominent image of God is as a father and sometimes I feel so loved by this father that I start crying and that's, well, those are maybe *the most beautiful experiences that I have.* I just treasure those. I don't want to analyze them.

Sometimes I say, ah, well, that's because you didn't have a relationship with your father. You know, so what? I don't care. That's where I'm at. Because it works. I showed you those pictures of me [before recovery and in recovery.] Those are all statements that it works. My life has gotten so much better. But I have part of me that wants to analyze crap like that. The presence of God. Sometimes I feel much closer to Him. God as the father, the lover, it's great. Then at a certain time I have to break, get away. I have a *fear of being close to God* [said slowly] and a *fear of being close to people*. There's a certain sense of drowning, losing self, that becomes real powerful.

I don't know if it's a principle, but somehow there's a theme throughout this whole *Course in Miracles* that I am studying that God loves me. It's not a punishing god of retribution. It's hard to pray to and trust something that you think is going to rap you. I think I have a faith today that is something that has grown, it's a trust. At first I trusted God because there was nothing else—I was desperate and destitute, why not? But over time, I am beginning to trust because I see it work over and over and over again. God makes stuff work out. He's the little kid in me who needs to be nurtured. I wouldn't want to hurt him. He helped me have this experience.

Joyce

One thing I'm trying to do is change my concept of what I envision God to be. It's always been a masculine person and I've tried to go more with a woman type. I haven't done it [before] because that's just not the way I think of it. But that has slowly been coming to me lately, more. That's real new, I'm not even sure where I am with that. That's just within the last week or so this has been happening. There's been some changes going on there. I found out that because I think of God as masculine that keeps the fear going, because I have a fear of men. Ernie Larsen [on these tapes I've been listening to] was talking about the different masks that God wears. He said that Abba is the same as papa, and how we should look on him as our loving father. Well, right away I got bad vibes [vibrations] with that, and that's the first time I recognized it, because my dad sort of deserted us and I had no role model for men. So to look on God as masculine seemed superior and strong. I like that when I want to be protected and cared for, but I resent that if I need help. Maybe that's why I don't ask for help. Ernie Larson said you could look on God as a lover. Now, I like that concept. I thought, well that sounds good. There's somebody to take care of you and everything. I haven't worked with that, but that appealed to me. But it's just in the last couple weeks that I can start maybe thinking of God more as feminine rather than masculine. I think if I can do that I could get closer. I think I could feel more comfortable in asking for things and being understood. As masculine he represents more authority to me and more punishing type things. It seems to me that in that book I was reading by the nuns, God was referred to as "She" in a couple instances, and that may have been why that change came for me. I'll have to look at that, because that allows me then what I always have been looking for.

John

My Higher Power is in me, out there, in other people, animals. Everywhere in all those places. Before the experience I had in treatment, I would not have located God within me. I didn't think of [God] at all before and if I did think about it, it wasn't in me, it was outside and it didn't care. It didn't care about me. I used a lot of things—like Nazi Germany and the Holocaust—as excuses. I read everything about that in my drinking days for examples of [godlessness]. I was always sort of fighting the concept of [a Higher Power], trying to disprove its existence. I wasn't raised with a concept of [God] and there I was with all this crap trying to disprove God existed, because if he did exist he would hate me for sure or something like that.

Spiritual longings started for me later in my drinking—when things were pretty bad. I suppose I do think of my Higher Power as a he—I can't help thinking of Jesus as a he just because there have been so many images of him. Some people do think of their Higher Power as female, or both male and female and neither male nor female. I think that's great.

Donald

Thomas Merton wrote about the feminine side of God. I believe that there is a feminine side of God. There is definitely a feminine side of God. [Before recovery], I didn't even think about that. It hadn't been brought to my attention. I think [an awareness of both aspects—male and female]—came through studying, although I guess it's been some time I've recognized it.

SUMMARY: PRACTICING PEACE WITH GOD OR HIGHER POWER

These stories provide evidence of a reconciliation between the individual self and a power greater than the finite self. A movement toward the closing of this gap is indicated in these participants' reports of increased awareness of a Higher Power within themselves, in others, and in the world around them, as well as their reports of more frequent communication with a Higher Power.

Each of the respondents reports experiencing a changing and expanding concept of a Higher Power, or at least openness to expand their understanding, even Paul who says he is still "hopping around" on the question of a Higher Power. While all reported lack of commitment to a spiritual life while drinking, they reported greater commitment in recovery. Each conceives of a loving Higher Power, even if the Higher Power is the group. *Bob,* with least cumulative daily abstinence, sees God as external. *Paul,* the next newest in sobriety, uses the group as his Higher Power, although he is open to other possibilities. *Jane* spoke of a union with a power greater than herself experienced as a sensation of warmth and waves. She reported the presence of a golden light: "I was surrounded in light and warmth. I didn't have to fight anymore."

Jean said, "I believe there is a loving and caring power in the Universe." *Jim* feels a strong sense of connection with a Higher Power and says he finds it particularly within himself and in nature. *Carol* reports experiences of feeling in the presence of a higher power which in turn helps her relate more intimately with other people. *Roger* described two periods of spiritual awakening; the first was the more dramatic of the two, but was in his opinion unsustained, due to lack of community. He says that during the first period he also was proselytizing, trying to impose his views on others, which increased rather than decreased the distance between himself and others. He observed that no matter how elating a spiritual awakening may be, "I can go off on my own and lose it."

Joyce's idea of a higher power is changing and expanding. At the time of the interview, she was considering the possibility of a feminine nature of God for the first time in her life. She smiled as she spoke of this possibility, and observed that one of the reasons she had always had a difficult time accepting God was that she thought of God as male, and she had a history of difficult relationships with men. *John,* before recovery, said, "I thought if there was a God, I'd be in trouble for sure." In recovery, he described a feeling of peace and reconciliation with a Higher Power while he was standing on a frozen lake outside of Hazelden. "It wasn't anything I did, for sure." *Donald* attributes his spiritual awakening to his involvement in A.A. "The [A.A.] program is the core. I prayed until I drank, and then I stopped. I had deep resentments. I had resistance." He describes two distinct spiritual experiences with a power greater than his finite self. The one that occurred while he was sitting in his living room was, he felt, a glimpse of the

123

more profound and lasting one that occurred while he was on a business trip. He associates his spiritual experiences with being on a plateau between spurts of self-will.

Bob, who responded to the questionnaire when he was in treatment and was still new in recovery when interviewed, questions whether God can intervene in our daily lives. Most of the others did believe such intervention was possible, with Jennifer saying her recovery was divine intervention, and most of the rest giving examples of what they consider to be miracles in their lives. Jean, Roger, and Joyce were studying or had studied from a *Course in Miracles*.[29] Each communicates with a Higher Power more now than either prior to active alcoholism or while actively drinking (including Paul, whose Higher Power at the time of the interview was the group).

Many of them specifically mentioned devoting time to meditation in one form or another. Several mentioned that they would like to increase the amount of time they devote to meditation in their lives. All who mentioned meditation stated that they had received positive benefits whenever they did set aside time to listen and be still. Jean, Paul, and Jim all had tried some form of meditation before recovery—Paul during a college experiment and Jim with Transcendental meditation. For Donald, it is meditative to sit outdoors as part of his daily routine, for John it is meditative to ride his bicycle.

PART III
PRACTICING PEACE WITH OTHERS

1.
Statements Illustrating the Nature of the Problem

From Meister Eckhart to Mary Daly, the sin behind all sin is seen as dualism. Separation. Subject/object relationships. Fractures and fissures in our relationships. Take any sin: war, burglary, rape, thievery. Every such action is treating another as an object outside of oneself. This is dualism. This is behind all sin. . . .

Gandhi held to the Buddhist and Jain view that all sins are modifications of himsā, that the basic sin, the only sin in the ultimate analysis, is the sin of separateness, or attavada. According to a Jain maxim, he who conquers this sin conquers all others.[1]

Matthew Fox

Wherever there is other, there is fear.[2]

Upanishads

There are hungry people everywhere. They have soup kitchens in New York, London, Canada. But poverty is not just being without food. It is the absence of love. I can tell you there is more warmth in Calcutta, where people are willing to share what there is, than in many places where they have everything.

There are people who have no one. They may not be dying of hunger, but they are dying of hunger for love. Especially the drunkards, the drug addicts. We give them tender love and care. Often in big cities, big countries, people simply die of loneliness, unwanted, unloved, forgotten. This is a much more bitter poverty than the poverty not to have food.

The only thing that can remove poverty is sharing.[3]

Mother Teresa

2.
Story Illustrating the Unity

"Do you know why the Center Pole in the Great [Renewal] Lodge is Forked?"

"No," answered Hawk. "No, I do not." "There is a twinness about man," began Yellow Robe. "A twinness of his nature. And there have always existed the twin parts of the People. It is always the Other Man who does not understand, or the Other Man who is the one at fault. This Other Man is represented by the Forked Tree, the Center Pole of the Sun Dance. It is Forked, but both parts of this are One Thing. Leaves are left upon the Forked Tree as a Sign to the People that these things of twinness mirror twinness again within the People. The Two Forks look exactly the same. And each Fork branches into many leaves that are exactly the same. But the question is always, which reflection is which? Which one am I? Or am I both? It is a great Teaching, and that is why it is symbolized in the building of the Sun Dance Lodge. It has healed the wounds between many divided Peoples, and has brought these many different kinds together in brotherhood within the Renewal Lodge."

"This twin part of myself is quite evident," Hawk offered. "I have found myself moved many times to do things that have become entangled in the lives of others and have been misunderstood by them. I have very seldom in my life set out to hurt someone else intentionally, but I have sometimes brought pain to people anyway."

"Yes," Yellow Robe agreed. "This is part of the Teaching. One half of you loves, and the other half of you at times hates. This is the Forked Medicine Pole of Man. The clever thing the Medicine has taught us here is this. One half of you must understand the other half or you will tear yourself apart. It is the same with the other half of any People who live together. One must understand the Other, or they will destroy each other. But remember! Both Halves must try to understand. Even within yourself it is hard to know which of the Forks is which. 'Now why did I do that?' One half of you asks the other half. You do things quite often which you do not mean to say or do, sometimes to yourself and sometimes to others. But you would not kill yourself for these mistakes, would you? I am quite certain that you would not. Yet there are those who have done this, who have killed either themselves or others. These are men who have not learned. An entire People can be like this. These People and men are not Full, they are not Whole."

"Tell me more," Hawk said. "I am interested."

"When Lightning Mouse and I visited the camp I was telling you about, we found a problem among them in their Understanding. It was a lesson to be learned in the Sign of the Forked Medicine Pole," Yellow Robe said.

He then called for his Pipe. Prairie Rose filled the Pipe and brought it to him. Yellow Robe lit the Pipe and took a long puff. He then handed the Pipe to Hawk. He began to speak again.

"These People had been taught . . . that good and evil existed as separate things. We talked with them about this philosophy and discovered their confusion. They had these two things set apart. But they are not separate. These things are found in the same Forked Tree. If one half tries to split itself from the other half, the Tree will become crippled or die. These People we discovered were trying to split this Tree with their law. But you cannot split these things with law. Rather than taking this barren Way, we must tie together the paradoxes of our Twin Nature with the things of one Universe.

"Before our Sun Dances can begin, many Forked Poles smaller than the great Center Pole must first be formed into a circle. This circle becomes the outside of the Medicine Lodge. The Forked Poles for the circle are given by the People, and they represent the People. But remember these are Forked also. This is the sign of their twinness. There are twelve of these placed to form the circle of the Great Lodge. They represent the Twelve Great Peoples of the world. Only the two at the opening that faces East represent the People of the Shields. The others represent the other Peoples in this world. One of these People is the whiteman.

"These smaller Forked Poles also represent all the things of this world. Let us pretend for a moment that they alternate as we go around the Lodge. The first one will be called good and the next bad. But the question will still be the same as before. Which is which? They are perfect twins and look exactly the same. They are all twins. . . .

"The answer to this conflict is the Give-Away. Whenever one gives from his heart, he also receives. Every man has his separate Way. And every man is a separate Way. But we all Dance within the Renewal Lodge in Renewal of the Brotherhood and in Giving. We, all of us, are the great Center Pole.[4]

Hyemeyohsts Storm

3.
Illustrative Excerpts from
Questionnaries and Interviews

I cannot harm someone else without harming myself.
59% of those in treatment agreed with this.
84% of those in on-going recovery agreed.

There are more differences than similarities between myself and others.
30% of those in treatment DISAGREED with this statement.
52% of those in recovery DISAGREED with this statement.

My own recovery depends on my willingness to pass on what I have to others.
64% of those in treatment agreed with this.
93% of those in on-going recovery agreed.

I tend to control or dominate the people I know.
25% of those in treatment DISAGREED with this statement.
32% of those in on-going recovery DISAGREED with this statement.

I am dependent on others in an unhealthy way.
30% of those in treatment DISAGREED with this statement.
36% of those in on-going recovery DISAGREED with this.

All minds are connected.
9% of those in treatment agreed with this statement.
24% of those in on-going recovery agreed with this.

I am satisfied with the quality or depth of the relationships I have with men.
23% of those in treatment agreed with this.
43% of those in on-going recovery agreed.

I am satisfied with the quality or depth of the relationship I have with women.
30% of those in treatment agreed with this.
57% of those in on-going recovery agreed.

Bob

I look to the A.A. group to be a Higher Power. One of the things I observed about myself in going to meetings is that just to attend meetings has a calming effect. I can come in really rattled and within fifteen or twenty minutes, I can feel a definite change in how I feel. I feel a definite peace. My Higher Power is mostly people, close friends. The A.A. group I belong to is certainly a Higher Power. The relationship I have with my wife and children is a definite, strong Higher Power. My relationships are more and more important; other things are becoming less important.

The company I've worked for has been almost more of a family than my family. I have been with the same company for nineteen years. For me to make a decision to leave is traumatic. I always felt a strong loyalty. At times I gave my company greater priority than I did my family. In the last year, I had to lay off a large percentage of people who worked for me. I no longer feel trust and loyalty to people I work for. I used to. That's stressful. I am reading a book called *Divorcing a Corporation*. It helps a lot. Severing that relationship with my company is almost like severing a marriage relationship. The company *has* been more of a family than my family. It is no longer.

Paul

I recall always being so *not* one with everyone. I always felt quite removed. Comparing myself before recovery and in recovery, I seem to be a lot more charitable about my conclusions concerning other people's motives. I don't think it's necessarily that I trust them any more, but I let them play out before I make a decision. I was a very bitterly sarcastic individual. It colored my perspective on everybody and everything. I guess I had really taken it to heart. In my family, you could say the most vicious things, but they had to be said very smartly [he laughs] and that's continued through my adult life. It got worse as [my drinking] got worse. Now seems sort of a return to precognitive innocence which I lost. I don't seem quite so angry anymore . . . [this said slowly]. I still think I'm right, but I don't seem so angry about it. The anger is there and informs a great deal of my behavior, but it is lifting a bit. The anger is lifting or is more properly channeled.

I have a new circle of friends. I have friends in A.A., I have friends who aren't in A.A., friends who were worried about me for years on end. So much of my business life is centered around socializing in bars and clubs, I find it essential to construct a new social life. Being with other people in the program is filling up the time I used to spend drinking. I like it. Part of me is learning that, yes, I'm lonely, but I don't have to be alone. I can go to [an A.A.] meeting. I don't have to sit at home, stewing. I can do something. No one can take away the loneliness, but . . . the people at the meetings are helping me fill up the hole and when it's not full, it doesn't mean there's something wrong at the moment. I *love* meetings. I *love* the stories. Our lives were really *awful* but they're really funny now because we're not doing it anymore. There's a great deal of affection at the meetings. I just love it. I just love the people there. All of a sudden, I'll go, "Oh, no, I'd forgotten I had done *that!*" This person would start qualifying, sharing his story. I *knew* this person's life. I thought, this is really familiar! You get so much of your own life back when you're at these meetings.

I've been an extremely suspicious person my entire life and very distrustful. In a sense there's a oneness with the people in meeting rooms. I really feel their pain, and it's not a sympathetic feeling, it's an empathetic one. It's *my* pain. And in many ways, if possible, I'd like to help them, you know. I've also learned a little bit each day that the pain in these instances causes the change. And that's the help—you're available to be supportive, but you can't make the pain go away.

One time I felt a connection with another person was when I was physically injured. [This man, whose name had been in the paper regarding an identical problem] two weeks prior was in the hospital room with me when I woke up. After he introduced himself, it occurred to me I was being punished for all the horrible jokes I had told about his problem for the previous two weeks. The rational part of me still believes that's not possible. But I believe that you get it back somehow or another—from simple egg on your face down to karma, fate.

My education in a Catholic school was a fabulous education. I think I learned a very strong moral responsibility. We all have to help change things, make them better. [It bothers me that] there are people who would completely pull the safety nets out of the social welfare system in the United States. [It bothers me] that we choose to ignore the real need to provide jobs, to provide money for the needed programs, for education programs, for housing. There is an attempt to reverse the consciousness— the conscience that Roosevelt brought in with the New Deal—under the guise of pulling back federal involvement, cutting budgets. It's up to the state and municipal governments to intervene wherever necessary so individuals are not without food, without proper shelter, without education, opportunities. What's really frightening is that I think there are certain people—and that Reagan is one of them—who really want to believe that there aren't people going hungry. Unfortunately, I'm sure there are people who are scamming their way through the welfare system, but I wouldn't want to determine who those are and then make the children suffer. This is a great country, it really is. You have to know the United States is an experiment in a government by and for the people. It behooves us as the wealthiest nation to take care of ourselves and other people for a variety of reasons. I'm coming from the standpoint that I couldn't get well on my own, I couldn't stop drinking or drugging, I needed help. I was fortunate, I could afford private treatment, but many people could not. I don't know if you noticed walking here that there are methadone clinics around here. I go by, day in and day out, and I see people's lives. I don't know if they're getting worse, if they're in this holding pattern, but their lives are just miserable. I would hope for someone coming forth who wants to help that situation. I could be out there on methadone. I didn't get there, but I could have. I work in the art community, and every day I crisscross one particular area of the city, and I see the people at the clinics. I say to myself, I wonder how long it would take me to get there? What would my family do to prevent me from getting there? And after they die, then what? It never occurred to me that I wouldn't get there. I couldn't do anything on my own. I knew I couldn't stop. I'm aware I'm in a somewhat privileged position on this, but help should be made available to everyone. My righteous indignation is inherited also, as well as my propensity for drinking and drugging. One of my relatives started a labor union in the city. My parents tend to vote very liberally on these types of issues. I grew up in the sixties. I always felt that we have responsibilities. . . .

Jane

I have more trouble feeling at one with people [than I do with my Higher Power]. My therapist tells me she's pleased that I'm more open now. I haven't had such a need to look all-together. I've been talking at meetings. I've gotten lots of support from people. I was talking about being upset about my job situation. This guy came up afterward and gave me a hug. I know I have to start looking at my attitude. He also said, take it easy on yourself. That was kind of neat [said with tears in her eyes]. I felt closer with the group. I didn't feel quite so alone. I have trouble connecting with people. I *was* feeling part of the group the times when I felt really in sync with the universe. I go through periods, especially lately, of gliding along, then I get down in the dumps again, then back. It seems to happen more often lately. I've been able to find myself not blaming people and situations so much. I have some choices. I've been having more power. Before, I felt I was a victim. I've had some real insights lately. I could see how I was trying to control this one guy. I didn't have to get into a power struggle with him. I've had a feeling of joy. I've been looking at old things. I've been on such a high, a feeling of harmony. Everything is just in sync. It goes up and down but I seem to rebound faster. I don't seem to stay down. I feel more a sense of hope. I'm starting to realize choices I can make. I do have power in a good sense, not in a controlling kind of way. I see myself as responsible. It makes it easier to accept things as they are. When I see myself as a victim, I get into controlling. It amazes me how many real friends I have. They say God works through people. I really see that. That's the biggest change in my life in the past eighteen months.

Jean

The whole [A.A.] program is about being receptive—accepting, relearning. You cannot manage life by yourself. It's also about being accepting of other people. It's also about unity with other people. There's an enormous cross section of people in A.A. There is enormous trust of other people in A.A.—bound together in the common human condition of being spiritually hungry. The whole program's about that.

I've felt at one with another person, with other people, several times. On three separate retreats I remember feeling at peace and close to all of those with me—that would have been maybe a dozen people. I feel calm and comfortable and I guess in a sense you feel you know how everyone else is feeling . . . but that's not the point. The point is however you're feeling. And everybody there is accepting however *you're* feeling. I have a best friend—I almost always feel that way with her. We don't have to explain anything to each other. There's absolutely no fear in our relationship. I've never felt this way in a romantic situation. I don't feel this way with my husband—I'm re-evaluating whether or not I should be married to him. I've felt close with a whole group when I worked [in an office on a shared project]. I always felt like that in that kind of creative effort with everybody doing what they have to do and doing it well and everybody trusting everybody else to do it well and everybody trusting everbody else to do it. I felt it in high school and college with key staff people. I feel it now with the man I work for. It's important to me. It's not just working hard and doing a job well. It's a step beyond that.

Jim

I would say the biggest change in me from when I was drinking to now is really priorities. Before, business was first, drinking was probably second, and what time was left was for the family. My father was a workaholic and I just fell into the exact same thing. I wanted closeness. I wanted to do things together. I really changed my priorities around. I used to get to work at 6:30. Now

I get to work at 8:30. I used to stay until 5:00 or 5:30, then stop at the bar and drink until 7:30 or something. Now, 4:00 or 4:30 rolls around and I'm gone. I'm very seldom there past 4:30. I used to consistently work weekends. Saturday was a common day to work. Summertime it wasn't unusual to be out there Sundays. Now I don't go to work on weekends. Period. Before I came home and worried about work. Now I don't even think about it. The family does things together.

I had a real hard time being close. I didn't take the time to get close. I never did the little things. The kids would walk up to me and ask, "Daddy, will you fix this?" and I would say, "Yeah, why don't you put it down and I'll get to it." Well, it never got done. Now they walk up to me and ask if I could help and I don't care what I'm doing. I'll stop and help. I spend time with them now, but I also have expectations that they never had before. They have to help in the house, have to keep their rooms clean, and so on. It's neat.

Ann

I don't know if there has been any one big change for me in recovery. There are a lot of changes. Before, I could never take anything anybody said at face value. I just didn't feel that close and loving and trusting. That's just how it was. I didn't need anybody that much. That's completely changed. I don't think I'd walk into a situation anymore ever where I assume that everybody there is trying to take advantage of me. At the very end I didn't trust anybody, and I put myself in a situation where I couldn't trust anybody I was around. I lived in an apartment where they stole from you if you walked out the door, and that's just the way things were. I always thought in this one city that everybody was out for themselves. I don't feel that way anymore.

I used to dislike living in a small community. Everybody knows everybody's name and my parents know everybody else's parents. My mother knows everybody's family history. I used to feel oppressed by this. I used to think that was why I was never doing good. Everybody knew everything that you did, even when I first went to treatment. There was a lot of asking questions: "Ah, what happened?" I don't feel oppressed by that sense that it's a small group anymore. It's really nice that there are all these people that I've known my whole life and that they will always be here.

In the past, I was never willing to surrender, never willing to compromise, never willing to say, okay, we'll try it your way. That has changed. If nothing else, I've learned that, and it works with so many people. Things go so well.

I don't know if there was any time I felt at one with someone else. That would take a lot of trust and I'm not sure I have that much trust yet.

Jennifer

I first felt love holding hands after an A.A. meeting as we were saying the Serenity Prayer. I felt so much love. After the first time I shared my own story with an A.A. group, I wanted to have love, not have sex, I wanted to make love to everybody in the room because at that point that was the only way I knew how to express love. It felt so natural to have that feeling of wanting to make love to everybody in the room, because up until that point that was how I expressed love—through sex. I confused the two.

Early in recovery, I'll never forget, I was asking people how you get self-esteem, and finally I heard the answer. You do estimable things to get self-esteem. If I'm feeling lousy, if I'm feeling like I don't have any friends on one day, I know now that instead of sitting there and sulking what I have to do is pick up the phone and call somebody, call a newcomer or somebody maybe I haven't spoken to [before]. Rather than isolate, I take an action. I find that giving, constantly giving, is an incredible form of feeling love for myself. I get so much when I'm giving. It's a very new thing to a relationship. The times I'm neediest, the times that I just want to be hugged and taken care of and loved, I'm really learning that those are the times that I have to give that love. A lot of times when I feel like that, I want [my partner] to fix me. I want him to make it better. It's kind of beyond me to even think of taking an action when I'm feeling like that, but the more and more times that I do take the action and get out of myself, go over to my husband and give him a hug, it works.

Roger

My basic orientation is that I'm less than other people. It's real deep stuff. It affects everything I do. It's gotten a lot, lot better. When I first came to A.A., I thought everybody wanted to kill me. For a year, my first year in A.A., I never looked up, never said a word. People would accept me, but not get too near me. It had to do with feelings of shame, a lot of still feeling different. There was this woman in treatment who seemed to know the hard time I was having. She put her hand on me. That touch. We hugged. Small things like that are so important. This other lady came over to me once in the Alano Club[5] when I was new in A.A.. No one would talk to me—I was putting out vibes that said "Stay away or I'll kill you." She came over to say hello. I would get real touched if someone would say something warm to me. I was so starved for love. I was amazed. I couldn't love myself, so I was amazed they could care.

I have a hard time trusting in groups. I don't talk in groups. I went to [Hazelden's Renewal Center] last year. I was in a group. The [facilitator] would get all this emotion to come out. He would take a couple of hours for each person. I wanted out by then. I waited until the last moment. I didn't think anything would happen. I didn't know how much anger, how much rage I had. I was in a chair. The chair went across the room. I was someone in agony, retching, wailing, throwing my body around, breathing so fast then quieting down. I remember struggling like something was breaking out. My body convulsed. One of the group members said it was like watching someone give birth, making sounds like I had given birth. I felt like I gave birth to my self. I had this tremendous feeling—I had the freedom of knowing I could feel. At the end I felt restored, very open, unafraid. I had this big smile and everyone was telling me I looked different. They compared it with a little kitten. I was free. Like busting out of prison. That has really opened up the world. The child abuser in me had done to the little kid in me what was done to me. I preached to the kid all the time. I thought I would fail. They [the group] ended up giving me a birthday card and a bracelet. That has changed my life a lot. I can't take it in at once. It's tough to hold on to it. Shortly after, I went back to the old way, but not totally. Within two hours after it happened, I started to deny it happened. I felt exuberance and a sense of freedom. I reaffirm that that happened. I try to keep that alive. Talking about it keeps it alive.

One of the principles that seems more and more true to me is that if any human being out there disturbs me—*if any human being out there disturbs me*—it's because I'm seeing something in them that's in me. That's been hard. Another principle that's important is that all fear is a form of attack. Every time I'm afraid of something, I'm projecting. It's all coming out of me—that's real important.

There's this guy in A.A. who's a preacher. By that I mean he editorializes. When he talks about the [Twelve] Steps he editorializes. He'll say, "If you work Steps Three, Nine, and Seven in this combination, then this or that will happen." I get angry with "preachers" in meetings who say you won't have a spiritual awakening until Step Nine. It drives me bananas. I feel they're attacking me because I was incessantly attacked when I was a kid. I was beat up mentally. This is not just sharing their [own] experience, it's editorializing. Well, this last week I got in touch with the child abuser in me. The child abuser in me is the preacher that preaches to this little kid in me. "Blah, blah, blah, you should do this, you shouldn't do that." It just hammers away. I think that's why this guy disturbs me so much. He's disturbing the little kid in me who doesn't want any more preachers, outside or in. Anyway, that's why I think I've been choking on that principle [that if I'm disturbed it's because I'm seeing something that's in me.] I hear it over and over. I generally do believe in that principle. It's evolving. It seems to be coming true. The problem is that there are lots of things I don't like and I haven't been able to see in myself yet. Or I don't want to see it, or the time isn't right—I believe in that—the time isn't right.

Probably the closest I ever felt to another human being is when I was making love during the year I had my first "spiritual awakening." There were a couple of cases. It wasn't just being in love—it was the first time I'd ever had sex with someone and we really connected for a number of hours. That's really what I wanted.

I think the most powerful experiences of my life have been when I was with another human being. I guess the word is intimacy. It's the thing I desire the most and fear the most. I'd go out of my way to get closer to people and then immediately back-pedal. I haven't even felt lonely for years, right? Now that I'm going out and meeting people, now I feel lonely. My mind is saying, this is not supposed to work this way. It's the same thing with God. God as the father, the lover, it's great. Then at a certain time I have to break, get away. It's that fear of being close.

I've been having dinner with this one guy every week. We connected like we were talking about—there was a sense of oneness. He and I even had similar experiences, similar fears. This is the person I've become most intimate with since I sobered up. We are going into this relationship with all this fear. We meet once a week. We see each other at other times, but this is a formal thing when we get together. We're both in these Adult Children of Alcoholics groups so we are experimenting with those ideas. It's been real frightening. I've felt real close. I've felt like I *love* [said slowly] this person. I've felt sexually attracted to this person and I've shared this with him. All this fear of homosexuality came up, but it's been just great. I guess I'm practicing getting closer to people. One of the most important parts of my week is connecting with him. I think one of the strongest forces in my life today is this desire to be close, but also this fear of getting close.

A real potent experience in my life was during the year after my first spiritual experience. I lived with a lady who was into mind control, alpha states. I was getting involved a lot with experiences that involved auras, Kirlian photography, pyramids. I took a class to practice relaxing. That's one of the hardest things I do. The reason I have a problem is that I start feeling close to people. At the end of these sessions on relaxation I took over several weekends, one of the things you try to do is heal. People would bring in the name of somebody. Somebody would then go into this alpha state, see this person's physiology, see the whole person, see what was wrong with him, diagnose him, and then you would try to heal what was wrong through seeing it in white light. I thought, this is just [magic-type] stuff, but I believed in it enough because of this other experience I had had. When it came to my turn, I had a real hard time imaging and I remember saying "I can't do that—I can conceptualize stuff, but I can't see pictures." The facilitator said, "Well then, conceptualize it." They gave me this freedom. "Have this lady put her head on your shoulder." And then—boom—this person was *there*. I don't know if I *ever* felt closer to another person. I felt real touched. I went on to diagnose this person [who I didn't know, and who wasn't physically present] correctly. That was the closest I've ever been to anyone. I remember saying at a certain point, I want this gone. All of a sudden there was a fear building. I get real confused as to why something so attractive and so warm and so rich creates in me this get-away-from-me response. I guess part of me felt like I could get lost in it and never return—that sense of drowning. It's not a lot different than the whole thing with God has been. Turning your will over. I guess the ego doesn't want to die or something. I don't want to get into intellectual stuff about it. That's the experience I had of oneness. It was that same incredible connection as when I was making love with the other woman I told you about, except this wasn't sensual, I wasn't sexually stimulated. I felt like I knew that person, not just physically—I knew what she was feeling, thinking. I never had that empathy for another person. There was no judgment. It was really accepting. I believe I judge people a lot. It's because I really don't know. If I could ever get that close to them, if I could ever connect with them like I did with this lady, I don't think I'd be judging them at all, because what I judge is all that exterior crap, and this was beyond how people look and the character traits. It was to the heart of something. I believe that all happened. I think it could happen a lot. I don't let it.

Joyce

When I first went in [to A.A.] there was a biker in my group. He wore the leather gloves, the fingers out, and the tattoos and the hair, and I was thinking "My God!" I consider myself a middle-class homemaker, and that was a new experience for me—finding out how people are loving and giving no matter what they look like.

I'll tell you an amusing story. My husband is a very negative person and he was always complaining, so I went to this one women's meeting [of Alcoholics Anonymous] and I was yelling about whatever it was. This friend of mine said, "Do me a favor. Why don't you pray for your husband every night for six weeks?" I said, "I can't stand to look at him, I'm not praying for him. No way." "I don't care if you want to throw up," she says. "You pray for him every night for six weeks and you let me know what happens." So I made a commitment to her and I did not want to. There was no way. So I thought, well, I'll pray that he's happy and that's all. I told God, "You know I'm doing this under protest, but, okay, I'll pray that he's happy." And I did, and four weeks later he bought a brand new van, four-wheel drive. Eighteen thousand dollars and he was ecstatic. So I went back to my friend and I said, "That's the last time I ever pray for him again." That was sort of where I figured I'll never pray for things. I'll just pray for God's will and let it go at that. Let Him decide where it's at. I feel comfortable praying for help with Weight Watchers, which I just joined because I do think it's God's will. I think my purpose right now in life is to help other recovering alcoholics, and I think it's God's will that you look good to do that, because if you want people to become interested you have to look good yourself. So I feel all right with that. I feel God's will is He wants me to be happy, and that was a long time with understanding that but I do feel that.

John

In recovery, I feel the sense of belonging that we talked about, for sure. That's something I never did have before.

I had been just drinking myself into some sort of oblivion for a long, long time. It was in the middle of the winter. I had a little cottage where I still live. This last winter of my drinking I couldn't afford to heat it and it was cold. I'd just go out and drink and panhandle in bars. Near where I lived there was a tavern that I could walk through the woods to get to—it's a rural area. There was another bar about five miles down the road—that was the one that opened at 7:00 in the morning. I'd often be there waiting for someone to come in, or maybe the bartender would even set me up because he saw me shaking. Sometimes I'd go home with a half a pint if I could squirrel the money out of somebody. That's how broke I was that last winter.

Anyway, this had been going on for some time. I had a couple friends that had known me in better days and still knew me. I never saw them. I hid from those kind of people. They were straight people. They weren't A.A. people, but both of them knew about [A.A. and treatment]. That's how this all came about. Jane and Susan joined forces one week and decided they were going to corner me and bring me to treatment. One woman lived quite far away and came up to spend the week with the other woman to get this job done. They kept coming over and I kept pretending I wasn't home. I'd see them coming. I sort of smelled a rat, I guess, and I was in awful shape and I didn't want them to see me. I just knew what I looked like and smelled like. I wasn't fit emotionally, and I was shaking all the time. I just couldn't see people like that. The only kind of people I could see were in a dark bar—and not even there until I had enough juice [alcohol] in me. But finally after three or four days of coming over and knocking on the door, they climbed in a window. They did this at eight o'clock in the morning. I had run out of pills I was using—I was a speed user—and I really needed those badly. They were the only way I could drink somehow.

I was a real dual addict. I had had about half a pint of rum and I was just a shaking mess. I ran and hid in the closet when I heard them coming in that window. I just didn't believe they would do it and they did. Needless to say, they found me in that closet. They walked around—my house is tiny—they walked right by me about four times and I thought "whew!" and then Susan said, "I'm going to have one more look" and she walked right over to that closet and opened it—there's a curtain on there—and pulled it back. I just went berserk when that happened. I was in a panic. I was like a wild animal they caught and ugh! I just yelled and cried and yelled at them, called them every dirty term I could think of, and these were two people who were really dear to me—and are. Then I just took off. I ran out the door and down through the woods, my path over to the bar, my tavern. I got halfway there and it was just like [a strangled sound] I thought *I cannot go in there I cannot go in there* and face anybody in there one more time. How am I going to? I didn't have any money. I couldn't go in there and beg for money one more time. I couldn't. There was a farmhouse nearby where I knew the people real well and I ran in there. They were drinking people. I said I had to use the phone. I called up a neighbor of mine and said "Could you get those people away from there [my house]?" and *she said "no!"* She was in on it! They'd gone next door! She said "You'd better go do what they're trying to get you to do." I went back and walked in and the next thing I did was say, "If you'd only loan me some money, I'd be all right." [He says this with laughter.] Which was fun thinking back on it. Anyway, Susan says, "You've put the touch on everybody you know and you're not putting the touch on me." She was real tough and, I don't know, I just broke down again. I didn't care what happened. I was thinking insane asylum, mental institution, that's what I was thinking. [I thought] it was going to be lockup, but that was all right, it didn't matter.

But that *surrender*. I think it happened when I got halfway across that field and realized I just couldn't do it. Also the feeling was, they've seen me at my worst—those two people—the cat was out of the bag. I couldn't hide my condition any longer. These straight people who actually I really loved a lot and who I'd been pretending I was all right to for so long—all of a sudden I knew they knew and I knew I wasn't drunk. At that moment, I mean, I saw it, just saw it, and they all knew and I didn't care. I just gave up. It was going across the field. The feeling was almost like being dead and not caring. There was no fight left. When I came back and asked for money, it wasn't even fighting, it was just a sort of token test [to see] if they were really resolved. But it wasn't fighting. It was maybe a week or two later that [I had a spiritual experience on the lake next to the treatment center].

The whole feeling was wonderful, coming out of the fog, and even though I don't remember any of the lectures in treatment or anything specifically said, I was just identifying with everybody. When I first got to treatment, I met this one man I identified with immediately. We didn't know each other, but we sort of did. He was this little skinny guy, kind of puny-looking. He could basically tell my story.

I was in a room with three other guys. We sat up all night talking about our drunken experiences. Before I had always felt separate . . . totally, like a weirdo, like I had things wrong with me, emotional problems that nobody would ever understand. I always felt separate. My whole life was a big *macho* act, sitting in bars swapping stories about your love lives. I'd always believe the other guys' stories, all the big bravado bull, but I knew I was lying when I did it and I was on real shaky ground in those areas. They really alienated me. They made me feel, "I'm sure weak. I'm not a real man like that guy." I didn't feel close to anybody. You wouldn't dare let anybody know—if they really knew. I'm close to crying. Whatever it was, drinking, drug using, sure helped me to put on an act. I'd start being cool. Drinking, using, did sometimes give me a feeling of temporarily belonging that I was certainly seeking. I would be able to somehow join the group. It would help me relax enough to be able to talk [to people].

In sobriety, there have been lots of moments over the years when I have felt a real sense of union with someone. Just talks with A.A. friends. Maybe that's what happened in treatment, too, right away. I don't even remember the names of those who I was in treatment with, except we sure were feeling close to each other. You know, we weren't doing any of that barroom bravado talk, it was real. Before I always suffered from "terminal uniqueness." That's the feeling of being a special case. That's got to go. Until someone gets rid of that, I feel they're in trouble. That goes for every area of my life. I can't think of any feeling that I'm having that's unique or special to me. That would give me an excuse to relapse—self-pity.

Now I'm able to interact with people, even outside of A.A. I've been missing that these last six months because I've been distancing myself. I've gotten so busy, to the exclusion of taking care of my A.A. program, maybe. Little by little, I've gotten a little superficial and phony on the outside. I go to A.A. and feel like something's expected of me. Maybe I was going to walk in and say, "Boy, it's been a lousy day, sobriety sucks!"—well, I've never felt *quite* like that—but I'm not going to say that when I see a newcomer. That's not being truthful. I've been around so long. I've also been going along with gossiping lately. I feel I can go back now and not be a part of that.

My life has gotten real good materially and I've done a lot of things—taken courses, went back to school—but recently I've also gotten a kind of greed about those things. Someone will call me up and want me to do something and I'll do it, but resent the intrusion. Someone will call up while I'm at work and want to talk twenty minutes, and again I feel it's an intrusion. I'll go visit someone [who is housebound] and they'll think I love them, but I'm feeling resentful about being there. I haven't liked myself for those reasons, for feeling selfish, not being more giving. Look at what I've been the recipient of. . . .

Donald

In recovery, about five or six years ago, I met a native American woman [while I was traveling in the Black Hills]. I stood [for a while] there with this young woman. I have always felt badly about how the white man has treated the Indian, and I wanted to make an amend as part of my A.A. program. I told her I was sorry for what we had done. I started to cry.

SUMMARY: SELF PRACTICING PEACE WITH OTHERS

A closing of the distance between *self and others* is indicated here by respondents' reports of a sense of separation from others while drinking and increased awareness of similarities and the coincidence of interests between the self and other in recovery.

Bob equates openness and willingness to ask for help from other people with spirituality. He says he feels closer now to his family than he did while drinking. *Paul* commented "I've been an extremely suspicious person my entire life, and very distrustful." "In recovery," he says "in a sense there's a oneness with the people in meeting rooms. I really feel their pain, and it's not a sympathetic feeling, it's an empathetic one. It's *my* pain." His greatest sense of connectedness is with A.A., his career, and gay communities. He also feels a strong sense of responsibility to the world community as a whole, and expresses a sensitivity to contemporary social and political issues. *Jane* says that while drinking she "built up walls." She connects her increased closeness with others with increased responsibility and not blaming others as much as she once did.

Jean gave several specific examples of times she had felt "at one" with others; some of these were before her active alcoholism, other times were in recovery. *Jim* said that before he got sober, he had "a hard time being close." In recovery, Jim's priorities changed. Whereas he described himself before as a "workaholic" as well as an alcoholic, he now takes time with his family.

Ann says she didn't feel that close and loving and trusting during active addiction. "I didn't need anybody that much. . . . I felt I had to do it myself." In recovery, she says she no longer feels that everybody is out for themselves. *Jennifer* spoke a lot of love. She feels that the times she feels "neediest" are the times that she "has to give that love." *Roger's* awareness of the importance of community is clear—he feels without it he would not be able to stay sober. He is actively involved in A.A. service positions. Roger finds that in his living situation he has the best of both worlds: his own apartment and close friends and members of A.A. who live in the same building. Roger describes specific instances of feeling at one with others, some of which were prior to his involvement in A.A., others of which were in recovery. *Paul* and *Carol* said they felt more comfortable with and had an easier time trusting other people than they did a Higher Power per se.

Joyce is sponsoring others in the A.A. program. Joyce noted it was a new experience for her in recovery to find out how "loving and giving" people are regardless of whether they are people she would ordinarily have come into contact with before on a social basis. *John* comments, "Before I always felt separate, totally, like a weirdo, like I had things wrong with me, emotional problems that nobody would ever understand. I always felt separate. In sobriety there have been lots of moments over the years when I have felt a real sense of union with someone." John was at the Renewal Center in part because he was concerned about being more self-centered than he would like to be. He expressed a desire to give freely. John's life-changing spiritual experience was closely connected to the feeling of belonging, which he says he felt for the first time in recovery. It was preceded by his surrender to those who joined forces to help get him help for his alcoholism. He notes a sense of union with non-A.A.s as well as with members of Alcoholics Anonymous. *Donald* said passing on what he received is a vital part of his recovery. "It's after the spiritual awakening that you begin to give the program away."

Part IV
Practicing Peace with the World as a Whole

Section A
Inner and Outer Worlds

1.
Statements Illustrating the Nature of the Problem

Both the key starting point and the goal of the Enlightenment . . . was autonomy . . . . Enlightenment thinkers labored mightily to attain for mankind freedom. First and foremost in this endeavor, they cast off as superstition all sense of mysteriously hidden forces beyond human understanding and control. To man belonged the responsibility as well as the right to determine and to shape human destiny.[1]

Ernest Kurtz

What we find as soon as we place ourselves in the perspective of religious man of the archaic societies is that the world exists because it was created by the gods, and that the existence of the world itself "means" something, "wants to say" something, that the world is neither mute nor opaque, that it is not an inert thing without purpose or significance. For religious man, the cosmos "lives and speaks."[2]

This means that traditional man felt . . . this Cosmos reveals itself in a cipher . . . it transmits its message by its formation, its states of being, its rhythms. Man "hears" or "reads" these messages and consequently behaves towards the Cosmos as towards a coherent system of significances."[3]

[In contrast,] desacralization pervades the entire experience of the nonreligious man of modern societies.[4]

Mircea Eliade

The belief in the primacy of cause and effect is one of the cardinal tenets of the Western view of life."[5]

Synchronistic events . . . hold an important clue to those "miraculous" occurrences that become the basis for religious traditions and mythologies.[6]

Ira Progoff

Coincidences . . . are manifestations of a universal principle in nature which operates independently from physical causation.[7]

[Synchronistic events are more aptly called "confluence," and are] causal manifestations of the Integrative Tendency. We may call this category of emotions, derived from the integrative tendency, the self-transcending emotions.[8]

According to Jung, all divinatory practices, from looking at tea-leaves to the complicated oracular methods of the I Ching, are based on the idea that random events are minor mysteries which can be used as pointers towards the one central mystery.[9]

Arthur Koestler

2.
Stories Illustrating the Unity

There was a great drought. For months there had not been a drop of rain and the situation became catastrophic. The Catholics made processions, the Protestants made prayers and the Chinese burned joss-sticks and shot off guns to frighten away the demons of the drought, but with no result. Finally the Chinese said, "We will fetch the rainmaker." And from another province a dried-up old man appeared. The only thing he asked for was a quiet little house somewhere, and there he locked himself in for three days. On the fourth day the clouds gathered and there was a great snow storm at the time of the year when no snow was expected, an unusual amount, and the town was so full of rumors about the wonderful rainmaker that Richard Wilhelm went to ask the man how he did it. He said, "They call you the rainmaker, will you tell me how you made the snow?" And the little Chinese man said, "I did not make the snow, I am not responsible." "But what have you done these three days?" "Oh, I can explain that. I come from another country where things are in order. Here they are out of order, they are not as they should be by the ordinance of heaven. Therefore the whole country is not in Tao, and I also am not in the natural order of things because I am in a disordered country. So I had to wait three days until I was back in Tao and then naturally the rain came.[10]

from Carl Jung
Re-told by Jean Shinoda-Bolen

Oscar Johnny spoke of Shoshone customs about food and clothing, marriages and wedding costumes. He talked of parents and grandparents and the stories the elders told. . . .

"A boy's grandparents usually find the wife for him. They make a buckskin outfit for him to wear at the wedding. They make it when he's a kid, and put it away for the wedding day. They make it the right size to fit on the wedding day, and they put it away."

"How do they know the right size?"

"They just know. They have to know, so they know. They know the wedding day and they know the size. It has to be right, so they have to know. They know the girl too, so they make her a dress—a wedding dress. It's a buckskin dress, a white buckskin dress, and it's the right size, too, and they put that away until the wedding day."

"You mean the grandparents always pick out the girl their grandson marries?"

"Well, they find her, they find the right girl."

"What about the girl's grandparents, do they agree?"

"Sure they agree. They say, 'Yes, that's the one.' "

"Do the girl's grandparents ever get to do the choosing?"

"Well, it's the same thing. If they choose the right one, it's the same."

"How do they know which person is the right one for another to marry?"

"Well, they just look into that and they find the one that a person's going to marry. They find out in advance. That's the way they pick it."

"Why don't they let the person pick his own partner?"

"Well, that's the one. That's the one he picks. That's what I meant by the right one, it's the one he picks. They just find her in advance. They have to find her because they have to make that buckskin dress."[11]

Passed on in Rolling Thunder

It was now the summer of 1982. This experience was one of synchronicity that Jung writes about. Jung sees this experience as holding an order beyond time and space, so to speak. Now then, I had had a fine discussion with a friend on spontaneity, and he told me about a way of living of persons who lived at the foot of Mt. Vesuvius in Italy. He said that the way of living was not controlled by cognitive, rational thought, but by a deeper sense of destiny, a deeper sense of spirit, so to speak. Thus, he said they lived in the present moment and they did not fear death, such that they would return to the little villas even when the volcanic ash had destroyed them. So then, I began to consider this view. I was contemplating on it the next afternoon as I walked on Brattle Street. I had a sense that I had little spontaneity within me. I was sorrowful over this, knowing this wasn't right. So, I was in this state when I went inside a little shop that had old prints. There I saw, in the back room of the shop, a picture of a woman in draped garments carrying flowers with joy, spontaneity, and grace. She was litheful, in full profile. I know this represented the part of me I had not yet been able to experience. I then bought the print for a small sum. I was going to (Lawrence) Kohlberg's home, and upon arriving went to his library, to the art section, and opened the first book I selected right to the picture! I was so amazed, so taken by this! Then, upon reading the background of the print I learned it was taken from murals in Pompei—at the foot of Mt. Vesuvius![12]

V. Lois Erickson

3.
Excerpts from Questionnaire and Interviews

I find my life is meaningful.
43% of those in treatment agreed with this statement.
72% of those in recovery agreed with this statement.

I am increasingly aware of meaningful coincidences.
43% of those in treatment agreed.
77% of those in recovery agreed.

I am aware of meaningful coincidences.
IN TERMS OF FREQUENCY,
34% of those in treatment responded with a 6 or 7
(with 7 being "all the time")
70% of those in recovery responded with a 6 or 7.

I think of meaningful coincidences as signs of a Higher Power in my life.
55% of those in treatment agreed.
75% of those in recovery agreed.

I find religious significance in ordinary places, things, events.
18% of those in treatment agreed with this statement.
48% of those in recovery agreed with this statement.

When a particular course of action seems right for me, things just seem to fall in place.
50% of those in treatment agreed.
86% of those in recovery agreed.

I am afraid of losing what I have.
11% of those in treatment DISAGREED.
27% of those in recovery DISAGREED.

I am afraid of not getting what I want.
16% of those in treatment DISAGREED.
35% of those in recovery DISAGREED.

The way the world looks to me is a reflection of my inner state.
41% of those in treatment agreed with this.
66% of those in ongoing recovery agreed.

Both the inner world and the outer world are in my imagination.
16% of those in treatment agreed.
27% of those in recovery agreed.

Heaven is a state of mind.
35% of those in treatment agreed.
55% of those in recovery agreed.

Paul

You ask about coincidences. You mean, "There *are* no coincidences?" [This in a theatrical tone, with laughter.] Part of me says, "Yes there are! There *are* some on this planet!" I think part of it is that things happen now. In the past I had a life full of coincidences and a great many opportunities and events that I took advantage of and used. I'm a firm believer that things happen to people who let things happen *to* them. Now different kinds of things are happening to me because I'm available to let them happen in a different way. My life used to be extremely grand. I was partying a lot. It was a real exciting life and I made myself available for certain things. Now I make myself available for different kinds of things. Like meeting new kinds of people, sober people. I make myself available by going to meetings, learning not to be so judgmental. In the past, after I left graduate school my career moved real quick because I listened to people, watched them do things. So within two years I [had a position with a lot of responsibility], an important position. Now I want to know more about what it's about to be sober. I think some of those good points—being willing to listen, to talk, to interact with sober people, is where I should be now. These are the people I want to know now. They have something I want.

It's that I listen to people. I don't think there's a mystery to coincidences. I think it's because we're sober, I'm sober, that things will happen, and you can make the choice to pursue it or not. That happens with everybody in the [A.A.] program. There are no coincidences. Well, I don't know if there are or not. [He laughs.] I mean, things do happen that don't seem to add up! Things that seem to be a coincidence. All of a sudden there are Alcoholics Anonymous meetings [right in my neighborhood], and I can choose to go there and I'm sober and available to do something. It's a coincidence that two people can connect and complement each other at any given moment.

When a particular course of action seems right to me, things fall into place. In many ways, my life has been charmed. In almost every instance I can think of, things have worked out. And not just that, they've worked out for the best or what appears to be a very good deal.

If you don't listen, you wouldn't hear of the wonderful—for lack of a better word—miracles. I have seen miracles in people's lives. Actually. I mean, they talk about them. It's a miracle that this person was once sick—I didn't know them then, I know them now. That's the difference between night and day. There's nothing else to say. It's the difference between night and day. Yes, I do see miracles in my own life, too. It's unbelievable. That we're not all *dead* is a miracle, first of all. That we're not all permanently miserable. It's truly unbelievable. It's unbelievable to me that I can discuss my life as a change. The changes *are* measurable for me. Certain things are very, very measurable. Simple things—that I can look people in the eye again. That I'm willing to make an effort about some things. It's not all gloom and doom. That's all I had left. What was the next bad thing that was going to happen? It's hard to imagine. In so many lives like my own, it wasn't so good, then it got bad, then it got worse, then it got *worse,* and unbelievably it kept getting worse than that! It tells that things change. Sometimes things just get different, sometimes they get better. If I had to define a miracle—if I got pinned—and I was avoiding that—I would say it is that for which absolutely no sleight of hand seems to have occurred. The things that just don't add up. Why if you do this, this, this, and this, logically, if you do A, B, and C you should get to D, but when we do A, B, C, and D we get N!!!! [Said with wonder, emphasis] And N is really good!!! The miracles in my life—I thought my mind was completely gone. I was worried. I thought I was insane, totally insane, and I was depressed. I was connected with the outside as a drunk. There's sort of external stuff. I've been asked to work again. That kind of thing, that's very external. To me, what's more important and harder to discuss are the feelings I have about myself, that I'm beginning to have. I didn't lose [a feeling of self-worth] while I was drinking—I think I just didn't have it. To take any joy in anything I've done. I've always had the feeling that you don't enjoy the good things you have because you're going to mess up and then have to grovel about it. Now I have this feeling of self-worth that's growing. I can look people in the eye. It's amazing. I know—*I know*—I haven't done anything the night before that I have to piece back together! Now I'm more relaxed than I've ever been—that's an external thing, also an internal thing. I find less dissatisfaction with the state of my life than I had in the past.

("*anyone out there?*")

ILLUSTRATION A: *Paul's Drawing*

When I took the questionnaire I drew a picture representing the relationship between myself, others, my Higher Power, and the universe. Looking back on it now, I feel, boy, is that a picture of being unconnected!!! I remember this [drawing]. There was a period when I was in treatment when I realized I wasn't going to be going home. I was feeling very, very alone. I felt very different from everybody out there. Really adrift. All my life I was really very popular, but it didn't mean anything to me—all that kind of stuff. I would use words to keep people at a distance. I would never want to let anybody in—ever. I had no Higher Power concept at all. You can see, a year later, I'm still hopping around on that one. [He laughs.] Would I draw that today? Depending on the hour, maybe. Get me coming out of a meeting, I wouldn't. I think this is me naturally, me left on my own. Without meetings, I could easily be like this again. I don't want to be, but I know it would happen. . . . I've always wanted to watch, look at people, have them around, but I never wanted them to know me.

Jane

I have been finding connections between my inner world and outer world more and more. I have to put myself out there and take those risks or nothing happens. If I play it safe, I stay in a situation which I think is secure, but really isn't. [When I put myself out there,] it just starts to happen. It's crazy. I have a much better relationship with my Higher Power than I did.

Making the choice to get out of the Service started it all. I started taking risks with my life. Things really started to happen. I had felt so stuck so long. I was stationed overseas. I had started graduate school. I was so crazy, I started going to meetings, but not to treatment. I was so stressed out. I didn't know how to stop. I was so busy trying to live up to other people's expectations. Then I looked at what *I* wanted to do and things fell in place.

I had stayed in the Service just because money was good. Staying in the service job was [being] dishonest with myself. Just taking their money was dishonesty. It is about control. When I present myself as something I'm not, I'm dishonest. As soon as I started to let go of some of that, things just started getting better. Now I just want to do something worthwhile. I feel I'm being directed that way. People I barely know were saying we're behind you. I get stuck in a situation I feel will never end and then a couple of hours later a call will come.

I looked at my financial situation. I sense it's a turning point. I think I wanted to know "Is there anything out there going to help me out?" I've had to develop a relationship with a Higher Power. I've been a lot closer to a Higher Power. Hopefully, that will keep getting better. When I am willing to cut loose, I grow more spiritually.

I wanted to take a trip overseas, I wanted to take courses. I finally decided, I'm going to do it, take the trip, take courses. I set about doing that, took action to make it happen. I had always been so passive. While others see me letting go, I was starting to be more active. I always tried to be what others want instead of who I am. It was a risk to do Outward Bound. I did it. People have been helping me lately. I knew the day would come when I would be out of money. I wondered if anyone would be there. There *are* people there. I see that as being a real message that I'll be taken care of. Just get out of there—get out of the way.

For the trip overseas, I wondered if it was right. I sent a deposit. I'll put it out there. I got a check I wasn't expecting. I [took it as a] message I was on the right track. The summer before I was trying to make extra money for another trip. When it seemed I wouldn't have the money, I would get a call and people would want to hire me. I was able to get enough. I was worried about it and decided to go to a meeting and see if I got a message there. The theme of the meeting was having fear. So often I go to a meeting and hear what I need to hear. So many little things. I put stuff out there. I pray, I ask God if I'm meant to do it, ask for help. Then I let go of it. I feel there's some sort of calling in life. I feel it's time for me to do that.

[I found out about this therapy group I wanted to be involved with.] I would have to pay for it. The therapist told me he would give me a discount. It felt symbolic. The therapist said you're finally beginning to let go, admitting you don't know everything.

Oh, yes, I feel there is such a thing as a miracle. I got back from one of my trips last fall. I found myself without money. Fear of economic insecurity[13] is the biggest fear for me. I couldn't get myself out of my job that paid $5.39 an hour, because I was so afraid I couldn't make it on my own. I was staying in a motel. I had no money. I was down in the dumps. I was ready to call Salvation Army. I was up to the limit in the motel. I was on a street corner. I was praying, if there's a God up there, help me now. I bumped into a friend. I had tried to call her before, frantically. Her number had changed. When I got out of money I was really worried whether I would be able to pay the bills. I got fifty dollars I didn't expect out of nowhere, just when I needed it. I've been able to make payments. I didn't know what to do last Thanksgiving. I went to the post office and there was a check for $50. I went to a pot luck. It all worked out. I got money and a dinner invitation. I didn't know anything about it ahead of time. A guy in the A.A. program told me he was in the same boat. He was to be a director of a place in January. The place burned down in December. He was out of work for fourteen months. He knocked around and always had enough money, a place to live in. It all worked out and that's just what I needed to hear.

I signed up with this temporary job service. They called and said we have this job. It's going to be working with the homeless. I felt a tingle. It seems that real coincidences happen. I feel there is spiritual significance in the job offer. [Before this call came,] I would send money up to a shelter for the homeless in another city. I put it out that if it was to happen, [I was open to it.] I feel there is some job out there waiting for me. I want some job where I can be of service. I'm trying to stay open to it. I feel I'll be directed to it.

It was my old pattern to feel sorry for myself. This guy wrote in to the magazine asking how to find meaning in his life. Try making it was the answer. I'm going to get myself out of this, I'm going to get into action. Things start to happen. I see I have choices. I can create the kind of life I want so much. It is open to me. I never thought it was possible. I feel I have choices and possibilities. I feel more of a willingness to take risks. It can change my life. I have a sense of purpose and meaning. Before I thought I was at the whim of others. I didn't think my dreams would come true. I have a sense of optimism. I feel more assertive. I feel better about myself. I feel a sense of hope and excitement. What's coming next? I now look forward to change. I can accept change better. I see it as good. I feel I'm being directed. I have confidence and excitement whereas before I thought life was something to get through. I am starting to enjoy life for the first time. I was praying I can continue like this. I am more willing to say I don't have the answers. The more contact I have with my Higher Power, the better things go. It builds on itself. I feel it's all happened in the past month. I was so afraid I couldn't take care of myself. I had no friends, I felt really isolated, afraid to go around the block. Now I put myself out there and am willing to face those things, not run away.

Being willing to *trust,* to take risks, is what makes the difference. I always had such a hard time trusting anyone, trusting that it would work out. It's been gradual. I take little risks, then more and more. The more willing you are, the better it gets. You are called on in life to take a series of risks. Basically what it comes down to is be willing to let go more and more. Therefore we're more flexible, not so rigid. When I'm not controlling, things fall into place. I had a fear I would end up in the streets and be a bag lady. I'm more willing now to listen. A.A. helps with that. I try to see what God wants me to do and be willing to do that. That's where meditation comes in. I want to work on meditation more and stay open to opportunity. It is an old thing to stay with what I know, even if I'm not happy. I'm more willing to try more things. I can have dreams and do things to help bring it about.

[Since I've been in recovery,] I've really tried to simplify my life. Since my last slip [use of alcohol] I had the Good Will come—they take used things to offer to those in need. I kept my bed and table. In the past I thought if I had all this stuff I was somebody. It felt so good to get rid of it. I felt like the stuff owned me. Before then, for my last move in the Service, it took me two days to pack up. I gave away a whole bunch of my clothes. I had the Service store my stuff for me. I had fancy stereo equipment. It was such a big thing to have a fancy stereo. I called Good Will to take it away. The same thing with TV. I have a little one in storage. I haven't had it since March.

Jean

Yes, I've had experiences of when the inner and the outer came together. It's hard to think of specific times. There have been a zillion times when I was thinking of someone and the phone rang, or thinking of someone and they showed up.

I have had dreams or visions of a spiritual nature. The first time I remember this happening is a situation when my parents said "na, na, na, na, na." It was a dream I had when I was about five and a half. I had never known anyone who died. My parents didn't discuss things with us. I dreamed of my grandfather. I interpreted that I dreamed that he died. I saw my grandfather like through a glass, through a really dark glass and he couldn't hear us and nobody would see him but me. I was trying to show him. . . . He turned and walked—it was strange—down this long hallway. He walked down the hallway and disappeared. I woke up and felt really like he was gone and he died that night. I tried to tell my mom about this dream before the call came telling us about his death and she said, just don't worry about it. She asked me about it later. She thought that someone had called during the night and I had answered the phone and knew that he died and forgotten. But nobody had called. Since then I've intermittently dreamed things that have happened. I really don't talk about it. It sounds foolish even to me. It sounds strange.

Another strange thing I could always do as a child—I could never do it for myself but I could do it to help others—was to find things. I don't know how to explain it. If something's missing I sort of get this picture of where it is. I've been able to do that since I've been a real small child. My parents just thought I had some phenomenal memory so I could remember things, but it wasn't that. One time—probably the most unusual case of it—I was working as a counselor in a camp. There is this huge all-camp picnic. It's out in the middle of hills and hills and a child was missing. A four-year-old. She was the little sister of a boy that I knew, and I hadn't even seen the child. I kind of just closed my eyes and saw a picture of this child on a ledge. Everybody is wandering around. It's getting close to dark. They're beginning to think they're going to start a search. I just knew this child was on this ledge and I knew the ledge. It was on the backside of a hill. I just said don't do anything, just a second, and we climbed back up and the child was on the ledge. There was no question in my mind that that was where she was. I *knew* that's where she was.

It's little things, too, like my little brother losing a toy, it was a Tonka truck. I saw it in a stream. I just walked to the spot and picked it up. My dad once couldn't find his keys. I was about seven years old. I knew where they were because I had seen this picture of them behind the furnace in our basement—it's like a still-frame photograph. I didn't want to say anything to him about where they were because he would say "You're nuts." I wasn't allowed to go by the furnace by myself. He always thought it was strange I knew where they were. Unfortunately, I can't do that when I lose my own stuff. [She laughs.]

Similar things have happened. I had two great aunts who lived a couple of hours away from me. One day I was at work, and I felt like I needed to leave work and drive to see them. I did. I was driving on a back road. I didn't let them know I was coming. An ambulance passes me and I just turned and followed the ambulance and it turned out it was my aunt. She had had a heart attack. My other aunt was at the hospital. She was in the hospital for months. She's still alive. It was comforting for my second aunt that I was there. I think that sort of thing has to happen to people more than they're aware. I don't try to understand.

This doesn't bother me at all. I never saw anything terrible. The dreams that someone was going to die have recurred and that's happened five times accurately. The dreams that somebody dies aren't ever terrible, violent things. I just know—that's all—that he's dead. I'm always looking first at their face and then they turn away and disappear and I know. It sounds really, really strange because there's nothing about that that says death, and yet when I wake up I know that it's death. The thing with my grandfather did bother me a lot at the time because nobody would really listen to me and I felt like I had made him die by dreaming that. The next time that happened I was thirteen, and I dreamed that a friend of mine died. Fortunately at that point, I talked a lot about it with my minister and I was old enough and rational enough not to think that I had caused it. I really didn't. He said that I shouldn't be afraid of my dreams.

While I was in college, I had an experience that involved a high school boyfriend I hadn't seen or thought about in three years. One night I could not go to sleep. I could not stop thinking about him. I sat down and wrote him a letter. Finally, at 4:30 in the morning, I felt okay and went to sleep. At eight o'clock in the morning, my mom called. His mom had called her. He's a bicycle racer and he had been hit by a car. He was having brain surgery from the time I had started thinking about him until 4:30 A.M. Isn't that strange?

I had experiences of [timeless time, connection of inner and outer worlds and joining of self and other] before recovery, but I did not experience these things while I was drinking. Not from the time I was 21 until in the last year. The experience I had when I was 20 was rape, which was really a crisis for me. I didn't tell anyone about that. I kept it to myself. I lost all the spiritual channels because I was angry. I had a real need to protect myself all of a sudden and I built up walls, even against God because of what happened because of having those walls down. I decided God was no longer my friend. Of course, it wasn't conscious at that time. Since that time, I've felt that I was just floundering, miserable. I went from one graduate school to another, not having a lot of direction. Before, I felt fearless. My ability and my trust in other people would get me through anything. After the rape, I felt I didn't have the right any more to take risks. I drifted into other things. I continued going to church, but just showed up. My heart wasn't there. Inside, I felt really alone. I felt like reliance on God or seeking God's will was childish—a luxury intelligent people and grown-ups couldn't afford. I am 29 now. The last nine years have been this terrible odyssey which has involved me starting to drink, becoming an alcoholic, becoming clinically depressed, and finally working back around to accepting spirituality.

This past fall, in recovery, when I was getting over this depression, I felt I had to do something. I woke up real early in the morning and I borrowed my neighbor's newspaper. I was going through the paper and clipping out all the big ads—anything that had to do with what I was specifically looking for. For some reason, over in the part-time secretaries section—I can't even type—were two itty bitty column lines in this huge newspaper. I called the number and said, "I have no idea why I'm calling this number." The guy who answered said, "Isn't that interesting." It's a small, small company and they were looking for ME! One of the owners is [a] recovering [alcoholic]. The place was located downtown, which is where I was living.

What they say at meetings is that coincidences are God's way of remaining anonymous.

ILLUSTRATION B: *Jean's Drawing*

Regarding the diagram, I see myself as part of others, almost always. I see myself as in God's care. I have seen myself as separate from others, too. This changes. I could have come up with a zillion other combinations. I see God in myself, too, though it's not drawn here that way. God is always in me, in others and in the universe.

Ann

[One way I find a connection between inner and outer] is having somebody say something that is just what you need to hear. The week I started taking anti-depressants [at a doctor's prescription] I just kept thinking well, am I using or not using?[14] I went to a meeting and it was the only time I'd ever been to that [particular] meeting. We got in a small group. The subject of taking medication came up. It turned out that everybody in that group had been on medication at one time or another in sobriety. And that would seem like some kind of Higher Power thing that I ended up in this group at this meeting where I felt really comfortable talking about it. Everybody had gone through different things. They said if you don't like it, you don't have to take it. It's your decision, but it's certainly okay. There are a lot of times when I've gone to meetings and something like that happens. I do see that as a sign of a Higher Power in my life. I end up hearing just what I need to hear, being just where I need to be. It happens more when I'm more open. Just little things that I notice. I know if I change my attitude, that can [change] the whole day. Sometimes I believe that more than other times.

I believe the way the world looks to me is a reflection of my inner state. When I'm feeling positive, the world around me looks a lot more positive. When I feel hopeless, everything looks hopeless. When I'm really depressed, I can't even try, I can't do anything. I can't possibly explain it to somebody how bad I feel. Nobody wants to hear it. Everything looks bleak.

I definitely believe in miracles. I think of some of the things that have happened in the last couple years—changes that have come about with me and my family. I would have said that it never could have happened. A miracle is when something happens that there was just no way it could have happened . . . and it just does. You can't explain why it did, it just did. It just happened.

Jennifer

The way I got sober is through divine intervention. I wrote a letter [in response to] a classified ad by a "recovered" man. I said "I'm not quite where you are yet, but if you'd like to meet somebody who's going in the right direction, the same direction as you, give me a call." It turns out he was in the program [A.A.]. He was just a few months' sober. It was divine intervention' to me. I was going to meetings with him to see what they were like. I started counting my days [sober] to myself. I didn't tell anybody I was counting my days. He implied I was an alcoholic. I was against religion. I was against labels. I started going to meetings and then I started counting my days [sober]. When the relationship ended, I was around four and a half months sober. I had to make a decision who I was sober for. I really wasn't that connected to the [A.A.] program at the time. I was kind of auditing the program. On my 90th day I said, I think I'm an alcoholic, and I would share a couple of times at meetings. Who am I sober for? The relationship ended—I could go out and drink again. That's my life.

I can give you an example of a time everything fell in place. My wedding was one big fight. I felt no one was cooperating with me. I knew the kind of wedding I wanted. I wanted a different kind of wedding. It wasn't working out. I found so much resistance, from my mother, from the man I was to marry. They weren't cooperating with my thoughts. I cried every day for a month probably. A few times we weren't going to have a wedding. I was so frustrated. In the end I let go of a lot of stuff, a lot of control. I just let go control. It was the best thing in my life, the happiest day of my life. I started wondering at a certain point what was I supposed to do? I really didn't know. Was I supposed to continue trying to get my way? I didn't really understand what the lesson was. This is my wedding and they weren't cooperating and I knew I had choices to go with it and fight it and be miserable. I think I just decided to just go with the flow at some point. It was black-tie. When it came to music for the ceremony, I wanted tapes: songs that were meaningful to me, and I wanted to use cassettes. I did not want live music being played during the ceremony. I wanted the original music. This is something that is not really normal to do; they usually have violins and maybe a flute or something and they just play. There was a party coordinator coordinating the party. I told everyone my idea. For weeks, I had it all planned out in my head. I orchestrated the entire production in my head. It didn't really excite anyone. It excited me so much I knew in my heart that it was what I wanted and I was fighting with them and they weren't cooperating. Again I had to really say to myself, what's going on? And I was really going to let it go. I decided, that's it. I can't do it anymore— it's not meant to be. All of a sudden the party coordinator said, "Why don't we try it out?" Here was that open door that I was waiting for. It just happened. We tried it and it worked. It was a little bit different from what everyone was used to, but it worked. I knew I was like the producer and there is danger in that—that was a big conflict. It worked out just at the point that I decided to let go.

I also know you can manifest things to happen by thoughts. I manifested the job that I have now. I manifested meeting a man and getting married. I don't manifest this by myself; it has been manifested for me. I mean, everything is a manifestation of your thoughts. If you're thinking positive thoughts, you create positive action. On this subject, I have to be a little bit careful. Maybe I'm not evolved to the point to explain this enough. I just feel I have to be careful when I talk about this, be careful about who's doing what. Am I doing this, or do I give credit to my Higher Power, which is a power greater than myself and guiding me? I want to be careful because it's not me that's creating. It's not me who would create the plane to crash. It's not Jennifer who got her job. There's my will, then there's God's will. I don't have all this figured out, I really don't. There's something there, but I just can't define it. But if I affirm health, the chances are I'll be healthy. It's a real miracle for me to be sitting here and not have all the answers but *know* and trust that there is a Higher Power and with that Higher Power I feel safe. I feel safe. I didn't feel safe on the plane, but I'm not a guru. [She laughs.] I've been at this two and a half years. I've got to give myself a break.

There are times in my life when ordinary things and circumstances seem to take on a religious or spiritual significance. That happens all the time. I think God speaks through people. So it's on a daily basis, being open to God speaking. Everything is lessons, so it's with me all the time. In making decisions, sometimes I'll open an [inspirational] book to a page. . . . I'm really not looking for decisions, but answers. I just try to pay attention, pay attention to my surroundings. I don't have any of the answers. I do believe the way the world looks to me is a reflection of my inner state. When I don't like myself—let's say I just ate sugar and I feel [terrible], I hate everything. All of a sudden, I hate everything about my life, I hate everything around me, hate everything, because I don't like myself.

ILLUSTRATION C: *Jennifer's Drawing*

I drew a diagram representing the relationship between myself, other people, my Higher Power, and the universe as a whole. The arrows going in two directions mean it's all flowing. From within and without. It's all never-ending. I did it very quickly. I decided to be spontaneous when I did it and just not think about how it would be or how it would look. I probably had second thoughts about doing those arrows because they don't look very pleasant. The arrows are there for direction. It's almost like having words in there, but instead it's in symbols. Arrows are hurtful, but these weren't meant like that—they were directional arrows.

Roger

Who hasn't heard of meaningful coincidences? It seems like it's something everyone has heard of.

From the moment I got on my knees and said "I give up," from that moment on, the coincidences started happening. I didn't get sober until February, but things changed. I saw my father in November and we made a little peace. I left feeling I connected with my father a little. In January, he died. I was able to get to the funeral and felt okay. While I was at the funeral, I met a guy who had been sober nine years. I had watched him for nine years to see if the [Alcoholics Anonymous] program worked. He asked me if I had a problem with alcohol. I was able to hear him because I had watched him be sober, not drink for nine years. It turns out this man had gone to treatment four weeks after my first treatment when I had been "inspired" about sobriety. I went into treatment after talking to him in February.

Another example of a coincidence happened once when I had to move from my apartment. This guy who had a reputation for helping people move showed up. I hadn't seen him in ten years. He helped me move.

I now go to Overeaters' Anonymous as well as Alcoholics Anonymous. How I got involved is a synchronicity. I had diabetes. I went to a couple of meetings. There was only one other man at the meetings—all the rest were women. I told the people there I didn't fit in. The night I told them that, I went to get in my car, and the whole car seat fell off. The bolts ripped off, I assume because I was so fat. I said "Thank you, God." I've been going ever since.

I'll give you another example. I had no memory of my childhood, so I hoped to visit old haunts on one of my visits to the state where I grew up. I didn't have a car, so I couldn't plan my own route. I was able to go along with others in a van on a short trip. The driver of the van had to take different routes. I came across more old places than I could have if I'd tried. My memory came back. I remember maybe ten things when I was a kid. I was led. If I show up, and just follow the lead, it's wonderful. That's why I don't want to plan. This is all God. I turn it over. I don't know what I'm walking into.

I'm very much a believer in listening to intuition. The year in my life that was so great for me was all intuitive. That's all it was. Maybe because I still don't totally trust people, I don't have a sponsor, maybe I have to trust in intuition a lot more. Or my God. That's how I hear what to do. That's how my God speaks to me. Maybe that's a better way of putting it. I don't see intuition itself as God—that's just the God in me. That thing has been telling me what to do all my life—it has never *not* been there. Has intuition ever *not* been there? Just think of one time! But when fear comes in, it says don't trust that. There's a leap to following intuition. Before, my life always centered around logic—I would never paint or draw or write or talk or do anything that would involve people or creative expression.

I had the intuition to take up roller skating. I broke my shoulder. I had to get help from people. That got me into asking for help. I believe that everything that happens is part of that synchronicity. In spite of the way it may seem, *all* of it connects. I just don't see it all. A lot of things don't happen right away. It happens in time, maybe twenty years. I've told you a lot of synchronistic stuff, and that's just a small percentage of the whole.

All my life I was so screwed up, I didn't notice the [connections]. When I got trusting, a lot of stuff was put in front of me. I use fear to guide me. Fear is like a flag. You want to grow? Come over here! Fear is blocking something in me that doesn't want to grow, to be happy. Now as I feel better, I plan too much. It works better if I'm open to it and things come up. It's more fun than the other way, planning consciously. Every day I pray. I realize how little I know. It's getting a proper perspective. I feel more dependent today and freer than ever. It's one of those paradoxes. It's not false modesty to say "I don't know," it's just true. If I start analyzing the [Twelve] Steps I fall apart.

Have you heard the definition of a miracle? A miracle is a coincidence in which God chooses to remain anonymous. I like it. It describes what I believe it is in a cutesy way. I believe in a

God, a higher force, or Higher Power, and all this stuff is flowing the way it's supposed to go. For some weird reason, the thing that makes human beings so incredibly weird is that they've got the choice to say "No, I don't want to go with the flow." I can say no. I'm so used to saying "no," that when I start saying "yes," the glorified [sic] wonderful things happen and I call them miracles. [He laughs.] Yet what is the miracle? It's just a natural thing. It just seems miraculous because we're used to crap, to put it bluntly. This one clergy says he heard somewhere that the good news is too good to be true. That also makes sense to me. *There really is a God! It really all makes sense—all this is really true! No, it can't be!!!* [Considerably louder, with a hint of laughter.] My whole sobriety has been nothing more than that more and more I've been coming to say, "Yeah, it *is* true, it really is true, a little bit more each day. Yeah, it really is true and a little less of 'Bull, bull, bull.'" Even as I tell you this, I can feel the tug in me. "Sure, Roger." The war is on. When we hear the good stuff, our reaction is "no"—we fight just accepting it. Now I'm aware of that, and I get to watch it. I don't think the experiences of [meaningful coincidences] are so unusual, but I think often the energy to deny that they're happening wins out.

Looking at the lights, looking at peoples' auras—that all seems spiritual to me. I could be in a room of twenty people. Most people would get into it—all that imaging. I never used one of those imaging techniques. All of a sudden I would connect, but I fight it. Any of the times I've let go I seem to have ended up connecting with something, whether it be a person, God, nature, or something. When I get into this meditation thing, I get a lot of different experiences that are not normal. I feel people next to me in the room, I feel closer. Feelings of the past come up. I start recalling childhood stuff and sometimes I don't want to. I think that all happened. I think it could happen a lot. I don't let it. I seem to have experiences like you'd have on acid (LSD). On acid, for some reason, I enjoyed it, because I thought, "Well, I'm on acid." When I do it off of acid, I think I have an editor in me that says, "Well, this is crazy." I'm not comfortable with having those experiences. I think I'm just afraid of them. They're too different. I'm afraid of being different like that. If I let them happen, they're real powerful stuff.

I first had some of those experiences when I was a kid. Even as a kid I had them. When I was a little kid one of the things I used to have happen to me is that I'd be lying in my room at night and everything would turn backwards—did you ever look at a telescope the wrong way? The whole room would become like that. With acid [LSD] you could get different views of things and it became okay. I believe in [altered states.] I don't know what to do with it. I'm not someone who throws a lot of interpretation on it. I don't want to make a religion out of it. It just happens. It's not the most important thing in my life, either, by any means. I'm trying to say something here and I'm not able to put my finger on it. I think part of me has a fear of being enveloped in that. In A.A., life is simple. Love is what's important, and all this other stuff is part of the whole picture. Those experiences can be so potent that you can get caught up into thinking you've got the answer or you're spiritually blessed. I had delusions of being Christ or the Son of God or something. I was thirty-three years old—that's when Christ got crucified—when I recovered and I was in treatment forty days and forty nights. My mind didn't hold onto that. What actually goes through my mind is, maybe you're something special. Ummm. I think what I'm saying is I have a fear of those kinds of experiences because I have a fear that they could be mentally unhealthy, or I could be caught in them, trapped in them, and be out there in some sort of deluded world. Probably a lot of people have those kinds of fears of anything unusual. I think it's a similar fear that I have of being close to people. I think those experiences seem to be beyond my normal ones. But you know, I'm letting them into my life more now. It seems as if as I go along, I have more confidence in this God that loves me, and none of that stuff seems as threatening. What I expect is that around the bend that stuff's going to happen more often, but I'm not going to see it so much as a threat.

Carol

You ask if I've felt in the presence of God or a Higher Power. I can tell you a few things that occurred that have no explanation, although when I heard in A.A. that coincidence was God's way of staying anonymous that made a certain amount of sense to me. I talk about miracles as mysteries—things that just happen. The way I use the word, it's a divinely natural occurrence that must be learned humanly. It's a miracle that I'm alive, maybe. There are more and more miracles in my life. I am learning.

I used to pray in boarding school from a very early age. I remember making a deal with God. This is all very embarrassing to talk about. I had this holy card my father had given me—Catholics have these pictures with little prayers on the back and you put them in your prayer book. He had had this card since he was a child. Grandmother had given it to him. This grandmother had raised me until I was three, and she was *the* person that gave me a little bit of love that I remember. I had a feeling she liked me. My mother was always terrified of me so she couldn't really surrender to my needs and demands, but my grandmother did. And so this holy card was passed on. It was terribly significant to me as a child. I remember wanting something very, very badly, and I can't even tell you what I wanted. Being a child of barter, I offered this holy card to get what I wanted, and as a matter of fact, I did get what I wanted, and the holy card was gone in the morning. You know, one doesn't know if this is childhood fantasy, or you know something practical probably happened. Dropped it or. . . . It doesn't matter, it was significant to me.

When I was five or six I was living overseas and my great grandmother was in America. I can remember (the whole family tells this story to this day, so of course this was not a figment of my imagination) that I started screaming and crying, "Oh, my grandmother's dead!" in the car on the way back from a trip. I remember them telling me to be quiet, it wasn't true, I should just go back to sleep, it was a dream. I had woken up screaming. We got back to the house and we did receive a telegram that my grandmother had died. I've always been able to be connected like that. You know, sensitive. You know Edison had an idea that he could connect with something of the spirit.

In the land I lived in overseas, we would have picnics in the cemetery. The dead were treated as living things. Ancestors were spoken to as if they were right there. We brought them little dumplings, persimmons. Maybe that gave me the idea that there was a connection between spirits. I'm not sure.

On Christmas Eve, my cousin died. We knew he was going to die for a long time, the whole year. The night before he died, I couldn't sleep. I just couldn't sleep. I had just spoken to him for an hour two days before and he was doing fine, making plans to go to parties, and to New Year's celebrations. Still I thought of him that night.

Who can say what's real? I know on acid (LSD), I saw lights all over and I saw auras and halos. Who can say what's real? I had hallucinations and heard voices and everything else.

I don't go for a day without coincidences. When it all seems to make sense. It's all there for a purpose. The problem sometimes is that there is something about it—I get frightened and get in my own way and want to stop it. I never go a day without something that happens for me.

[When I took the questionnaire for this study,] I agreed that the way the world looks to me is a reflection of my inner state, although I'm happy to tell you that I have acquired a certain detachment, so that it's not so much anymore a *projection* of my inner state. I don't mean that there is less of a connection, just less of a projection. Even if I'm feeling peaceful, the world might really be nuts! [Laughter.] That's okay, I don't have to be nuts with it. I can be peaceful and it can still be nuts. But there was a time when probably I wrote that if I was peaceful, it had to be peaceful, and I couldn't see it as anything else. But most of the time that wasn't true. If I was upset, then it would be upset. In other words, the delusions are becoming less, and so the projections are becoming less. The detachment's a result of this.

Joyce

There are a lot of things that happened. Even like smoking. I had no intention to quit smoking. Matter of fact, if anything I was going to keep it up because my family was bugging me and it was like "Well, God, how perfect do you want me to be?" More in defiance than anything. I had attended a seminar on the *Course in Miracles* I do some work on that and they had something else called masterminding that I didn't know anything about. This was just a Saturday deal, and there was a psychologist who facilitated it. At the end of the day we were to write ourselves a letter to be mailed back to us, and we would ask anything we wanted. So the paper was passed out and we went through a forgiveness-type thing—I can't remember it all—then we had to write. Well, I get real leery. I don't like to ask for things because I say I don't know enough and I may not want them. I've had that happen. So I thought, well, okay, I'll write that somebody close to me shows an expression of their love. That can't be too bad. I don't know what else I put in there, but I had a hard time with it. I only had a couple things on there, so I was going to put smoking, and I thought, no, I'm not going to do that. Then I was sitting there and sort of twiddling my thumbs and the girl next to me is writing frantically and she's got this whole sheet filled, and I've just got these couple things, and I thought "Gee, look at all of the stuff she's got." Just before we were going to pass it in, I just scribbled on there, "Help me quit smoking," or something like that. I quit, which was six months later, and I don't know to this day why I did it. There was an article in the paper about the gum and I got the gum, but there was something more. I didn't have a problem with it. I had tried to quit many times. And when I got home from that seminar in the afternoon it was five o'clock, and I pulled in the yard and my one daughter who lives nearby was there, and I thought, what's she doing here? and I came in and it turned out that my daughter from Oklahoma was there. She had flown up. It was a complete surprise, and it came to my mind right away that that was the expression of love that I had asked for, and the smoking was there. I also asked to lose twenty pounds, but that hasn't happened.

I don't remember what I was thinking of when I strongly agreed [with the item on the questionnaire, "The way the world looks to me is a reflection of my inner state."] I do strongly agree if I'm feeling happy within me, then the world looks good. When I go to work in the morning, as I'm driving, I ask God to let anything that happens be a lesson to learn that day, and I always tack on "Don't give me too many lessons." [Laughter.] I remember at an [A.A.] meeting one time somebody said that every time they get depressed and they ask God for help, He sends them another drunk to take care of. [Laughter.]

I definitely believe that God speaks through people. There's just no doubt about that. I see that time and time again. I believe that in reading, in opening up a book and doing a meditation, reading one of my meditations for the day, I feel there are real messages in that. I think there are a lot of messages I'm just not capable of understanding yet. I think there are messages in music and all this kind of stuff, but I haven't advanced enough to understand. I think it's all around me, but I can't recognize it.

I do believe in miracles. I think basically they're a change in attitude, that's what miracles are.

I find miracles in a lot of small ways. I do think that big ones can happen. I mean, I feel real strong, even with all this turmoil that I've been going through as far as trying to find serenity. Just fighting the whole way for it and everything, and I was told . . . that I'm still trying to control, now I'm trying to control God. Well, see, I still think a lot of people in A.A. feel that it takes years to get to a certain point. I don't feel that way. I feel that you can be there, I can be there, tomorrow. There'll be an attitude change, but I do think it can happen. If I thought I had to wait around five years, well forget it. I probably wouldn't do it then. The attitude change, if I could be the way I wanted to be, it would be with giving unconditional love. I'm not there, but that's what it would be. I have a lot more self-confidence in myself that I didn't have before, that's an attitude change. I think an attitude of miracles is one of self-acceptance—I think confidence comes along with it. I have a difficult time with the phrase "learning to love yourself." It isn't that I don't believe in it, but I can't quite pinpoint it. To love myself at first seemed contrary to my teachings. To love myself, in my mind, I pictured as being conceited and self-centered. And now I've grown enough that, no, I know that that's not the case. I think I love myself and, you know, I'm not sure where that's at, nor how to find that. The biggest before-miracle attitude I think would be resentments, having resentments before and then being able to let go of them. I have a problem right now with old resentments that I can't let go of, and I'm trying. I need to forgive or else I can't grow any more.

In my life, there have been miracles. The attitude changes to be able to give up alcohol are a miracle. It's a miracle that I quit smoking. I had also asked God—I think it was in that letter—that I would make $20,000 a year, and this year I made $20,184. I laughed when I saw my W-2 [income tax form]. Wow! I don't believe this! Even [my going to] therapy is a miracle, because it's certainly not cheap and it's something I felt real strong that I had to do. There were some areas of my life that I was still having problems with and I wanted to work on them. Now that was something that I let go of, now that I think of it. My husband and I've been married for thirty-two years and it's been constant chaos, so I was in real turmoil about the need to do something about this marriage. It was going on internally with me all the time. I'd think this, then that. I finally let go of it. I thought, I can't handle this anymore. I'm turning it over to God. [The next thing that happened was I met this women who helped me a great deal with that—she had been through a similar situation.] Last fall I found an apartment and said, I'm leaving. Then everybody said, "Something's wrong with Mom." And that's when therapy started. It would have never started if I hadn't let go. It's a miracle, because I let go of the problem and it worked out the way it did, which is much better. I think that's God working. Whether I stay in the marriage or not isn't even the issue—who knows down the line? I guess I feel that if I don't belong here, I'll know, and I've let go of that part.

My studying the *Course in Miracles* was a miracle. Someone recommended that I go to it. At that point I would not drive at night, I would not drive out of the city. I mean there's just no way. It turns out a group of people in a personal growth group I started going to met one-half block from my house. Some were in A.A., some weren't. What they all had in common was they studied the *Course in Miracles*. That's when I started checking into it. I had a lot of trouble with the words, and I had a lot of doubt as far as my faith as being Catholic—should I be doing this, you know. So there was a lot of that. I was doing it because I felt I needed to know more about it, but I was not open and receptive and I've just picked it up again because of the fact that it seemed to be a fairly happy time when I was doing that.

John

You ask for examples of when my inner state and outer circumstances came together. I'll tell you a weird one. Well, it happened when I first came back from treatment. I don't know how often I'd go to bed in my little cottage on one side of the woods and I'd been thinking of my Higher Power and this flash of light would come! The room would light up—and I thought wow! [He says with laughter and excitement in his voice.] Again, as with my spiritual awakening, I never, ever told anybody. This was my own spiritual experience. The whole winter when I got back from treatment until the summer came, I would see the room light up! Great! I'd be thinking about the power of God or whatever. I have a flash and it would happen. This happened quite often. It was great, really great. *Oh!* This all stopped happening in the summer, and I kept trying to make it happen again. It worried me a little bit that it had stopped. [He laughs.] Where did it go? [His voice is full with laughter.] Well, it wasn't until a year later I was out on the road—which is about a half a mile away from where I live—and coming from somewhere, that I realized . . . it was cars coming down this road. There's a dead end here. . . . [He quickly draws a map and points to it.] Their headlights had been shining through these trees into my bedroom window! [Laughter.] In wintertime, of course, there are no leaves on the trees . . . but what is a spiritual experience anyway? *It worked! By the time I found out, it didn't matter anymore!* In fact, it was funny. I got a kick out of it. I still feel like maybe it *was* some sort of . . . why not . . . it worked. It *did* seem to happen at particular times. It was usually while I was awake before I went to sleep. I *do* know it was the cars . . . but where does the spiritual feeling come from? *I* interpreted it the way I did. It sure helped me during that time. I didn't need that afterwards. In fact, it was almost a relief to find out that that's what it was, that it hadn't stopped. I mean, it was always there anyway. Obviously life was fine. The compulsion of drinking and drug taking was gone. It was just tremendous. It's so obvious that that was such a miracle. I didn't need anything else. There sure have been coincidences, things that seem to work without much trouble when I'm not controlling, like I have been for the last year or so. What comes into mind is just running into people . . . meeting people at the right times in your life. Going to an A.A. meeting, hearing just what is needed. That's happened so many times. *Not* wanting to go, dragging myself and being real glad I went. That has happened countless times. Those experiences have *always* been beneficial.

There are times in my life when ordinary things take on a spiritual or religious significance. I must say that that has happened to me. Again, in nature and beauty. I'm a bike rider. I bike-ride for miles—thirty or forty or fifty miles or so. I can either be by myself or be with a group of guys and just really have a flash of "Boy, I'm so lucky! It's so beautiful and thank you, God." The exhilaration, the outdoors and the physical exercise. It's real hilly, so you fly down the hills. One time it was the end of autumn. The trees still have leaves on them but they're brown. The colors are muted, but they're so beautiful, even more beautiful than when they're vivid. Somehow there's another beauty. The burning smells of leaves in the little villages you go through . . . all those kitschy, old romantic feelings of thanksgiving and apple pie or pumpkin pie or something. That took on spiritual significance. Yeah! Wow! I'm so lucky! I was feeling a part of it. Yeah! Here it is! You're right in it. You're not in it driving somehow, but you're on the bike feeling air. The bike is silent. It's great. I'm not a meditator as such, except maybe how I just described. Just being overwhelmed by the look of nature and also with appreciation of the architecture and what man can do beautifully! You see that on the bike rides even in these old Victorian farmhouses. Each one is a kind of a work of art and they get prettier with age. You know they sort of speak of God to me. There's something real nice about that . . . that I feel that way. I don't think I would have before treatment so much. I wouldn't have had time to look or even do that sort of thing. What also takes on a spiritual significance is a sense of community. Belonging is the biggest part I think. That happens a lot even outside of A.A. I was thinking of bike riding with the other guys. They're not in A.A., and they don't even necessarily know about it. It's nice, it's real nice to be able to interact.

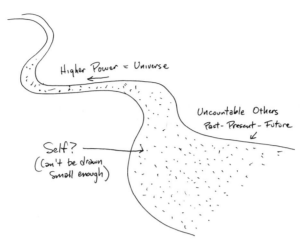

ILLUSTRATION D: *John's Drawing*

Donald

Sure there have been meaningful coincidences. I just accept them. I suppose I accept it as part of the larger picture. I think that there's a possibility of minds connecting on a level. I wouldn't preclude that. I haven't given it much thought, but I wouldn't want to have a closed mind.

SECTION B
PAST AND FUTURE

1.
Statements Illustrating the Nature of the Problem

Everything within the field of time is dual.[15]

Joseph Campbell

Duality is nothing more or less than the way in which American-European cultures categorize virtually everything. Physics and anthropology tell quite a different story. But the reader should know that duality is, as Einstein put it, something which one "imbibes with one's mother's milk."[16]

Modern . . . people of American-European heritage . . . have some difficulty understanding sacred or mythic time, because this type of time is imaginary—one is in the time. It is repeatable and reversible, and it does not change. In mythic time people do not age, for they are magic. This kind of time is like a story.[17, 18] *. . .*

Edward Hall

The perspective [on time] changes completely when the sense of the religiousness of the cosmos becomes lost. This is what occurs when, in certain more highly evolved societies, the intellectual elites progressively detach themselves from the patterns of the traditional religion. The periodical sanctification of cosmic time then proves useless and without meaning. The gods are no longer accessible through the cosmic rhythms. The religious meaning of the repetition of paradigmatic gestures is forgotten. But repetition emptied of its religious content necessarily leads to a pessimistic vision of existence. When it is no longer a vehicle for reintegrating a primordial situation, and hence for revering the mysterious presence of the gods, that is, when it is desacralized, cyclic time becomes terrifying; it is seen as a circle forever turning on itself, repeating itself to infinity.[19]

Mircea Eliade

The opinions of Marx and the findings of [Lewis] Mumford that the clock made possible the development of production and regulation, and that it marked the perfection toward which other machines had to aspire, may be seen in retrospect as a symbol of the Christian, especially the Protestant, pragmatic ethics. From the sixteenth century on the clockwork became the bourgeois, later the communist ideal, a quasi-religious object for both, and the paradigm of praiseworthy conduct. The history of the machine civilization which culminated in techno-logical man, and of which the clock is such a distinguished citizen, is the story of a powerful efferent adaptive pressure by man upon his environment.[20]

J. T. Fraser

We have only one word for time; the Greeks had two, each one describing a difference in the experience and quality of time. One was kronos, time as we usually "watch it," measured time passing. It is our scheduled life, when we must get to work, when our appointments are, time we must account for, Father Time. The second, kairos, was very different. Rather than measured time, it is participation in time; time that so engrosses us that we lose track of time; timeless time; moments when the clock stands still; nourishing, renewing, more maternal time. . . . It happens when we are completely involved in what we are doing. It always accompanies moments of emotional meaning or spiritual significance—time when we feel "one with," rather than separate from, the Self, the Tao, the love that connects us to others.[21]

Jean Shinoda Bolen

Phenomenal existence, according to Advaita Vedanta and Buddhism, is existence in the grip of the all-consuming temporality. In other words, everything that exists in time is, by the very nature of such existence, subject to change, decay, and death. As such, all attempts to overcome pain and death by means and methods which are themselves time-bound are doomed to failure. . . . Man overcomes the pain and suffering of time-bound existence by the knowledge of the eternal and timeless. . . . In both Advaita Vedanta and Buddhism time is of the essence of the phenomenal world. And since the phenomenal world has no independent reality, time too is not an independent reality. History is part and parcel of the phenomenal world, that is, of time-bound existence. . . . It is a truism that all history takes place in time. . . . According to Advaita Vedanta and Buddhism, what the study of history reveals to us is man in bondage, not man in his primordial reality; what history shows us is man in the state of ignorance, not the liberated man. Further, as long as he labors under the illusion of the ultimacy of historical reality and seeks freedom through history, man will remain in ignorance and bondage. Liberating knowledge can only be attained by transcending the time-bound existence of the empirical world.[22]

Puligandla

Like space, time could never be perceived without the distinctions we impose upon it. But we have fortified ourselves with a welter of temporal systems and distinctions. . . . We create the year, academic and fiscal, and the day, whether holiday or workday, in terms of events and situations that make them significant and worthwhile . . . and we do so by predicting them and then seeing how the events and situations impinge on our expectations. Calendars, schedules, timetables and seasonal expectations and routines are all "predictive" devices for precipitating . . . time. They are a means of setting up expectations. . . . [23]

We know time (and its brothers "growth," "life" and the "weather") by its stealthy habit of creeping up on us. We make it creep up by assuming that we are able to predict and prepare for it. [24]

Roy Wagner

Thought must take place in time, but vision can transcend it. [25]

Fritjof Capra

2.
Stories Illustrating the Unity

No Zen student would presume to teach others until he had lived with his master for at least ten years.

Tenno, having completed his ten years of apprenticeship, acquired the rank of teacher.
One day he went to visit the master Nan-in. It was a rainy day, so Tenno wore wooden clogs and carried an umbrella.

When he walked in, Nan-in greeted him with "You left your wooden clogs and umbrella on the porch, didn't you? Tell me, did you place your umbrella on the right side of the clogs or on the left?"

Tenno was embarrassed, for he did not know the answer. He realized he lacked awareness. So he became Nan-in's student and labored for another ten years to acquire constant awareness. [26]

Told by Anthony DeMello

She, Christa T., made a great discovery that summer, not without knowing that she'd done so, but without knowing that it was great. Suddenly she saw something like a link between herself—this life which did strike her as being too ordinary and often even narrow—and these free magnanimous moments. She began to realize that one must create the moments oneself and that she had the means for doing so.

When, if not now? [27]

Christa Wolf

3.
Illustrative Excerpts from Questionnaire and Interviews

I experience or have experienced timeless time (timeless moments or periods).
5% of those in treatment responded with a "6" or "7," with 7 being all the time.
14% of those in recovery responded with a "6" or "7," with 7 being all the time.

I live one day at a time.
36% of those in treatment said this is true for them all the time or nearly all the time.
48% of those in recovery said this is true for them all the time or nearly all the time.

Bob

In sobriety, at times when I was meditating if I felt real successful, I would become quite detached from the world, able almost to float and be detached from physical surroundings.

Paul

At times, at moments, my vision of time, my concept of time has differed greatly from others'. I'm not really all that convinced that—how can I put it?— I'm not that convinced that time runs consecutively. I think it might be concurrent? That's even though I'm not aware that other things are going on. Part of me still thinks that there are time warps that I could walk through. I haven't experienced any. Even when I was doing drugs in college, doing hallucinogens. I'm very drawn to artistic things, but I've been very skeptical about things like that happening, astral projecting and all this kind of stuff. I've always wondered, if I'm willing to pursue the creation of art, why I'm not open to pursue all that other stuff. It's not like one's concrete and the other isn't, because art itself is not concrete. I believe in the stock market, but I can't believe in the other.

I tried a little Transcendental Meditation back in college. It was something I really liked. I was involved in some psychology student's experiment, which was the measurement of alpha-wave production. We spent half an hour to forty-five minutes every day wired for sound. We were talked through to the alpha state eventually. I found it extremely restful. It would be after class, about 5:30 or 6:00 every night. It was the most restful kind of time I ever spent. It went on for about six months. Then they turned in the results and the experiment stopped. [He laughed.] I didn't pursue it. I think part of it was that I liked the idea of being measured. It didn't seem so flaky. I was doing this for an experiment. This wasn't behavior on my part. I always thought I was sleeping, but the experimenter told me I wasn't. The only other timeless time I can think of [was with] the sodium pentothol-valium mixture they used on me for surgery. I loved it. My body was in the most wretched, pained condition. They put you under, they paralyze you, put you under respirators, they can talk to you, interact at times. That's what I wanted from my drugs and alcohol. I never wanted to remember, I wanted to *obliterate*. Timelessness was involved in that. On my own, I don't think I experienced timeless time, except while at the ocean or swimming.

Jane

I have a little clock radio. I don't ever want a watch anymore.

Jean

[My experiences of being in the presence of God] mostly have to do with being aware of the natural sort of timeless moments in nature. I've also had timeless moments in church. The most striking instance I've had of timeless moments in nature—and I've since realized it's sort of a universal feeling—was when I was at this one camp. It was really an intense mountaineering camp. One of the things I did was a thirty-six hour mountaineering solo. You're out in the Rockies and you get dumped in a spot with a knife and you don't see anybody, talk to anybody.

You don't have a watch. You have some water in a stream and what you wear for thirty-six hours. Oh yeah, you had a pen and a pad—they thought it was important that if you wanted to journal you could do journaling. I wrote something about being able to think an eternity before sundown because I had no concept of time passing at all. It could have been a second, it could have been days. It was a phenomenal experience.

The same sort of feeling of not being aware of time has happened since. Last week there was a terrible, really thick fog. I was driving across this high bridge. It's a strange bridge. It goes uphill and with the fog, driving across the bridge and these lights on the side of them, it made this whole huge wall of light going up into the sky. I had the sense that I was driving over that bridge for about an hour and a half. It wasn't so unusual—I feel ridiculous talking about it. Things like that happen frequently and always make me feel beyond myself.

I experience timeless time too when I'm alone and I paint. Not every time I paint, but when I'm doing it right, twelve hours can pass and I won't be aware of it. I'll be completely absorbed in what I'm doing.

Ann

In order to stay one day at a time, I look at whatever's happening and accept it as God's will. If I'm doing my best, if I'm doing what I'm supposed to do, then whatever happens is God's will. That is God's will. I never could do that before.[28]

Jennifer

I believe that right now everything is okay. I can give you one example of having a hard time putting into practice what I believe. I have an incredible fear of flying. I really had an intention of practicing these principles I believe on the plane, and I had so much fear on the plane that it was overwhelming. It would leave for a moment. I would try to use the tools from A.A. that I have at my fingertips today. I wouldn't have an hysteria attack, but I was so conscious of being full of fear. When the plane took off the only thing that helped me feel a little bit safe is putting a blanket over my head. I felt very cocoon-like. I had incredible visualizations of crashing, of colliding with another plane in midair. I know today in my process of recovery, all I have to do with fear is change my thoughts. I was projecting. I had to keep getting right back into the now. Every time I felt myself drifting and getting panicky—I was panic-stricken—I had to consciously get back into the now, constantly, constantly. But on this plane, every five minutes I was slipping into projected states. That was the largest scale of fear that I have felt in a long time. I've allowed the projection of what will happen or what can happen. I know today that all I have to do is change my thoughts. Right now, I am safe, I am safe.

Roger

When I was in treatment, I was living one day at a time, moment to moment—whatever chunk of moment I could handle. I sliced it down to what I could handle without a drink. One minute at a time. If someone saw me in treatment, they probably wouldn't think I was living in the now because I was anxious, worried about never getting out, but I stayed in the here and now with effort. I would repeat phrases like "everything is just the way it's supposed to be." "I'm right where I'm supposed to be." "There is nothing to lose."

I feel I do well with that. It's critical. I took up roller skating to help me be in the here and now. I would be disturbed and go skating—go around in a circle. Something demanded one to stay in the moment. All that big stuff in your head. Here you have to turn or you go into the wall.

Donald

I have some experiences [of timeless time] when I can concentrate on something—I have very strong concentration. I forget what's going on. I can become so involved in what I'm doing. It's really an artistic thing, that I lose all sense of time. I don't look at the clock. I focus right here doing it. Creating. That's what I'm talking about.

I walk in the woods a lot. I have what I call my stump-sitting-and-staring time. I'd go out and read—the Big Book [of Alcoholics Anonymous]. I knew how far away I was from things just by timing the length of time it took me to start to become aware of where I was, to hear a bird singing, hear noises, become one with the woods, nature. If that took two hours then I knew that I was going too strong. I better slow down. If it took thirty minutes, maybe I wasn't so bad. How long does it take to clean the mind of the world and let the present moment come in? That's what I'm talking about. As I said, if it took me two hours to be aware the birds are singing, maybe I better cut out what I'm doing . . . spend some more time listening to some of the birds.

Section C
Life and Death

1.
Statements Illustrating the Nature of the Problem

In the West, we have a culture which in recent history has virtually prohibited all thought about death.[29]

George D. Bond

What is most fundamental in a culture, I think, is the culture's solution to the problem of death. . . . Working against time, we work against death.[30]

John S. Dunne

[Addicts] are desperate and they know there is something really wrong. A lot of them wish they were dead. They are on a self-destructive course, and they know it. The world as it is is intolerable, and their lives are intolerable, because they aren't really living their own lives. . . . [It does have a very creative aspect.] Death and resurrection. And they do go through the death.

People are terrified of death. . . . Life is a series of deaths and rebirths. You out-grow patterns, you outgrow people, you outgrow work. But if you are frightened and do not have a flexible personality, when you have to face the death of what you've always known, you are pitched into terror.[31]

Marion Woodman

In Hiroshima, a defense mechanism called forth by people exposed to the horrors of the bomb was simply to cease to feel, that is, to become psychologically desensitized. Virtually every survivor I spoke to told of some such psychological state at the time the bomb fell. They described being fully aware of dying in horrible ways, but of simply losing their emotional involvement in it all. They used such phrases as "paralysis of the mind" or "I simply became insensitive to human death," and [many other forms] . . . of psychic closing off. . . . Psychic numbing was necessary to Hiroshima survivors, as it is for anyone exposed to extreme catastrophe. It is a protection against overwhelming and unacceptable stimuli, and it is associated with an inner imagery that goes something like this: "If I feel nothing, then death is not taking place;" or "If I feel nothing, I cannot be threatened by the death all around me;" or "If I feel nothing, then I am not responsible for you or your death."[32]

Jay Lifton

Everywhere we have found the symbolism of death as the ground of all spiritual birth— that is, of regeneration. In all these contexts death signifies the surpassing of the profane, non-sanctified condition, the condition of the "natural man," ignorant of religion and blind to the spiritual. . . . Let us remember this fact, for it is important—that access to the spiritual is expressed in archaic societies by a symbolism of death.[33]

Mircea Eliade

Now the soldier as well as the civilian has to anticipate weapons of mass destruction which offer no one a reasonable chance, often not even an awareness of their approach. Destruction can strike out of the blue skies and destroy thousands like the bomb at Hiroshima; it may come in the form of gases or other means of chemical warfare— invisible, crippling, killing. It is no longer the man who fights for his rights, his convictions, or the safety or honor of his family; it is the nation including its women and children who are in the war, affected directly or indirectly without a chance of survival. This is how science and technology have contributed to an ever-increasing fear of destruction and therefore fear of death. . . .

If all of us would make an all-out effort to contemplate our own death, to deal with our anxieties surrounding the concept of our death, and to help others familiarize themselves with these thoughts, perhaps there could be less destructiveness around us. . . .

I think that with rapid technological advancement and new scientific achievements men have been able to develop not only new skills but also new weapons of mass destruction which increase the fear of a violent, catastrophic death. Man has to defend himself psychologically in many ways against this increased fear of death and increased inability to foresee and protect himself against it. Psychologically he can deny the reality of his own death for a while.

If . . . denial is no longer possible, we can attempt to master death by challenging it. . . . If a whole nation, a whole society suffers from such a fear and denial of death, it has to use defenses which can only be destructive. Wars, riots, and increasing numbers of murders and other crimes may be indicators of our decreasing ability to face death with acceptance and dignity. Perhaps we have to come back to the individual human being and start from scratch, to attempt to conceive our own death and learn to face this tragic but inevitable happening with less irrationality and fear.

Though every man will attempt in his own way to postpone such questions and issues until he is forced to face them, he will only be able to change things if he can start to conceive of his own death. This cannot be done on a mass level. This cannot be done by computers. This has to be done by every human being alone. Each one of us has the need to avoid this issue,

161

yet each one of us has to face it sooner or later. If all of us could make a start by contemplating the possibility of our own personal death, we may effect many things, most important of all the welfare of our patients, our families and finally perhaps our nation. . . .

Finally, we may achieve peace—our own inner peace as well as peace between nations—by facing and accepting the reality of our own death.[34]

Elisabeth Kübler-Ross

2.
Stories Illustrating the Unity

The third lodge is called the Lodge of the Thunderbird. This was the lodge of death and birth.

The People learned within the teaching of the Black Shield that it was important for them to wean their children from themselves and from their camp circle. If they did not do this, their children would live, but their spirits would die.

When each girl or boy returned from their Vision Quest they entered the Lodge of the Thunderbird. When they entered, the People of the camp mourned and wept. They lamented because the seeker they had known had died. But when the seeker came out from the Lodge of the Thunderbird there was rejoicing and singing, because a new person had been born among them! A shield was painted, and the newcomer was given a name. This new person was celebrated.[35]

Hyemeyohsts Storm

She knew things that nobody had ever told her. . . . She knew that God tore down the old world every evening and built a new one by sun-up. It was wonderful to see it take form with the sun and emerge from the gray dust of its making.[36]

Zora Neale Hurston

3.
Illustrative Excerpts from Questionnaire and Interviews

I recall or was told I had at least one near-death experience.
52% of those in treatment agreed.
59% of those in recovery agreed

I have made peace with death.
21% of those in treatment agreed.
48% of those in recovery agreed.

I feel comfortable being around a person who seems near to death.
23% of those in treatment agreed.
41% of those in recovery agreed.

Paul

I was dead when I went to detox. I used to wake up every morning and wonder why the *hell* I was alive, why I hadn't been killed the night before, feeling like death and knowing being dead would be more comfortable. I was dead . . . spiritually. I was shut down completely on art. I couldn't even look at a Rothko and get into it. I had become so highly emotionally removed. I would do an intellectual number on it. So I was spiritually dead there. That's where my spirituality is I guess. I wanted to die, but I wasn't brave enough to commit suicide. You know, death was not coming. I did really stupid things also which would ensure death which never happened. I don't know why. So my surrender was just like they say. People in the program said "If you do it this way, you might be happy." I did it. It wasn't conscious on my part. I was just sort of grasping at anything and I think that's where the surrender is for me. I can't give you a specific moment. I cannot. I thought of that in the writing I've done while I was in treatment, but I can't come up with a moment where I was—this was it—because it doesn't make sense. You know, in one way it does not make sense . . . it's just too simple . . . but part of me was so desperate that I kept saying "yes" to whatever was suggested. Therein is evidence of surrender, even though I cannot pinpoint a moment of it. [He laughs.] It won! I don't want to play another round with it! I don't want to. It's bigger than I am! I mean alcohol, drugs! *Life* is bigger than I am! I cannot beat life. In fact I didn't even come to a draw with it. It beat me because I'd been doing it wrong. I was behaving in ways . . . I was killing myself with the alcohol and I didn't know how to behave in any other way. I did not know how not to drink. It was just something that was impossible for me. I had tried to take life on my terms, and my terms didn't cut it.

There's a great deal of pain these days, and it's about death and dying. God knows what I would do without A.A. Quite honestly. I'm completely surrounded by death and dying. My friends are too. I know if I was still out drinking and drugging, I would stay completely anesthetized even more than I was previously. You know, I was reading the paper today. I read about some of my friends. They're dead of AIDS. The circle draws closer and closer. I found out recently that my ex-lover probably isn't well. He has shingles. Thirty-one years old. You don't get shingles when you're thirty-one. These things add up. I know I couldn't deal with it without being in A.A. I could not. First of all by being sober. I'm physically healthy myself. I'm not knocking my system all the time. I have to get the results of another blood work-up tomorrow. Being sober helps me stay well. It's all buying time. Something good will happen in AIDS treatment, but if you're sick now, it won't do you any good.

There's an incredible sense of despair. Last week I got a letter from my best friend who is living abroad. He's sick, had pneumonia. He has not seen me sober. He has been extremely excited, very happy and very proud for me, and my despair is that I don't know if I'll be able to see him while he's still healthy. I don't want to see him dead, I want to see him sober. I want him to know the joy that's in my life. I can think clearly about what his choices are. From here I found out the doctors over there who are familiar with his problem. I found treatment centers over there. It may only be helping *me* feel better, but I *can* do something. Last year I wouldn't have been able to. I would reach for another bottle.

Recently I went to a memorial service and saw people I hadn't seen in a while. When you're gay these days and you disappear for [the length of time I had been in treatment] the community just writes you off. You're dead! It's not an unreasonable thought. And people were remarking that I looked remarkably good in the middle of all this death around me. I had gained thirty-five pounds while I was in treatment. I'm sure I *looked* like death the last time they had seen me.

I think about that oneness. . . . There is a feeling of hope in the face of this disaster that we're living through. I know that if I was hanging out with people who weren't sober, the reaction would be complete misery and hopelessness and helplessness. The manifestation of behavior would be completely nihilistic. Let's sing and dance because tomorrow may never come. For so many people, tomorrow *isn't* coming, the death bells are tolling. That's a cliché, but. . . . I'm choosing not to live that way. [Long silence.] People in the [A.A.] rooms are also choosing that.

[Long silence.] It's amazing, the consistency with which other people in the rooms have been able to help other drunks through this. None of these people are dying alone. They're there, they're in the hospitals, they're helping setting up care. They're *there,* helping other drunks who are sick come to grips, work through, live through their death. I don't know any other way to put it. [Long silence.] I continue to choose not drinking and going to the meetings.

I've always been very annoyed that I have to die. My mortality is always something I've been very angry at. I hate the fact that I'm going to die.

Jean

There was one time I was actually considered technically dead. I was fifteen. I had always had problems with my lungs. I came from a real stoic family. I had a bronchial infection which ended up a full-blown case of pneumonia. I had passed out. My heart actually stopped. I was given an IV. My heart started again. I remember being out of my body. I remember watching the ambulance. . . . It was sort of an aerial view driving to the hospital. It may all sound very strange. I remember being up in the corner of the emergency room. I remember watching these people mess with my body, but I don't remember brilliant white lights or seeing other people or any of that. I remember watching my body as though I was outside of it. I know it will sound really strange. I remember it was sort of like watching a kind of TV show. I watched the heart monitor. When I saw it go back to normal, I knew I was alive. I thought, I guess I'm not dead. I didn't consciously say "Well, I guess I'll crawl back into my body." I saw the heart monitor. I wasn't drinking then. I didn't drink until I was 21.

One time after I had been in an outpatient program for my drinking, I didn't drink for several months. I didn't drink, I went to meetings, I went through a bunch of emotional crises. I had been fighting it and fighting it and fighting it. One night I just said "what the hell" and went out and bought vodka and started drinking it. I never drank vodka. My husband had been out of town. He came back into town the following afternoon and found me curled up in a ball in the back of a closet with my wrist slit. I had done this the night before. That is something that violated my prior spiritual code, my religious code, and also my ethical code. It was something so horrifying to me, and I do not remember doing it. It was a blackout. The fact that I could do something violent—violence just makes me sick. The fact that I could consider trying to kill myself, the fact that I couldn't remember and all of that were just all of the things I had said I had never done yet [as a result of my drinking].

Jennifer

My old life was so horrible that I couldn't go back there. That was suicide. So I was carried, I was carried to kind of like forge ahead. I felt like a sinking ship being thrown a life preserver and I really clung to the program. I didn't drink a day at a time. Slowly the process started happening. The rest is just the rest of my story. But that's divine intervention.

I used to tell my therapist there was a war raging inside of me. A war raging between living and not living. That war's ended. I'm not terrified of dying. I don't think dying is the end. It takes a lot of trust. I don't feel comfortable with violent death. If I was totally at peace with death, I wouldn't care.

When I was drinking, I thought the rest of the world was living and I was doomed to die. I was doomed to this life without happiness. I would always be on the outskirts watching life. I would watch mothers with their babies and I would watch couples and I would watch life happening. People laughing was a big one. I would just watch life and never be a participant because I was so miserable. Everything was opposite. Now in recovery, I feel joy, I feel love. I don't feel doom. It's completely changed. I felt miserable and different. Now I feel more connected. I think being a recovering alcoholic is a gift. I was looking at people in the bus tonight and I know that my face is happy. I have a happy face. People used to stop me in the street and ask me why I was so sad. I know that I don't have that same face any more. I feel joy. I was looking around at people on the bus and seeing misery and sadness on people. It's just times like that I feel so much gratitude. I feel so grateful that I was given this gift. Not everybody gets it. Not everybody has a gift. Maybe some just humdrum through life. This is it, you know. I make this life the best I can.

Roger

I would shoot coke and heroin. I would go into convulsions behind it. My heart would be going so fast. I would wake up forty minutes later and not know where the time went.

Carol

Ten years before I came into the program, I was in the middle of the woods. I had a partner. He was the man I supported financially most of the time. I considered him my best friend, the person I trusted, that kind of thing. I didn't treat him very nicely. He hated me by the end. Anyway, I was going through a lot. He brought over a shotgun. He told me to go shoot myself and just get it over with, and I did bring out that shotgun. I was just going to end it. The gun went off at my feet. Something *else* shot that gun. I walked back into the house.

I've walked out of totalled-car accidents. I've walked out of hospitals. They told me I have cancer. I'm fine. I've really felt in the presence of God during one of my car accidents, as well as during the gun incident. I was in the car and there was a truck in front of me. It was snowing. It was January and the roads were very icy. I was traveling back up to school and pulled to pass a truck and there was this car coming down on the wrong side of the thruway, right toward me. There's a truck on my right, and a car coming towards me. I didn't know what to do. I moved over. I guess the car pulled off to the side. It took off the entire front fender as if it was paper. I wasn't touched. I mean, I've watched my whole life rolling over as I rolled over in a car. There is actually no reason. . . . I shouldn't be alive. It happened a number of times. I took absolute chances.

Donald

You hear so often people say, I'm not afraid to die. My surface answer is "Yeah, I am and I'm not afraid to admit it." Then after that my faith pumps in and settles that down, you see. I don't know if I'm different. If you ask me, I'll say, "Yeah, I'm afraid. It's the unknown." Then I have this spiritual life which is building, and the more I build that, it diminishes that fear or equalizes it or balances it. To say that we're not afraid. . . . I can't speak for other people, but I hear that all the time. I always question it. I question if they're telling the truth. I don't think I am [when I say that I'm not afraid]. I don't think they're quite telling the truth because I think maybe they've never been confronted with death. I've been confronted with death three or four times, come very close to it. I cracked up in an airplane once. There was also a time when I went through the ice when I was a child. There have been several instances where I've had death right here. [He puts his hand on his chest.] It's pretty much like alcoholism. [He laughs.] You try and keep control as long as you can and then when you see the inevitable, you surrender! When I did surrender, well, then it's peaceful, quiet, peaceful. Somehow acceptable. When I flew into that hillside, it didn't seem like I had much of a chance of walking out of there. After it was over, it didn't have any particular effect. It still doesn't. It was one of those unpleasant experiences . . . sober. That happened just a few years ago. I recall sitting on the ground there and thanking God for getting me through it.

SECTION D
SELF AND NATURE

1.

Statements Illustrating the Nature of the Problem

For most, the desacralized world is doomed to become an obstacle inviting conquest, a mere object. Like the animal or the slave who is understood to have no soul, it becomes a thing of subhuman status to be worked, used up, exploited. . . . Today, when "realistic" people look at nature around them—mountains, forests, lakes, rivers—what is it they see? Not divine epiphanies, but cash values, investments, potential contributions to the GNP, great glowing heaps of money . . . [something] that only exists to be taken manfully in hand and made over into something human greed will find "valuable."[37]

Theodore Roszak

Behind the apparent kinship between animals, reptiles, birds, and human beings in the Indian way stands a great conception shared by a great majority of the tribes. Other living things are not regarded as insensitive species. Rather they are "peoples" in the same manner as the various tribes of men are people. . . . Equality is thus not simply a human attribute but a recognition of the creatureness of all creation. . . . The awareness of the meaning of life comes from observing how the various living things appear to mesh to provide a whole tapestry.[38]

Vine Deloria, Jr.

The earth is a living organism, the body of a higher individual who has a will and wants to be well, who is at times less healthy or more healthy, physically and mentally. People should treat their own bodies with respect. It's the same thing with the earth. Too many people don't know that when they harm the earth they harm themselves, nor do they realize that when they harm themselves they harm the earth. Some of these people interested in ecology want to protect the earth, and yet they will cram anything into their mouths. . . . .

It's not very easy for you people to understand these things because understanding is not knowing the kind of facts that your books and teachers talk about. I can tell you that understanding begins with love and respect. It begins with respect for the Great Spirit, and the Great Spirit is the life that is in all things—all the creatures and the plants and even the rocks and the minerals. All things—and I mean all things—have their own will and their own way and their own purpose; this is what is to be respected.

Such respect is not a feeling or an attitude only. It's a way of life. Such respect means that we never stop realizing and never neglect to carry out our obligation to ourselves and our environment.[39]

Rolling Thunder

2.
Stories Illustrating the Unity

Anyway, we went to get horehound plants up there near the old ranch. Rolling Thunder knew right where they were. He agreed to show me because he knew I needed horehounds. As soon as we got there Rolling Thunder made his prayer and his offering. Then I saw that the plants were absolutely covered with bees. I'm deathly afraid of bees; it frightens me just to look at them and they always sting me. So I just didn't know what to do. I was just ready to leave. Well, Rolling Thunder talked to me; he was so kind and gentle. He sensed what I was feeling, without my saying anything. He told me I was really not afraid of animals or any living thing. I only thought I was. And he reminded me how I had always loved animals and had taken care of them on a farm in my childhood.

He told me that the fear of any living thing is based on misunderstanding. He said, "Now, Alice, I want you to talk to those bees. I saw how you talked to the dogs just a little while ago. You talked to the babies and to the mother and you said the right things in the right way. If you can talk to dogs that way, you can talk to bees, and they will understand. They won't understand the English language, but they'll understand your meaning just as you say it."

So he told me what to say to the bees. I was supposed to ask the bees to share the plants with me, to tell them I wouldn't harm them, and to explain that I needed the plants for good medicine, but I would leave enough for the bees and for seeds for the coming year. He told me to say it loud and clear. He said he would be sitting behind me, and he wanted to be able to hear my voice. I did as he said, and, do you know, the bees actually understood me, and they moved! I just can't describe how I felt. All the bees on the plant I was looking at moved. They all moved together to the back of the plant. I took only the front half of the plant which they had left me, and then I moved to another plant covered with bees, and the same thing happened again! On one of the plants, when the bees moved back and I started to cut, they all made the strangest buzzing sound. It felt as though they were somehow speaking, telling me to stop, and I was understanding. I looked at Rolling Thunder and he said, "There now, you see? You and the bees have agreed to share and now you're cutting back too far. They'll expect you, now, to do as you said." So I cut only the front half very carefully. Then Rolling Thunder came up to me . . . .And he said that this was a gift of the Great Spirit![40]

Told in Rolling Thunder

". . . By Messer Sun, my brother above all,
Who by his rays lights us and lights the day—

". . . By Sister Moon and stars my Lord is praised,
Where clear and fair they in the heavens are raised.

"By Brother Wind . . . Thy praise is said,
By air and clouds and the blue sky o'verhead,
By which Thy creatures all are kept and fed.

"By one most humble, useful, precious, chaste,

By Sister Water . . . Thou art praised. . . .

". . . By Brother Fire—he who lights up the night
Jocund, robust is he, and strong and bright.

"Praised art thou . . . by Mother Earth—
Thou who . . . to her flowers, fruit, herbs, dost colour give and birth."[41]

*from The Canticle of the Sun
by Francis of Assisi*

167

3.
Illustrative Excerpts from Questionnaires and Interviews

God is or is in nature.
77% of those in treatment agreed.
86% of those in recovery agreed.

I can harm the earth without harming myself.
59% of those in treatment DISAGREED with this statement.
75% of those in recovery DISAGREED with this statement.

There has been a time when I experienced an overwhelming sense of unity or harmony
with the universe while free of alcohol and/or other drugs.
64% of those in treatment agreed with this.
77% of those in on-going recovery agreed.

I have felt a sense of communion with a flower or a tree.
30% of those in treatment agreed with this.
48% of those in on-going recovery argeed.

I have tried, at least for an instant, to put myself in the place of
a bird, or a cat or dog and tried to view the world with their eyes.
48% of those in treatment agreed with this.
48% of those in on-going recovery agreed.

I feel a sense of reverence, wonder or awe in the presence of nature.
54% of those in treatment responded with a "6" or "7," with 7 being "all the time."
64% of those in on-going recovery responded with a "6" or "7," with 7 being "all the time."

Bob

I view nature as closer and can relate to it easier than God.

Paul

You *can* harm the earth without harming yourself. I would hope I wouldn't do that, but I think
I can, I think I can. I'm capable of that. We can do simple ecological damage. If everybody
behaved in a certain way, *we* might not be affected by it, but in 150 years people will be. Part
of me believes that you're going to get back what you do, somewhere along the line.

Jane

I did a [camping] solo in the desert. I felt one with nature there. It was a three-day solo. I found
myself being real quiet. I lay under a palm tree. I just lay there. I got the idea of going to
Minnesota [to do a winter solo] while lying in the desert. In the sleeping bag at about dawn,
Why not go to Minnesota? popped into my head. I felt that to be a spiritual experience. Before
I didn't know where I wanted to go, what I wanted to do.

I had always wanted to go on an Outward Bound trip. To go climbing, back-packing. I really
enjoyed that. It was so neat to know I could be outdoors and it wasn't threatening. I could take
care of myself. They gave us tarp, an axe, a bag of macaroni. I cut fire wood and built a fire.
I set the tarp out. I guessed just right where it would go. It was so quiet and peaceful. I'd like

to do more. During that solo in Minnesota, I felt oneness. Everything was so still. I got to a point I got so quiet I could just watch the snow fall. I could have sat there for days. I felt a part of it, not separate from it, not trying to control. As a girl, my parents put me in a program at church where we would go out hiking in the woods. I felt at peace—it wasn't something you had to be frightened of. Like I belonged there. Camping during the winter was wonderful. They showed us how to dry clothes overnight. It's such a simple way to live.

Jean

[My experiences of being in the presence of God] mostly have to do with being aware of the natural sort of timeless moments in nature.

Jim

You ask me if I see God in nature. I first realized, really realized that Christ is within me, God is within me, when I was at Hazelden looking out at the lake. I am a contractor. I could see this lake out there and I could see the development [that could go on] around there—apartments or condominiums or town houses, you know. That's what I knew when I came up here—[development]. Three or four weeks later it dawned on me *that this is not a place of town houses or condos, this is a place of Christ out here. This is a work of nature. It was just like that! Boom! It just hit me in the head. Hey!* You don't want to build townhouses! This is a place you want to *be* at. This is a place you come to sit and relax and get in touch with yourself and get the answers. A lot of times I will reflect back to that exact thing that happened. Up here, it's a work of God. It did a lot for me. It just happened. Boom. It was just there. I can't tell you. I just looked out the window and I said, "That's nuts—you don't build townhouses here. You don't build apartment buildings here. This is a work of God out here." I can go away from here and I can say, yeah, this is a good piece of land, a good piece of land, but I can't up here. I reflect back. . . . You ask do I see God in nature? Here is where I see it probably more than anything else. I get out in the west hunting or I get out snowmobiling. I'm in heaven when I'm out west snowmobiling and I see the beauty of it. There is no reason I would destroy any of it. It's so serene and so quiet. You get out there in the mountains in a snowmobile, you turn it off and out there . . . pine trees, light fluffy snow. It's like heaven. Just perfect. God's all around, all around.

Carol

I have felt in the presence of a Higher Power mostly in nature. I always believed in nature. Always.

I just always would bring home animals. Bring them to school. Always liked them. I had a parakeet that only had one leg. I like little lame things. I always liked lame men, too, but anyway. . . . So the little parakeet would always do what I wanted it to do. There was a two-legged cat I had. I had this goose I just loved and it was shot in the head and one day I was coming home—I have a little place in the country—and the goose was right on the side of the road. Some kid had shot it through the head. It was still alive so I put it in the goose house with the other geese and ducks. It started to peck, so I brought it inside and put it in my bathtub. I cleaned up the bedroom and forgot about it. I thought it would be dead and here it was floating around in the bathtub having a grand time in the bathtub. The next morning it ate a little something out of my hand and you could see the hole straight through the goose's head. I took it to the vet and he said, "Well, there's no reason for it to be alive. I don't know what you're going to do with it. I can't do anything for it—it's got a hole in its head." [Laughter.] I took care of it for weeks and then I had to go away and my partner just kept the goose in the bathtub. It couldn't walk very well because its equilibrium was totally shot, but it could float, it could swim around in the bathtub. So it stayed alive for a few weeks when I went away. I came back and he said it died and he buried it, but we got along just fine, that goose and I. You just know those kinds of things. The goose used to follow me all around and the little cat did, too. My dog kind of protected me in the middle of my drinking. He was there right at the end. And I tell you, after he died three months later I was in my first meeting. Animals, you know, are kind of like angels, they have no choice. They just love you or they don't. That's all.

I was walking in this park in the city. There was a red-tailed hawk with an oak leaf in its mouth—it flies right over me, my dog and I. That's significant for me. The hawk was significant. He just flew over my head. They are very strong symbols—the hawk and the oak. Building its nest. It was as if I was living in, living through a dream. It could have been a dream—but it happened.

Up in the country I was very much in love with this person. He had a red-tailed hawk that kind of lived on his property and I was always happy to see it. It came to symbolize love and freedom. It just kind of awakened things when I saw them. A bird of prey, with a wonderful majesty about it. What's a hawk doing in this city?

Nature's the closest personification of the idea of God. Indians thought hawks were a good omen. Falcons are majestic birds. Communication can be established between you and them. Yes, I absolutely have felt like I could fly or put myself in the place of a bird or animal. I can remember standing in towers in large buildings and thinking that I could fly. Angels have always fascinated me. Lewis Carroll says " 'The time has come,' the Walrus said,'to talk of many things: Of shoes—and ships—and sealing wax—of cabbages—and kings—and why the sea is boiling hot—And whether pigs have wings.' "[42] I remember my first English class my teacher wrote "Why do pigs have wings?" on the board and said just write something, and I thought, I love this woman. Who could ask for more? Incorrigible as I was, she also was incorrigible— bringing coffee and Irish whiskey in a thermos.

Joyce

I have fought nature all my life. My husband is a nature lover and we have a cabin up north. He wanted to retire up there which I was deathly against. Therefore, I never gave into the beauties of nature because I thought if I give in, then my husband will think I'm ready to go up north. So all my life I have fought nature, and it has just been the last couple years that I have felt okay to say yeah, I really like some things. But I fought it for so long that I have a hard time getting real enthused about it and I work on fighting things.

Donald

In sobriety there has been a time when I felt totally absorbed with nature. Oh, yeah. I have a deep appreciation for God's creations. I walk through the woods a lot. Once every week or two, I go finding specimens of wood I'll turn into a walking stick. I'm aware of the connection between nature and myself.

SUMMARY: PRACTICING PEACE WITH THE WORLD AS A WHOLE

Inner and Outer

Respondents were able to cite specific examples of times of confluence between their inner and outer worlds. For the purpose of this study, movement toward healing of this separation are indicated by self-reports of an awareness of a connection between the inner state and outer circumstance. *Paul,* for example, noted the presence of A.A. meetings in his neighborhood when he was ready to attend. *Jane,* newly abstinent, spoke of finding a friend on the street corner when she had been unsuccessfully trying to reach her through other means in a time of crisis. *Roger,* who had described his world prior to recovery as hostile, gave evidence of believing in a friendlier universe with his example of a time in recovery when he was moving from one house to another and a man who had helped others in the A.A. program move just showed up. *Joyce* noted the coincidence between her asking to earn $20,000 a year and later finding her income was $20,184.

Past and Future

Respondents were able to give examples of times they were living in the present moment. For the purpose of this study, evidence of healing of the split between past and future is indicated by self-reports of living in the present moment as well as by experiences with "timeless time." A majority of respondents reported at least one experience of non-kronos time which was memorable to them in recovery. For example, *Jean* driving over the bridge in the fog; *Jane* while she was alone on a camping trip.

Life and Death

Respondents were able to give examples of times they experienced the confluence of life and death. A number of respondents reported encounters with physical death (e.g., *Jean* when she was a teenager, and then again after a suicide attempt; *Carol* with her gun incident and car accidents; *Donald* with his plane accident). Two (*Carol* and *Jean*) reported knowledge of the deaths of those they knew through dreams in childhood or young adulthood. *Paul* seems particularly sensitive to the pain of those dying with AIDS and is grateful that alcoholics with AIDS are at least not dying alone. He says he is grateful too that he is able to be one of those available to support the dying. While once, he says, "I used to wonder why the hell I was alive," he is now taking his place in a community of survivors—some of whom are dying of still another disease.

Self and Nature

Respondents were able to give examples of times when they had felt a communion with nature. *Jane,* for example, gave instances of when she had been alone in the desert or in the winter of Minnesota. She associates trying not to control with a feeling of belonging in the universe. *Jim* said his life-changing spiritual experience was a transformed way of relating with nature. He is a contractor and always before had seen nature as something to be converted into cash profits, and became aware for the first time of nature as a place of God. *Joyce* said she was uncomfortable with nature most her life, but says she no longer wants to fight it.

Chapter Five

A Pattern of Recovery from Alcoholism

Summaries and Conclusions

This has been a study of some of the spiritual ideas, practices, and experiences of certain individuals who are recovering from alcoholism with the help of the program of Alcoholics Anonymous. It has been an exploration of their ways of being and seeing, an exploration of what William James describes as conversion—the religious reunifying of a discordant personality.

In chapter 1, I described an imbalance toward dualism over unity which may occur within alcoholics and in the mainstream of American society. My description of the problem of separation in society and culture relied primarily on my interpretation of the findings of Bellah, Madsen, Sullivan, Swidler, and Tipton. For the description of the problem of separation in the lives of alcoholics, I offered ideas from psychiatrist and A.A. advocate Harry Tiebout. I included a poem that spoke of an overt imbalance toward separation over unity as it may exist *in extremis* in contemporary mainstream American society and culture. I also included a poem that spoke of separation, the associated imbalance, and longing for reconciliation in the voice of an alcoholic. Key terms such as "the way of the two" and "the way of the one" were clarified.[1] In chapter 2 there was a synopsis of the main ideas of other scholars writing on addiction in general and Alcoholics Anonymous in particular, selected on the basis of their relevance to this study and reviewed in that context, along with a brief description of how this entire story was gathered.

In chapter 3, evidence was presented to indicate that Alcoholics Anonymous serves as a revitalization movement congruent with the universal pattern described by Anthony Wallace. Chapter 4, which consisted of four main parts, presented some of the ideas and experiences of people practicing the principles and program of Alcoholics Anonymous. The stories were told by alcohol addicts with varying periods of abstinence from mood-changing chemicals who during the initial phase of the research were either (1) residents of Hazelden Foundation's Residential Treatment program for adults, or (2) guests at Hazelden's Renewal Center.[2] I offered evidence to indicate that the twelve individuals who were involved in the second and primary phase of the research (i.e., the case studies or interviews) were finding increased balance and connections in their relationships between one aspect of themselves and another, themselves and a Higher Power, themselves and others, and themselves and the world as a whole.

In this chapter, I will first summarize the responses to the primary questions asked in this thesis, and then draw some conclusions and advance some ideas about possible implications. Both conclusions and ideas are based on prior direct experience and ideas, research in alcoholism and other fields, the literature and legacy of Alcoholics Anonymous, the case study portion of this project, and responses to the primarily quantifiable questionnaire designed for this study.

The questions considered were these: What evidence is there to indicate that Alcoholics Anonymous on an organic or organizational level serves as a revitalization movement as defined by Anthony Wallace, helping members create a more satisfying culture or way of life? What evidence is there to suggest that the alcoholics in recovery with Alcoholics Anonymous involved in this study experience a transition from a relatively discordant, dualistic way of being in the world to a more harmonious, unified one?

Part I
Question One: Summary and Conclusions

1.
Summary

In chapter 3, evidence was presented to indicate Alcoholics Anonymous is a deliberate, organized effort by members of a society to create a more satisfying culture or way of life. A.A. began, as do most revitalizations studied by Wallace, with a transformative dream or vision. A.A. performs all the tasks of revitalization, including mazeway reformulation, communication, organization, adaptation, cultural transformation, and routinization. The principles, program, and people of A.A. provide a context for a way of life that equally honors power and powerlessness, body and mind, self and community, self and Higher Power, past and future, and life and death, providing members with a program and a set of principles that allow them to balance in the center between often opposed pairs.

2.
Conclusion

Meeting the above cited criteria, Alcoholics Anonymous may be considered a revitalization movement in accordance with the pattern described by Wallace. Although there are significant differences between the movements he describes in the 1956 *American Anthropologist* article and the birth and growth of Alcoholics Anonymous,[3] the A.A. movement does appear to fall well within the relatively permeable parameters of revitalization movements he identifies. I have chosen to consider A.A. as one variation of this theme for a number of reasons: It provides a common language with which to acknowledge and share ideas about this phenomenon; it provides a larger cultural context within which the contributions of Alcoholics Anonymous and similar movements may be appreciated; and it may stimulate the sharing of ideas about similar patterns within individuals, the community as a whole, and in other fields of study.

Revitalization movements in general and A.A. in particular help its followers insofar as the movements acknowledge, provide permission for, and cultivate an appreciation of the powerlessness of separate selves. In so doing, they legitimize the way of receptivity and validate the individual's need to connect with a power source greater than the separate self. This source may be conceived of in anyone of an infinite variety of ways—as the group, the greater good of society, the Creative Intelligence of the Universe, Divine Providence, an untapped inner resource which transcends the finite personality, and so on.[4]

The context and community offered by A.A. support a way of life which values the intangible, inexplicable, uncontrollable. Bill Wilson describes this way and the condition of entry. He says, "We [alcoholics] have to find a life in the world of grace and spirit, and this is certainly a new dimension for most of us. Surprisingly, our quest for this realm of being is not too difficult. Our conscious entry into it usually begins as soon as we have deeply confessed our personal powerlessness to go on alone, and have made our appeal to whatever God we think there is—or may be. The gift of faith and the consciousness of a higher power is the outcome."[5]

PART II
QUESTION TWO: SUMMARY AND CONCLUSIONS

1.
Summary

In chapter 4 evidence was presented to indicate that the recovering alcoholics involved in this study are experiencing a more harmonious, unified way of being in the world in sobriety than they did while drinking. As a group, they report experiences of greater balance and/or confluence where before there was conflict between at least one of the following pairs: active ways and receptive ways of being in the world, and the associated male and female aspects of themselves; themselves and a Higher Power; themselves and others; inner worlds and outer worlds; past and future; life and death; themselves and nature. I clustered these pairs somewhat arbitrarily into four primary pairs: one aspect of the self and another, the self and God or Higher Power, the self and other, and the self and the world as a whole.

All of the twelve interviewed have known and were able to tell of at least one time when boundaries dissolved, decreasing the distance between their separate selves and at least one of the following: an aspect of themselves formerly discounted or denied; God or Higher Power; other people; and the world as a whole. All twelve were able to give one or more specific example(s) of instant(s) when they felt in communion with God as they understand God (e.g., Donald with his experiences of light in his living room and in Boston, Jane with her experiences of light and warmth and waves); communion with other people (e.g., Paul and his strong bonding with those in meeting rooms, as well as with those dying of AIDS, Jennifer with her feeling of love for everyone in the A.A. meeting rooms); and communion with nature (e.g., Jim and his experience of the land surrounding Hazelden as a place of God rather than as a potential site for condominiums, Jane during her Outward Bound adventure, John while bicycling through the countryside). Many also gave specific examples of times of communion between their inner states and outer circumstances. The most frequently reported experiences of communion between inner states and outer circumstances were experiences in recovery of what are variously called "meaningful coincidences," "synchronicity," "serendipity," or less commonly and more aptly "confluence." Roger, Jane, Jean and Carol were among those able to give many examples of these. Others said they experienced such coincidences frequently as well, but were to recall only a few specific examples at the time of our interview.

Some of the reported experiences of communion occurred prior to the period of active addiction (e.g., Paul's being in the right place at the right time prior to active addiction, Jean's dreams of deaths which mirrored actual deaths, Carol's similar dream experience with the death of her grandmother). Some moments of communion were experienced during the period of addiction under the direct or rebound influence of alcohol and/or other drugs (e.g., Roger's report of seeing auras under the influence of LSD). Most of those reported, however, were experienced in recovery. Of the latter, some experiences occurred initially in a receptive, solitary state (e.g., Donald's two experiences, John's experience on the lake, and Carol's experience while on retreat), others were experiences in ongoing recovery (e.g., Jennifer's feeling of love and communion while holding hands in a circle after an A.A. meeting). The relevance of these findings will be explored later in this chapter.

There is additional support for the idea that there is a general change from a sense of alienation and discord in the direction of harmony in the comparison of frequencies of response between those in treatment just beginning abstinence (not all for the first time) and those in the Renewal Center who reported longer cumulative and consecutive daily abstinence. For example, in terms of the relationship between one aspect of the self and another, 43 percent of those in treatment agreed with the statement "Strength comes out of weakness" while 73 percent of those in the Renewal Center agreed.[6] In terms of the relationship between self and a Higher Power, 66 percent of those in treatment agreed with the statement "There has been at least one time when I have felt in the presence of God," while 82 percent of those in the Renewal Center agreed with this statement. In terms of the relationship between the individual self and other, 59 percent of those in treatment agreed with the statement "I cannot harm someone else without harming myself," while 84 percent of those in the Renewal Center agreed with that statement. In terms of the relationship between the individual self and the world, 59 percent of those in treatment disagreed with the statement "I can harm the Earth without harming myself," while 75 percent of those in the Renewal Center disagreed; 43 percent of those in treatment said they are increasingly aware of meaningful coincidences, while 77 percent in Renewal agreed.

2.
Conclusions

CONCLUSION AS TO PRACTICING PEACE WITH THEMSELVES

Recovery involves a healing of splits within the self. During active addiction those splits include the separation of active from receptive ways of being in the world and subsequent swinging between the two.[7] This condition of conflict gives way in recovery to acknowledgment of both halves of what Emerson calls a "bipolar Unity."[8] Recovery from alcoholism for those relying on the program and society of Alcoholics Anonymous involves a shift to a greater appreciation for and attention to listening and receptivity than was experienced during active alcoholism, thus balancing the previous weightedness in the direction of activity and control such as Tiebout described in his alcoholic patients.

As to the stories of the twelve, each spoke of the importance of listening and being receptive in their recovery. Most respondents explicitly associate this change with the program and society of A.A. John said "I feel recovery was given to me. It's all a gift." Jane commented, "A lot has happened without me trying to make it happen." The responses of those interviewed indicate that preceding each experience of communion or confluence is a surrender, an experience of powerlessness, a willingness to ask for and receive help—regardless of whether that communion was initially with God as they understand God, with others, or with nature. This was the case for John as he finally gave up trying to run from friends who were there to help him; for Donald who felt that right before his first spiritual experience he had likely hit a plateau when struggle had momentarily ceased and he had "gotten out of the way" and then again in Boston for his second and more profound experience when he reports having "let go"; for Jim when he decided to take time out for a retreat and realized that nature is a place of God. For those initiatory experiences of unity, each entailed reports of frustration, then apathy or exhaustion followed by relief and release. The perennial nature of these elements in the conversion process are identified by William James quoting Carlyle's Teufelsdröckh, who says one "passes from the everlasting No to the everlasting Yes through a 'Center of Indifference.' "[9]

If nothing else, the increased valuing of receptivity is both the cause and effect of expansion beyond the limits of separates selves, no insignificant change for alcoholics described in A.A. literature as self-centered in the extreme. This connectedness with a greater power provides some detachment from the finite personality and provides a concomitant sense of safety. The increased valuing of receptivity is commonsensibly associated with increased acceptance of the self *as is,* which allows for admission of both personal assets and shortcomings. This in turn reduces the tendency to project unwanted traits onto others, and likewise reduces the tendency to find desirable attributes within others which are felt lacking within. All of this in turn decreases the attachment to a world out there which when active makes for bondage through attraction or bondage through aversion, both of which are associated with unequal relationships. An example of this increasing acceptance of "good" and "bad" aspects of the self may be found in Paul's "I'd always expect fifteen out of twenty of them, but then I'd expect twenty out of ten from myself. . . . I'm not as dreadfully hard on myself as I used to be."

Since in the case of many alcoholics, emotions rather than intellect are considered unacceptable and the body (rather than the mind)[10] is considered unacceptable, a greater self-acceptance means greater valuing of emotions and body.

In recovery there is implicitly at least some reconciliation as well between the mind and the body as the toxic substance, alcohol, is jettisoned. Even an initial phase of reconciliation between body and mind which begins with abstinence from alcohol has a ripple effect and functions at least as one individual's contribution to cleansing our environent.[11]

CONCLUSION AS TO SELF AND GOD OR HIGHER POWER

With a balancing of these two basic ways of being in the world—active-dualistic-scientific and receptive-unified-spiritual—comes a greater place for grace. As Starbuck finds, "Faith comes in [when] . . . the soul is in a receptive attitude, [when] it is left open, so that the new currents of mental activity may flow together into one great stream."[12]

What is remarkable here is that the will of separate selves is less and less opposed (intentionally at least) to the will of God or Higher Power. The recovering alcoholic knows clearly that his or her own willpower was totally ineffective when it came to the use of or abstinence from alcohol. The recovering alcoholic knows just as clearly exactly the condition in which self-will landed him or her. Recovering alcoholics are open to another way, and are promised that once their life is turned over to the care of a Higher Power, they will experience a new dimension of life. The prayers of A.A. are prayers in which the will of the individual is aligned with the will of God or Higher Power. For example, it is suggested on page 63 of the book *Alcoholics Anonymous* that as part of the Third Step of Alcoholics Anonymous, the individual say something like this: "God, I offer myself to Thee—to build with me and do with me as Thou wilt. Relieve me of the bondage of self, that I may better do Thy will. Take away my difficulties, that victory over them may bear witness to those I would help of Thy Power, Thy Love, and Thy Way of life. May I do Thy will always!" And what is known as the Seventh Step prayer in Alcoholics Anonymous asks that shortcomings be removed so that the individual may be of greater service to God and others. With prayers such as these, the seesawing between a desire for the will of one's separate self and a desire for the will of God diminishes. Free flow of energy is restored as it inheres from a power source greater than the finite self. It seems to inhere most fully when the two wills, human and divine, are aligned.

It is suggested here that at least the initial conscious contact with the transcendent may occur through different agencies, singly or in combination. For some individuals it may be through nature, for some through an awareness of the higher (and/or deeper) self, for some through their relationship with others.[13] The contact serves as an affirmation that there is an order to the universe, exquisite if inexplicable. It makes possible further trust on a higher,deeper, greater power and less reliance on the will of separate selves.

CONCLUSION AS TO PRACTICING PEACE WITH OTHERS

It is the collective experience of these alcoholics that they do not link through mastery and inequality. None of the experiences of communion occurred during successful attempts at controlling another person, place, or situation. As Kurtz emphasizes, we cannot link as closed systems, gods unto ourselves. We bond in pain, bond in what Kurtz calls the dynamic of the *"shared honesty of mutual vulnerability openly acknowledged."*[14] Both the willingness to be vulnerable and the ability to relate to others as equals are facilitated by the tools of Alcoholics Anonymous, including anonymity, emphasis upon identification with—rather than comparison with—others, taking personal inventory, asking that defects of character be removed, making amends, and so on. Once an individual comes to know powerlessness, that person knows that even if she or he didn't actually commit a particular harmful act, she or he *could* have done anything. In this position, it is harder to judge others and thereby distance oneself from them. Recovery depends to a large degree on the individual's willingness and ability to sense his or her connection with others—to gain, often for the first time, a true sense of community and shared interests. Members hear and find through experience with A.A. that "we can do together what we can't do in separation."[15]

The previously perceived dichotomy of self-interest versus interest in others begins to be resolved. Rather than the "therapeutic contractualism" described by Bellah as characteristic of contemporary American culture mentioned in chapter 1, the relationship between one A.A. member and another is contingent on freedom and awareness of absolute equality. A contractual relationship is bound by offer and acceptance; that is, "I'll do this for you if you do that for me, but if you don't, I won't either." In Alcoholics Anonymous there is an offer that may or may not be accepted. The offer stands regardless of outcome, the benefit is received regardless of outcome. The A.A. member is responsible for simply "sowing the seed," a phrase frequently heard in meeting rooms. This frees relationships from what Meister Eckhart refers to as a "merchant mentality,"[16] in which you give to get from an objectified reality. In A.A., the giving and receiving are one and the same. The A.A. member is not dependent on any one person or outcome for fulfillment of his or her offer and thus is unbound by exclusive relationships.

In another context, John S. Dunne wrote that when someone "is free to leave the message without expectation of repayment," the interaction does not contain the "element of desire and demand which would leave him unfree. His state is not one of mere autonomy and unrelatedness, for he has touched their minds and their hearts. It is a state of freedom and relatedness, it is a state in which freedom and relatedness can go together."[17] This describes well the nature of relationships between alcoholics in recovery with Alcoholics Anonymous.

One of the most common critiques of A.A. is that members become dependent on A.A. itself, thereby substituting one dependency for another. I believe that there is only a dependency when there is other, and the people who make up A.A. are not other; rather they are truly "members of the same body," to use John Winthrop's phrase.[18] *They experience interdependence,* as one organ of the body relies on another. Lois Wilson's remark that "it was not a question of getting on with Bob and Anne, they were a part of you" illustrates this idea well. Another example of this sense of unity can be found in Paul's remark that he feels *empathy* rather than sympathy for those in Alcoholics Anonymous meeting rooms. Respondents without exception expressed a heightened awareness of their interdependence with others. Roger, for example, knew he needed the context of community to be able to integrate the gifts he had received and to fulfill his responsibility to pass them on to others. The manner of relationship learned in Alcoholics Anonymous is applied to relationships with the larger community as well, as evidenced, for example, in Donald's story of his visit to the Dakotas.

As members increasingly give up attempts to alternately dominate or depend and to control or feel controlled, as they increasingly find themselves in others and others in themselves (e.g., Joyce's experience with the biker in her A.A. group), relationships are equalized, and in appreciation of that equality is peace.

CONCLUSION AS TO PRACTICING PEACE WITH THE WORLD AS A WHOLE

In recovery, the individuals interviewed for this study report experiencing greater harmony between themselves and the world as a whole. This is indicated in part by increased reliance on and valuing of intuition joining heart and head. Comfortability with paradox, attention to and experience with synchronicity or confluence, a time orientation increasingly in the present, increased experience of an immanent God or a Higher Power with God found in nature, in others, in ordinary events, and often, finally, in themselves are some other indications of greater harmony.

SELF AND NATURE

As to reconciliation between the individual and nature, this can be appreciated most clearly in the case of Jim, who once viewed the land as a potential building site, a place to master and turn into monetary profit, and who came to view the land as a place of God. The decreased distance in one pair may well decrease the distance in others as well. Joyce, who says she is now more accepting of nature, is now also more accepting of her body and is taking steps to correct what she considers her overeating. She is also considering for the first time a feminine aspect of God and says she is coming to trust more in receptivity. Three of those who expressed a great appreciation for nature were also among those most comfortable with receptivity (Jane, Carol, and Jean).

PAST AND FUTURE

There is evidence as well of healing of the split that alcoholics experience in time between past and future (except for "absent present" moments in drug-influenced periods), with respondents indicating that they value and are making some progress toward living in the present moment (e.g., Donald's communion in the woods and getting back into the rhythm of nature).

As respondents begin to reconcile the past and future, and value living in the present, one day at a time, their future is freed of outcome expectations and so, according to Gerald May, is available for the influx of grace. Also, living in the present, which embraces both past and future, they are more respectful of both children and elders (e.g., Jennifer's greater attention to the needs of her mother) and now see the need to act in a manner responsible to both future and former generations.

LIFE AND DEATH

As to reconciliation of life and death, if Ken Wilbur and Ernest Becker among others are correct in believing we seek substitutes for our own death, then dealing with death would naturally reduce the level of aggressiveness in relationships with others. There is evidence as well to suggest that individuals in recovery come to make at least an ideological peace with death (e.g., despite Paul's attitude of defiance of death, he is actively involved with those dying of AIDS; Donald's statement that while initially he says he is afraid of death, his more considered answer would be that he has made some peace with death as a result of practicing the A.A. program).

INNER AND OUTER

It is experiences of confluence between inner and outer worlds that I find most interesting. This is also the area in which there is a great difference between responses of the group new in recovery and the responses of those who have enjoyed a longer period of daily abstinence. Each of the instances reported here also involved receptive states. What I find significant is that (1) the instances of synchronicity or confluence were meaningful to the person reporting them, however commonplace they may sound to an "objective" listener, (2) the instances could not possibly have been manipulated by the separate self and are outside the realm of cause-and-effect as we ordinarily understand it, (3) they are instances when the time dimension is absolutely synchronous with the dimension of space, and the issue of control or causation by a separate self is immaterial. I believe it is no coincidence that awareness of these occurrences seem more frequent by those who at least ask to do the will of God as they understand God. These occurrences may well be related to decreased attachment, which occurs first through letting go of attachment to alcohol, then by letting go of other attachments as well. It is accompanied by increased attention to process rather than outcome (e.g., Jennifer's experience with the planning of her wedding). This orientation toward process rather than outcome became possible with increased trust found through reliance on a Higher Power when all other remedies had been tried and found wanting. This reliance on the universe is not possible as long as the individual retains attempts at mastery of an objectified universe. Roger is an example of this as he identifies an extreme rebound state which invariably accompanies attempts at mastery. He says that during his active addiction and attachment to control, he used to feel strongly that "the world was hostile, it was attacking me." Letting go of attempts to arrange situations to suit the finite desires of separate selves brings peace.

The phenomenon Carl Jung believes allows for occurrences of synchronicity is remarkably like the phenomenon Tiebout believes is a condition for recovery from alcoholism. In treating the subject of how such events as synchronicity come to pass, Ira Progoff says, "Jung makes use of a deceptively simple psychological conception that he derives from Pierre Janet and refers to as the partial *abaissement du niveau mental*, a partial 'lowering of the mental level.' " As the mental level is partially lowered on one side, there is a heightening on the other. As Jung put it, "Owing to the restriction of consciousness produced by the affect so long as it lasts, there is a corresponding lowering of orientation which in its turn gives the unconscious a favorable opportunity to slip into the space vacated."[19] Tiebout describes this same process in terms of surrender in exhaustion. Respondents to this study have indicated considerable familiarity with such a process.

In *The Language of the Heart*, Bill Wilson uses the term "Providence" or "Divine Providence" in place of the name God or phrase Higher Power at least nine times. The providential nature of God becomes increasingly evident through meaningful coincidences for those who freely want to do the will of God as they understand God. That means a willingness to let go of outcome expectations and cause and effect. It means learning to trust the mystery, the unpredictable. Progoff feels that synchronistic events that occur in such situations "hold an important clue to those 'miraculous' occurrences that become the basis for religious traditions and mythologies."[20] If, as May believes, addiction is a condition of normality, recovery from one or more addictions implies a willingness to allow for unforeseen events. Progoff notes that "the unpremeditatedness of spontaneity is one of the distinguishing characteristics of synchronistic events."[21] An often-repeated slogan in A.A. which seems to characterize those respondents who are most in touch with connections between inner and outer is this: Don't leave five minutes before the miracle. Another phrase, used by two of the respondents here and heard frequently in Alcoholics Anonymous, is that "coincidences are God's way of remaining anonymous."

Eliade suggests that modern societies live in a de-sacralized cosmos.[22] If this is true then the reports of these recovering alcoholics when considered in conjunction with others likely sharing similar experiences may indicate a significant cultural change. If the reports of the respondents to this study are representative of experiences in recovery, it may well be that recovering alcoholics believe with William Blake that "God lives in the details."

CONCLUSION: QUESTION 2 AS A WHOLE

A state of imbalance with an associated sense of separation is the starting point of recovery. Roger, for example, says "I am a creature of imbalance. That is my problem." Jennifer says "Before, my whole life was imbalanced. The greatest imbalance was in the area of self-centeredness and control. I've made a little progress. A.A. helps with everything." Joyce says she still doesn't lead a balanced life, but it's gotten better. Donald says one of the most important things in recovery is to lead a balanced life.

Such imbalance and associated separation is characteristic of an active-dualistic way of relating to the world. This state of separation, which is the result of a dualistic way in *the absence of attention to, acknowledgement of, and appreciation for the underlying unity,* is inherently an imbalanced state due at least in part to dependencies upon attraction or aversion and the related power struggles.

Balance is found with the help of the program and society of A.A. with its emphasis on the receptive-spiritual mode in which at least initiatory experiences of communion occur. The great variety of means by which the program helps members balance previously opposed pairs have been detailed in the body of this study in the chapter devoted specifically to A.A. Additional examples have been given in the diagrams which precede each "Practicing Peace" section.

Recovery from alcoholism involves finding whole what was previously believed to be divided. The fundamental division is between the way of the two and the way of the one. The problem is the inability to hold *both* the way and the view of the two and the way and experience of the one. The division derives from splits in awareness, with one half of a pair resisted or dismissed, resulting in imbalance in the pairs of opposites and inevitable rebound states. The experience of these splits is characteristic of an active-dualistic-scientific way of knowing the world. The healing occurs with an admission of inability to control at least one major area of life and subsequent willingness, however reluctant, to try another way. The experience of wholeness is synonymous with a receptive-unitive-spiritual way. Implicit in the active way is control; implicit in the spiritual way is letting go. The first holds a judgmental stance—i.e., things are not as they ought to be; the second is characterized by an accepting stance—everything is fine as is.[23]

The distance between one part of the whole and another is decreased through an admission of the personal powerlessness of the finite ego self as the individual, however begrudgingly, admits the need for help from a greater power. The distance is decreased with an increased willingness to be receptive and ask for and act on guidance. The distance is decreased as God or a power greater than the finite self is seen by many to have fewer and fewer boundaries—is known as not exclusively male, not exclusively above, not exclusively in one place or another, not exclusively a repository for special favors. The distance is decreased as recovering alcoholics come to find themselves in others and others in themselves, and to appreciate others as equals.

With equality comes a decrease in distance, a collapse of time and cause and effect. So acceptance of equality is related to decreased distance which is related to awareness of unity which is related to decreased distance. It is in the shifting from a "scientific" way to the way of spirit and reconciliation between them that splits in space and time and power-cause dissolve. Bill Wilson's declaration in A.A.'s Big Book that "most of us feel we need look no further for Utopia. We have it with us right here and now" hints that the shift is epistemological rather than ontological.

In recovery, two ways of knowing and experiencing the world may be held simultaneously. One of the staple prayers of A.A., now known as the Serenity Prayer, specifically addresses itself to the balancing between the active and the receptive ways. It is only in the balancing of active with receptive that splits are healed: receptivity opens us up to the larger whole. As Meister Eckhart, a fourteenth-century mystic, notes,[24] there can be no true relationship without equality. With equality comes decreased distance, with decreased distance, equality. There can be no true relationship with others as long as there are attempts to dominate or depend, with rebounds between one and the other; no true relationship with a power greater than the finite self as long as this Higher Power is exclusively distant and detached and there is a background battle between God's will and one's own; no true relationship with the animal, bird, reptile, insect, vegetable, or mineral kingdoms as long as attempts at mastery by separate selves are retained; no relationship with the "outer world" as long the outer world is perceived of as alien from and hostile to the self, an object which exists to control or be controlled.

Recovery involves reconciliation of these previously opposed pairs—acceptable self and unacceptable self; self and Higher Power, self and others, self and the world as a whole.

Each of the stories told by the twelve, to one degree or another, like the accounts in *The Varieties of Religious Experience* by William James, allows for "the divided self and the struggle; they involve the change of personal centre and the surrender of the lower self" and a subsequent experience of communion. While admittedly these reports of confluence may be no more than what James describes as a "subjective way of feeling things, a mood of . . . fancy, in spite of the effects produced,"[25] they are nonetheless of "enormous biological worth. Spiritual strength really increases in the subject when he has them, a new life opens for him, and they seem to him a place of conflux where the forces of two universes meet."[26]

Harry Tiebout believed that the changes which take place in the conversion process

> *may be summed up by saying that the person who has achieved the positive frame of mind has lost his tense, aggressive, demanding, conscience-ridden self which feels isolated and at odds with the world, and has become, instead, a relaxed, natural, more realistic individual who can dwell in the world on a 'live and let live' basis.*[27]

Tiebout says that he knows that a positive phase comes after surrender, but he does not know "just why" it comes. "Surrender," he says, "means cessation of fight and cessation of fight seems logically to be followed by internal peace and quiet." But "why the whole feeling tone switches from negative to positive, with all the concomitant changes, is not clear." He adds that "despite my inability to explain the phenomenon, there is no question that the change does take place and that it may be initiated by an act of surrender."[28] Sandra Schnall wonders along similar lines. She feels that what is lacking in the various explanations of how participating in A.A. effects change "is a theoretical framework pertaining to what change is, how it occurs, and what types of change the alcoholic needs to make."[29]

I find that the switch Tiebout refers to from a relatively combative relationship with the world to one of relative peace and quiet as well as the change which Schnall wonders about occur in recovery as a result of a glimpse of the unity, no matter how brief or in what form. It may occur initially through any agency, such as other people, nature, or an experience of light or sound. In any case, the individual has experienced some connection which before was overtly absent, now made possible through receptivity in the form of surrender, as letting go, or as a state of being. Tiebout equates the act of surrender with an admission of the need for help. This act in itself, if done truly, is a step in the breaking down of the wall erected to keep himself or herself in, thus protecting others, or to keep others out, thus protecting himself or herself. Ongoing glimpses of the wholeness may occur with increased frequency in the form of confluence or meaningful coincidences— events which reveal the exquisite pattern of connections between ourselves and other beings and events in the world. These experiences provide evidence of the matrix of unity which manifests as diversity. What causes *that* is another matter for which I have no explanation at all.[30]

When attempts at mastery are surrendered, recovering alcoholics find that "God is doing for [them] what [they] could not do for themselves." Awareness that this is the case frequently comes in the form of meaningful coincidences which could not possibly have been planned by the finite self and self-will contemptuous of the greater peace. With less and less defiance of and opposition to the will of God, there is a flow. In the absence of control, energy inheres. Intuition, which the Big Book of Alcoholics Anonymous promises will become an increasing part of the mind, is the partner of synchronicity or confluence. It is the link between inner and outer worlds. In a state of being of practicing peace with the self, practicing peace with God, practicing peace with others, and practicing peace with the world as a whole there is increasingly lack of what Chinese philosopher Mo Dsi refers to as "doubleness."[31] This is a new realm for most active alcoholics.

If time and space and power-cause are the fundamental categories of any culture, and alcohol addicts experience in more extreme form and similar pattern the bifurcations and imbalances of their cultural environment, then a consideration of their ideas about and experiences with time and space and causation may well offer a fertile field for further inquiry.

Gerald May confesses that he had hoped to understand the cause of "unitive experiences" in order to *make* them happen. He concludes that this is not possible. I confess to a similar wish, and similarly acknowledge that such moments and such a way of life are not subject to willful manipulation. I do feel that it is possible to *cultivate conditions conducive to the influx of grace.* May and others discuss this as well. That is the considerable contribution of the principles and program and people of Alcoholics Anonymous. I believe that these same principles are at the core of and may be found in a great many of the major religious, spiritual, and philosophical systems in the world.

PART III
OTHER DISCOVERIES

I had expected to hear about experiences of unity in recovery from alcoholism associated with surrender, letting go, and receptive states which follow. It didn't occur to me that the folks I talked with would tell of other unitive experiences prior to alcohol addiction and recovery as well. As I listened, I became intrigued and was quite unwilling to ask them to confine their responses to experiences in recovery. Carol was one of those with vivid recollections of a time in childhood when she felt outer and inner were one (e.g., the card memory she described, and her extrasensory knowledge of the death of her grandmother). So too with Jean and her dreams of the deaths of relatives or acquaintances and her reports of locating missing entities with images in her mind. Aside from accounts by Carol and Jean of particular instants of unity, some spoke of an ongoing sensitivity to the underlying unity and reported a history of finding wholeness where others found pieces. You may recall Donald's declaration that he was always able to "see the whole where others saw parts." Then too, there is Paul's report that even in the past he was open to "a life full of opportunities and events."

These reports, along with other ideas and experiences, lead me to believe that many alcoholics, among others, are sensitive to the whole[32] and lack a cultural context which validates such beliefs and experiences.[33] Jean, for example, said her family responded with disbelief when she told them about her knowledge of the death of her grandfather.

For many alcoholics, any experiences of unity that do occur in states of intoxication result in sober re-bound states characterized by a sense of separation and loneliness even deeper than the initial state.[34] Without a drug-free context to help make sense of and validate and integrate experiences of unity in his or her daily life, the individual may have difficulty integrating experiences of communion and knowledge received in receptive states. Integrating this inner knowledge and experience and passing it on are mutually self-sustaining. Without a context, it may be exceedingly difficult to hold both the intuitive appreciation for the way of the one and the way of the two. In recovery from alcoholism with Alcoholics Anonymous, free flow may occur between one and the other with the help of balancing prayers such as the Prayer of St. Francis included in one of A.A.'s basic texts and the Serenity Prayer attributed to Reinhold Niebuhr, along with a host of other instruments.

Julian Jaynes emphasized the importance of validation of experience in his book, *The Origin of Consciousness in the Breakdown of the Bicameral Mind*, and during a symposium in Canada. It was likewise something he pointedly made reference to in our conversations. He says, for example, that the bicameral mind, which he believes was characterized by auditory hallucinations, is innate but not inevitable. He says that 'it means [there is] an inborn potentiality that can be made actual in a particular environment." He says that "a child from bicameral times brought up in our culture would be normally conscious, while a modern child if brought up in the Ur of 3000 B.C. under the sovereignty of Marduk in his *giginu* in the great ziggurat would be bicameral."[35]

All this leads me to conclude that one of the greatest contributions A.A. makes to recovering alcoholics in particular and society and culture in general is its acceptance and nurturance of powerlessness, receptivity and letting go. Alcoholics get the message that it's all right to be powerless. They *are* powerless, at least over alcohol. They are not in control. A.A. offers permission for states other than the dualistic one common to our culture. Paul, for example, previously sought legitimization of unitive states by participating in a college experiment. Roger found validation of a unitive state in the drug LSD.

These findings made it clear that for many respondents, experiences of receptivity or unity are not entirely new in recovery. Unitive states reportedly occurred in the lives of some of the respondents even prior to recovery with Alcoholics Anonymous, but for those who specifically mentioned them, they lacked validation. In any case, whether experiences of receptivity and unity were new in recovery or not, respondents without exception feel that receptivity or listening is a capacity nurtured and valued in recovery with A.A. Jean and Carol specifically mention how it was eclipsed during the period of active addiction and, according to their own reports, would not have been recovered without the program of A.A.

The experiences of unity *in recovery* seem to fall into two basic categories. I did not anticipate this, despite the fact that I had read Stephanie Brown's book, in which one criterion she uses to distinguish early from ongoing recovery (aside from cumulative daily abstinence) is that of

This is an exploratory map, proposing a cycle which follows the conventional A.A. wisdom that recovery is physical, intellectual, emotional, and spiritual.[38] Such motion is represented on this map in terms of four quadrants within a circle, the physical being represented in the first quadrant, the intellectual-scientific in the second, the emotional-religious in the third, and the conjunction in confluence or coherence[39] of intellectual-scientific and emotional-religious in the physical in the fourth.

The spiral cycle of recovery from alcoholism would involve (1) attempts to control an objectified physical world (represented in the diagram as Quadrant One) followed sooner or later by frustration and (2) progression into the emotional/religious sphere where the tasks are (a) admission of powerlessness of the finite self (b) surrender to a power greater than the finite self (willingness to accept help) and (c) recognition of the unity of self and other with acceptance of the shadow[40] so one can admit what was formerly believed to be object as subject. It is suggested that "loss of control" (which is according to many the hallmark of addiction) marks the transition into the third quadrant. The pain experienced in this quadrant would be due to persistent attempts to control and apply the ways of scientific subject-object splits which no longer work. Surrender and peace comes with acceptance of this powerlessness. The *act* of surrender may usher in what Tiebout calls a *state* of surrender and I call receptivity, in which the individual remains open and willing to receive.

Realization of all three tasks in quadrant three may restore a balance to the spheres and lead to the fourth quadrant where the tasks are to (1) offer the gifts received in the emotional/religious sphere to equals (2) reconcile the two spheres of scientific/intellectual and religious/emotional through attitudes and behavior consonant with the insights and deeper knowledge received in the religious/emotional sphere. In quadrant four there is increasing reliance on intuition rather than intellect or feelings alone, and experiences of what Carl Jung called *meaningful coincidences* or *synchronicity,* Koestler called *confluence,* and others have called *serendipity*.

As this cycle is completed, another round would begin, each time with concentrated attempts to control still another aspect of an objectified world. The spirals of recovery would continue to expand until all are known as subjects *in a state of non-attachment*. With each cycle is experienced less mass, more space.

It seems that each cycle is increasingly expansive, embracing more and more of a formerly "objectified" world as subject (for example, Joyce's identification with the "biker" in her group). And it is likely increasingly contracted as well. The expansive part or increasing identification may occur, for example, as the alcoholic identifies with an A.A. sponsor, with different individuals in his or her "home group,"[41] with individuals with whom he or she may not otherwise have had contact, and possibly with all members of A.A., with all groups, with those in other Twelve Step programs, with neighbors, with those in increasingly inclusive geographical communities, and with the family of origin. This may occur in any order, with varying particulars, but the overall process is one frequently described in meetings.

The simultaneous contraction and *dis*-identification occurs with a detachment from all that is temporal, possibly first the letting go of alcohol, then the letting go of other addictions which surface as the last is jettisoned or released (for example, Roger letting go of attachment to alcohol, to other drugs, to compulsive use of food, and to smoking). As one Northern California Alcoholics Anonymous member (Ann) put it: "Whatever stands between me and my Higher Power is the next thing to go." Or as one East Coast member reported hearing at a meeting: "A.A. lets you hit bottom in *all* areas, not just with alcohol." As Ram Dass explained this universal process, "You can go in and in and in saying 'I am not that, I am not that [*neti neti*] or out and out and out saying 'I am that, I am that' [*tat twam asi*] embracing everything and you come to the exact same place."[42] I believe recovering alcoholics do both.

With each letting go of an attempt to control one facet of "out there," an attempt to control another facet surfaces—possibly the next most subtle until less and less stands in the way of the individual and God or a power greater than the finite self. This process continues until everything that has been objectified in the process of an attached dis-identification is known as subject—everything that has been falsely identified as "self" is known in its true nature. This may be done all at once, or as big chunks together and/or incrementally.

If the process is experienced incrementally, it occurs in stages such as those described by James Fowler, Jane Loevinger, and Lawrence Kohlberg. In each cycle, the recovering individual would increasingly be able to appreciate the standpoint of other beings. That is, he or she would increasingly be able to imagine himself or herself in place not only of other people (first of one other, then two, then of a group, and so on) but also in the place of animals, birds, reptiles, minerals, and so on, possibly in the place of a Higher Power. If this process occurs simultaneously, the individual may bypass developmental stages or zip through them in an instant—a possibility refreshingly advanced by Sam Keen.[43] The change may occur *both* incrementally and in a flash.

Again, as Principal Caird finds, "religious life is progressive . . . [it] is not progress *towards*, but *within* the sphere of the Infinite."[44] It is cyclical progress.

Alcohol addicts find their way from experiencing the world in separate and unrelated pieces to experiencing it in combination with awareness of unity in the religious one—the gift of powerlessness. Or they don't. They may be caught in separation, denying the loss of control they felt they had, denying the need for a power greater than the personal self. They may fail to pass through initiation trials by carrying over the belief in duality that characterized the separation stage. They may attempt to control emotions through use of addictions and continue to experience divisive emotions such as those mentioned by Lewis Hyde. They may refuse the return—refuse to pass on the gifts of the spirit. Or they may return from the death to their separate selves, choosing to share the gifts and experience rebirth in community. This is the task that Joseph Campbell describes as bringing the gifts of the unconscious to consciousness.

The program and fellowship of A.A. helps bridge each pivotal juncture.

Such movement towards spirit and reconciliation of science and religion is consonant with the progression involved in the nuclear unit of the monomyth as described by Joseph Campbell.

According to Campbell, "The standard path of the mythological adventure of the hero is a magnification of the formula represented in the rites of passage: *separation—initiation—return:* which might be named the nuclear unit of the monomyth."[45]

ILLUSTRATION F: *Joseph Campbell's Circular Map*
Copyright © 1949 by Bollingen Foundation, Inc.;
Copyright © 1976 by Princeton University Press

"Elpenor"[46] has suggested such a possibility. So has Charles Whitfield and his colleague, Schreder.[47] Recovery is one variation on the theme of the monomyth with its three stages: separation, initiation, and return.

Separation
This phase for the alcoholic would involve increasing isolation. This is the time perhaps in which the discriminatory function of the ego is developed. This may be a period characterized by a sense of the disappearance of God, by the development and dominance of a scientific point of view based on subject-object splits *in the absence of attention to, acceptance of, appreciation for, and reliance on the underlying unity,* growth in self-consciousness, and ability to distinguish between oneself and others. It is imagined that this separation is that which is experienced in Quadrant Two of the exploratory map offered in Illustration E.

Initiation
This is the second stage of the monomyth, located on the exploratory map proposed here as Quadrant Three [Illustration E]. Campbell says that

> *if anyone—in whatever society—undertakes for himself the perilous journey into the darkness by descending, either intentionally or unintentionally, into the crooked lands of his own spiritual labyrinth, he soon finds himself in a landscape of symbolical figures (any one of which may swallow him). . . . In the vocabulary of the mystics, this is the second stage of the Way, that of the "purification of the self," when the senses are "cleansed and humbled." . . . this is the process of dissolving, transcending or transmuting the infantile images of our personal past. . . . The hero, whether god or goddess, man or woman, the figure in a myth or the dreamer of a dream, discovers and assimilates his opposite (his own unsuspected self) either by swallowing it or by being swallowed. One by one the resistances are broken. He must put aside his pride, his virtue, beauty, and life, and bow or submit to the absolutely intolerable. Then he finds that he and his opposite are not of differing species, but one flesh.*[48]

It is here where he meets the "tyrant-monster" whose characteristics are everywhere essentially the same:

> He is the hoarder of the general benefit. He is the monster avid for the greedy rights of "my
> and mine." The havoc wrought by him is described in mythology and fairy tale as being
> universal through his domain. This may be no more than his household, his own tortured
> psyche, or the lives that he blights with the touch of his friendship and assistance, or it may
> amount to the extent of his civilization. The inflated ego of the tyrant is a curse to himself and
> his world—no matter how his affairs may seem to prosper. Self-terrorized, fear-haunted,
> alert at every hand to meet and battle back the anticipated aggressions of his environment,
> which are primarily the reflections of the uncontrollable impulses to acquisition within
> himself, the giant of self-achieved independence is the world's messenger of disaster, even
> though, in his mind, he may entertain himself with humane intentions.[49]

The question here, Campbell suggests, is whether the ego can put itself to death. He observes
that

> many-headed is this surrounding Hydra; one head cut off, two more appear—unless the right
> caustic is applied to the mutilated stump. . . . . Dragons have now to be slain and surprising
> barriers passed—again, again, and again. Meanwhile there will be a multitude of preliminary
> victories, unretainable ecstasies and momentary glimpses of the wonderful land.[50]

This phase of initiation involves entry into the world of small-r religion, religion in the sense
of binding together. This is the region of the heart and the emotions. "Religion is feeling," it is
said in Starbuck's *Psychology of Religion*.[51] The entry phase of initiation may involve trying to
meet trials on one's own, a continuation of what is known in the program of Alcoholics
Anonymous as a life lived on the basis of self-propulsion, self-will, belief in objects apart from
subject. If such is the case, "the results are nil, until we let go absolutely." The mythological
monsters encountered in this region have names such as Sticky Hair and Holdfast. They are
defeated only as it is recognized that the well-being of the would-be hero and the monsters are
inextricably bound.[52]

Return
Campbell observes that when the hero-quest has been accomplished, "through penetration to
the source, or through the grace of some male or female, human or animal, personification, the
adventurer still must return with his life-transmuting trophy. The full round, the norm of the
monomyth, requires that the hero shall now begin the labor of bringing the runes of wisdom,
the Golden Fleece, or his sleeping princess, back into the kingdom of humanity, where the boon
may redound to the renewing of the community, the nation, the planet, or the ten thousand
worlds."[53]

For the alcoholic, full and rich recovery depends on the "return," the sharing of the gifts of
unitive experiences, acting on awareness of the coincidence of interest. This is known in A.A.
circles as "passing it on." Without this, the individual may well be caught up in beliefs of his
or her uniqueness and become attached to the spiritual experiences as ends in themselves rather
than insights, symbols, and guidance to be shared through changed attitudes and behavior. The
return is shown in Illustration E as the Fourth Quadrant.

Successful negotiation of the passage from ego-death in the spirit world (Quadrant Three)
to reconciliation, in Quadrant Four, of the spirit world with science depends on at least two
conditions. One is a willingness to give freely rather than attempt to either hoard the boons or
to pass on gifts received through letting go through the use of power or force. The second related
condition of full return is to give with awareness of the equality of giver and receiver, rather

than attempt to pass on gifts with an attitude of *noblesse oblige.* At least one recovering alcoholic has found that attempts to pass on gifts with an attitude of superiority and pity *don't work.* They are to pass on gifts with an awareness that they *themselves* need to do so. This awareness may disappear as a motivation and simply remain as an awareness of essential equality. Ernest Kurtz notes that Bill W., in the year after his spiritual experience in Towns Hospital in New York, approached forty to fifty drunks and no one was interested in his message until he realized, right before his meeting with Dr. Bob Smith, that *he needed to offer help to another drunk because Bill himself needed help.* In A.A. there are constant reminders that the separate self is "not-god,"[54] such as the telling of and listening to stories in which the would-be hero is clearly monster as well, and sober only with the help of a power greater than his or her finite self.

The movement of the recovery as proposed here, as well as the dynamics of the monomyth are consonant with the stages of revitalization movements identified and described by anthropologist Anthony Wallace and discussed here in chapters 1 and 3.

Applying the stages of Anthony Wallace, as identified elsewhere in this study, to the level of the individual organism, the physical quadrant of Illustration E would be equivalent to Wallace's steady state; the separation (Quadrant Two) would be equivalent to Wallace's time of stress; the increased cultural distortion may indicate attempts to make the old way (i.e., control and the implicit subject–object splits) work in a new realm (Quadrant Three). Revitalization (Wallace's stage four) would occur with surrender and receptivity within the realm of initiation or religion/emotion, and the return in Quadrant Four would involve accomplishment of the tasks of revitalization: mazeway reformulation, organization, communication, adaptation, cultural transformation, and routinization, which helps constellate a new steady state, also in Quadrant Four of Illustration E. The steady state would be one in which all four quadrants are at least temporarily in balance—physical, mental, emotional, spiritual. And from here begins another departure, another round of attempts to make old ways work in still one more area, followed by a new cycle. (The application of the revitalization process to the exploratory model isn't exactly neat, with the base and starting-point steady state being in Quadrant One, the new steady state in Four.)

The movement of recovery, the movement of the monomyth, and the movement inherent in revitalizations are consonant with the process involved in the origin of consciousness[55] as identified and described by Julian Jaynes.

Jaynes, who began as a psychobiologist and is currently examining consciousness through the use of "historical analysis, introspection, and the study of language and metaphor,"[56] states that his task is to explain "the contrast, so obvious to a child, between all the inner covert world of imaginings and memories and thoughts and the external public world around us."[57] He begins with what he calls the bicameral mind, characterized by and identified with auditory hallucinations, known then as the voice or voices of the gods. He says that "human mentality [at one time] was in two parts, a decision-making part and a follower part. . . . In everyday life [humans were] creature[s] of habit, but when some problem arose that needed a new decision or a more complicated solution than habit could provide, that decision stress was sufficient to instigate an auditory hallucination. Because such individuals had no mind-space in which to question or rebel, such voices had to be obeyed."[58] According to Jaynes, the bicameral mind *is* what it *does:* it produces "answers to problems and decisions."[59] Some of the factors Jaynes identifies as contributing to or associated with the origin of consciousness away from a bicameral mind (in which there is no space for free choice between the God-part of mentality and human-part of mentality, and the God-part is in charge), include (1) the use of written language and an associated shift from what he qualifiedly calls an "auditory" mind to a "visual" and spatial mind,[60] (2) observation of differences, and (3) the practice of long-term deceit.[61]

In describing the ways in which the separation from the presence of the voice or voices of God or gods occurred, he implicitly describes the process by which the ways of consciousness may be rejoined with the ways of the bicameral mind, i.e., ways in which the sphere of science (what Jaynes refers to as the man-part of mentality) and which I imagine to be associated with the left hemisphere of the brain, may be rejoined with the sphere of religion (the God-part), which I imagine to be associated with the right hemisphere of the brain. So that for the shift into Quadrant Three—the realm of religion—the process is inversely symmetrical to the one described by Jaynes as occurring in the creation of consciousness from the bicameral mind. That is, following Jayne's reasoning and evidence, re-connection would at least in part involve (1) emphasis and reliance on and appreciation of auditory communication, (2) attention to similarity, and (3) increased honesty. This time, however, these changes would occur in the presence of a constellated "analog I" which has the capacity to imagine and to choose.[62]

Following Jaynes further, as written language seems to have played a key role in the transformation from bicameral mind to consciousness, a de-emphasis on written communication and increased reliance on oral communication would presumably facilitate a reconciliation with the God-side initially lost in the origin of consciousness. Improved auditory communication would in turn depend variously on both internal and external silence to allow reception of messages. Observation of difference, which he also feels played a part in the origin of consciousness,[63] now balanced with attention to similarities may likewise contribute to greater conscious contact with a Higher Power. As long-term deceit seems to have played a key role in the transformation from the bicameral mind to consciousness, honesty is vital for re-entry into "God-side" of the brain, or the sphere of religion (Quadrant Three). So in place of the distancing which occurs with long term deceit comes the greater closeness that follows from increased honesty with (1) *the self* through breaking of denial of what Carl Jung refers to as the "shadow" aspect of oneself (2) *others* through awareness of equality and the coincidence of interests, and (3) *God* with an awareness of God within. The increased honesty and related cleansing of making amends for harm done may help clear the multitude of voices so that one still voice may be heard. In place of the strengthening of what Jaynes calls the analog I comes a relaxation, now that it has "gelled," and an interior mind space-time-power is established. The return is a return to valuing the functions and attributes ascribed to the brain's right hemisphere—that which Jaynes associates with the "god-side"—now coupled with consciousness, which differs primarily from the bicameral era in that the post-conscious mind is characterized by the potential for freedom of conscious choice. Those initiated may at least fumblingly, or skillfully (as shamans, for example), decide when to enter the right brain for the benefit of the community. They may also enter at any time effortlessly through grace.

This describes the process of recovery from alcoholism with Alcoholics Anonymous. A renewed awareness of the connection between the "human-side" and the "god-side" occurs with decreased distancing. Wedges between the spheres are gradually removed with practice of the steps of A.A. Resentments, which distance; deceit, which distances; judgments, which distance; defiance, which distances; self-pity, which distances; and pride. These distances invariably diminish for those practicing the program of recovery.[64]

The re-establishment of balance between the left and right hemispheres may be due in part to what Jaynes calls *consilience* and *narratization*[65] on a collective rather than individual level—the gathering together of mind-space and time through finding connections. This happens in recovery from alcoholism through the sharing of stories. It may also occur through a balancing of active with receptive ways through a disengagement of the human-side of mentality by "letting go" (what Pierre Janet and Carl Jung refer to as *abaissement du niveau mental*) so that the God-side of mentality may perform its ancient function of "fitting all the disparate parts together . . . in a grand design."[66] The rite of story-telling in a mythic formula (what it was like, what happened, and what it is like now) helps fuse the intellect and emotion, helps to heal splits in what Jaynes calls "mind-space" through identification with other story-teller-alcoholics,[67] and helps to fuse the splits in "mind-time" through the gathering of personal history into the security of the present moment. This fusion brings us full circle, connecting the self over time with other, the self with a power greater than self, and end with beginning.

This understanding does not depend on any particular understanding of God or a greater power source, since the right hemisphere of the brain associated with the voice of a Higher Power or powers may be understood either as a receptor and/or transmission site through which the voice of God may be heard.

The description offered by Jaynes as the movement from bicameral mind to consciousness would likewise be an apt description of the transition from the physical quandrant (Quandrant One) on the symbol-map of Illustration E to the quadrant of separation (Quandrant Two). The movement into the realm of religion (Quadrant Three) is imagined to be a continuation of and inversely identical to the process which Jaynes finds occurs in the origin of consciousness. Reconciliation of the characteristics of consciousness and the characteristics of bicamerality may occur with a re-establishment of communication between the two spheres (Quadrant Four).

The process of recovery, the process of the monomyth, the stages of revitalization movements, and the process described by Jaynes are likewise consonant with the "transpersonal view of human development" described by psychologist Ken Wilbur.

Wilbur says that the two dynamic factors in development are Eros and Thanatos, Life and Death. He says that at each stage of development, "the subject is terrified of real transcendence, because transcendence entails the 'death' of his isolated and separate-self sense. The subject can find the prior Whole only by letting go of the *boundary* between subject and object—that is, by dying to the exclusive subject."[68] He suggests that

> *because man wants real transcendence above all else, but because he cannot or will not accept the necessary death of his separate-self sense, he goes about seeking transcendence in ways, or through structures, that actually prevent it and force symbolic substitutes. And these substitutes come in all varieties: sex, food, money, fame, knowledge, power . . . [The process proceeds until] all substitutes for Unity are tried and found wanting, and only Unity itself remains. [The process proceeds] . . . .as long as the Eros . . . exceeds Thanatos—as long as the grasping exceeds the emptiness (sunyata), as long as the new structure serves as a substitute gratification and does not go tasteless in its desire. But once that occurs, once Thanatos outweighs Eros, then the self accepts the "death" of that level—and thereby switches its identity to the next higher emergent structure, which itself then possesses new forms of Eros, and faces new seizures of Thanatos and death. . . . When these substitutes cease to satisfy, then the lower level is abandoned . . . .[69]*

In this case, the point of origin would be Quadrant One in Illustration E, Eros would be analogous to Quadrant Two, Thanatos analogous to Quadrant Three, and the steady state preceding a new round would be Quadrant Four.

In the field of alcohol studies, this model would visually fit with and slightly modify the spiral of Stephanie Brown's developmental model of recovery.

It would be in concert with her description of early recovery as characterized by a primarily receptive state followed by an ongoing recovery of three or more years characterized by reciprocity. The circle shown in Illustration E may offer a cross section of the spiral recovery process she proposes:[70]

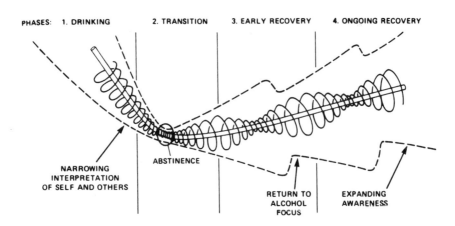

PHASES: 1. DRINKING   2. TRANSITION   3. EARLY RECOVERY   4. ONGOING RECOVERY

NARROWING INTERPRETATION OF SELF AND OTHERS

ABSTINENCE

RETURN TO ALCOHOL FOCUS

EXPANDING AWARENESS

ILLUSTRATION G: *Stephanie Brown's Model of Recovery*
Reprinted by permission of John Wiley & Sons, Inc. Copyright © 1985.

The axis symbolic of alcohol which Brown feels remains a constant is perhaps symbolic of powerlessness over any *objectified reality* in the absence of a working knowledge and acceptance of the unity. A receptive way to be, once learned, is not one to be given up at a later stage of recovery. It is simply to be balanced by and integrated with activity.

The pattern of recovery proposed here is consonant with the movement or process or pattern described in many other fields or traditions by many other researchers.[71] Once this basic pattern is discerned, it is possible to find comparable patterns in a variety of fields.[72] Those selected for consideration here were the movement of the monomyth described by Joseph Campbell, the progression of revitalization movements described by Anthony Wallace, the movements involved in the origin of consciousness as identified by Julian Jaynes, the developmental process identified by Ken Wilbur, and the developmental model of recovery from alcoholism proposed by Stephanie Brown.

If the experiences, feelings, and ideas of the recovering alcoholics who participated in this study are at all representative, it may well be that A.A. is one expression of a perennial pattern which facilitates the flow from the "problem" or separation stage (Quadrant Two) through Quadrant One to a sense of unity within the "initiation" or religious-emotional stage (Quadrant Three) and from there to the return of reconciliation in the Fourth Quadrant. The separation stage involves the constellation of consciousness. The initiation phase involves experience of death to at least one aspect of the small separate self and reconciliation with a power greater than the finite self. The return involves a return from death with an acceptance of responsibility and an ability to hold both the way of the two and the way of the one.

A.A. is instrumental in helping members progress through the cycle of the monomyth, to progress from a scientific way of being in the world to a spiritual one, to progress from a way of life based on separation to a way of life based on coherence, accompanied by an improved ability to choose appropriately between the two with help from a Higher Power. It does this through its appreciation of powerlessness and receptivity in balance with activity, through provision of a context of community in balance with individuality, and through its injunction to pass on what was received and simultaneously received again regardless of the outcome. A.A. helps balance the active with the receptive in its various forms through honoring the "feminine" in each pair of commonly imagined polarities: feminine myth with masculine history; feminine community with masculine individual; feminine small-r religion with masculine science; feminine inner world with masculine outer world. This happens as members "Don't drink. Go to meetings." This happens through practicing the Twelve Steps of A.A. over and over.

This cycle allows a transcendence of an *exclusively* dualistic separatist perspective, a transition to a unified experience of the world which itself may allow both free flow and integration of the two. This occurs with embracing what in general has historically been undervalued and/or discounted and/or disregarded and/or feared in Occidental cultures—personal powerlessness and the feminine receptive.

In Campbell's monomyth,

> *a hero ventures forth from the world of common day into a region of supernatural wonder: fabulous forces are there encountered and a decisive victory is won: the hero comes back from this mysterious adventure with the power to bestow boons on his fellow man.*[73]

A variation on this theme expressed in the A.A. stories might read: a hero ventures forth from the world of common day into a region of supernatural terror and wonder: fabulous forces beyond the finite self are there encountered along with the monster who turns out to be himself or herself, and a temporary and decisive victory is won through loss: the hero comes back from this mysterious adventure with the power to bestow boons on his or her fellow beings, if these fellow beings choose to receive them and as long as he or she remembers that the gifts may be claimed only by passing them on—freely as they were received. And somewhere along the journey, he or she discovers one of the greatest mysteries—how, in the words of Schopenhauer, one can be "the hero of his own drama while simultaneously figuring into a drama foreign to him."[74]

The return involves balancing the "way of the two" with "the way of the one." This is done in A.A. with the help of a number of practices. One is through the use of the "Peace Prayer" of St. Francis,[75] which is reprinted in *Twelve Steps and Twelve Traditions* and seeks to bring imbalance in the direction of self-centeredness and separation to the peace of the whole. Another is through reliance on the Serenity Prayer, cited here in plural form:

> *God Grant us the serenity to accept the things we cannot change,*
> *the courage to change the things we can,*
> *and the wisdom to know the difference.*[76]

Frederick Hampden-Turner calls this Serenity Prayer of A.A. "a hymn to the ecology of mind, to constant movement between fused values—risk and security, power and surrender, dependence and independence—to heal the splits between them and develop all synergistically."[77]

There are those among us
courageous
for all their insecurity
willing
for all their resistance
open

for all their defensiveness

Those who gather
shards and
splinters
into the story

of their life

gather them
with other stories

gather mind-time
and mind-space
gently pull them in

Free of outcome expectations
they learn to tame time
round time out
until it's full and rich

connect
end with beginning

Learn that the line
in its fullness
circles back
upon itself

There are those
learning to be still and
rest in center space

With swinging ceased
they find the chasm
between
science and spirit
active and receptive
time and space
west and east
male and female
outer and inner
is a channel
between
earth and heaven

Those
rebirthed
in the time and space and power place
of male and female joined

the space
between the spheres

There are those who find
that
A.A. offers

bridges braided
with traditions
across the distance
from one side to the other

Find these are ladder rungs as well
reaching up and free

the structure of sobriety

When they let go
their weight

balance gravity
with levity

they can leap too
and lifted
fly

find
time collapses
with collapse
in the space
of distance
separating
good self from bad
self from others
self from nature world
self from God

and in the vacuum
energy
inheres

flows
freely
once
again

Free of distance

they find
they are
already
there:

Here.
At home
at last.

Chapter Six

Parallels and Patterns in the Larger Community

Implications and Recommendations

In this Chapter, I set forth some ideas about the similarities that may exist between two emerging patterns. The first is a pattern of change for individuals in recovery from alcoholism. The second is a pattern of change within the larger community. I also assess the implications of this study for recovery from the pain of dualism and make recommendations for further research.

PART I
PARALLELS

Cultural anthropologist Gregory Bateson concurs with Bill Wilson's observation that "the errors of the alcoholic are the same as the 'forces which are today ripping the world apart at its seams.' "[1] Bill W., who Aldous Huxley felt was the "greatest social architect of the century,"[2] noted that "like other men and women, we AAs look with deep apprehension upon the vast power struggle about us, a struggle in myriad forms that invades every level, tearing society apart." He believes that if those same forces were to operate among the community of recovering alcoholics in Alcoholics Anonymous, the A.A. community might "perish altogether."[3] He says "how best to live and work together as groups became the prime question" for alcoholics. "In the world about us we saw personalities destroying whole peoples. The struggle for wealth, power, and prestige was tearing humanity apart as never before."[4] He says, "All history affords us the spectacle of striving nations and groups finally torn asunder because they were designed for, or tempted into, controversy. Others fell apart because of sheer self-righteousness while trying to enforce upon the rest of mankind some millennium of their own specification. In our own times, we have seen millions die in political and economic wars often spurred by religious and racial difference. We live in the imminent possibility of a fresh holocaust to determine how men shall be governed, and how the products of nature and toil shall be divided among them."[5] Bill says, "We think that AA should offer its experience to the whole world for whatever use can be made of it. . . . Let us of AA therefore resolve that we shall always be inclusive and never exclusive, offering all we have to all."[6]

There is evidence to support the idea that there are parallels between the path of the alcoholic and the path of mainstream American culture. According to Tiebout, for example, *alcoholics experience their world in pieces*. The authors of *Habits of the Heart* suggest this is true for mainstream American society as well. One of Kurtz's main messages is that alcoholics set their separate selves up as God, as the absolute, as the omnipotent. Recovery with A.A. involves an acceptance of limits. Richard Madsen says American society needs to recognize our need to limit our desires. *Alcoholics keep trying harder and harder to control their use of alcohol.* Historian Gene Wise notes Perry Miller's observation that we as a nation suffer from a try-harder syndrome on which we rely to get us from a state of declension and pain to one of paradise. *Alcoholics are toxic,* having little or no regard for the impact of their toxicity on their environment. Theodore Roszak says we are living in a toxic culture. Jim, one of the recovering alcoholics who contributed to this study, says *"I suffered from terminal uniqueness."* Historian Bercovitch is among those who say the United States considers itself unique as well. Bercovitch says that from the very start the America of the European-Americans has believed itself to be the "holy land." This depends, he says, "on other lands not being holy; the chosenness of the chosen people implies their antagonism to the *goyim,* the profane 'nations of the earth.' "[7] Alcoholics learn to identify rather than compare in listening to the stories of others. Paul, another recovering alcoholic involved in this study, says, "I *empathize, not sympathize.*" Rollo May in Berkeley, CA, (1987) said that for "rebornment we will have to build a new society aware of poverty and hunger based on a creative capacity to understand and listen to another's woes." Ralph Waldo Emerson invites all of his listeners to "deny every distinction" *beween themselves and others* and "make individuation an endless process of incorporation."[8] *Self-centeredness is the root of our problems,* Bill Wilson says. Jennifer says she was imbalanced in the direction of self-centeredness and control. Ram Dass says nationalism is Ego writ large. William Appleman Williams declares "the nation-state [is] a major mechanism used by prideful people in their attempts to impose their will on the diversity of human experience."[9] According to Kurtz, *alcoholics repeatedly attempt to satisfy spiritual needs by material means.* William Appleman Williams says the United States defines itself and the world in economic terms. *Alcoholics attempt to annex and engulf an objectified world other than itself to serve their needs.* Williams says the happiness of mercantile countries such as the United States comes at the expense of others. Kurtz describes the *compulsion of the alcoholic for more and again.* Historians Turner and Beard and Hofstadter are among those who discuss expansionism as our national solution to all problems. Roger says *he felt the world was a hostile place.* Sam Keen says that the notion that we must control everything leads to paranoia and to the destruction of the body. He says, "Untrust can destroy us. . . . The national humiliation of Vietnam is the end result of a paranoid policy, of the effort to be warriors and men of power. . . . Most disease is, like the Pentagon, a symptom of our paranoid way of dealing with the world."[10] Jennifer says, *"My old life was so horrible I couldn't go back there. That was suicide."* Rollo May says, "Despair is prerequisite not only to the curing of the alcoholic, but also to the forming of a new society." *Active alcoholics seek the extreme of perfection* rather than contentment with what is. Marion Woodman and Anne Wilson Schaef are among others who note the perfectionism that characterizes American society.

If the imbalances of active addiction are similar to those experienced by the mainstream culture, the tasks that face us as a people may be similar as well. For the society as well as for individual addicts, the problem may be part of an emerging pattern. The state of separation described above may simply be a phase of the perennial pattern proposed before.

Nations too may traverse the cycle. A society also may take the path of separation-initiation-return.

Part II
Patterns

Section A
Separation

1.
Absence of Peace among Ourselves?

There is some evidence to support the idea that the dominant culture is concerned with control, an active-dualistic way of relating *to* the world.

Howard Stein is an anthropologist who explicitly compares the attitudes and behavior of the nation with the attitudes and behavior of alcoholics. He says that "while the personal grandiosity, intoxication with power, and out-of-control aggressivity of alcoholism are under attack within American culture from all quarters, at the group level, national grandiosity, intoxication with power, and out-of-control aggressivity are constantly inflamed and acted out. One thinks, for instance, of American foreign adventurism, provocation in foreign policy, and gearing up for the prospect of nuclear war with the Soviet Union. What in the alcoholic we condemn and wish to curb, in the national mood we applaud as renewed patriotism and hope to escalate even further! While we crack down on the slaughter on the highways, we embark dangerously upon the slaughter of the human species. One form of intoxication receives our undivided attention and opprobrium; another form of intoxication is met with denial and further acting out."[11]

For over a hundred years, say the authors of *Habits of the Heart*,

> *a large part of the American people, the middle class, has imagined that the virtual meaning of life lies in the acquisition of ever-increasing status, income, and authority, from which genuine freedom is supposed to come. Our achievements have been enormous. They permit us the aspiration to become a genuinely humane society in a genuinely decent world, and provide many of the means to attain that aspiration. Yet we seem to be hovering on the very brink of disaster, not only from international conflict but from the internal incoherence of our own society . . . . We have imagined ourselves a special creation, set apart from other humans. In the late twentieth century, we see that our poverty is as absolute as that of the poorest of nations. We have attempted to deny the human condition in our quest for power after power.*[12]

Kurtz too notes this preference for "power after power" for control. He argues that beyond geography, "most people readily agree . . . that one meaning of 'America' is 'modern.' . . . The United States is the one political entity founded as *new* in the age of the Enlightenment out of commitment to the living out of Enlightenment insights." And, he says, "Both the key starting-point and the goal of the Enlightenment, expressed in one word, was *autonomy*—the essential independence of each human individual. Every person, as rational, was to use his own reason to set and to achieve his own goals." From this supposition flowed one of the dominant assumptions of all modern thought: "the exercise and extension of rationalization and control as the purpose of human life."[13] He believes Enlightenment thinkers "labored mightily to attain for mankind *freedom*," and "first and foremost . . . cast off as superstition all sense of mysteriously hidden forces beyond human understanding and control. To man belonged the responsibility as well as the right to determine and to shape human destiny."[14]

There is some evidence to support the idea that we as a nation have been divided within ourselves: one community in conflict with another, one community in isolation from others. For example, *Habits'* authors note a tendency for those Americans whom they interviewed to confine their social interaction to what Bellah et al. term *social enclaves*—people who share most closely their own values and backgrounds to the exclusion of social interaction with heterogeneous groups. What we need, they feel, is a true community, a community in the strong sense of the world which "attempts to be an inclusive whole, celebrating the interdependence of public and private life and of the different callings of all."[15]

There is evidence to support the idea that the ways and values of the dominant culture in America have permeated quantitatively smaller cultures and native nations, groups which traditionally have honored many different values. For example, Vine Deloria, Jr., notes that

> *tribal religions . . . face the task of entrenching themselves in a contemporary Indian society that is becoming increasingly accustomed to the life-style of contemporary America. While traditional Indians speak of a reverence for the earth, Indian reservations continue to pile up junk cars and beer cans at an alarming rate.*[16]

2.
Absence of Peace with Higher Power/God?

It is the collective experience of many recovering alcoholics that we can't find peace with God or a Higher Power as long as we are or make our own gods. Alcoholics have been known to mistake liquid spirits for spirit, a tendency expressed in Carl Jung's formula for recovery: *spiritus contra spiritum.* [Please refer to the Appendix for a copy of Carl Jung's letter to Bill Wilson in which Jung uses this phrase.] They have learned through experience the truth of Ananda Coomarsaswamy's observation passed on through Mircea Eliade that "when the mind is no longer capable of perceiving the metaphysical significance of a symbol, it is understood at levels which become increasingly coarse."[17]

Gerald May offers some fine insights in this area for society as a whole. Addictions, he believes, are what we make more important than God. The objects of our addictions become our false gods, our idols.[18]

Roland Delattre provides a description of how we make our own gods in his discussion of an American culture of procurement with its "compulsive dependence upon spending and acquiring." He speaks of a "whole network of addictions" which nourish and sustain the "culture of procurement."[19] He says the "culture of procurement, constituted at its core by addictive acquisition, nourished and sustained by a whole network of addictions, is a powerful presence in the life of the nation. It is a culture in itself, and not merely a cultural theme. It offers a fabric of meaning and a framework of interpretation, a sense of how the world is and of how things are done among us." He says the key to addiction "is not found in the substances or activities that are the objects of addiction, but in the experience and the pattern of dependence."[20]

For many, these external sources of satisfaction may be substitutes for God as traditionally understood.[21] And as long as we remain dependent in this manner, what Meister Eckhart calls a "merchant mentality" will prevail, a mentality which may apply equally to our relations with God as well as with other nations.

3.
Absence of Peace with Others?

There is evidence to support the idea that the dominant culture in America has affected not only those quantitively smaller societies on this soil, but the ways of all cultures and creatures of the Earth. For example, Carlos Fuentes, Mexican novelist-diplomat, says he has two great fears about the twenty-first century with which "humanity must come to terms." The first is fear of nuclear annihilation. The second is fear that the developing nations will either be crushed out or swallowed up by the developed world."[22] According to Rushmore Kidder, who interviewed Fuentes, Fuentes is concerned with " 'the enormous gap' between the political, economic, social and the technological conditions of industrial nations and those of developing nations. As a result, he says, the latter will face in the twenty-first century a clash between what he calls the 'project of independence'—their ongoing efforts to shed what was once a colonial status—and the 'project of interdependence' that increasingly makes the worlds' nations reliant on one another." He voices a fear that " 'our national projects will be swallowed up by transnational companies, . . . [and] . . . that we will have little say in our own destiny.' " He hopes in the twenty-first century "to see 'the disintegration of bipolar politics as the dominating factor' in world affairs."[23]

Theodore Roszak asserts that America led the whole world into an urban industrial culture in which we are now embedded. Within one generation, he believes, there will be no "primitive" cultures, no agrarian cultures. There will be power lines everywhere. There will be no air and no water left unpolluted. He says we live in a culture of "compulsive masculinity." He believes that the primary questions of such an industrial society are "who will hold and run it?" He says that our dominant culture is deeply addictive and we are hooked on it. He makes a simple observation that Rome could fall without Asia falling, but if our culture falls, all go down with it.[24]

4.

Absence of Peace with the World?

Peace with the world as a whole is here considered as distinct from peace with others in that it is more inclusive. In this view, in the words of Deloria, we are dealing with "a complexity of relationships in which no particular object is given primacy over any other object or entity."[25] It is a theory of relativity that "hardly means that all things are relative. It rather means that all things are related."[26]

At present, there is ample evidence that people in the main stream of America relate to the world around them from a preference for mastery. Kluckhohn and Stodtbeck suggest that starting with the United States as one example of a total culture, we can easily see how its dominant value orientations of individualism, future, time, mastery-over-nature, [and] doing . . . make for a high evaluation of the occupational world, conceived as a world of technology, business and economic affairs in general."[27] There is a preference among "main-stream" Americans for mastery over others through individualism preferred to either collateral or lineal relations with others, mastery over the future with attempts to predict and control rather than value present or past; mastery through doing, i.e., making things happen, preferred to simply being, and mastery over nature preferred to harmony with or subjugation to nature.

In Madsen's view, modernity needs and is looking for "an integrative kind of thing." He explains, "You can't think of finding yourself on your own. You can only be sustained and nurtured by involvement in a larger movement, in a community. To be individual in the best sense of the word is to see oneself as part of the larger whole that is rooted in the past. We need to emphasize things that enable us to reach out and link."[28]

Along lines parallel to the thought of Roszak and others, Fuentes observes that

> *throughout history we've always known that man and woman can destroy themselves. But we have always known, throughout the ages, that nature would remain while we disappeared . . . if only to bear witness to our folly and our pride. Today I think for the first time in history we have the consciousness that nature can disappear along with us, and it really shakes your soul. [This knowledge] unites us as human beings through fear as we have never been united before.*[29]

Fuentes believes that "high on the agenda for the 21st century . . . will be the need to restore some kind of tragic consciousness." He believes we need a view of the world reflected in "the most ancient wisdom of the West" which is that "progress does not assure happiness" and the world is "not divided into good guys and bad guys." He says "the world is made of grace . . . and the important thing is to understand that . . . we are all struggling between values." He says his hope as a friend of the United States is that "the democracy [will] coincide inside and out. And then the power of the United States in the Western Hemisphere will be such as it has never imagined."[30]

Gregory Bateson asserts that the non-alcoholic world has many lessons which it might learn from the epistemology of systems theory and from the ways of Alcoholics Anonymous. He says that "if we continue to operate in terms of a Cartesian dualism of mind versus matter, we shall probably also continue to see the world in terms of God *versus* man; elite *versus* people; chosen race *versus* others; nation *versus* nation; and man *versus* environment. It is doubtful whether a species having *both* an advanced technology *and* this strange way of looking at its world can endure."[31]

Section B
Initiation

From the state of separation described above between one community within the political borders of the United States and another, between ourselves and a Higher Power, between ourselves and other nations, and ourselves and the world as a whole, we may now find ourselves nationally in the phase of initiation. We may be stuck in the phase of initiation, persisting in a number of dubious assumptions.

1.
We Are Alone; We Can Do It On Our Own

We as a nation are on our own, we can do anything that is worthwhile doing alone. We as a separate nation-state-self are not really powerless, despite considerable evidence to the contrary. The authors of *Habits of the Heart* are among those who offer evidence which contests this long-held belief. They say that the culture of separation "with its concern for instrumental control is no longer viable apart from a culture of coherence."[32] Norman Cousins is among those who argues that the first problem in our northern-western-white-male modern society is denial of its problems.[33]

There is evidence to support the idea that we as a nation are being confronted with limits to our ability to control. Kurtz traces this theme in a historical sketch of Twentieth Century America:

> The twentieth century began in American with the "Progressive Era"— a self conscious quickening of hope in the possibilities of extending rationalization and control in service to human happiness and fulfillment. The era's philosophers and economists agreed in identifying "doing" and "making" with being—that is, with being "American." . . . The Progressives sought to apply rationalization and control, so successful in the technological and economic spheres, to the political and psychological lives of their fellow citizens. . . .

> The idealism invigorated by American intervention in World War I broke down in the aftermath of the contagious cynicism of Versailles, and a population accustomed to the deflationary economy of the late nineteenth century found it impossible to comprehend, much less to cope with, the inflationary underside of their very modernity. Pained and confused, Americans retreated, internationally into isolationism and domestically into privacies. Even the abundance was for most illusory. At the height of the twenties' "boom," over sixty per cent of American wage earners supported their families on less than the income required for a minimum standard of decent living.

Still, in the twenties, some roared and some soared until the Crash of 1929. The thirties brought depression to all, and new attempts at community for almost all. In the forties, surprise attack led to a war that ended in hollow triumph as new fears emerged. Then, in the 1950s, there was Korea with its hint of limitation; and there flourished a curious mixture of suspicion and complacency rendered tolerable only by denial that it existed. The decade of the sixties brought in every way too much for even the insatiable. There were the enthusiastic idealism of Camelot and the New Frontier, the confidence-shattering violence of assassinations, and an increasing mistrust of government not unrelated to increasing immersion in an increasingly unpopular war.

A sense of limitation was clearly and distinctly born. A "consumer movement" arose and soon sired offspring that made earlier concerns for conservation look amateurish. Adversarial relationships began to displace the presumption of even the existence of a "common good" . . . ."Doing good" itself became suspect as the sixties turned into the seventies, and the spectacle of a virtually impeached vice-president, then president, shattered lingering altruisms. Dedication to rationalization and control had led, paradoxically, to the sense that, in human affairs at least, the only rational understanding was that there could be no effective control over all the contingencies and complexities so newly and carefully made understandable.[34]

Sam Keen observed that

at America's bicentennial, she is dead. Vietnam was America's midlife crisis. Capitalism as a total way of organizing the world has been shown to be corrupt. The unequal distribution of wealth, our carelessness of the environment, and our insane military responses to minor crises have made this clear.[35]

According to David Noble and colleagues, during the Vietnam crisis, Lyndon Johnson's Informal Advisory Group of twelve men supported Senator Fulbright's 1965 observation that the nation was "losing its perspective on what exactly is within the realm of its power and what is beyond it."[36]

Failure to acknowledge powerlessness on a national level translates into inability to appreciate the grace that inheres with receptivity. As a nation we remain caught in our try-harder syndrome, a legacy of our Puritan past.[37] Persistence in the old ways of subject-object splits, the way of dualism and the "instrumental control" that *Habits* authors associate with the culture of separation, results in unilateral actions upon the world-as-object which are increasingly doomed to frustration. This persistence in the active dualistic way (associated with control) results in lack of openness to inventory ourselves and a consequent projection of fears and desires.

V. Lois Erickson, who worked with Lawrence Kohlberg at Harvard on stages of moral and ethical growth, is among those who have noted that "in early European history . . . persons began to view their minds as separate from their bodies . . . thus, a split occurred in the mind/body link of many at this time. . . . [There began to be] . . . an imbalance in the way persons processed information. We, in the West in particular, hold that we need to compare, contrast, and analyze the differences we observe. This analytical mode of thought is a problem to us in that it creates disease; thus, feelings of a lack of ease." She adds that "we have taught for separateness, and allowed this view to be considered the normal way to be on Earth."[38]

2.

We Are Heroes Alone

This involves the national tendency to overlook our tyrant-monster selves, not totally unlike children who close their eyes so others won't see them. Recovering alcoholics discover that they are the monster Holdfast *as well as* the hero of their own drama. Those observing our culture from another perspective, like those who live with alcoholics, are quite aware of our short-comings. There is evidence to indicate that we believe ourselves a heroic nation, unwilling to acknowledge our tyrant-monster selves.

Carl Jung says, "The crux of the matter is man's own dualism. . . . Even today people are largely unconscious of the fact that every individual is a cell in the structure of various international organisms and is therefore causally implicated in their conflicts. . . . It is in the nature of political bodies always to see the evil in the opposite group, just as the individual has an ineradicable tendency to get rid of everything he does not know and does not want to know about himself by foisting it off on somebody else."[39] Sam Keen, observing such a tendency in the United States, reflects, "We need to battle social evil but not to project it outward. Vietnam is not something *they* did. It is something we did. We *all* laid waste the children. This includes the Vietcong. We *all* did it. It is necessary to remain in touch with the murderous parts of ourselves." Keen describes that "American capitalism and the Marlboro man personality it produces have a definite hierarchy of values. The highest value is assigned to mind, head, reason, control, rationality, technique—that is, to what traditionally have been the 'masculine' virtues. The 'feminine' virtues, which are associated with body knowledge, touch, emotion, surrender, and art, are less highly valued. Control is up. Being controlled is down. . . . Our problem is character armor."[40]

Bercovitch identifies and calls into question a "self-justification myth of America." Reinhold Niebuhr calls to our attention the national proclivity to draw distinctions between a corrupt Old World (Europe) and an innocent New One (the United States), and denies persistent beliefs that we are a virtuous New World that needs to be segregated from an evil old one.

3.

We Alone Are Heroes

Other nations are subordinates waiting to be saved by us—or existing to be exploited by us, they being less blessed and hardly equal. Fuentes wonders why the United States—"seem[s] so bent on 'imposing' its own solutions to the problems in the developing world."[41]

Regarding individual Americans, the authors of *Habits of the Heart* observe that "the American dream is often a very private dream of being the star, the uniquely successful and admirable one, the one who stands out from the crowd of ordinary folk who don't know how. And since we have believed in that dream for a long time and worked very hard to make it come true, it is hard for us to give it up, even though it contradicts another dream that we have—that of living in a society that would really be worth living in."[42]

Alcoholics recovering with the help of A.A. discover that we are all in this together, all equal one with the other. If there's any service to be done, it needs to be in the form of an offer given with the awareness that the giver is benefited in the giving, regardless of the response of those to whom the idea or help is offered. This is a non-contractual relationship. The gift is not something that can be imposed. It can only be offered freely without expectation of outcome.

Whether for the alcoholic or a society, return requires humility. Awareness that, as David Noble observes, we may have arrived at the end of American history, that is, at the end of clinging to a belief in the exclusive uniqueness of America, would help humble us as we acknowledged our similarities and connectedness with the rest of the world. With humility such as this, we may find that we are, as Joseph Campbell believes, in a new era of human history, "when it is time to rediscover an experience of the entire earth as the holy land, here and now."[43]

4.

Our Gifts Are Ours Alone

We may persist in a belief that it is possible to abscond with the boons. This is a refusal to share our resources with the larger community. Refusing the return, the system remains in runaway, as described by Gregory Bateson in his book *Ecology of Mind*. This runaway is the logical result of our worship of unlimited expansion, tantamount to the individual attempting a getaway with the boons. It is associated with the "more and again" syndrome described so well by Kurtz. We remain complacent in our hoarding and attachments[44] today, vowing, as have one or two alcoholics, that we'll "quit tomorrow."[45] Refusing the return is a refusal of responsibility, refusing to pass from the stage of cultural childhood to maturity. As an antidote, Bellah, Madsen, Sullivan, Swidler, and Tipton recommend that we "rejoin the human race, to accept our essential poverty as a gift, and to share our material wealth with those in need."[46]

Section C
Return

William McLoughlin's research in the history of religion indicates that there may already be some segments of society that to one degree or another have chosen the return. He describes the collective effect of their experiences and ideas as America's Fourth Great Awakening. He says it began in the 1960s and has distinctive countercultural features:

> *It has rejected the dualistic view of man and nature, man and God, this world and the next, that is so ingrained in Western thought. It espouses a new sense of time, or timelessness. . . . It admires the East instead of considering its wisdom backward, quaint, or incomplete. It prefers to think of humanity in terms of "the family of man" instead of in terms of particular ethnic groups, races, classes, or "chosen" people; it tends also to think of man as merely one form of life among all the others, not necessarily superior to them or empowered to have dominion over them. Finally, it would rather be passive than activist in the current crisis, [waiting] . . . to get reoriented in time and space, spirit and life. . .* [47]

Theodore Roszak says that the period of the sixties in our history is qualitatively different from other periods of reform in that it "for the first time began calling into question the basic structures and premises of industrial society."[48] He observes that of the three major periods of protest in twentieth century American history—1900–1914, 1933–1941 and 1955–74—the first two produced party platforms, laws, constitutional amendments, policies and programs that were political in character, and stayed within fairly well-defined cultural limits. The third, he says, which coalesced in the sixties, "raised issues that transcended politics and reached to the level of culture. It raised questions about our cultural framework. It asked questions about what is sane, what is not sane. It asked for the first time whether we are killing the planet and ourselves." He says we can learn from traditional societies that are closer to nature and have

209

a spiritual foundation. He notes, as does McLoughlin, that religions of this period were concerned with experience rather than doctrines.[49]

Steven Tipton studied what he called "alternative religious movements" among sixties folks and identified themes in each that were more or less consonant with those discussed by McLoughlin and Roszak. He found, for example, that alternative religions such as Zen encouraged the "softening" of self, and attempted to help its adherents fit into the world rather than attempt to change it.[50]

June Singer believes that "a new consciousness is rising out of the morass of a decline in society that has bent too far toward rationalism, toward technology and toward the acquisition of power through unbridled competition—or whatever other means have been considered necessary by those in charge to achieve dominance and control. . . . The new consciousness takes note that our society has become over-balanced in favor of the so-called masculine qualities of character. The new orientation that is gaining in influence may be characterized as emphasizing values that in the past, at least, have been associated more with the feminine than with the masculine. Among these values is a preference for cooperation rather than competition, for a team approach to problems rather than a strictly individualistic approach, for giving credit to intuition at times over and above a deliberate thinking process, and for emphasizing sexuality and relationship over and above power and violence."[51]

Carl Degler says that until after World War II, American history was the history of the white Anglo-American male. He gives an account of a recent change in the content of American history as well as in the personal backgrounds of historians that is in keeping with the themes McLoughlin identifies as part of a Fourth Great Awakening. Degler finds that since WWII there has been a "rather profound reshaping of American history." He says the shift to a healthier mixture of races and genders among historians that we have today [1980] is associated with the alteration in the content of American history. He adds that he is not referring "to changes in interpretations of the past, but to changes in the boundaries of the past, in the definition of what constitutes American history."[52] He says that "this remaking of the content of the American past can be explained in large part by the new self-consciousness among various social groups during the 1960s. Group after group followed the example set by blacks during the late 1950s and early 1960s. The result has been a new recognition by the [historical] profession of the diversity of the population in the American past."[53]

Historian David Noble would likely concur. He speaks of the sixties as a time when the barriers between the sacred and profane began to be broken, a time that saw the emergence of changes including the beginning of the women's movement. He sees it as a time when natives, blacks, gays and other minorities were just beginning to be heard, a time when we as a people were beginning to talk openly about death with the help of such pioneers as Elisabeth Kübler-Ross.[54]

V. Lois Erickson also notes this changing consciousness. She says "on Earth we are only now beginning to hold a view of our connectedness. Thus, we are now recognizing that our world is interconnected, and our universe is such that we are each a part of the all. . . . With conscious experiencing of our connectedness, we then will be able to remember the intuitive voice. It will be remembered by all, for it has been the belief in a separation of specialness in our minds that has not allowed the voice in each of us to be received from wholeness. So, the phase just ahead of us will be one of demonstration . . . . This is my intuitive view of the way we will lift the feminine voice to a balance with the masculine voice, as they are commonly called. In this balance the stance will be a receptive one. The masculine voice, in each of us, will offer a supportive stance. Thus, from my intuitive view, now, the masculine voice in each of us will offer a cognitive stance to support the flow of the voice from our receptive self."[55]

Each of these individuals finds evidence that there are at least some people living within the borders of the United States who are questioning the exclusively dualistic, masculine ways of the past and beginning to appreciate qualities and values traditionally associated with the feminine.[56] They are not alone.

These themes are consonant with those of Alcoholics Anonymous as well. Alcoholics Anonymous is something old and something new. It is firmly grounded in American religious tradition. It is a unique blend of heart and head, self and other, self and god, self and world. With its acceptance of pragmatism, pluralism, and paradox, it incorporates those elements in our American mythology that McLoughlin feels can be revitalized, including "our emphasis on the sanctity of the individual and the importance of the general welfare," as well as "our sense of the holiness of life and the need to find it by losing it."[57] Despite its repeated reference to God with masculine pronouns, the frequently expressed view of A.A. members about a Higher Power as nurturing, empathetic, and accepting is in keeping with McLoughlin's prediction that the godhead in the Fourth Great Awakening will be defined in less dualistic terms.[58]

For Ernest Kurtz, A.A.'s contribution to American culture lies precisely in its philosophy of and program for balancing in the middle. He says that "recovery from alcoholism, then—as disease or as metaphor— meant quite simply for Alcoholics Anonymous the living of a *life* of temperance . . . [and temperance] may be the hinge virtue that allows opening the door to a new, long-delayed age. . . ."[59]

For Ralph Waldo Emerson, "Above all, 'America' wed the ideals of individualism, community and continuing revolution."[60] According to Bercovitch, "Far from pressing the conflict between individual and society, Emerson obviated all conflict whatever by defining inward revolt and social revolution in identical terms. . . . His vision of the good society invited the individual to deny every secular distinction between himself and others" and develop by means of "an endless process of incorporation."[61] This precisely describes some of the key tasks accepted by those who have chosen the return, and key tasks of recovery from alcoholism as well.

Alcoholics Anonymous helps reconcile one of the greatest guiding individual and collective secular myths in American society—the myth of the hero, etc.—and one of the greatest guiding individual and collective spiritual myths—that of re-birth. A.A. helps uncover the underside, or the more subtle side, of the myth of the hero in American culture. The prevailing notion of hero as all-powerful and in control, like Keen's Marlboro man, saving others from a position of superiority, gives way to a hero who needs others as they need him or her, a hero who himself or herself is reliant on a power source greater than the finite self. The hero needs to give, to be of service to embrace his or her healing gifts. The alcoholic continues to suffer as long as he or she operates from the related premises "I can do it alone. I am in control." As Ernest Becker and Jay Lifton, among others, suggest, the task of the hero today is to confront death—to die to the exclusive self and reconnect with community. In transmuting the cycles alcoholics discover unwittingly the flip side of the myths they were teethed on. They find it is ultimately impossible to control an object out there; there are no heroes without monsters; it is impossible to abscond with the boons and be free; and there are no poor helpless victims to be saved, only other hero/monsters to be recognized at different stages of hero/monsterdom. Accepting death to separate selves, alcoholics are free to be re-birthed.

Acknowledging and appreciating the myth in its entirety allow us as a people to move beyond the problems of history to reconciliation, and to peace.

As Campbell notes, "Looking back at what had promised to be our own unique, unpredictable, and dangerous adventure, all we find in the end is such a series of standard metamorphoses as men and women have undergone in every quarter of the world, in all recorded centuries and under every odd disguise of civilization."[62]

Imagine	*Imagine*
a society	*in the balance*
so tired	
from	*of the*
trying	*way of two*
to hold it all together	*with one*
to keep the world in line	*the seeming splits are healed*
that effort ceases	*The problem*
and in frustration	*emerges*
in exhaustion	*as*
its members ooze on through	*one phase*
to Spirit	*of a perennial pattern.*

PART III
RECOMMENDATIONS

PROGRAMMATIC

Regarding Alcoholics

For those in recovery from alcoholism it may be helpful to identify the varieties of ways we ingeniously split ourselves, observe the greatest gaps, and be willing to do or let be done whatever is needed to close the distance.

For Society

Bellah, Madsen, Sullivan, Swidler, and Tipton insist that personal transformation, including transformation of consciousness, among large numbers is essential for the transformation of our culture and our society.

The tasks in many respects are the collective equivalent of those addressed by alcoholics recovering with the help of Alcoholics Anonymous. If they are left undone, we may die, and with us the rest of the world.

Imagine this: The United States practices the Twelve Steps of recovery. . .

FURTHER RESEARCH

I. Possibly now in America we are in the fourth phase of a pattern that may occur in recovery from addictions. The first three phases may be the three great religious awakenings in America identified by McLoughlin. Maybe with each round our society becomes more inclusive, moving from an "ethnocentric" godly utopia[63] to one that increasingly embraces diverse religious and spiritual beliefs. Indicative of a full return and the connection of end with beginning may be the renewal of interest in Native American ways, which both McLoughlin and Roszak note in this half of the 20th century.

It may be that this Fourth Great Awakening, which reconciles formerly perceived dualities, brings with it entry into the fourth quadrant of the proposed spiral cycle. It is possible that further studies of the nature of this awakening would reveal the nature of the fourth dimension of existence as discussed by such writers as Ouspensky, who suggests that the

> *fourth dimension is unknowable. If it exists and if at the same time we cannot know it, it evidently means that something is lacking in our psychic apparatus, in our faculties of perception; in other words, phenomena of the region of the fourth dimension are not reflected in our organs of sense. We must examine why this should be so, what are our defects on which this non-receptivity depends, and must find the conditions (even if only theoretically) which would make the fourth dimension comprehensible and accessible to us.*[64]

Such a dimension could not, as Ouspensky acknowledges, be known through ordinary cumulative knowledge; it may be known only through the process of subtraction. It could be known through what in Indian philosophical systems is referred to as the higher knowledge— *prajna*—a Sanskrit word that roughly translates into English as intuition. In the Indian philosophical systems of Vedanta and Buddhism, the mundane world and nirvana are said to be ontologically the same. What differs is our way of knowing.

Again, an inquiry into the experiences of alcoholics recovering with the help of A.A. might be useful because of the extremity of their experiences. Such a study may well prove fruitful ground for some tentative ventures into the Fourth Dimension—"even if only theoretically." This is a dimension roughly analogous to the Fourth Quadrant on the exploratory symbol-map (Illustration E).

The phrase "Fourth Dimension" is mentioned two times in the Big Book, once in Bill W.'s story when he says he was "catapulted into what [he likes] to call the fourth dimension of existence." The second time is in a promise to others recovering with the help of A.A.: "we have found much of heaven and we have been rocketed into a fourth dimension of existence." He seems to equate the two. "Follow the dictates of a Higher Power," the Big Book says, "and you will presently live in a new and wonderful world, no matter what your present circumstances!" Bill Wilson makes frequent reference to intuition and promises that recovering alcoholics will increasingly rely on this—a sixth sense. This he seems to associate with the paired promise that "God is doing for us what we could not do for ourselves."

I would suggest that Bill Wilson neither used the term "fourth dimension" lightly, nor relied solely on theoretical constructs in this promise made to those who would follow on the path of the pioneer members of Alcoholics Anonymous.

In a sense it could be said that Bill believed the promised land at least was here. "We found much of heaven" right here on this good old earth. It could be implied by Bill's use of these phrases and by his own reports of spiritual experiences that he would agree that the difference between mundane and supramundane existence was epistemological rather than

213

ontological—in accord with the central tenets of such philosophical systems as Avaita Vedanta and Buddhism. There are parallels here too in the Kabballah tradition in Judaism, and with Sufism within the Islamic tradition as well as with Christian mysticism with a mystic such as Meister Eckhart.

Of particular interest may be the nature of the prior "non-receptivity" mentioned by Ouspensky and the receptivity called for in Alcoholics Anonymous. What conditions make the fourth dimension comprehensible and accessible? The experiences of those recovering from alcoholism and other drug addictions with the help of the program and society of Alcoholics Anonymous may suggest that it is an admission of personal powerlessness, a surrender or letting go, and entry into a receptive state along with acceptance of responsibility and equality that opens us to tentative forays into this new dimension.

For alcoholics, perhaps, entry into this realm is gradual. It happens as they begin to find the sacred in the profane, begin to find signs of a Higher Power right here, speaking through other alcoholics, speaking through our neighbors. It happens as they interpret "meaningful coincidences" or synchronicities or serendipities or confluential events as signs of a higher power acting in their lives right here at this moment, and as they learn very gradually and often (usually? invariably?) painfully to live in the present moment.

Entry into this realm happens as splits in mind-space are healed through what Julian Jaynes, adapting a term of Whewell's, calls *consilience*—appreciating similarities between ourselves and others. It happens as splits in mind-time are healed through the telling of stories and gathering the past into the present. It happens with the healing of a split in mind-power, as the will of the separate self is aligned with the will of a greater power. This occurs as the alcoholic begins to become increasingly aware of powerlessness over an objectified universe—first perhaps powerlessness over alcohol, then over other drugs like nicotine, and then maybe food or money or so on, any one or all of which had become deified, ends unto themselves.

The pivotal tasks for the alcoholic are an admission of the powerlessness of his or her separate self, which begins with surrender as described by Tiebout; a willingness to pass on what was received in surrender states, or states of receptivity; and balancing the way of the two with the way of the one.

It is interesting to speculate as to the characteristics of this fourth dimension. To wonder if it is not the place where we know the flow of space–time—power/cause, a place we access as our splits in perception are healed. It is interesting to wonder whether it is a space where time and space collapse without distance, and cause and effect are abridged in the absence of space and time and the opposition of wills—in the absence of the distance which comes from the bifurcation of subject and object.

The situation we find ourselves in may be inversely analogous to the one in Mesopotamia around 1400 B.C. described by Julian Jaynes. Jaynes says that in the graphics of that period gods are no longer depicted. They had disappeared: "In some instances kings beg in front of empty gods' thrones."[65] The idea of heaven, he suggests, emerged to explain where the gods had gone. The reasons for the breakdown—overpopulation, conflicting voices—are similar to the diversity and overwhelming number of choices that "Elpenor" finds as the demon encountered by alcoholics.

So many possibilities can breed confusion, and much confusion can lead to surrender. The very multiplicity of choices that Bellah suggests characterizes the last stage of religious growth may become only two—to accept or resist. And then does it become only one as the will of the separate self is attuned with a cosmic blueprint as we respond to the invitation to return. Does a Higher Power return as asked? With an increased reliance on an "auditory " heart as well as a "visual" mind, it is possible to realize with Bill Wilson that " . . . we need look no further for Utopia. We have it with us right here and now."

II. Would there be any significant differences in the way diverse populations would respond to questions such as those raised in this study?

What similarities and/or differences might there be in response to these questions from within the diverse population of Native Americans?

III. Would there be significant differences in the ways chronological adolescents respond to questions such as those raised in this study? How would their responses compare with a study such as the one done by Edwin Starbuck in the 1800s? Is it possible that traditional time frames need necessarily no longer apply? Maybe, like Vonnegut's Billy Pilgrim, we have become unstuck in time.

Research on adult children of alcoholics indicates that today, at least in many alcoholics' homes, the child has become the parent, the parent the child. It is not uncommon for an alcoholic who began recovery at age 60 to speak of having an extended adolescence. As one recovering alcoholic woman expressed it, "I am experiencing adolescence and menopause at the same time."[66] Similarly, the individual who begins recovery at age 14 may speak of a telescoped adolescence.

Maybe conversion is, as Starbuck suggests, a distinctly adolescent phenomenon, a phenomenon of distinctly adolescent cultures of adolescent adults with dichotomous thought patterns, a need for security and consistency in a world of "mixed messages" they are inexperienced with, or a lack of context for reconciliation. Maybe one who is mature is one who at any age has accepted responsibility and the call to service.

IV. What similarities and/or differences are there between the *Gaiwiio* today and Alcoholics Anonymous? Do followers of this way find A.A. compatible with their teachings and practices? What practices and teachings of Alcoholics Anonymous, if any, do various Native American nations and peoples find compatible with their own traditions? What practices and teachings may they find problematic?

V. Would the responses of those interviewed or surveyed for this study be significantly different than the response for "middle America" on the Kluckhohn and Strodtbeck value orientation scale? If the ideas and experiences reported here are representative, then there may well be a shift in the "mainstream" values in the direction of present orientation from future preference, harmony with nature rather than mastery over nature, and the equal selection of individualism, collateral and lineal relations rather than a preference for individualism, at least within the community of recovering alcoholics. The key splits are identified in somewhat different form by Kluckhohn and Strodtbeck than I have identified them here, but they are basically the same "five crucial universal problems for assessment" described in their studies.[67]

VI. Is there a shift to what Gregory Bateson refers to as Level III learning among alcoholics in recovery with A.A.? Do the responses to the questions in this study corroborate such a shift? If so, it would be expected, for example, that the Renewal Center Group would agree more strongly with paradoxical statements than do those new in recovery. (Morris Berman in *The Reenchantment of the World* has already made a considerable contribution to research in this area. Dr. Daniel Anderson raises the question of Level III Learning among alcoholics in some of his lectures.)

VII. What are the physiological implications of a model such as that proposed by Kohn? What does the occurrence of Wernicke's disease in many chronic alcoholics tell us in light of Jaynes' research and theory?

VIII. How common is attention to synchronicity or confluence among those in recovery from alcoholism? Are there any apparent common denominators in their experiences (even such simple things as paying attention)? Is there anything individuals do or cease to do which seems to encourage or reveal these experiences? Is it possible to investigate causation when cause and effect are one? Is the awareness of confluential events greater among recovering alcoholics than it seems to be in the general population?

IX. How has recovery with Alcoholics Anonymous affected the politics of the recovering individual? How has recovery affected their respective families? What are the spiritual beliefs, practices, and experiences of family members?

X. What is the connection between alcoholism and schizophrenia? Julian Jaynes remarked that it is occasionally informally observed that alcoholism may be a compensation for schizophrenia. What research has already been done? Individuals recovering from alcoholism, as well as schizophrenics, may serve as a fertile source for studies on bicamerality, and the implications of bicamerality for involution and evolution.

EPILOGUE

Imagine our male-and-female man   to
in the tale told by William James   pass
with which this story began   it
at the foot of this cliff   on—
bedraggled
fancy clothes coated with sweat and soil   now
head held in one hand   willing
uprooted tree in the other   to
                                               pass

imagine   truth
this Being   on
knowing the way of the two
finding the way of the one   willing
finding the two and the one to be one   to
                                               pass

imagine this Being   love
now   on
willing
to ask for help   now
                                               willing

willing to accept it   to
                                               pass

and   peace
this time   on

willing

APPENDIXES

Appendix 1

TWELVE STEPS OF ALCOHOLICS ANONYMOUS

1. We admitted we were powerless over alcohol—that our lives had become unmanageable.

2. Came to believe that a Power greater than ourselves could restore us to sanity.

3. Made a decision to turn our will and our lives over to the care of God *as we understood Him.*

4. Made a searching and fearless moral inventory of ourselves.

5. Admitted to God, to ourselves, and to another human being the exact nature of our wrongs.

6. Were entirely ready to have God remove all these defects of character.

7. Humbly asked Him to remove our shortcomings.

8. Made a list of all persons we had harmed, and became willing to make amends to them all.

9. Made direct amends to such people wherever possible, except when to do so would injure them or others.

10. Continued to take personal inventory and when we were wrong promptly admitted it.

11. Sought through prayer and meditation to improve our conscious contact with God *as we understood Him,* praying only for knowledge of His will for us and the power to carry that out.

12. Having had a spiritual awakening as the result of these steps, we tried to carry this message to alcoholics, and to practice these principles in all our affairs.

    These steps appear in the book *Alcoholics Anonymous,* on pages 59–60 of the Third Edition. Reprinted with permission of Alcoholics Anonymous World Services, Inc.

APPENDIX 2

THE TWELVE TRADITIONS OF ALCOHOLICS ANONYMOUS

1. Our common welfare should come first; personal recovery depends upon A.A. unity.

2. For our group purpose there is but one ultimate authority—a loving God as He may express Himself in our group conscience. Our leaders are but trusted servants; they do not govern.

3. The only requirement for A.A. membership is a desire to stop drinking.

4. Each group should be autonomous except in matters affecting other groups or A.A. as a whole.

5. Each group has but one primary purpose—to carry its message to the alcoholic who still suffers.

6. An A.A. group ought never endorse, finance, or lend the A.A. name to any related facility or outside enterprise, lest problems of money, property, and prestige divert us from our primary purpose.

7. Every A.A. group ought to be fully self-supporting, declining outside contributions.

8. Alcoholics Anonymous should remain forever nonprofessional, but our service centers may employ special workers.

9. A.A., as such, ought never be organized; but we may create service boards or committees directly responsible to those they serve.

10. Alcoholics Anonymous has no opinion on outside issues; hence the A.A. name ought never be drawn into public controversy.

11. Our public relations policy is based on attraction rather than promotion; we need always maintain personal anonymity at the level of press, radio, and films.

12. Anonymity is the spiritual foundation of all our traditions, ever reminding us to place principles before personalities.

    These Traditions appear on pages 9–13 of *Twelve Steps and Twelve Traditions*. Reprinted with permission of Alcoholics Anonymous World Services, Inc.

APPENDIX 3

THE BILL W.—CARL JUNG LETTERS
Printed in the A.A. Grapevine, January 1963

Here is a vital chapter of A.A.'s early history never before published. Before Bill brought the message to Bob, even before Ebbie carried the message to Bill, there was one—known as Roland H.—who had taken the messages to Ebbie. Roland H., a helpless, hopeless alcoholic, had been set on the spiritual path to recovery by the celebrated psychiatrist, Dr. Carl Jung of Zurich. This extraordinary exchange of letters reveals for the first time not only the direct historical ancestry of A.A., but the bizarre situation wherein Jung, deeply involved with scientists and with a scientific reputation at stake, felt he had to be cautious about revealing his profound and lasting belief that the ultimate sources of recovery are spiritual sources. Permission to publish Dr. Jung's letter has been granted to the Grapevine by the Jung estate.

January 23, 1961

Professor, Dr. C. G. Jung
Kusnacht-Zurich
Seestrasse 228
Switzerland
My dear Dr. Jung:

This letter of great appreciation has been very long overdue.

May I first introduce myself as Bill W., a co-founder of the society of Alcoholics Anonymous. Though you have surely heard of us, I doubt if you are aware that a certain conversation you once had with one of your patients, a Mr. Roland H., back in the early 1930's, did play a critical role in the founding of our fellowship.

Though Roland H. has long since passed away, the recollections of his remarkable experience while under treatment by you has definitely become part of A.A. history. Our remembrance of Roland H.'s statements about his experience with you is as follows:

Having exhausted other means of recovery from his alcoholism, it was about 1931 that he became your patient. I believe he remained under your care for perhaps a year. His admiration for you was boundless, and he left you with a feeling of much confidence.

To his great consternation, he soon relapsed into intoxication. Certain that you were his "court of last resort," he again returned to your care. Then followed the conversation between you that was to become the first link in the chain of events that led to the founding of Alcoholics Anonymous.

My recollection of his account of that conversation is this: First of all, you frankly told him of his hopelessness, so far as any further medical or psychiatric treatment might be concerned. This candid and humble statement of yours was beyond doubt the first foundation stone upon which our society has since been built.

Coming from you, one he so trusted and admired, the impact upon him was immense.

When he then asked you if there was any other hope, you told him that there might be, provided he could become the subject of a spiritual or religious experience—in short, a genuine conversion. You pointed out how such an experience, if brought about, might re-motivate him when nothing else could. But you did caution, though, that while such experiences had sometimes brought recovery to alcoholics, they were, nevertheless, comparatively rare. You recommended that he place himself in a religious atmosphere and hope for the best. This I believe was the substance of your advice.

Shortly thereafter, Mr. H. joined the Oxford Groups, an evangelical movement then at the height of its success in Europe, and one with which you are doubtless familiar. You will remember their large emphasis upon the principles of self-survey, confession, restitution and the giving of oneself in service to others. They strongly stressed meditation and prayer. In these surroundings, Roland H. did find a conversion experience that released him for the time being from his compulsion to drink.

Returning to New York, he became very active with the "O.G." here, then led by an Episcopal clergyman, Dr. Samuel Shoemaker. Dr. Shoemaker had been one of the founders of that movement, and his was a powerful personality that carried immense sincerity and conviction.

At this time (1932–34) the Oxford Groups had already sobered a number of alcoholics, and Roland, feeling that he could especially identify with these sufferers, addressed himself to the help of still others. One of these chanced to be an old schoolmate of mine, named Edwin T. ("Ebby"-Ed.). He had been threatened with commitment to an institution, but Mr. H. and another ex-alcoholic "O.G." member, procured his parole and helped to bring about his sobriety.

Meanwhile, I had run the course of alcoholism and was threatened with commitment myself. Fortunately I had fallen under the care of a physician—a Dr. William D. Silkworth—who was wonderfully capable of understanding alcoholics. But just as you had given up on Roland, so had he given me up. It was his theory that alcoholism had two components—an obsession that compelled the sufferer to drink against his will and interest, and some sort of metabolism difficulty which he then called an allergy. The alcoholic's compulsion guaranteed that. The alcoholic's drinking would go on, and the allergy made sure that the sufferer would finally deteriorate, go insane, or die. Though I had been one of the few he had thought it possible to help, he was finally obliged to tell me of my hopelessness; I, too, would have to be locked up. To me, this was a shattering blow. Just as Roland had been made ready for his conversion experience by you, so had my wonderful friend, Dr. Silkworth, prepared me.

Hearing of my plight, my friend Edwin T. came to see me at my home where I was drinking. By then, it was November 1934. I had long marked my friend Edwin for a hopeless case. Yet here he was in a very evident state of "release" which could by no means be accounted for by his mere association for a very short time with the Oxford Groups. Yet this obvious state of release, as distinguished from the usual depression, was tremendously convincing. Because he was a kindred sufferer, he could unquestionably communicate with me at great depth. I knew at once I must find an experience like his, or die.

Again I returned to Dr. Silkworth's care where I could be once more sobered and so gain a clearer view of my friend's experience of release, and of Roland H.'s approach to him.

Clear once more of alcohol, I found myself terribly depressed. This seemed to be caused by my inability to gain the slightest faith. Edwin T. again visited me and repeated the simple Oxford Groups' formulas. Soon after he left me I became even more depressed. In utter despair I cried out, "If there be a God, will He show Himself." There immediately came to me an illumination of enormous impact and dimension, something which I had since tried to describe in the book, "Alcoholics Anonymous," and also in "A.A. Comes of Age," basic texts which I am sending to you.

My release from the alcohol obsession was immediate. At once I knew I was a free man.

Shortly following my experience, my friend Edwin came to the hospital, bringing me a copy of William James' "Varieties of Religious Experience." This book gave me the realization that most conversion experiences, whatever their variety, do have a common denominator of ego collapse at depth. The individual faces an impossible dilemma. In my case the dilemma had been created by my compulsive drinking and the deep feeling of hopelessness had been vastly deepened by my doctor. It was deepened still more by my alcoholic friend when he acquainted me with your verdict of hopelessness respecting Roland H.

In the wake of my spiritual experience there came a vision of a society of alcoholics, each identifying with, and transmitting his experience to the next—chain style. If each sufferer were to carry the news of the scientific hopelessness of alcoholism to each new prospect, he might be able to lay every newcomer wide open to a transforming spiritual experience. This concept proved to be the foundation of such success as Alcoholics Anonymous has since achieved. This has made conversion experiences—nearly every variety reported by James—available on almost wholesale basis. Our sustained recoveries over the last quarter century number about 300,000. In America and through the world there are today 8,000 A.A. groups.

So to you, to Dr. Shoemaker of the Oxford Groups, to William James and to my own physician Dr. Silkworth, we of A.A. owe this tremendous benefaction. As you will now clearly see, this astonishing chain of events actually started long ago in your consulting room, and it was directly founded upon your own humility and deep perception.

Very many thoughtful A.A.s are students of your writings. Because of your conviction that man is something more than intellect, emotion and two dollars worth of chemicals, you have especially endeared yourself to us.

How our society grew, developed its traditions for unity and structured its functioning, will be seen in the texts and pamphlet material that I am sending you.

You will also be interested to learn that in addition to the "Spiritual experience," many A.A.s report a great variety of psychic phenomena, the cumulative weight of which is very considerable. Other members have—following their recovery in A.A.—been much helped by your practitioners. A few have been intrigued by the "I Ching" and your remarkable introduction to that work.

Please be certain that your place in the affection, and in the history of our fellowship, is like no other.

Gratefully yours,
William G. W.
Co-founder
Alcoholics Anonymous

Mr. William G. W.
Alcoholics Anonymous
Box 459 Grand Central Station
New York 17, New York
Dear Mr. W.

Your letter has been very welcome indeed.

I had no news from Roland H. anymore and often wondered what had been his fate. Our conversation which he has adequately reported to you had an aspect of which he did not know. The reason that I could not tell him everything was that those days I had to be exceedingly careful of what I said. I had found out that I was misunderstood in every possible way. Thus I was very careful when I talked to Roland H. But what I really thought about, was the result of many experiences with men of his kind.

His craving for alcohol was the equivalent, on a low level, of the spiritual thirst of our being for wholeness, expressed in medievel language: the union with God.°

How could one formulate such an insight in a language that is not misunderstood in our days?

The only right and legitimate way to such an experience is, that it happens to you in reality and it can only happen to you when you walk on a path which leads you to higher understanding. You might be led to that goal by an act of grace or through a personal and honest contact with friends, or through a higher education of the mind beyond the confines of mere rationalism. I see from your letter that Roland H. has chosen the second way, which was, under the circumstances, obviously the best one.

I am strongly convinced that the evil principle prevailing in this world leads the unrecognized spiritual need into perdition, if it is not counteracted either by real religious insight or by the protective wall of human community. And ordinary man, not protected by an action from above and isolated in society, cannot resist the power of evil, which is called very aptly the Devil. But the use of such words arouses so many mistakes that one can only keep aloof from them as much as possible.

These are the reasons why I could not give a full and sufficient explanation to Roland H. but I am risking it with you because I conclude from your very decent and honest letter that you have acquired a point of view above the misleading platitudes one usually hears about alcoholism.

You see, Alcohol in Latin is "spiritus" and you use the same word for the highest religious experience as well as for the most depraving poison. The helpful formula therefore is: *spiritus contra spiritum*.

Thanking you again for your kind letter

I remain
yours sincerely
C. G. Jung

°*"As the hart panteth after the water brooks, so panteth my soul after thee, O God." (Psalm 42.1)*

Notes

References
Notes to Chapter One
Polarizing and the Imbalance of Pairs Apart

[1]One of those who responded to the written questionnaire designed for this study responded with both "yes" and "unsure" to the question as to whether he or she considered him or herself to be an alcoholic.

[2]Hazelden Foundation is a not-for-profit corporation. The philosophy of Hazelden's primary treatment program for chemical dependency, as described in a statement of its philosophy, is based on the belief that "chemically dependent persons have the capacity to abstain from mood-altering chemicals and the capacity to actualize human potential: the capacity to demonstrate personal freedom and responsibility, to exercise self-determination, to realize personal growth and to form meaningful relations." The mission is to help the chemically dependent person achieve two long-term goals: (1) abstinence from mood-altering chemicals and (2) an improved life style. Its short-term goals are "to help the chemically dependent person recognize the illness and its implications; admit that he or she needs help and then realize that he or she will be able to cope with his or her illness; identification with others who share the condition; identify specifically what needs to change; translate that understanding into action." The purpose of Hazelden's Renewal Center as described in one of their brochures is "to provide an environment of hospitality and serenity where 12 Step spirituality can be strengthened or renewed through discovery, reflection and the mutual sharing of skills to improve the quality of one's life."

[3]Jean Kinney and Gwen Leaton, *Loosening the Grip* (St. Louis, Missouri: C.V. Mosby Company, 1978), 76. The illustration from which this description was taken was by Stuart Copans, M.D.

[4]The sole requirement for membership in Alcoholics Anonymous is a desire to stop drinking. Some of those who attend meetings consider themselves to be addicted to drugs other than alcohol *as well as to alcohol*. Some individuals with drugs of choice *other* than alcohol (e.g. heroin) participate in Twelve Step Programs modeled after Alcoholics Anonymous such as Narcotics Anonymous. Each of the twelve individuals interviewed for this study considers him or herself to be a member of Alcoholics Anonymous.

[5]Those who participated in this study are clients of Hazelden Foundation and also consider themselves members of Alcoholics Anonymous. There is no *organizational* affiliation at all between these groups. The Sixth Tradition of Alcoholics Anonymous states that "An A.A. group ought never endorse, finance, or lend the A.A. name to any related facility or outside enterprise, lest problems of money, property, and prestige divert us from our primary purpose." Hazelden Foundation does rely on the Twelve Step Program of Alcoholics Anonymous as the core of their treatment program, and recommends involvement in A.A. and/or other Twelve Step Programs for alumni of Hazelden programs.

[6]Bill Wilson, *Language of the Heart* (New York: The AA Grapevine, Inc., 1988), 276.

[7]This was adapted from the quotation "God chooses one man with a shout, another with a song, another with a whisper "(Rabbi Hahman, qtd. in Lawrence Le Shan *How to Meditate: A Guide to Self-Discovery* [Toronto: Bantam Books, 1974], 33). The quotation was changed to make it more inclusive.

[8]James M. Curtis, *Culture as Polyphony: An Essay on the Nature of Paradigms* (Columbia: University of Missouri Press, 1978), 4–9. Curtis refers here to Thomas Kuhn's work pioneering

the concept of paradigm analysis and Kuhn's reference to the importance which expectations play in the sustaining of paradigms.

[9]The text *Loosening the Grip* mentioned above categorizes and summarizes some theories of causation. George Kohn does a good job of categorizing and summarizing the different modes of treatment in his article "Toward a Model for Spirituality and Alcoholism." In a lecture given as part of the Counselor Training Program at Hazelden, Dr. Daniel Anderson, President Emeritus of the Foundation, describes five theoretical models of Chemical Dependency: (1) Moral/Ethical, (2) Social, (3) Psychological-Psychiatric, (4) Biomedical, and (5) Metaphorical/Existential/Spiritual. He says there are four major treatment models in the United States: (1) Detox (2) Psychiatric (3) Behavior Modification, and (4) Comprehensive.

[10]Fritjof Capra, "The New Physics Revisited," Esalen Conference, 15 November 1985. Tape recording.

[11]Many members of A.A. are careful to distinguish between spirituality and religion. One of the first times the issue surfaced was when liberal, conservative, and radical contingents of A.A. debated over ideas to be expressed in A.A.'s first publication, *Alcoholics Anonymous*. The debate is described in a later publication, *Alcoholics Anonymous Comes of Age:*

> The liberals were the largest contingent and they had no objection to the use of the word "God" throughout the book, but they were dead set against any other theological proposition. They would have nothing to do with doctrinal issues. Spirituality, yes. But religion, no—positively no. Most of our members, they pointed out, believed in some sort of deity. But when it came to theology we could not possibly agree among ourselves, so how could we write a book that contained any such matter? There was no such thing as group opinion in these areas and there never could be. Alcoholics who had tried the missions were forever complaining about this very thing. The alcoholic's unreasoning rebellion against the specifically religious approach had severely handicapped the missions. . . . The atheists and agnostics, our radical left wing, . . . at first . . . wanted the word "God" deleted from the book entirely. (Alcoholics Anonymous, *Alcoholics Anonymous Comes of Age: A Brief History of A.A.* [New York: Alcoholics Anonymous World Services, Inc., 1957], 162–63).

[12]Carl Jung, *Psychological Types,* a revision by R.F.C. Hull of the translation by H.C. Baynes, The Collected Works of C.G. Jung, vol. 6, Bollingen Series XX (Princeton, New Jersey: Princeton University Press, 1976), 273.

[13] William James, *The Varieties of Religious Experience* (New York: The New American Library, nc., 1958), 368. The story of a man falling off a cliff at the beginning of this book is from *Varieties,* 99.

[14]William Bateson, cited in Morris Berman, *The Reenchantment of the World* (Ithaca, New York: Cornell University Press, 1981), 198.

[15]Elpenor, Charles Whitfield, and Schreder are among those who have compared recovery from alcoholism with a mythic quest.

[16] The findings of sociologist Robert Bellah and his colleagues reveal that a sense of separation and related imbalance characterize mainstream American society. A discussion of their findings follows in a later section of this chapter. Bellah et al. say that "a study of [a people's] mores gives us insight into the state of society, its coherence, and its long-term viability. Secondly, it is in the sphere of the mores, and the climates of opinion they express, that we are apt to discern incipient changes of vision—those new flights of the social imagination that may indicate where society is heading." Bellah et al., *Habits of the Heart* (Berkeley, California: University of California

Press, 1985; reprint, New York: Harper & Row, Publishers, 1986), 275 (page references are to reprint edition.) Copyright © 1985 The Regents of the University of California. This sense of separation and imbalance may be comparable to that experienced by alcoholics.

[17]Mircea Eliade, *The Two and the One* (London: Harvill Press, 1965), 122.

[18]György Doczi, *The Power of Limits* (Boston: Shambhala, 1981), 139.

[19]Matthew Arnold, "Stanzas from the Grand Chartreuse" (1855); qtd. in Bellah et al., 277.

[20]Bellah et al., 277; ibid., 124.

[21]Ibid., 277–78; 111.

[22]Alexis de Tocqueville says that Americans "clutch everything and hold nothing fast" Alexis de Tocqueville, *Democracy in America,* trans. George Lawrence, ed. J.P. Mayer (New York: Doubleday, Anchor Books, 1969], 565, 536, 538, qtd. in Bellah et al., 117, 37).

[23]Bellah et al., 46.

[24]Bellah et al. state that Puritan theologian John Winthrop (1703-58) "had seen religion . . . as located in the 'affections.' " Bellah et al., 46.

[25]Ibid., 223; idem, 82; idem, 87.

[26]Ibid., 223.

[27]Ibid.

[28]Ibid., 222.

[29]Ibid., 223, citing Donald M. Scott, *From Office to Profession: The New England Ministry, 1750–1850* (Philadelphia: University of Pennsylvania Press, 1978), 149.

[30]Ibid., 232–33.

[31]Ibid.,234; idem, 245–46.

[32]Ibid., 220–21.

[33]Ibid., 114.

[34]Ibid., 133.

[35]Ibid., 83; idem, 83.

[36]Richard Madsen, Lecture on *Habits of the Heart* given at a Progressive Roundtable program, 9 November 1985, Minneapolis, Minn.

[37]Bellah et al., 144.

[38]Ibid., 236–37.

[39]Some of the problems Bellah et al. find to be associated with mysticism and religious individualism include the following: (1) members find it difficult to sustain their own beliefs "when their only support is from transient associations of the like-minded"; (2) individuals "have difficulty transmitting their own sense of moral integrity to their children in the absence of such a [religious] community"; (3) even the "romantic individualism" of Emerson, and Wordsworth, and others is "remarkably thin when it comes to any but the vaguest prescriptions about how to live in an actual society" (Bellah et al., 247; idem, 81).

[40]Karen R. Staubus offers an interesting discussion of Massachusetts community and the relative isolation of European settlers in colonial Virginia in the context of their respective attitudes and practices in connection with "drunkards." Karen R. Staubus, " 'The Good Creatures': Drinking Law and Custom in Seventeenth Century Massachusetts and Virginia," (Ph.D. diss., Rutgers, 1984).

[41]This dynamic on a collective level is not unlike the dynamic in which females, whom the authors of *Habits* say have traditionally thought more in terms of relationships than in terms of isolated individuals, are now being enjoined to be aware with men primarily of their assertive selves.

[42]Bellah et al., 144, vii.

[43]The relationship between the individual self and nature is noted in *Habits'* section on social ecology in their concluding chapter; the relationship between the individual and time is mentioned in their section on the culture of coherence and also in their concluding chapter; the relationship between the self and a power greater than the self (referred to most frequently as God in *Habits of the Heart*) and the presence or absence of a Higher Power in the world (sacred-profane) in contemporary America is explored in the section on religion. The relationship between the individual self and his or her inner world and outer world is discussed in terms of the separation between public life and private.

[44]June Singer refers to the two different ways of being in the world as the mechanical and the mystical. June Singer, *Androgyny: A New Theory of Sexuality* (Garden City, New York: Anchor Press, 1976).

[45]Gerald M. May, *Will and Spirit* (San Francisco: Harper & Row, Publishers, 1982), 55. May says that "in our willful, manipulation-addicted society it is not surprising that one would try to make unitive experiences happen. It is even less surprising in view of the fact that such experiences so often seem to be 'triggered' by certain environmental or psychological situations. This observation makes it almost impossible for us *not* to jump to the conclusion that some cause-and-effect relationship does exist and that we could master and control it if we only knew how. To date however, such attempts have at best succeeded in achieving only pieces of unitive experience. The full thing has not been, and the contemplatives would say *cannot* be, achieved" (Idem, 58).

[46]Anthony Wallace, "Revitalization Movements," *American Anthropologist* 58 (April 1956): 265. Reproduced by permission of the American Anthropological Association from American Anthropologist 58:2, April 1956. Not for further reproduction.

[47]Wallace, *The Death and Rebirth of the Seneca,* with the assistance of Sheila C. Steen, (New York: Random House, 1972), 301; idem, 307–309. Anthony Wallace says that the difficulties of Handsome Lake "mirrored" those of his community.

[48]This will be discussed further in chapter 3, "Principles and Program for Practicing Peace."

[49]Wilson, "A.A. Tradition: How It Developed," pamphlet, (New York: The A.A. Grapevine, Inc., 1955; reprint, New York: Alcoholics Anonymous Publishing, Inc., 1983), 3.

[50]Wilson, *Language of the Heart: Bill W.'s Grapevine Writings* (New York: The A.A. Grapevine, Inc., 1988), 95.

[51]Ibid., 116.

[52]Ernest Kurtz, *Not-God: A History of Alcoholics Anonymous* (Center City, Minnesota: Hazelden Educational Services, 1979), 202.

[53]Ibid., 203–04.

[54]Tiebout also served as a therapist to Marty Mann, and introduced her to Alcoholics Anonymous. She became not only one of the first female members of Alcoholics Anonymous, but also subsequently helped found the National Council on Alcoholism. (Kurtz, 119).

[55]Harry M. Tiebout, M.D., "Conversion as a Psychological Phenomenon," *Pastoral Psychology,* No. 13 (1951): 28–29.

[56]Ibid., 33–34.

[57]Tiebout, "Therapeutic Mechanisms of Alcoholics Anonymous" (Paper presented at the Ninety-Ninth Annual Meeting of The American Psychiatric Association, Detroit, Michigan, 10–13 May 1943), 469.

[58]Ibid., 471.

[59]Tiebout, "Conversion," 31.

[60]Ibid., 32.

[61]Ibid.

[62]Ibid., 29.

[63]Tiebout, "Therapeutic Mechanisms," 469.

[64]Ibid., 471.

[65]Tiebout, "Conversion," 32.

[66]Tiebout, "Therapeutic Mechanisms," 471.

[67]Ibid.

[68]Tiebout, "Conversion," 29.

[69]Ibid., 29.

[70]Ibid., 33.

[71]Ibid., 31.

[72]Ibid., 33.

[73]Tiebout, "Therapeutic Mechanisms," 472–73; ibid.

[74]Tiebout, "The Act of Surrender in the Therapeutic Process: With Special Reference to Alcoholism." *Quarterly Journal of Studies on Alcohol* 10, no. 1 (June 1949), 50.

[75]Ibid, 48.

[76]Tiebout, "Conversion," 29.

[77]Ibid., 29–30.

[78]Ibid. Tiebout quotes Bill Wilson as saying that "roughly 10 per cent enter Alcoholics Anonymous on the strength of such an experience. The remaining 90 per cent who stay dry achieve the same result by developing slowly and much more gradually the spiritual side of their nature through following the various steps in the program already outlined" (Tiebout, "Therapeutic Mechanisms," 469).

[79]I first came upon this phrase in Mircea Eliade's book *The Two and the One.*

[80]Jung, *Civilization in Transition*, The Collected Works of C.G. Jung, vol. 10, Bollingen Series XX (Princeton, New Jersey: Princeton University Press, 1964), 464.

[81]Eliade, *The Two and the One*, 97.

[82]Kai Erikson, *Everything in its Path: Destruction of Community in the Buffalo Creek Flood* (New York: Simon and Schuster, 1976), 79. Erikson also comments that when considering the culture of a people, "if one wants to understand how any given culture works, one should inquire into its characteristic counterpoints as well as its central values . . . the axes of variation cutting across a culture are not only sources of tension but gradients along which responses to social change are likely to take place. When individual persons or whole groups of people undergo what appear to be dramatic shifts in character, skidding across the entire spectrum of human experience from one extreme to another, it is only reasonable to suspect that the potential had been there all along—hidden away in the folds of the culture, perhaps, but an intrinsic element of the larger pattern nonetheless" (Ibid., 83–84).

[83]Dr. Anderson uses this description in the lectures he gives as part of Hazelden Foundation's Counselor Training Program.

[84]The dualistic way is comparable to what Bellah et al. describe as a culture of separation; the unitive way is comparable to what these authors refer to as a culture of coherence. The difference between a culture predicated upon a dualistic way and a culture traditionally based on a unitive one is illustrated in a passage from William O'Kane in which he compares Northwestern civilization with the civilization of the Hopi Nation in Arizona. See *Walter Collins O'Kane, The Hopis: Portrait of a Desert People* (Norman, Oklahoma: University of Oklahoma Press, 1953), 190–91.

[85]Swami Shantanand, "Science and Spirituality," at *The Twelfth International Congress: The Union of Science and Spirituality, the Himalayan International Institute of Yoga Science and Philosophy of the U.S.A., Honesdale, Pennsylvania, 19 June 1987.*

[86]Steven M. Tipton, *Getting Saved from the Sixties*, with a foreword by Robert N. Bellah (Berkeley, California: University of California Press, 1982), 232. Copyright © 1982 by the Regents of the University of California.

[87]Vine Deloria, Jr., *God is Red* (New York: Grosset & Dunlap, 1973), 300–301.

[88]Tiebout, "Therapeutic Mechanisms," 473.

[89]Tiebout, "Conversion," 35.

[90]Bellah et al. referring to Jonathan Edwards association of religion with the affections, 46. See also footnote 24.

[91]Alcoholics Anonymous, *Alcoholics Anonymous*, 3rd ed. (New York: Alcoholics Anonymous World Services, Inc., 1976), 535. This book will hereinafter be referred to as the Big Book, as it is frequently referred to in A.A. circles.

[92]Kinney and Leaton, 43. Charles Jackson in *The Lost Weekend* describes this condition well: *The curse of the thing, and the blessing too, was that he promised himself to take one drink, or at the most a couple, only to relieve the fright of his tension and stave off collapse; he took it as a medicine; and the, the medicine in him, he was whole again, ready once more to start out. An endless chain, of course; a vicious circle if ever there was one; a helpless series of processes in which the original disorder creates a second which aggravates the first and leads to a third, a third which makes inevitable and necessary a fourth, and so on till the nadir of*

such a day as today is reached—and THIS *is not the bottom, this unhuman torture of now, this wanting to start all over again, even though he well knew that a fifth depth and a sixth were yet to be sounded. He knew all that, he was no fool like other people (they who believed his promises when he knew better than to believe them himself); and knowing it, he yet craved the drink that would bring the whole ruin down upon him again.*

(Charles Jackson, *The Lost Weekend* [New York: Farrar & Rinehart, Inc., 1944], 193–96. Copyright © 1944 by Charles Jackson. Renewal copyright © 1971 by Miss Rhoda Jackson. Reprinted by permission of Farrar, Straus and Giroux, Inc.)

[93]Huston Smith, *The Religions of Man* (New York: Harper & Row, Publishers, 1958), 212.

[94]James, 22

Notes to Chapter Two
Stories from Scholarly Sources

[1]Kurtz, 164.

[2]James, 297.

[3]Ibid.

[4]Ibid., 298.

[5]Ibid., 93.

[6]Ibid., 298.

[7]Ibid., 99.

[8]Ibid., 137.

[9]Ibid., 171.

[10]Ibid., 147.

[11]Ibid., 53.

[12]Ibid., 396.

[13]Despite repeated reference to a Higher Power as God with masculine pronouns, it is also clearly stated that members are free to find their own conception of God or a Higher Power. For example, in the Big Book's "Chapter to Agnostics," it says (using masculine pronouns for all individuals as was the common usage of the day), "In our personal stories you will find a wide variation in the way each teller approaches and conceives of the Power which is greater than himself. Whether we agree with a particular approach or conception seems to make little difference. Experience has taught us that these are matters about which, for our purpose, we need not be worried. They are questions for each individual to settle for himself." Alcoholics Anonymous, p. 50. In most cases I have retained the original language of the A.A. literature despite the fact that it is not always gender-inclusive. I have reproduced the Twelve Steps and Twelve Traditions in the form now used in the Third Edition of *Alcoholics Anonymous*. In some meetings, when the Steps are read, they are read with the word or name "God" replacing "Him." Rachel V. has made such a revision [which she notes that she did with the permission of Alcoholics Anonymous General Service in New York] in the appendix of her book *A Woman*

Like You: Life Stories of Women Recovering from Alcoholism and Addiction (San Francisco: Harper & Row, Publishers, 1985).

[14]James, 329, 323.

[15]Ibid., 143.

[16]Ibid., 344.

[17]Ibid., 343.

[18]Ibid., 129.

[19]Ibid., 49.

[20]May defines grace as an active expression of love (Seminar, "Addiction and Grace," Tiburon, California, 22 November 1988). Jointly sponsored by the Pacific Center for Spiritual Formation of San Rafael, California, the Pacific School of Religion, and the San Francisco Theological Union.

[21]May, *Addiction and Grace* (San Francisco, California: Harper & Row, Publishers, 1988), 10.

[22]Ibid., viii.

[23]Ibid., 13.

[24]Ibid., 24.

[25]Ibid., 27.

[26]Ibid., 132, 52.

[27]I believe the oversimplification that accompanies such categorization is warranted at least in part because of the felt need for a common language, a need discussed repeatedly, for example, by Bellah et al. in *Habits of the Heart*. The decision to refer to masculine and feminine principles as active and receptive ways was made for a number of reasons. Use of the words "masculine" and "feminine" often understandably evoke gender association and possibly defensiveness. The most vital distinction between the two ways seems to be one of function. This is not to imply there are no other aspects of feminine and masculine principles, simply that active and receptive expressions are most significant for those in recovery from alcoholism. It seems each individual, each researcher on this subject speaks of the same general principle and same basic polarity but uses different terms to represent varying degrees of activity or passivity. David Bakan, for example, uses the terms *agency* and *communion;* José Argüelles uses the terms *techne* and *psyche;* June Singer uses the phrases *mechanical* and *mystical;* Gerald May uses the terms *will* and *spirit*. The words do not all mean exactly the same thing; however, I feel each author alludes to the same basic dynamic.

[28]Marion Woodman, "Worshipping Illusions," *Parabola* (Summer 1987): 59.

[29]Ibid., 60.

[30]Ibid., 57.

[31]Woodman, *Pregnant Virgin,* (Toronto, Canada: Inner City Books, 1985), 148–49. This book was recommended to me by Jean, one of the women I interviewed for this dissertation.

[32]Ibid., 30.

[33]Ibid., 81.

[34]Ibid., 83.

[35]Woodman, "Worshipping Illusions," 61.

[36]Anne Wilson Schaef, *When Society Becomes an Addict* (San Francisco: Harper & Row, Publishers, 1987), 14. Excerpt from *When Society Becomes an Addict,* Copyright © 1987 by Anne Wilson Schaef, reprinted by permission of HarperCollins Publishers.

[37]Ibid., 83.

[38]Ibid., 50.

[39]Roland Delattre, "The Culture of Procurement," *Soundings* LXIX, no. 1–2 (Spring-Summer, 1986): 131.

[40]Ibid., 131.

[41]Ibid., 128. Wilson Schaef refers to two types of addictions, which she calls "process" and "substance" addictions.

[42]Ibid., 138.

[43]The powerlessness here is not one of openness to a new way, accompanied by awareness of the futility of attempts to control objectified reality, but experienced rather as a rebound and unwitting powerlessness.

[44]Gregory Bateson, "The Cybernetics of 'Self': A Theory of Alcoholism," *Psychiatry* 34 (February 1971): 11.

[45]Ibid., 16.

[46]Ibid.

[47]Elpenor, "A Drunkard's Progress," *Harper's Magazine,* October 1986, 43–44. Copyright © 1986 by *Harper's* magazine. All rights reserved. Reprinted from the October issue by special permission.

[48]Ibid., 43.

[49]Ibid., 46.

[50]Ibid., 47, 46.

[51]Ibid., 46, 45.

[52]Ibid., 48.

[53]Ibid., 45.

[54]Ibid., 48.

[55]George Kohn, "Toward a Model for Spirituality and Alcoholism," *Journal of Religion and Health* 23, no. 3 (Fall 1984): 253.

[56]Ibid., 257.

[57]Ibid., 254.

[58]Ibid., 257.

[59]Stephanie Brown, *Treating the Alcoholic: A Developmental Model of Recovery* (New York: John Wiley & Sons, 1985), 14. Copyright © reprinted by permission of John Wiley & Sons, Inc.

[60]Ibid., 32.

[61]Ibid., 134.

[62]Ibid., 135.

[63]Ibid., 50.

[64]Ibid., 141.

[65]Brown, "Defining a Continuum of Recovery in Alcoholism" (Ph.D. diss., California School of Professional Psychology, 1977), 60.

[66]Ibid., 3. Dr. Brown's study attempts to determine whether there is a pattern of increasingly high self-esteem as Bean suggests and whether that pattern is determined by length of sobriety as Carroll and Fuller indicate, ibid., 23. She divides recovery into four phases. After the drinking phase, she looks at the following time frames: (1) up to one year of sobriety, (2) 1-3 years of sobriety, (3) 3-5 years of sobriety, and (4) 5 years of sobriety or more. Ibid, 24–25. There were 80 participants in her study from the San Francisco Bay area chapters of Alcoholics Anonymous. Ibid., 27.

[67]Margery Leithliter Jackson, "Actualization of Alcoholics Anonymous Members" (Ph.D. diss., United States International University, 1980), 4, University Microfilms International, Ann Arbor, Michigan #8019033.

[68]Ibid.

[69]Ibid., 37.

[70]Ibid., 42, 58.

[71]Sandra Schnall, "An Interpersonal Approach to Alcoholism: The Transformation of Self through Alcoholics Anonymous," (Ph.D. diss., University of Massachusetts, 1980), 1, University Microfilms International, Ann Arbor, Michigan #8101393.

[72]Ibid., 230.

[73]Ibid., 28.

[74]Ibid., 72.

[75]Ibid., 76.

[76]Ibid., 75.

[77]Ibid., 74–75.

[78]Ibid., 78.

[79]Ibid., 99–100.

[80]Tiebout, "Alcoholics Anonymous—An Experiment of Nature," *Pastoral Psychology* 13 (April 1962): 46.

[81]Ibid., 49.

[82]Tiebout, "Therapeutic Mechanisms," 469.

[83]Ibid., 470, 472.

[84]James F. Rooney and Joan N. Volpe, "The Role on Androgyny in Alcoholism Recovery," (Paper presented at the annual meeting of the Society for the Study of Social Problems, New York, August 1980).

[85]Whitfield, *Alcoholism and Spirituality* (Baltimore, Maryland: The Resource Group, 1985), 45.

[86]Ibid, 19.

[87]Ibid., 84.

[88]Ibid., 39.

[89]Ibid., 67.

[90]Homer Alexander Hall, "The Role of Faith in the Process of Recovery from Alcoholism," (D.Min. diss., Drew University, 1984), 101, 3.

[91]Ibid., 105.

[92]Greg Martin, "The Gospel of Christ and the Gospel of Alcoholics Anonymous: Divergent Paths of Human Liberation" (Ph.D. diss., San Francisco Theological Seminary, 1983), 181, 2 (Abstract).

[93]S. James Roessler, "The Role of Spiritual Values in the Recovery of Alcoholics" (D.Min. diss., Wesley Theological Seminary, 1982), 104.

[94]Edward Sellner, "The Event of Self-Revelation in the Reconciliation Process: A Pastoral Theological Comparison of A.A.'s Fifth Step and the Sacrament of Penance" (Ph.D. diss., University of Notre Dame, 1981), 2.

[95]C. Roy Woodruff, *Alcoholism and Christian Experience* (Philadelphia: The Westminster Press, 1968), 25.

[96]Ibid., 95.

[97]The idea to do this came after seeing a questionnaire on spirituality and recovery by Dr. Charles Whitfield. (There is a copy in his book *Alcoholism and Spirituality* on pages 12–13.) The areas explored in the questionnaire are also similar to those explored by Edwin Starbuck in the *Psychology of Religion* and Steven Tipton in *Getting Saved from the Sixties*.

[98]While no attempt was made to match the group of respondents with the characteristics of Alcoholics Anonymous members as a whole, I will provide as some basis of comparison figures cited by the Alcoholics Anonymous General Serice Organization based on a 1986 survey in which almost 7,000 A.A. members from the United States and Canada participated. In terms of length of sobriety, 33% of A.A. members surveyed were sober less than one year (compared with 25% of the 12 in this study); 38% were sober between one to five years (compared with 50% of those in this study) and 29% were sober over five years (compared with 25% of the twelve in this study). The 1986 survey of A.A. members revealed that 38% of Alcoholics Anonymous members are also addicted to drugs other than alcohol (compared with 42% of those in this study). In terms of the age, 3% of members of Alcoholics Anonymous are aged 20 and younger (compared with 0% of those in this study); eighteen per cent are aged 21–30 (compared with 17% of those interviewed in this study); 52% are aged 31 through 50 (compared with 58% of those in this study) and 27% were aged 51 and older (compared with 25% of those in this study). "AA Membership Survey" pamphlet (New York: Alcoholics Anonymous World Services, Inc., 1987).

[99]James, 358, citing C. Hilty, *Gluck: Dritter Thiel,* 1900, 92ff.

[100]Emerson, cited in Sarcan Bercovitch, *The Puritan Origins of the American Self* (New Haven, Connecticut: Yale University Press, 1975), 182.

[101]One article which addresses the issue of boundaries is by Michael Kerr, entitled "Chronic Anxiety and Defining a Self: An Introduction to Murray Bowen's Theory of Human Emotional Functioning." It appeared in *The Atlantic,* September 1988.

[102]Helen M. Luke, "Letting Go," an interview by Lorraine Kisly, *Parabola* (February 1985), 24.

[103]Jay Lifton, *Boundaries* (New York: Simon and Schuster, 1967), xii.

[104]Julian Jaynes, with Daniel Dennett, Jonathan Miller, and George Ojemann, "Consciousness and Voices of the Mind," McMaster-Bauer Symposium on Consciousness, ed. S.F. Witelson and A.A. Kristofferson, eds., in *Canadian Psychology/Psychologie Canadienne* 27 (Ottawa, Ontario: 1986): 131. Annie Dillard also speaks on this issue:

> *Many of us are still living in the universe of Newtonian physics, and fondly imagine that real, hard scientists have no use for these misty ramblings, dealing as scientists do with the measurable and known. We think that at least the physical causes of physical events are perfectly knowable, and that, as the results of various experiments keep coming in, we gradually roll back the cloud of unknowing. We remove the veils one by one, painstakingly, adding knowledge to knowledge and whisking away veil after veil, until at last we reveal the nub of things, the sparkling equation from whom all blessings flow. . . . All we need do is perfect our instruments and our methods, and we can collect enough data like birds on a string to predict physical events from physical causes.*
>
> *But in 1927 Heisenberg pulled out the rug, and our whole understanding of the universe toppled and collapsed. For some reason it has not yet trickled down to the man on the street that some physicists now are a bunch of wild-eyed raving mystics. For they have perfected their instruments and methods just enough to whisk away the crucial vein and what stands revealed is the cheshire cat's grin.*
>
> *The Principle of Indeterminacy, which saw the light in the summer of 1927, says in effect that you cannot know both a particle's velocity and position. You can guess statistically what any batch of electrons might do, but you cannot predict the career of any one particle. They seem to be as free as dragonflies. You can perfect your instruments and your methods till the cows come home, and you will never ever be able to measure this one basic thing. It cannot be done. The electron is a muskrat; it cannot be perfectly stalked. . . .*
>
> *It is not that we lack sufficient information to know both a particle's velocity and its position; that would have been a perfectly ordinary situation well within the understanding of classical physics. Rather, we know now for sure that there is no knowing. You can determine the position, and your figure for the velocity blurs into vagueness; or, you can determine the velocity, but whooops, there goes the position. The use of instruments and the very fact of an observer seem to bollix the obeservations; as a consequence, physicists are saying that they cannot study nature per se, but only their own investigation of nature. And I can only see blue-gills within my own blue shadow, from which they immediately flee.*
>
> (Annie Dillard, *Pilgrim at Tinker's Creek* [Toronto: Bantam Books, Inc., 1975], 206–207.)

NOTES TO CHAPTER THREE
PRINCIPLES AND PROGRAM FOR PRACTICING PEACE

[1]As of April 17, 1989, the General Service Office of Alcoholics Anonymous gives membership figures as 835,489 individuals in 40,693 groups in the United States alone. It estimates the

number of groups worldwide as 85,270 with 1,734,734 members. At least one group has begun in the Soviet Union. (There was an article about this latter group in *Time* magazine 10 April 1989: 32.) I understand this group recently celebrated its first-year anniversary.

[2]Dr. Daniel J. Anderson, President Emeritus of Hazelden Foundation, in his lecture "Theoretical Aspects of Chemical Dependency" for the Hazelden Counselor Training Program, uses these terms to describe the behavioral patterns of individuals addicted to the beverage alcohol.

[3]This same description of the Fellowship appears in much of the A.A. literature. It is copyrighted by the AA Grapevine and reprinted here with permission.

[4]Kurtz, 162, 229, 228.

[5]Ibid., 169.

[6]Kurtz, 180, says his ideas on this are drawn from Sidney Ahlstrom, "whose phrase is '*annus mirabilis*' " and also from William R. Hutchison, *The Modernist Impulse in American Protestantism* (Cambridge, Massachusetts: Harvard University Press, 1976), 195.

[7]Please refer to the Wilson-Jung-Wilson letters [Appendix 3] for a succinct history of the founding of A.A. The invaluable roles of Lois Wilson and Anne Smith are discussed elsewhere. See, for example, *Lois Remembers* and *Dr. Bob and the Good Oldtimers*.

[8]Wallace, "Revitalization Movements," 265.

[9]Alcoholics Anonymous, *Dr. Bob and the Good Oldtimers,* (New York: Alcoholics Anonymous World Services, Inc., 1952), 40. Page 40 of this book was also the source of information on Dr. Bob's hiding places for alcohol cited in the poem about the origin of Alcoholics Anonymous.

[10]Alcoholics Anonymous, *"Pass It On,"* (New York: Alcoholics Anonymous World Services, Inc., 1984), 90.

[11]Ibid., 106.

[12]Wilson, "The Society of Alcoholics Anonymous," *American Journal of Psychiatry* 106, No. 5, (November 1949): 374. Read at the 105th annual meeting of The American Psychiatric Association, Montreal, Quebec, May 23–27, 1949. Reprinted by permission of the American Psychiatric Association.

[13]Alcoholics Anonymous, *Twelve Steps and Twelve Traditions,* (New York: Alcoholics Anonymous World Services, Inc., 1952), 24. This book will hereinafter be referred to as *Twelve and Twelve*.

[14]Wallace, "Revitalization Movements," 271.

[15]Robert Thomsen, *Bill W.* (New York: Harper & Row, Publishers, 1975), 193.

[16]Bill Pittman, "Alternative Explanations for the Beginnings of Alcoholics Anonymous 1934–1939" (Master's thesis, University of Minnesota, 1983), 205.

[17]Alcoholics Anonymous *"Pass It On,"* 108.

[18]Pittman, 221.

[19]Wallace, "Revitalization Movements," 267.

[20]Ibid., 270–71.

[21]This account is a combination of three versions Bill Wilson gave of his spiritual experience.

One is found in *Language of the Heart,* 284; the second is in *"Pass It On,"* 121; and the third is in *Alcoholics Anonymous Comes of Age: A Brief History of A.A.* (New York: Alcoholics Anonymous World Services, 1957), 63.

[22]Bill Wilson, "The Society of Alcoholics Anonymous," 371.

[23]Wilson, *Language of the Heart,* 285.

[24]Nell Wing was the first receptionist and archivist for Alcoholics Anonymous and worked with Bill Wilson from 1950 until 1971. Nell was also an associate and close family friend of both Bill and Lois Wilson until the death of Bill in 1971, and the death of Lois in 1988. Alcoholics Anonymous, *"Pass It On,"* 294; Nell Wing, interview by author, 29 December 1987, tape recording, New York, New York.

[25]Lois Wilson, interview by author, 1 January 1988, tape recording, Stepping Stones, Bedford Hills, New York. Al-Anon is a mutual help group based on the Twelve Steps of Alcoholics Anonymous for people concerned about the alcoholism of a loved one, friend, or any significant other person in their lives.

[26]Wallace, "Revitalization Movements," 266.

[27]Ibid., 267.

[28]A.A., Big Book, 68.

[29]Ibid., 151.

[30]Ibid., 60–1.

[31]Ibid., 62.

[32]Wilson, *Language of the Heart,* 270.

[33]Wilson, *As Bill Sees It: The A.A. Way of Life . . . Selected writings of A.A.'s co-founder* (New York: Alcoholics Anonymous World Services Inc., 1967), selection No. 217. This passage appeared in the AA Grapevine, January 1963, and is reprinted with permission.

[34]Wilson, *Language of the Heart,* 99.

[35]A.A., Big Book, 45.

[36]Wilson, *Language of the Heart,* 273.

[37]Wilson, *Language of the Heart,* 270.

[38]A.A., Big Book, 73.

[39]A.A., *Twelve and Twelve,* 80.

[40]Ibid., 90.

[41]A.A., Big Book, 59–60.

[42]Wallace, "Revitalization Movements," 267.

[43]Wilson, *Language of the Heart,* 283.

[44]Ibid.

[45]It is noted that many alcoholics continue to smoke nicotine, drink caffeine, and so on. Still, the trend even here may be towards increasing abstinence. For example, of those who answered the questionnaire designed for this study, 59 percent of those in treatment said they still felt

they were using nicotine abusively, compared with 39 percent in the Renewal Center. Similarly, 11 percent of those in treatment said they once had a problem with, but are currently abstinent from, abusive use of nicotine, compared with 32 percent of those in the Renewal Center, who said they had once abused nicotine and were currently abstinent. An A.A. sponsor reports that she heard that "being in A.A. lets you hit bottom in all other areas as well." And my friend Joyce quite pointedly remarked (to one in the throes of heroic attempts to single-handedly control financial affairs) that *she* was told *all* addictions have to go.

[46]Consider the quantities of grapes, potatoes, grain consumed by alcoholics! Consider the wastes excreted in one form or another.

[47]Wallace, "Revitalization Movements," 270.

[48]A.A., Big Book, 12,13.

[49]Ibid., 46.

[50]Wilson, "Society of Alcoholics Anonymous," 374.

[51]Wilson, *Language of the Heart,* 302.

[52]Wallace, "Revitalization Movements," 270.

[53]A.A., Big Book, 84.

[54] Ibid., 62.

[55]Wilson, *Language of the Heart,* 302.

[56]A.A., Big Book, 102.

[57]Kurtz, 214.

[58]Nell Wing adds that "if there is any relaxing of that principle, it will make a great deal of difference because the newcomer would not be getting the full philosophy of the meaning in that word 'anonymity.' It encompasses what it's all about—what they're all about or wanting to be about. It wasn't for nothing that Bill [Wilson] used anonymity as his last message. I just think that the whole base of the fellowship stands tall on anonymity, on that plank" (Interview with author, December 1987).

[59]Ibid.

[60]Wallace, "Revitalization Movements, 267.

[61]Wilson, *Language of the Heart;* A.A., *Twelve and Twelve,* 130.

[62]A.A., *Twelve and Twelve,* 129.

[63]Wilson, *Language of the Heart,* 32.

[64]Lois Wilson, interview by author, January 1988.

[65]A.A., *Twelve and Twelve,* 77.

[66]Ibid., 93.

[67]A.A., Big Book, 84.

[68]Kurtz defines his use of "not-God": "The program of Alcoholics Anonymous . . . teaches first and foremost that the alcoholic is *not* God. . . . Because the alcoholic is not God, not absolute, not infinite, he or she is essentially limited. Yet from this very limitation—from the

alcoholic's *acceptance* of personal limitation—arises the beginning of healing and wholeness. It is this facet of the message of 'not-God' that Alcoholics Anonymous as fellowship lives out" (Kurtz, 3–4).

[69]Elpenor, 44.

[70]Ibid., 47.

[71]Ibid., 46.

[72]Mythologers note that in many societies the dragon is symbolic of the Ego.

[73]Wilson, *Language of the Heart,* 166. Kurtz speaks of this in terms of merging Pietist and Humanistic traditions. He says that "both appear in the fellowship and program of Alcoholics Anonymous." He says, "The first of these . . . concentrates upon the separation of the human individual from the fulfilling Other. . . . [It] . . . stresses 'salvation' as from outside the self, and because of its root perception of awe and sense of humility is well-termed 'Pietist.' " The second "stresses human participation in human salvation, and because of its profound respect for human possibility, rejoices in the name 'Humanist.' Because of its faith in human freedom, the style is also well-termed 'Liberal' " (Kurtz, 179).

[74]A.A., Big Book, 188.

[75]Ibid., 86–88.

[76]Ibid., 83–84.

[77]Ibid., 569–70.

[78]Wallace, "Revitalization Movements," 265.

[79]Ibid.

[80]A.A., Big Book, 59.

[81]A.A., *Twelve and Twelve,* 122.

[82]Some of the measures taken within the organization of Alcoholics Anonymous to ensure that money matters are kept in perspective include the refusal to accept donations from other than A.A. members; limiting even those donations; and leasing rather than owning office equipment and furniture.

[83]Wallace, "Revitalization Movements," 274.

[84]Wilson, *Language of the Heart,* 94.

[85]A.A., *Twelve and Twelve,* 9–10.

[86]A.A., *Comes of Age,* 270.

[87]Wing, interview by author.

[88]Wilson, *Language of the Heart,* 81.

[89]Ibid., 89.

[90]Wilson, "Society of Alcoholics Anonymous," 374.

[91]Wilson, *Language of the Heart,* 78.

[92]Ibid., 88. Bill also comments that when the newcomer asks, " 'Are there any conditions?' we joyfully reply, 'No, not a one.' When skeptically he comes back saying, 'But certainly there must

be things that I have to do and believe,' we quickly answer, 'In Alcoholics Anonymous there are no *musts*.' Cynically, perhaps, he then inquires,'What is this all going to cost me?' We are able to laugh and say, 'Nothing at all, there are no fees and dues.' . . . For Alcoholics Anonymous is saying,'We have something priceless to give, if only you will receive.' That is all" (Ibid., 79).

[93]Wilson, "Society of Alcoholics Anonymous," 374.

[94]A.A., "Questions and Answers on Sponsorship," pamphlet (New York: Alcoholics Anonymous World Services, Inc. 1976), 5.

[95]Wallace, "Revitalization Movements, 274.

[96]Tipton, *Getting Saved from the Sixties,* foreword by Robert Bellah (Berkeley, California: University of California Press, 1982), 240. In this interesting study, Steven Tipton identified and described "alternative religious movements" in America today. There are many parallels between these movements and A.A.

[97]A.A., Big Book, 149.

[98]Ibid., 150.

[99]Tipton, *Getting Saved,* 237.

[100]Wilson, *As Bill Sees It,* Selection No. 44. This passage appeared in the AA Grapevine, March 1962, and is reprinted with permission.

[101]A.A., *Twelve and Twelve,* 124.

[102]A.A., Big Book, 452.

[103]Tipton, *Getting Saved,* 232.

[104]William McLoughlin, *Revivals, Awakenings and Reforms* (Chicago: The University of Chicago Press, 1978), 86. Copyright © 1978 by the University of Chicago Press. Quotations are reprinted with permission.

[105]According to Wallace, Handsome Lake is the Indian prophet who conceived *Gaiwiio* or Good Word. He says that the *Gaiwiio* is still practiced today by about seven thousand of the approximately fifteen thousand Iroquois Indians in New York State and Ontario. Wallace, "Handsome Lake and the Great Revival," 150. There is an article which mentions the role of the *Gaiwiio* as it exists today in *National Geographic* (September 1987), 370–403.

[106]Wallace, *Death and Rebirth of the Seneca* (New York: Random House, 1972) 307–09. Copyright © 1969 by Anthony Wallace. Used by permission of Alfred A. Knopf, Inc.

[107]Ibid., 301.

[108]Ibid., 309.

[109]Ibid., 253.

[110]Ibid., 324.

[111]Ibid., 279.

[112]Ibid., 308–09; 329.

[113]Ibid.

[114]Ibid., 279.

[115]There are other similarities as well, such as the use of preceptors or spiritual guides who are in some ways similar to A.A.'s sponsors.

[116]A.A.'s beauty is also in its borrowing of what works, and omitting what did not seem to work for other movements. For example, it learned from the Washingtonian Movement to avoid alignment with political causes which may dilute the primary purpose of the organization. From the Oxford Group, in addition to many of the fine ideas adapted to the program of A.A., it learned to rely on attraction rather than promotion as a policy for expanded membership. (Dr. Silkworth is said to have had a strong influence in this direction, advising Bill early on that a "drunk must be led, not pushed.") Another mainstay of the Oxford Group changed in A.A. was the Oxford Group's advocacy of "Four Absolutes" (absolute honesty, absolute purity, absolute unselfishness, absolute love). In A.A., this idea of absolutes was replaced with the goal of spiritual progress rather than spiritual perfection.

[117]McLoughlin, 105.

[118]Ibid., 112–13.

[119]Ibid., 128.

[120]William Clebsch, *American Religious Thought: A History,* Chicago History of American Religion, Series ed. Martin E. Marty (Chicago: The University of Chicago Press, 1973), 125 ff.

[121]Kurtz, 164.

[122]Wing, interview by author.

[123]Kurtz, 183.

[124]McLoughlin, 128.

[125]Ibid., 129.

[126]Ibid.

[127]A.A., *Comes of Age,* 39.

[128]This practice was subsequently modified in A.A., whose early members felt it was important to be even more careful than they felt the Oxford Group was at that time to emphasize the rights and honor the guidance of the individual member.

[129]Kurtz, 49.

[130]Ibid.

[131]A.A., *Comes of Age,* 231.

[132]Wilson, "The Society of A.A.," 375.

[133]Wilson, *Language of the Heart,* 151.

[134]Mac Marshall, "Social Thought, Cultural Belief and Alcohol," *Journal of Drug Issues* 15 (Winter 1985): 68.

[135]The distinction between involution and evolution as considered here is described by Swami Rama in the *Perennial Philosophy of the Bhagavad Gita.* He says that

> the human being goes through two distinct stages in this journey to Self-awakening. The first stage is traditionally referred to as evolution. In this process consciousness travels from its subtlemost aspect through ever more gross aspects of existence, obscuring all awareness of

oneself as pure Consciousness. Finally one becomes completely identified with the external world. In the second stage, which is traditionally referred to as involution, one reverses direction: he turns inward and commences a journey in which he rediscovers and experiences ever more subtle aspects of his being, finally coming to realize himself as pure Consciousness. Sensory withdrawal is one of the first important steps in the process of involution, . . . and that is just like going against the currents of a river. One needs to be well equipped for such an undertaking, for his habits and past experiences continually pull the mind outward.

(Swami Rama, *Perennial Psychology of the Bhagavad Gita* [Honesdale, Pennsylvania: The Himalayan International Institute of Yoga Science and Philosophy of the U.S.A., 1985], 108.)

[136]A.A., *Twelve and Twelve,* 55.

[137]This prayer appears in Reinhold Niebuhr's article "A View from the Sidelines," as "God, give us grace to accept with serenity the things that cannot be changed, courage to change the things that should be changed, and the wisdom to distinguish the one from the other" (*The Christian Century,* [19–26 December 1984]: 1195).

[138]John Bierhorst, ed. *The Red Swan: Myths and Tales of the American Indians,* (New York: Farrar, Straus and Giroux, 1976) 6–7.

[139]A.A. is in concert with many Indian philosophical traditions, particularly as they find expression in the Vedantic and Mahayana Buddhist traditions, which scholar Puligandla feels in many ways are most representative of the world perspective of Indian philosophical traditions. Some shared themes include the following: (1) The importance of the role of attachment. One of the most well-known verses from the Bhagavad Gita, a sacred text, is compatible with A.A. philosophy and A.A. with it: "The person who wanders free of attachment, having abandoned all desire, devoid of ego and of the concept of 'mine,' he attains peace" [Verse 71]. Swami Rama, 116. A central concern of individual A.A.s and A.A. as a whole involves the process of letting go of a primary attachment—that of the alcoholic to alcohol. The A.A. program fosters disidentification with the small separate self—the ego in the popular sense. It is said in one of the basic texts of A.A. that "all of A.A.'s Twelve Steps ask us to go contrary to our natural desires . . . they all deflate our egos." (2) The emphasis on the role of ignorance. The term for this in A.A. language is *denial, (ignore-ance* as Alan Watts hyphenates it)—one of the hallmarks of addiction according to Dr. Daniel J. Anderson, President Emeritus of Hazelden, and others. (3) The concern with alleviating suffering right here, right now. Bill Wilson and Dr. Bob Smith were, in their way, as was Buddha, concerned primarily with practical effects of tenets; little concerned with theory divorced from experience and alleviation of pain. (4) The concentration on internal causation. This is evident in A.A. with its belief that *"After all, our problems were of our own making."* A.A., Big Book, 103. (5) The importance of purification. Provision for purification in A.A. occurs throughout the entire program, with all the steps, in particular Steps Four through Ten. The Seventh Step prayer specifically addresses itself to this need. The authors of the Big Book comment on the Seventh Step on page 76: "When ready, we say something like this: "My Creator, I am now willing that you should have all of me, good and bad. I pray that you now remove from me every single defect of character which stands in the way of my usefulness to you and my fellows. Grant me strength, as I go out from here, to do your bidding. Amen." (6) The role of surrender. This is evident in A.A. through such practices as the repetition of the Lord's Prayer and the Third Step Prayer. The Big Book suggests that members say a prayer similar to this as they practice the Third Step: "Many of us said to our Maker, *as we understood Him:* 'God, I offer myself to Thee—to build with me and to do with me as Thou wilt. Relieve me of the bondage of self, that I may better do Thy will. Take away my difficulties, that victory over them may bear witness to those I would help of Thy

Power, Thy Love, and Thy Way of life. May I do Thy will always!" A.A., Big Book, 63. (7) Value of intuitive knowledge, known as *prajñā* in Sanskrit. Recovering alcoholics are promised that they will "intuitively know how to handle situations which used to baffle [them]" (A.A., Big Book, 84). (8) Each of the "five sheaths" identified in Advaita Vedānta are addressed in A.A. The Yoga Sutras refer to these sheaths as "*kleshas*—the five afflictions; they are sheaths that cover the real nature of the Self. They are said to be the five forms of wrong cognition: ignorance, egoism, attraction, aversion, and the fear of death. According to yoga philosophy and psychology these five are the afflictions that deepen man's bondage to the ever changing world with all its pains and miseries." Michael Klein, "The Role of Self-Effort and Grace on the Spiritual Path," Master's thesis, August 1986, Himalayan Institute, Honesdale, Pennsylvania, 48. A.A. teaches of the impermanence of life. "This too shall pass" is one of the most often cited slogans in A.A.

This is not to suggest that these are the only similarities, nor to suggest that these similarities are shared with the Eastern philosophical traditions alone. Those parallels cited are simply meant to be exemplary. Some of the parallels with a Native American People are identified in the section which compares the rebirth of the Seneca in the nineteenth century with the movement of A.A. The roots of A.A. in Christianity is a subject explored in depth in many other books and papers. (Some of these works, e.g., those by Sellner, Martin, and Woodruff, are cited in chapter 2.) A survey of the literature frequently read by and considered as important by early A.A.s makes clear the influence of Christianity on the program of A.A. A bibliography of works read by early A.A.s is available in Bill Pittman's book, *AA: The Way It Began* (Seattle: Glen Abbey Books, 1988). Kurtz discusses the relationship between Christian ideas and practices in depth in *Not-God*. While it is said there are so many forms of Christianity it is difficult to identify any one form, the A.A. program does revolve around one of the commonly agreed upon tenets: loving one's neighbor as one's self.

In connection with A.A.'s conjuction of modern and traditional values, I find it interesting that the symbol of A.A. is a triangle in a circle—the triangle which in mathematical notations stands for change, the circle which stands in Nell Wing's words for eternity. The circle, she says, "came down from ancient beliefs. The circle represents the whole, it represents the universe, it represents the continuation of life, the never-ending circle of spirituality" (Interview by author). Maybe the triangle is a pyramid within the circle as vortex, which likely encloses a more inward vortex. And so on.

If we imagine traditional societies to be our collective feminine, and modern ones our collective masculine, it may be said that A.A. embraces the cultural as well as personal feminine. It may be helpful to consider this possibility in so far as it may help identify similar dynamics between male and female principles on the levels of culture and of inter-personal and intrapersonal relationships.

[140]Wing, interview with author. Kurt Vonnegut, Jr., in response to an interview question said that "Alcoholics Anonymous gives you an extended family that's very close to a blood brotherhood, because everybody has endured the same catastrophe. And one of the enchanting aspects of Alcoholics Anonymous is that many people who aren't drunks [practice the program] because the social and spiritual benefits are so large" (Kurt Vonnegut, Junior, *Wampeters, Foma, and Granfalloons* [New York: Dell Publishing Co., Inc., 1974] 240–41).

[141]Figures given by General Service Office of Alcoholics Anonymous, New York, NY, 1989.

[1]A.A. "birthdays" are anniversaries of the date when the individual began daily abstinence from alcohol. In some parts of the countries, these dates are referred to as anniversaries, in other parts of the country as birthdays.

[2]A "beginners' meeting" in A.A. is one specifically devoted to members new in the program in which concerns about being new in sobriety and questions about the program are discussed.

[3]"AIDS" is the acronym for Acquired Immunodeficiency Syndrome; "ARC" the acronym for AIDS-Related Complex.

[4]This is an excerpt from what is known in A.A. as the Third Step prayer, cited above.

Notes to Chapter Four
People Practicing Peace
Part I
Practicing Peace with Themselves

[1]May, "Spirituality and Addiction."

[2]Frederick Hampden-Turner, *Maps of the Mind,* (New York: Collier Books, 1981), 168.

[3]Swami Ajaya, Ph.D., *Psychotherapy East and West: A Unifying Paradigm* (Honesdale, Pennsylvania: The Himalayan International Institute of Yoga Science and Philosophy of the U.S.A, 1983), 55, 56.

[4]Ernest Becker, *The Denial of Death* (New York: The Free Press, 1973), 23.

[5]Wendell Berry, Excerpt from "Envoy," a poem in *Openings: Poems by Wendell Berry* (New York: Harcourt, Brace & World, Inc., 1968), 67. Copyright © 1968 by Wendell Berry, reprinted by permission of Harcourt Brace Javonovich, Inc.

[6]Thomas Merton, citing I Cor. 1:17 in *Zen and the Birds of Appetite* (New York: New Directios, 1968), 55.

[7]R. Puligandla, *Fundamentals of Indian Philosophy* (Nashville, Tennessee: Abingdon Press, 1975), 245–46.

[8]Hazrat Inayat Khan, *The Sufi Message of Hazrat Inayat Khan* (London: Barrie and Jenkins, 1962), Vol. 8, *Struggle and Resignation,* 72.

[9]Louis Sullivan, *Democracy: A Man-Search* (Detroit: Wayne State University Press, 1961), 211; *The Testament of Stone: Themes of Idealism and Indignation from the Writings of Louis Sullivan,* ed. Maurice English (Chicago: Northwestern University Press, 1963), 16.

[10]Woodman, "Worshipping Illusions," 61, 63, 64.

[11]A.A., *Twelve and Twelve,* 21–22.

[12]Hyemeyohsts Storm, *Song of Heyoehkah* (San Francisco: Harper & Row, Publishers, Inc, 1981), 76–77. Excerpt from Song of Heyoehkah by Hyemeyohsts Storm. Copyright © 1981 by Hyemeyohsts Storm. Reprinted by permission of Harper Collins Publishers.

[13]Boy George is a British entertainer.

[14]James W. Fowler and Sam Keen, *Life Maps: Conversations on the Journey of Faith,* ed. Jerome Berryman. Copyright © 1978, 1985 Word Publishing, a division of Word, Inc., Dallas, Texas. Used by permission.

[15]Theodore Roszak, *Where the Wasteland Ends* (New York: Doubleday & Company, Inc., 1973), 89.

[16]A.A., Big Book, 535.

[17]Lewis Hyde, *Alcohol and Poetry: John Berryman and the Booze Talking* (Dallas, Texas: Dallas Institute Publications, 1986), 10.

[18]Eleanor Bertine, *Jung's Contribution to Our Time* (New York: G.P. Putnam's Sons, 1967), 17.

[19]Jung, *Memories, Dreams, Reflections* (New York: Vintage Books, 1961), 247–48.

[20]Storm, *Song of Heyoehkah* (San Francisco: Harper & Row, Publishers, 1981), 207.

[21]Paul associates surrender with death and says he does not believe in an afterlife.

[22]This would be in keeping with the findings of Edward Sellner, whose whole study, also done in part with Hazelden clients, was an investigation of the significance of what he calls the "event" of the Fifth Step [of Alcoholics Anonymous.]

Notes to Chapter Four
People Practicing Peace
Part II
Practicing Peace with God or Higher Power

[1]Khan, *The Unity of Religious Ideals,* vol. IX, The Sufi Message of Hazrat Inayat Khan (London: Barrie and Rockliff, 1963; reprint ed. London: Barrie and Jenkins, 1974),11; idem, vol. VII, (London: Barrie and Rockliff, 1962; reprint ed. London: Barrie and Jenkins), 178; idem, vol. IX, 12.

[2]Vine Deloria, Jr., *God is Red* (New York: Grosset & Dunlap, 1973), 104.

[3]Khan, *The Unity of Religious Ideals,* 11, 247, 12.

[4]Acts 17: 26–29.

[5]Matthew Fox, *The Coming of the Cosmic Christ: The Healing of Mother Earth and the Birth of a Global Renaissance* (San Francisco: Harper & Row, Publishers, Inc., 1980), 228.

[6]Earnie Larsen has written several books on recovery from alcoholism and has made available several cassette tapes. He also does workshops on this subject.

[7]Catherine L. Albanese, *America: Religions and Religion,* The Wadsworth Series in Religious Studies, ed. Robert S. Michaelsen (Belmont, California: Wadsworth Publishing Company, 1981), 25, 22.

[8]Carroll and Noble, *The Free and the Unfree,* 50.

[9]Teilhard de Chardin, cited in Henri de Lubac, S.J., *The Religion of Teilhard de Chardin: The Spiritual Teaching of Teilhard de Chardin and its Influence on His Over-all Thought,* trans. Rene Hague (Garden City, New York: Doubleday & Company, Inc.), 292–93.

[10]John 13:20.

[11]The First Step of A.A.: We admitted we were powerless over alcohol—that our lives had become unmanageable.

[12]The Fifth Step of A.A.: "Admitted to God, to ourselves, and to another human being the exact nature of our wrongs."

[13]This was an assessment for chemical dependency.

[14]This is religious practice in the Catholic Church.

[15]The Fourth Step of A.A.: "Made a searching and fearless moral inventory of ourselves."

[16]Julian Jaynes, *The Origin of Consciousness in the Breakdown of the Bicameral Mind* (Boston: Houghton Mifflin Company, 1976), 225.

[17]Jaynes, Symposium, 139, 138, 136.

[18]Zora Neale Hurston, *Their Eyes Were Watching God* in *I Love Myself When I am Laughing . . . And Then Again When I am Looking Mean and Impressive,* Alice Walker, ed., (Old Westbury, New York: The Feminist Press, 1979), 248.

[19]Ruby Modesto, and Guy Mount, "Autobiography of a Cahuilla Pul," *Shaman's Drum* (Spring 1987), 44.

[20]Evelyn Eaton, *Snowy Earth Comes Gliding* (Independence, California: Draco Foundation, 1874), 29.

[21]May, *Addiction and Grace,* 116.

[22]The Eleventh Step of A.A.: "Sought through prayer and meditation to improve our conscious contact with God *as we understood Him,* praying only for knowledge of His will for us and the power to carry that out."

[23]Please refer to Reference Notes, chapter 4.

[24]Mary Farrell Bednarowski, "Outside the Mainstream: Women's Religions and Women Religious Leaders in Nineteeth Century America," *Journal of the American Academy of Religion.* XLVIII/2, 208, 225, cited in Gayle Graham Yates, *Women in Contemporary American Religion,* Course Manual for Independent Study (Minneapolis, Minnesota: University of Minnesota, 1985), 157, 174.

[25]Rita M. Gross, "Hindu Female Deities as a Resource for the Contemporary Rediscovery of the Goddess," *Journal of the American Academy of Religion* XLVI/3,271, cited in Yates, 223.

[26]Alice Walker, *The Color Purple* (New York: Simon & Schuster, Inc., 1982), 203. Excerpt from *The Color Purple.* Copyright 1982 by Alice Walker. Reprinted by permission of Harcourt Brace Jovanovich, Inc.

[27]Mahatma Gandhi, *All Men Are Brothers: Autobiographical Reflections,* 72. Copyright 1958 by Columbia University Press. Reprinted by permission of the Continuum Publishing Company.

[28]Ann stated that she felt she was still using food abusively at the time of our interview.

[29]Key concepts of the *Course in Miracles* appear on the the first pages of the text: "Nothing real can be threatened. Nothing unreal exists. Therein lies the peace of God" (*A Course in Miracles* [Farmington, New York: Foundation for Inner Peace, 1975]). Gerald Jampolsky, in his book *Love is Letting Go of Fear,* summarizes the basic teachings of this text. How the Course was written and came to be published is the subject of Robert Skutch's *Journey Without Distance.*

Notes to Chapter Four
People Practicing Peace
Part III
Practicing Peace with Others

[1]Fox, *Original Blessing,* (Sante Fe, New Mexico: Bear & Company, 1983), 49. The second paragraph cited from Matthew Fox, is Fox's citation of Raghavan Iyer, *The Moral and Political Thought of Mahatma Gandhi* (Oxford University Press, 1978), 181.

[2]The Upanishads, cited in Ken Wilbur, *The Atman Project* (Wheaton, Illinois: The Theosophical Publishing House, 1980), 191.

[3]Mother Teresa, interview by Courtney Tower, *Reader's Digest,* December 1987, 227, 175. Excerpted with permission from "Mother Teresa's Work of Grace" by Courtney Tower, *Reader's Digest,* December 1987. Copyright © 1987 by The Reader's Digest Assn., Inc.

[4]Storm, *Seven Arrows* (New York: Harper & Row Publishers, 1972). 125–29. Excerpt from *Seven Arrows* by Hyemeyohsts Storm. Copyright © 1972 by Hyemeyohsts Storm. Reprinted by permission of HarperCollins Publishers.

[5]Some towns or cities in the United States have what are called Alano Clubs (neither owned nor operated by Alcoholics Anonymous as an organization), where some A.A. meetings may be held and which may serve as a social meeting place for some members.

Notes to Chapter Four
People Practicing Peace
Part IV
Practicing Peace with the World

[1]Kurtz, 165–66.

[2]Eliade, *The Sacred and the Profane,* trans. Willard R. Trask (New York: Harcourt, Brace & World, Inc., 1957), 165.

[3]Eliade, *The Two and the One,* (London: Harvill Press, 1965), 158.

[4]Eliade, *The Sacred and the Profane,* 13. David Noble comments that moderns *do* have a sense of the sacred; however it is a sacred that exists in the future, a state to be arrived at progressively.

[5]Progoff, *Jung, Synchronicity and Human Destiny: C.G. Jung's Theory of Meaningful Coincidence* (New York: The Julian Press, Inc., 1973), 46. Arthur Koestler says that it was

> only in the eighteenth century that, in the wake of the Newtonian revolution, causality was enthroned as the absolute ruler of matter and mind only to be dethroned in the first decades of the twentieth, as a consequence of the revolution in physics. But even in the middle of the materialistic nineteenth century that lone giant, Arthur Schopenhaur—who had a decisive influence on both Freud and Jung—proclaimed that physical causality was only one of the rulers of the world; the other was a metaphysical entity, a kind of universal consciousness, compared to which individual consciousness is as a dream compared to wakefulness; "coincidence," Schopenhaur wrote, "is the simultaneous occurrence of causally unconnected events. . . ."

(Arthur Koestler, *Roots of Coincidence,* with a postscript by Renee Haynes [New York: Random House, 1973], 107. Copyright © 1972 by Arthur Koestler. Reprinted by permission of Random House Inc.) While Koestler comments that causality was "dethroned" in the first decades of the twentieth century, I believe it is important to note in this context what Anthony Wallace terms the "Principle of Conservation of Cognitive Structure." According to David Born, Wallace states than "an individual will not abandon any portion of his mazeway structure unless he has available a substitute conception. Furthermore, an individual will often cling tenaciously to outmoded mazeway structures long after evidence has been presented indicating their total ineffectiveness" (Anthony Wallace, *Culture and Personality* [New York: Random House, 1961], 161, cited in David Born, "Psychological Adaptation and Development under Acculturative Stress"), 533.

[6]Progoff, 121.

[7]Koestler, 85.

[8]Koestler, 119, 122. Koestler says there is a basic polarity between what he calls the "Self-assertive Tendency" and the "Integrative Tendency." Ibid., 112–113.

[9]Koestler, 108. Reprinted with permission of Sterling Lord Literistic, Inc. Copyright © 1972 by Arthur Koestler.

[10]Jung, *Mysterium Coniunctionis*, 419–20, cited in Jean Shinoda Bolen, *The Tao of Psychology* (San Francisco, Harper & Row, Publishers, 1979), 98.

[11]Doug Boyd, *Rolling Thunder* (New York: Dell Publishing Company, Inc., 1974), 54–55.

[12]V. Lois Erickson, "The Nature of the Self: Integrating the Spiritual Order," speech presented to the Educational Psychology Department, University of Minnesota, 13 May 1988.

[13]One of the promises given in A.A.'s Big Book on page 83 is that "fear of economic insecurity will leave us."

[14]She wasn't sure if taking prescription medication as prescribed would mean she still could consider herself abstinent.

[15]Joseph Campbell, interviewed by Bill Moyers. Aired on public television June 13, 1988 in California.

[16]Edward Hall, *Dance of Life: The Other Dimensions of Time* (New York: Anchor Press, Doubleday, 1984), 135.

[17]Ibid., 25.

[18]Hall notes that there are many kinds of time, including personal time, biological time and profane time. He is one of those who observe that people all over the world report transcending time and space. Ibid., 24.

[19]Eliade, *Myth and Reality,* trans. Willard R. Trask (New York: Harper & Row, Publishers, 1963), 107.

[20]J.T. Fraser, *Of Time, Passion and Knowledge: Reflections on Strategy of Existence* (New York: George Braziller, 1975), 377.

[21]Shinoda Bolen, 93. Excerpt of text from *The Tao of Psychology* by Jean Shinoda Bolen, Copyright © 1979 by Jean Shinoda Bolen. Reprinted by permission of HarperCollins Publishers.

[22]Puligandla, *Fundamentals of Indian Philosophy* (Nashville, Tennessee: Abingdon Press, 1975), 248–55.

[23]Roy Wagner, *The Invention of Culture* (Englewood Cliffs, New Jersey: Prentice-Hall, Inc., 1975), 73.

[24]Ibid., 73, 74.

[25]Capra, *The Tao of Physics: An Exploration of the Parallels Between Modern Physics and Eastern Mysticism* (Boulder, Colorado: Shambhala Publications, Inc., 1976), 173.

[26]Anthony deMello, The Song of the Bird (New York: Doubleday, 1984), 20. Excerpt from *The Song of the Bird* by Anthony deMello, copyright © 1982 by Anthony deMello, S.J. Used by permission of Doubleday, a division of Bantam Doubleday Dell Publishing Group, Inc.

[27]Christa Wolf, *The Quest for Christa T.,* Translated by Christopher Middleton (New York: Farrar, Straus & Giroux, 1970), 88, 185.

[28]Both Ann and Bob give examples of what they felt was timeless time in depressed states. Bob: "During the period of my depression, I lost track of where I was once. I found myself driving one day with no recollection how I got to a particular place although I had been drinking during that period of time. It was frightening. I didn't know how or why or where I was. I had been in that state for probably an hour or two hours. I know time had elapsed because I was about 100 miles from home. I didn't recall where I was going. I was mentally detached." Ann: "I got to the point where I was so depressed that I could not plan ahead more than whatever little thing that I had said I would do that day. The next thing I knew it got better and I could still not worry about what might happen actually. If I catch myself doing that, I'm really conscious to not let it control my behavior and if I don't then it seems to settle down again and I can say if I'm doing my best, if I'm doing what I am supposed to do, then whatever happens is God's will."

[29]George D. Bond, "Theravada Buddhism's Meditations on Death and the Symbolism of Initiatory Death," *History of Religions* 19 (August 1979–May 1980): 249.

[30]John S. Dunne, *The Way of All the Earth: Experiments in Truth and Religion* (Notre Dame, Indiana: University of Notre Dame Press, 1978), 70; idem, 155.

[31]Woodman, "Worshipping Illusions," 61, 66.

[32]Lifton, 31, 32.

[33]Eliade, Myths, p. 200, cited in Bond, "Meditations on Death," 249.

[34]Elisabeth Kübler-Ross, *On Death and Dying* (New York: Macmillan Publishing Co., Inc., 1969), 12–18. Reprinted with permission of Macmillan Publishing Company from *On Death and Dying* by Elisabeth Kübler-Ross. Copyright © 1969 by Elisabeth Kübler-Ross. Reprinted with permission courtesy of Tavistock Publications in England as well.

[35]Storm, *Song of Heyoehkah* (San Francisco: Harper & Row Publishers, 1981), 243.

[36]Hurston, 249.

[37]Theodore Roszak, *Where the Wasteland Ends* (New York: Doubleday & Company, Inc., 1973), 118–19.

[38]Deloria, Jr., 103–04; idem, 102.

[39]Rolling Thunder quoted in Doug Boyd's *Rolling Thunder* (New York: Dell Publishing Company, Inc., 1974), 51–52. Copyright © 1974 by Robert Briggs Assoc. Reprinted by permission of Random House, Inc.

[40]Doug Boyd in *Rolling Thunder* recounting a story he was told by Alice in *Rolling Thunder*, 114–15.

[41]Mrs. Oliphant, *Francis of Assisi* (London: Macmillan and Co., 1907) 230-31.

[42]Lewis Carroll, *Alice's Adventures in Wonderland & Through the Looking-Glass* (New York: Bantam Books, 1981), 145.

NOTES TO CHAPTER FIVE
A PATTERN OF RECOVERY FROM ALCOHOLISM

[1]In Chapter One, it was stated that for the purpose of this study, the scientific way will be considered as a dualistic way characterized by (1) dichotomous thought based on subject-object splits, (2) perceived need for change, (3) resistance, and (4) control. Such a way would characterize a culture of separation as described by Bellah et al.; it would likewise characterize what James Curtis refers to as a "linear" paradigm, associated with a visual mode. For the purpose of this study, the way of the spirit is considered as a unified way characterized by (1) awareness of unity beneath surface variety, (2) belief that all is well, (3) acceptance, and (4) letting go. Such a way would characterize what Bellah refers to as a culture of coherence; it would likewise characterize what James Curtis refers to as a "nonlinear" paradigm, which he associates with an auditory mode. James Curtis, *Culture as Polyphony*. See especially chapters 2 and 3.

[2]There were two exceptions. Two Renewal Center guests completed the questionnaire after our personal conversations.

[3]One primary difference between the Seneca community and the community of Alcoholics Anonymous is that the latter is more heterogeneous and widely dispersed. The members of the latter society here considered are identifiable by self-reports of what Dr. Daniel J. Anderson describes as "repetitive, stereotypical mal- or unadaptive patterns of behaviors in connection with their use of alcohol and/or other mood-changing chemicals." Wallace initially identified the cycle of revitalization within traditional societies; A.A. grew in the midst of a modern one. It seems easier to identify change against a background of stability than to find stability in background of a culture which is predicated on continual change.

[4]William James states that "the practical needs and experiences of religion seem to me

sufficiently met by the belief that beyond each man and in a fashion continuous with him there exists a larger power which is friendly to him and to his ideals. All that the facts require is that the power should be both other and larger than our conscious selves. Anything larger will do, if only it be large enough to trust for the next step." James, 396. (Additional discussion of some of James' ideas may be found in chapter 2 of this work.)

[5]Wilson, *Language of the Heart*, 267.

[6]The term treatment here refers to those who were in Hazelden's residential treatment program for alcoholism and who voluntarily completed the questionnaire designed for this study; the phrase "those in recovery" refers to those who were guests at Hazelden's Renewal Center and who voluntarily completed this questionnaire. The phrase "agreed with" means that they responded with a "six" or a "seven" on a seven-point Likert scale, with "one" equal to strongly disagree and "seven" equal to strongly agree. The phrase "disagreed with" means that they responded with a "one" or a "two" on a seven-point Likert scale, with "one" equal to strongly disagree and "seven" equal to strongly agree. [Please refer to chapter 2 for further information about the questionnaire and respondents.]

[7]Please refer to chapter 2 for Roland Delattre's observation of this phenomenon within the mainstream of American society and culture.

[8]See Bercovitch, *Puritan Origins of the American Self* (New Haven, Connecticut: Yale University Press, 1975), 179.

[9]James, 173–74.

[10]Marion Woodman offers a clear discussion of this tendency in her book *The Pregnant Virgin*.

[11]As was previously acknowledged, many in recovery from alcoholism continue to smoke cigarettes, eat compulsively, and so on, so that the pollution on the individual level is usually only reduced rather than eliminated.

[12]Edwin Diller Starbuck, *The Psychology of Religion*, 3rd ed., with a preface by William James (New York: Charles Scribner's Sons, 1912), 117.

[13]A similar dynamic may occur in the world's major religions or spiritual beliefs. For example, for Christians in general, the way of experiencing the unity may be primarily in relationship with others; for Eastern philosophies and religions, in relationship with the higher self within; for Native peoples, in relationship with Nature and her animal, reptile, bird, insect, fish, mineral, and vegetable kingdoms. This is not to say this is to the exclusion of other ways, simply that it may be the "home" mode that most of the literature, most of the stories, mechanics or technology, treatises or teachings are concerned with as an entry point. There are simply different emphases. Possibly what stands out, too, about different religious or spiritual traditions are those aspects not as frequently discussed in our own.

[14]Kurtz, 61.

[15]Wilson, *Language of the Heart*, 302.

[16]Meister Eckhart, *Breakthrough: Meister Eckhart's Creation Spirituality in New Translation* with Introduction and Commentaries by Matthew Fox (Garden City, New York: Doubleday & Company, Inc., 1980), 459–60.

[17]Dunne, *Way of All the Earth: Experiments in Truth and Religion* (Notre Dame, Indiana: University of Notre Dame Press, 1978), 49. It is not suggested here that members of Alcoholics Anonymous practice this principle, or any other principle of the A.A. program perfectly, nor

that members are equally committed to practicing the principles of Alcoholics Anonymous in "all [their] affairs."

[18]This phrase of his was revived in *Habits of the Heart* (p. 285) and referenced in chapter 1.

[19]Progoff, 108–09.

[20]Ibid., 120–21.

[21]Ibid.

[22]Eliade, *Sacred and Profane* (New York: Harcourt, Brace & World, Inc. 1957), 17.

[23]Imbalance in either direction may have its harmful consequences. Swami Shantanand, for example, says his native India has been imbalanced in the direction of a spiritual way to be in the world, and as a consequence has been repeatedly subjugated to other nations.

[24]Eckhart, *Breakthrough,* 523.

[25]James, 384.

[26]Ibid.

[27]Tiebout, "Act of Surrender," 48.

[28]Ibid., 54.

[29]Schnall, 28.

[30]I do not mean to imply that this process is a one-shot deal, with conflict prior to recovery and peace and light and all that afterward. More than one alcoholic in recovery, as well as prior to and during the throes of active addiction to alcohol, has done his or her part to contribute to a dualistic culture. It is the painful experience of more than one alcoholic that the fight comes and goes, as does the feeling of peace. Still, with Starbuck, I don't believe the fundamental change in orientation is ever wholly lost.

[31]Mo Dsi, cited in Marie-Louise VonFranz, *On Divination and Synchronicity: The Psychology of Meaningful Chance* (Toronto, Canada: Inner City Books, 1980), 110.

[32]Kohn (255) says that "as early as 1973 there were incidental findings of a 'high incidence of left-handedness in a group of male alcoholics.' A 1980 study associated right hemisphericity with alcoholism. A 1981 study found three times the number of right-hemisphere-dominant individuals among a group of alcohol abusers than in general population control groups." His notes as to the source of the first quotation: Bakan, P. "Left-Handedness and Alcoholism," *Perceptual and Motor Skill*, 1980, 89, 3, 514. His note as to the second citation: Sandel, A. and Alcorn, J.D., "Individual Hemisphericity and Maladaptive Behaviors." *Journal of Abnormal Psychology,* 1980, 89, 514–17.

[33]Anthony Wallace's observation about some of the more subtle effects Anglo-American culture had on the Iroquois may illustrate a somewhat an analogous situation on a larger, deeper, communal scale from the perspective of a traditional culture. He says that after the advent of European-Americans, the Iroquois faced a moral crisis: "They wanted still to be men and women of dignity, but they knew only the old ways, which no longer led to honor but only to poverty and despair; to abandon these old ways meant undertaking customs that were strange, in some matters repugnant, and in any case uncertain of success." Wallace, *Religion, An Anthropological View* (New York: Random House, Inc., 1966), 31.

[34]This rebound phenomenon is discussed in physiological terms by both pioneer Stanley

Gitlow and more recently by Gerald May in *Addiction and Grace*. Any drug-induced unitive experience when boundaries are dissolved is followed by a rebound or hangover period in which the body compensates to restore homeostasis. For those using a depressant such as alcohol, the compensatory stimulant lasts even longer and is experienced as jitters or tremors. With this condition found unbearable, more depressants are ingested and so on.

[35]Jaynes, "Symposium on Consciousness," 145. Jaynes says that "the social, verbal, behavioural environment of a child today and the peer pressure to be and think like other children does not encourage or reward a child in a bicameral direction. Back before 1000 B.C., that social, verbal, behavioural environment plus peer pressure would encourage [a child's experience of an] imaginary playmate towards the status of a personal god and a full-fledged bicameral mind" (Ibid.).

[36]Both men tend to discuss pre-conversion and post-conversion states in somewhat dualistic terms. James, for example, gives one definition of conversion as a process "either gradual or sudden, . . . by which a self hitherto divided, and consciously wrong, inferior and unhappy, becomes unified and consciously right, superior and happy in consequence of its firmer hold upon religious realities." Tiebout describes the change as being one from a negative state to a positive one.

[37]Wilson, *Language of the Heart,* 36.

[38]Throughout A.A. literature, and in literature about A.A. (e.g. Kurtz' N*ot-God),* recovery is most often referred to as physical, *mental,* and spiritual. However, sometimes informally in A.A., recovery is considered as physical, mental, emotional and spiritual. In this study, the "mental" aspect of recovery will be considered as having two components—one, the intellect (called mental) and the other emotions. Intellectual-mental in this instance is equated with an epistemology based on subject-object splits.

[39]Here confluence refers to unity in a state of flux; coherence refers to unity in a state of rest.

[40]Carl Jung says, "By shadow I mean the 'negative' side of the personality, the sum of all those unpleasant qualities we like to hide, together with the insufficiently developed functions and the contents of the personal unconscious." (Carl Jung, vol. 7, p. 65, cited by Rychlak, *Introduction to Personality and Psychotherapy,* 2d ed. [Boston: Houghton Mifflin Company, 1981], 140).

[41]A "home group" is usually an A.A. group that the individual attends with regularity and to which he or she feels the strongest ties.

[42]Ram Dass, Seminar, "Blessed are the Peacemakers," seminar coordinated by Anthea Francine, Starr King School, Graduate Theological Union, Berkeley, California, Fall, 1987. Neti neti roughly translated means "not this, not this"; tat twam asi means "Thou art that."

[43]Fowler and Keen, *Life Maps: Conversations on the Journey of Faith,* ed. Jerome Berryman (Dallas, Texas: Word, Inc., Publishers, 1978). Change may also be experienced gradually over time *as well as* suddenly and effortlessly.

[44]James citing Principal Caird, 344.

[45]Campbell, *The Hero with a Thousand Faces,* 2d ed., Bollingen Series XVII (Princeton, New Jersey: Princeton University Press, 1949), 30. Illustration F is on p. 245 © 1949 Bollingen Foundation, Inc., New York, New York, Published by Princeton University Press. © 1976 Princeton University Press. Reprinted with permission. Campbell notes that the word "monomyth" is from James Joyce's *Finnegans Wake* (New York: Viking Press, Inc., 1939), 581.

[46]Please refer to chapter 2 for comments on his article.

[47]I quote almost in entirety the section Whitfield has on the connection between recovery and myth in *Alcoholism and Spirituality* [which he says is currently in process for publication.] Whitfield says "the classical story or myth is similar or even identical to our stories in self-help groups." In a map of the hero or heroine's journey in *Alcoholism and Spirituality*, he locates both separation and initiation in the unconscious. In the text, he says that

> *as the hero or heroine enters the phase of separation and initiation, a period of extreme stress, "sacred blunders," betrayals or symptoms occur. Separation represents the break with the ego's world and a journey into a sacred place, from which the traveler can eventually reach a completion and learn transcendence. . . . We frequently encounter the shadow side of our personality, which is often accompanied by experiencing confusion and paradox. A series of trials must be faced along the way, including the fear of losing control or losing our self. To meet the challenge, the hero has to surrender to the trial, i.e. drop previous belief systems and behaviors. After the surrender, the hero transcends the duality, and there is a sacred union of hero and God as one. Thus, the hero/heroine learns from the initiation-adventure, with all of its struggling, discomfort and frustration, and returns a more whole person. At this time he shares the knowledge with fellow humans (Campbell 1949). The curse becomes a gift in a "fall upward." . . . It is the cycle of death and rebirth, of involution and evolution.*

(Whitfield, *Alcoholism and Spirituality*, 84–85.) In his book, *Healing the Child Within: Discovery and Recovery for Adult Children of Dysfunctional Families* (Baltimore, Maryland: The Resource Group, 1987), 98, he offers the following map of the hero-heroine's journey:

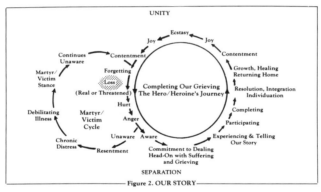

Figure 2. OUR STORY

[48]Campbell, 101, 108.

[49]Ibid., 15.

[50]Ibid., 109.

[51]Starbuck, *The Psychology of Religion*, 322.

[52]In the diagram reprinted from Campbell's *Hero with a Thousand Faces*, dismemberment and so forth, listed on the left side of his circle, would, in the exploratory cycle proposed in this dissertation, be included in the stage of initiation (my Quadrant Three) rather than the stage of separation where it may begin. Powerlessness would mark the entry to this initiatory stage. I believe such a designation is consistent with Campbell's text. The stage of separation would be largely conscious, while the stage of initiation is marked by entry into the unconscious.

[53]Campbell, 193.

[54]Kurtz gave this figure of between forty and fifty in a talk sponsored by Hazelden Foundation

on the 50th Anniversary of A.A. Kurtz originates the term "not-God" and explains the concept as it relates to members of A.A. Kurtz, "Fiftieth A.A. Anniversary Salute," O'Shaughnessy Auditorium, College of St. Thomas, St. Paul, Minnesota, 9 June 1985; Kurtz, *Not-God: A History of Alcoholics Anonymous*.

[55]Jaynes identifies the following features of consciousness: (1) mind-space, (2) analog "I" (3) narratization. Other characteristics include concentration, suppression, excerption, and consilience. Jaynes, "Symposium on Consciousness," 132–33.

[56]Ibid., 128.

[57]Ibid.

[58]Ibid., 134.

[59]Ibid., 138.

[60]During a conversation with Dr. Jaynes in his office, it seemed that he was apparently uncomfortable with the imprecision of these terms.

[61]Jaynes' model includes but is not dependent upon his apparently reluctant references to right and left hemispheres of the brain. Jaynes associates the left hemisphere of the brain with the "man-side" and the right hemisphere of the brain with the "God-side." He identifies the four ideas or "modules" of his theory: "First is the nature of consciousness and its origin in language . . . . Second . . . is the bicameral mind, which can be studied directly in ancient texts and indirectly in modern schizophrenia. Third is the idea that consciousness followed bicamerality, which can be studied in the artifacts and texts of history. And the fourth is that the neurological model for the bicameral mind is related to the two hemispheres. And this can be studied in laterality differences today" (Jaynes, "Symposium on Consciousness," 139).

[62]Jaynes says this about analogs in general: "An analog is a model, but a model of a special kind. It is not like a scientific model, whose source may be anything at all and whose purpose is to act as an hypothesis of explanation or understanding. Instead, an analog is at every point generated by the thing it is an analog of. A map is a good example" *Origin, 54*. He says this about the "analog I": "A most important 'feature' of this metaphor 'world' is the metaphor we have of ourselves, the analog "I," which can 'move about' vicarially in our 'imagination', 'doing' things that we are not actually doing. There are of course many uses for such an analog 'I'. We imagine 'ourselves' 'doing' this or that, and thus 'make' decisions on the basis of imagined 'outcomes' that would be impossible if we did not have an imagined 'self' behaving in an imagined 'world'." (*Origin*, 62–63).

[63]Jaynes, *Origin*, 217.

[64]Lewis Hyde refers to divisive emotions in *Alcohol and Poetry: John Berryman and the Booze Talking*.

[65]Jaynes says that consilience is a feature of consciousness. He notes in his book that he uses the term conciliation, but "consilience is Whewell's, 1858, better term for my intended meaning of mental processes that make things compatible with each other." Consilience is "the conscious analog of perceptual assimilations where ambiguity is made to conform to some previously learned schema. Consilience is in mind-space what narratization is in mind-time, making things compatible with each other" ("Symposium on Consciousness," 146).

[66]Jaynes, *Origin*, 117–18.

[67]I have adopted Julian Jaynes' use of the terms "mind-space" and "mind-time."

[68]Wilbur, 102.

[69]Ibid., 102–11.

[70]Brown, *Developmental Model*, 49, her figure 2–7. Reprinted by permission of John Wiley & Sons, Inc. Copyright © 1985 by John Wiley & Sons, Inc.

[71]Julian Jaynes is most helpful in an explication of the transition from the physical quadrant (Quadrant One) to Quadrant Two of the exploratory map (Illustration E) and by extension and reversal of this theory helps identify the tasks involved in the transition from Quadrant Two to Three as well. Harry Tiebout (whose work was briefly described in chapters 1 and 2) in conjunction with Jaynes helps explain the shift into Quadrant Three and the conditions of this receptive state. Joseph Campbell is particularly sensitive to the tasks involved in the synapse between initiation and return (here Quadrants Three and Four) as well as the inherent dangers of refusing the return. (A refusal of the return is a refusal to share and exclusive hoarding of the "boons" or gifts of the spiritual state, and thrusts the individual into run-away. Refusal of the return is a refusal to accept the limit or context of community.) Campbell is particularly sensitive to the rigors of crossing the threshold from initiation to return as well—the crossing of which requires no less than return from death. It requires grieving, letting it go. Anthony Wallace is most helpful in providing an understanding of the tasks of the fourth quadrant. Those tasks are the same as those he identifies for revitalization movements: organization, communication, adaptation, cultural transformation, and routinization.

[72]The movement of the recovery as suggested here, the movement of the monomyth of Joseph Campbell, the revitalization movements identified by Anthony Wallace, the process involved in the origin of consciousness as described by Jaynes, and the developmental process described by Ken Wilbur are similar to the pattern described in Richard M. Bucke's theory that there are four stages of intellect. Bucke believes that

> *we have four distinct stages of intellect, all abundantly illustrated in the animal and human worlds about us—all equally illustrated in the individual growth of the cosmic conscious mind and all four existing together in that mind as the first three exist together in the ordinary human mind. These four stages are, first, the perceptual mind—the mind made up of percepts or sense impressions; second, the mind made up of these and recepts—the so-called receptual mind, or in other words the mind of simple consciousness; third, we have the mind made up of percepts, recepts and concepts, called sometimes the conceptual mind or otherwise the self conscious mind—the mind of self consciousness; and, fourth and last, we have the intuitional mind—the mind whose highest element is not a recept nor a concept but an intuition. This is the mind in which sensation, simple consciousness and self consciousness are supplemented and crowned with cosmic consciousness.* (Bucke, *Cosmic Consciousness,* [New York: E.P. Dutton and Company, Inc., Publishers, 1901], 16).

Following this theory of transition from Simple Consciousness (Quadrant One of Illustration E) to Self-Consciousness (Quadrant Two of Illustration E) to Cosmic Consciousness (Quadrant Three inclusive of Quadrants Two and One), with his first construct possibly unrepresented on this map. His simple consciousness may be analogous to undifferentiated consciousness, in Quadrant One, or the Third Quadrant *before* experience with Quadrant Two, his self-consciousness analogous to the science sphere or Jayne's conscious "man-side" of the brain, and what he refers to as cosmic consciousness analogous to re-entry into awareness of the "god-side" of the brain in conjunction with consciousness.

So his receptual mind may be analogous to Jayne's bicameral mind, in which the "voices" of the right brain were simply obeyed, without deceit, without dissent, without what Jaynes calls an "analog I." As Bucke describes the state of cosmic consciousness, it could encompass both Quadrants Three and Four of the exploratory map (Illustration E). Some of the case studies he cites would seem to fall into the Third, others into the Fourth, depending on whether or not the incidence of unity occurred in a purely receptive state or reciprocal state. In any case, it seems at the minimum, cosmic consciousness would be analogous to the Third Quadrant *after* experience with Quadrant Two (Bucke, 16). Bucke goes on to say that simple consciousness is "to be conscious of the things about one, but not to be conscious of one's self. [In self consciousness] one is not only conscious of what I see, but I know I am conscious of it. Also I am conscious of myself as a separate entity and personality and I can stand apart from myself and contemplate myself, and can analyze and judge the operations of my own mind as I would analyze and judge anything else. This self consciousness is only possible after the formation of concepts and the consequent birth of language. . . . The philosophy of the birth of cosmic consciousness in the individual is very similar to that of the birth of self consciousness—the mind becomes overcrowded (as it were) with concepts and these are constantly becoming larger, more numerous and more and more complex; some day (the conditions being all favorable) the fusion, or what might be called the chemical union, of several of them and of certain moral elements takes place; the result is an intuition and the establishment of the intuitional mind, or, in other words, cosmic consciousness" (Bucke, 17–18).

One of the case studies in cosmic consciousness cited by Bucke is that of Honoré de Balzac. According to Balzac, "The world of ideas divides itself into three spheres—that of instinct; that of abstraction; that of specialism." Bucke equates these three with his simple consciousness, self consciousness and cosmic consciousness. Balzac says that "specialism consists in seeing the things of the material world as well as those of the spiritual world. . . . Specialism carries with it intuition. Intuition is a faculty of the inner man, of whom specialism is an attribute." Balzac continues: "Between the sphere of specialism [which I would associate with Quadrant Three] and the sphere of abstraction [which I would associate with Quadrant Two] and likewise between those spheres and that of instinctivity, [Quadrant One] we find beings in whom the diverse attributes of the two kingdoms are mingled. . ." (Bucke citing Balzac, 211–13).

Although Bucke identified only a few individuals he felt met his criteria for cosmic consciousness, he believed that "cases of cosmic consciousness should become more numerous from age to age, and not only so but that they should become . . . more pronounced." He commented that "all cases of Cosmic Consciousness are not on the same plane." He stated that the range of self-consciousness *in any given species* on its plane is far greater than the range of simple consciousness, and so must the range of cosmic consciousness be "very much greater both in kind and degree. . . ." He goes on to say that "given a world peopled with men [sic] having Cosmic Consciousness, they would vary both in the way of greater and less intellectual ability, and greater and less moral and spiritual elevation, and also in the way of variety of character, more than would the inhabitants of a planet on the plane of Self Consciousness." Bucke predicts that what he refers to as cosmic consciousness "awaits the whole race" (Bucke, 66).

He suggests that when a person who was self-conscious only, enters into cosmic consciousness

> (a) he knows without learning (from the mere fact of illumination) certain things, as, for instance: (1) that the universe is not a dead machine but a living presence; (2) that in its essence and tendency it is infinitely good; (3) that individual existence is continuous beyond what is called death. At the same time: (b) he takes on enormously greater capacity both for learning and initiating. (Bucke, 76)

Bucke seems primarily to address that which comes of receptivity, the spiritual experience per se, rather than the daily life (the return) and the "passing it on" which may follow such experience(s). It seems that possibly his assertion that the cases would be more pronounced would take the form of distinguishing between what might be singular or initiatory experiences of cosmic consciousness in what are referred to as "altered states" and the *application* of the awareness internalized during this or these states. This is to suggest that cosmic consciousness may occur in the proposed Third Quadrant, and as in the monomyth proposed by Campbell, remain to be translated within the Fourth Quadrant.

This may fit into the pattern of recovery for alcoholics using the program and society of A.A. in a number of ways. The entry "into the world of the spirit" referenced in the Big Book of A.A. may be equated on some level with Bucke's cosmic consciousness. Bucke equates cosmic consciousness with the intuitional mind, and the development of intuition is one of the promises made to recovering alcoholics; for example, "we will intuitively know how to handle situations which used to baffle us. We will suddenly realize God is doing for us what we could not do for ourselves."

The idea of a movement from intellect, to feeling, and then to intuition is also supported by the identification of three distinct epistemologies by Sufi mystics: those of intellect, feeling, and intuition.

The pattern Gayle Graham Yates discerned within the women's movement is also illustrative of this proposed generic pattern. She examines the women's movement from the perspective of paradigm shifts and describes three basic constellations. The first to emerge she describes as being characterized by women advocating their equality to men; the second, women over and above men; and the third, women and men equal to each other, or androgynous. Here the women equal to men would be analogous to the Second Quadrant, with women cultivating those traits traditionally associated with the masculine; the women over and above men analogous to the Third Quadrant, valuing and nurturing traits traditionally associated with the feminine; and the third—women and men equal to each other—would be analogous to the Fourth Quadrant of my Illustration E. Yates, *What Women Want; The Ideas of the Movement* (Cambridge, Massachusetts: Harvard University Press, 1975).

The same pattern may occur in the economic sphere as well. The first stage may be feudalism, which was characterized by hierarchical master-servant relationships as was bicamerality, still with a sense of all being a part of same organism. This is followed by a split into capitalism and communism with some cultures preferring capitalism, discounting the other, some cultures preferring communism, discounting the other. To be followed by unforced giving based on awareness of the self and other having same interest in the presence of and valuation of uniqueness, individuality?

[73]Campbell, 30.

[74]Koestler, page 108, citing Schopenhauer, (1850), p. 224.

[75]Maria Pushpam, in "Peace-Prayer of St. Francis in the Context of Santi-Mantra," says, "This prayer originated before World War I in Normandy. It was printed on one side of a picture of St. Francis holding a book, bearing the clear inscription 'this is the Rule of the Third Order.' On the card there was no indication that the prayer was composed by St. Francis. By the year 1936, in England, an English translation of the same prayer came to light. With the post-World War II experiences, the prayer became very popular. Since the name of Francis was attached to the prayer it gained brush-fire diffusion through the world. In fact the prayer had its origin in a Franciscan milieu: hence it rightly evoked the spirit of Francis." (Pushpam, *Journal of*

Dharma X No. 3, July-September 1985, 331). It may have been composed by Francis and shared without a claim of authorship.

[76]Bill Wilson repeated this prayer in plural form at least at the conclusion of at least two conventions.

[77]Hampden-Turner, *Maps of the Mind* (New York: Collier Books, 1981), 169.

Notes to Chapter Six
Parallels and Patterns in the Larger Community

[1]Bateson, "Cybernetics of Self," 15.

[2]A.A., *"Pass It On,"* 368.

[3]A.A., *"Pass It On,"* 312.

[4]A.A., *Twelve and Twelve,* 130.

[5]A.A., *Twelve and Twelve,* 176-77. Ibid., 180–181. A distinction is then made between A.A. as a whole and individual A.A. members. It says that this "does not mean that the members of Alcoholics Anonymous now restored as citizens of the world, are going to back away from their individual responsibility to act as they see the right upon issues of our time. But when it comes to A.A. as a whole, that's quite a different matter."

[6]Wilson, *Language of the Heart,* 80. Bill does qualify this saying that one thing which will not be offered is the A.A. name.

[7]Bercovitch, *The American Jeremiad* (Madison, Wisconsin; University of Wisconsin Press, 1978), 178-79. The quotation from Rollo May was from a lecture he gave all the First Congregational Church in Berkeley in November 1987. When I contacted May to request permission to quote this line, and the other at the end of this paragraph, he graciously agreed and suggested that I add five exclamation marks!

[8]Ibid., 184.

[9]Noble, *End of American History* (Minneapolis, Minnesota: University of Minnesota Press, 1985), 136-37.

[10]Fowler and Keen, *Life Maps,* 111.

[11]Howard Stein, "Alcoholism as Metaphor in American Culture: Ritual Desecration as Social Integration," *Ethos: Journal of the Society for Psychological Anthropology* 13, No. 3 (Fall 1985): 210–11. Reproduced by permission of the American Anthropological Association. Not for further reproduction. Stein looks at alcoholism as a cultural disorder. I believe he offers many interesting insights into the relationship between alcoholism and culture.

[12]Bellah et al., 284; idem, 296.

[13]Kurtz, 165.

[14]Kurtz, 166.

[15]Bellah et al, 72, 74. The authors of *Habits* add that they do not wish to exaggerate this tendency.

[16]Deloria, 260.

[17]Eliade, *The Two and the One,* 100.

[18]Gerald May, *Addiction and Grace,* 13.

[19]Delattre, 129.

[20]Ibid. He finds the "quintessential expression" of a culture of procurement to be the military-industrial complex (Delattre, 129).

[21]It follows from this that at the same time this makes for a culture of displacement where those things undesired are discarded.

[22]These quotations are from Rushmore M. Kidder reporting on the views of Carlos Fuentes, interviewed by Rushworth M. Kidder, *Christian Science Monitor,* 28 November 1986, 28.

[23]Ibid.

[24]Roszak, "The Counter-Culture," lecture, Sonoma State University, Rohnert Park, California, 4 December 1987.

[25]Deloria, 109.

[26]Ibid., 299.

[27]Kluckhohn and Strodtbeck, *Variations in Value Orientation,* p. 29. David Born describes the Kluckhohn and Strodtbeck study in his dissertation,"Value Orientation and Immigrant Assimilation in a Southern Illinois Community" (Ph.D. diss., Southern Illinois University, 1970). He says that these researchers make three basic assumptions:

> 1. There is [sic] a limited number of common human problems for which all peoples at all times must find some solution.
> 2. While there is variability in solutions of all the problems, it is neither limitless nor random but is definitely variable within a range of possible solutions.
> 3. All alternatives of all solutions are present in all societies but are differentially preferred. (Kluckhohn and Strodtbeck, 1961: 10)

He then states the questions "posed by each of these problems" along with their shortened titles:

> 1. What is the character of innate human nature? (Human Nature Orientation)
> 2. What is the relation of man to nature (and supernature)? (Man-Nature Orientation)
> 3. What is the temporal focus of life? (Time Orientation)
> 4. What is the modality of human activity? (Activity Orientation)
> 5. What is the modality of man's relationship to other men? (Relational Orientation) (Kluckhohn and Strodtbeck 1961:11)

Born explains that Kluckhohn and Strodtbeck developed an instrument to determine variations of value orientations to these problems "which has been used in a variety of testing situations which focused on identifying socio-cultural discontinuities. . . . An initial field testing of the instrument with five cultural groups, Spanish-American, Navaho, Mormon, Texan, and Zuni demonstrated its viability" (Born, 35–6).

[28]Richard Madsen, Progressive Roundtable Seminar, Minneapolis, Minnesota, 9 November 1985.

[29]Fuentes, 28.

[30]Ibid., 29.

[31]Bateson, "Cybernetics of Self," 17, 18.

[32]Some of the harmful consequences of such a separation are discussed by the authors of *Habits* and summarized in Part I of this study. Their findings are supported by the observations of other scholars and public figures.

[33]Norman Cousins, qtd. in Rushworth M. Kidder, *Christian Science Monitor,* 12 November 1986, 28. In this article, Kidder states that "in fact, what occupies Cousins' attention these days is not so much the specific problems facing the world, serious though they are, as the lack of structures through which to deal with them. . . . 'The Institutions that we have,' he says, 'tend to pull us back rather than enable us to cope with these problems.' The reason: 'Those institutions not only are incapable of meeting the need, but actually intensify the need.' "

[34]Kurtz, 169, 170–71.

[35]Keen, 147.

[36]Noble, Horowitz and Carroll, *Twentieth Century Limited: World War Two to the Present,* vol. II., (Boston: Houghton Mifflin Company, 1980), 487.

[37]Bercovitch describes the American Jeremiad (which David Noble believes is the *modern* Jeremiad) as a political sermon which conveyed "the dual nature of [the New England Puritans'] calling, as practical and as spiritual guides. . . ." Bercovitch uses the sermons as a key source of evidence in his discussion of early New England (Bercovitch, *American Jeremiad,* xiv). Bercovitch believes the jeremiad has had a "pervasive impact upon our culture" (*American Jeremiad,* xv). He says that "the traditional . . . European jeremiad, was a lament over the ways of the world. . . . But from the start the American Jeremiads invert the doctrine of vengeance into a promise of ultimate success. . . " (Bercovitch, *American Jeremiad,* 7). David Noble says this Jeremiad has three basic components: the first is the promise of the sacred realized, the second is the declension, i.e., the immediate experience of the profane, and the third is the prophecy which speaks of moving toward fulfillment of the original promise. He notes that the only concrete experiences is with declension. Noble, conversation with author, 28 February 1989.

[38]V. Lois Erickson, "A Way to View the Lifting of the Intuitive Voice" (Paper presented to the Department of Educational Psychology, University of Minnesota [5 November 1988]: 5,8,9,11). Draft copy.

[39]Jung, *Civilization in Transition,* 299.

[40]Keen, 109, 111.

[41]Fuentes, 29.

[42]Bellah et al., 285.

[43]David Noble says this change began with the "closing of the frontier at the turn of this century and [was] felt even more deeply after WW II" (Noble, *The End of American History;* Joan Marler, "A Tribute to Mythologist Joseph Campbell," *Folio: Program Guide for KPFA and KFCF* [January 1988]: 5).

[44]Fox, Breakthrough, 459. Matthew Fox says that the word Meister Eckhart uses for attachment is *ownership*.

[45]*"I'll Quit Tomorrow"* is the title of a book by Vernon Johnson (New York: Harper & Row, Publishers, 1973).

[46]Bellah et al, 296.

[47]McLoughlin, 199. McLoughlin uses masculine pronouns in accordance with the common usage of the day of publication.

[48]Roszak, "The Counter-Culture."

[49]Ibid.

[50]Tipton, 237.

[51]Singer, 15.

[52]Carl Degler, "Remaking American History," *Journal of American History,* 67 no. 1 (June 1980): 7.

[53]Ibid., 9.

[54]David Noble, Conversation with author, 28 February 1989, University of Minnesota, Minneapolis, Minnesota.

[55]V. Lois Erickson, "Ethics: A Way to View the Lifting of the Intuitive Voice," 2, 14, 15.

[56]Gayle Graham Yates observes that the same stages which she identified in the emergence of the women's movement may likewise apply to historical situations. The stages simplified are these: women-equal-to-men, women-over-and-above-men, women and men equal to each other. Yates, *What Women Want: The Ideas of the Movement* (Cambridge, Massachusetts: Harvard University Press, 1975), 175.

[57]McLoughlin, 215.

[58]Ibid., 214.

[59]Kurtz, 229, 230.

[60]Bercovitch, *American Jeremiad,* 183.

[61]Ibid., Bercovitch citing Ralph Waldo Emerson, 184.

[62]Campbell, 12–13.

[63]Carroll and Noble, *Free and the Unfree,* 57.

[64]Ouspensky, *A New Model of the Universe* (New York: Vintage Books, 1971), 68.

[65]Jaynes, "Symposium on Consciousness," 136.

[66]Observation offered by a member of A.A. in California.

[67]Born, "Value Orientation and Immigrant Assimilation," 35.

Sources Consulted

Ajaya, Swami. *Psychotherapy East and West.* Honesdale, Pennsylvania: The Himalayan International Institute of Yoga Science and Philosophy of the U.S.A., 1983.

Albanese, Catherine L. *America: Religions and Religion.* The Wadsworth Series in Religious Studies. Edited by Robert S. Michaelsen. Belmont, California: Wadsworth Publishing Company, 1981.

Alcoholics Anonymous. *Alcoholics Anonymous.* Third Edition, New and Revised. First Edition published in 1939. New York: Alcoholics Anonymous World Services, Inc., 1976.

_____. *Alcoholics Anonymous Comes of Age: A Brief History of A.A.* New York: Alcoholics Anonymous World Services, Inc., 1957.

_____. "The A.A. Membership Survey." Pamphlet. New York: Alcoholics Anonymous World Services, Inc., 1987.

_____. *Best of the Grapevine.* New York: The AA Grapevine, Inc. 1985.

_____. *Came to Believe.* New York: Alcoholics Anonymous World Services, Inc., 1973.

_____. *Dr. Bob and the Good Oldtimers.* New York: Alcoholics Anonymous World Services, Inc., 1980.

_____. *"Pass It On."* New York: Alcoholics Anonymous World Services, Inc., 1984.

_____. "Questions and Answers on Sponsorship." Pamphlet. New York: Alcoholics Anonymous World Services, Inc., 1976.

_____. *Twelve Steps and Twelve Traditions.* New York: Alcoholics Anonymous World Services, Inc., 1952.

Bateson, Gregory. "The Cybernetics of 'Self': A Theory of Alcoholism." *Psychiatry 34* (February 1971): 1-18.

Becker, Ernest. *The Denial of Death.* New York: The Free Press, A Division of Macmillan Publishing Co., Inc., 1973.

Bellah, Robert N., Richard Madsen, William M. Sullivan, Ann Swidler, and Steven M. Tipton, eds. *Habits of the Heart.* New York: Harper & Row, Publishers; Berkeley, California: University of California Press, Ltd., 1985. The Regents of the University of California.

Bellah, Robert N. "Religious Evolution." In *Reader in Comparative Religion,* 36-52. Edited by William A. Lessa and Evon Z. Vogt. New York: Harper & Row, Publishers, 1958.

Bercovitch, Sacvan. *The American Jeremiad.* Madison, Wisconsin: University of Wisconsin Press, 1978.

_____. *The Puritan Origins of the American Self.* New Haven, Connecticut: Yale University Press, 1975.

Berman, Morris. *The Reenchantment of the World.* Ithaca, New York: Cornell University Press, 1981.

Berry, Wendell. *Openings: Poems by Wendell Berry.* New York: Harcourt, Brace and World, Inc., 1968.

Bertine, Eleanor. *Jung's Contribution to Our Time.* New York: G.P. Putnam's Sons, 1967.

Bierhorst, John, ed. *The Red Swan: Myths and Tales of the American Indians.* New York: Farrar, Straus and Giroux, 1976.

Boissiere, Robert. *Meditations with the Hopi*. Sante Fe: Bear & Company, Inc., 1986.

Bolen, Jean Shinoda. *The Tao of Psychology*. San Francisco: Harper & Row, Publishers, 1979.

Born, David Omar. "Mid-Life Crisis Index" (Unpublished Psychological Instrument). Personal Communication. University of Minnesota, Minneapolis, Minnesota.

————. "Psychological Adaptation and Devlopment Under Acculturative Stress: Toward a General Model." *Social Science and Medicine* 3 (1970): 529-547.

————. "Value Orientation and Immigrant Assimilation in a Southern Illinois Community." Ph.D. diss., Southern Illinois University, 1970.

Boyd, Doug. *Rolling Thunder*. New York: Dell Publishing Company, Inc., 1974.

Brown, Stephanie. "Defining a Continuum of Recovery in Alcoholism." Ph.D. diss., California School of Professional Psychology, 1977.

————. *Treating the Alcoholic: A Developmental Model of Recovery*. New York: John Wiley & Sons, 1985.

Bucke, Richard Maurice. *Cosmic Consciousness*. New York: E.P. Dutton and Company, Inc., Publishers, 1901.

Burkette, Tyronne Louis. "Spiritual Renewal in the Midst of Crisis: An Alcoholics Anonymous Twelve Steps Approach." D.Min. diss., United Theological Seminary, 1983.

Campbell, Joseph. *The Hero with a Thousand Faces*. Princeton: Princeton University Press, 1949. First Princeton/Bollingen Paperback Printing, 1972.

Capra, Fritjof. *The Tao of Physics: An Exploration of the Parallels Between Modern Physics and Eastern Mysticism*. Boulder, Colorado: Shambhala Publications, Inc., 1976; reprint, New York: Bantam Books, 1977.

————. "The New Physics Revisited." Esalen Conference, 15 November 1985. Tape recording.

Carroll, Peter N., and David W. Noble. *The Free and the Unfree: A New History of the United States*. New York: Penguin Books, 1977.

Clebsch, William A. *American Religious Thought: A History*. Chicago History of American Religion, edited by Martin E. Marty. Chicago: The University of Chicago Press, 1973.

Cousins, Norman. Interview by Rushworth M. Kidder. *Christian Science Monitor,* 12 November 1986, 28-29.

Curtis, James. *Culture as Polyphony: An Essay in the Nature of Paradigms*. Columbia: University of Missouri Press, 1978.

Degler, Carl. "Remaking American History." *Journal of American History* 67, no. 1 (June 1980).

Delattre, Roland. "The Culture of Procurement: Reflections on Addiction and the Dynamics of American Culture." Symposium: *Habits of the Heart. Soundings* LXIX, No. 1-2 (Spring/Summer, 1986): 127-144.

Deloria, Vine, Jr. *God is Red*. New York: Grosset & Dunlap, 1973.

Dillard, Annie. *Pilgrim at Tinker Creek*. Toronto: Bantam Books, Inc., 1975.

Deikman, Arthur J. "Bimodal Consciousness." *Archives of General Psychiatry* 25 (December 1971): 481-489.

Doczi, György. *The Power of Limits*. Boston: Shambhala, 1981.

Dunne, John S. *The Way of All the Earth: Experiments in Truth and Religion*. Notre Dame, Indiana: University of Notre Dame Press, 1978.

Eaton, Evelyn. *Snowy Earth Comes Gliding*. Independence, California: Draco Foundation, 1974.

Eckhart, Meister. *Breakthrough: Meister Eckhart's Creation Spirituality in New Translation*. Introduction and Commentaries by Matthew Fox. Garden City, New York: Doubleday & Company, Inc., 1980.

Eliade, Mircea. *Cosmos and History*. Translated from the French by Willard R. Trask. New York, Harper & Row, Publishers, Inc., 1959.

_____. *Myth and Reality*. Translated from the French by Willard R. Trask. New York: Harper & Row, Publishers, 1963.

_____. *The Sacred and the Profane*. Translated from the French by Willard R. Trask. New York: Harcourt, Brace & World, Inc., 1957.

_____. *The Two and the One*. London: Harvill Press, 1965.

Elpenor, [pseud.]. "A Drunkard's Progress." *Harper's Magazine,* October 1986, 42-48.

Erickson, V. Lois.. "Ethics: A Way to View the Lifting of the Intuitive Voice." Paper presented to the Department of Educational Psychology, University of Minnesota 5 November 1988. Draft copy.

_____"The Nature of the Self: Integrating the Spiritual Order." Speech presented to the Educational Psychology Department, University of Minnesota, 13 May 1988.

Erikson, Kai T. *Everything in its Path: Destruction of Community in the Buffalo Creek Flood*. New York: Simon and Schuster, 1976.

Forman, Robert F. and Michael J. Fassino. "Spiritual Beliefs, 12 Step Programs and Contentment: A Preliminary Investigation." *Addictionary* 2, no. 6 (November 1987). Alvernia College, Reading, Pennsylvania.

Fowler, James. *Stages of Faith*. San Francisco: Harper & Row, Publishers, 1981.

Fowler, James and Sam Keen. *Life Maps: Conversations on the Journey of Faith*. Edited by Jerome Berryman. Waco, Texas: Word Books, Publishers, 1978.

Fox, Matthew. *Breakthrough: Meister Eckharts's Creation Spirituality in New Translation*. [See Eckhart.]

_____. *The Coming of the Cosmic Christ: The Healing of Mother Earth and the Birth of a Global Renaissance*. San Francisco: Harper & Row, 1980.

_____. Original Blessing: *A Primer in Creation Spirituality Presented in Four Paths, Twenty-Six Themes, and Two Questions*. Sante Fe, New Mexico: Bear & Company, 1984.

Fraser, J.T. *Of Time, Passion and Knowledge: Reflections on Strategy of Existence*. New York: George Braziller, 1975.

Fuentes, Carlos. Interview by Rushworth M. Kidder. *Christian Science Monitor,* 28 November 1986, 28-29.

Gallup, George. *Religion in America: 50 Years: 1935-1985. The Gallup Report,* May 1985, no. 236.

Gandhi, Mahatma. *All Men Are Brothers: Autobiographical Reflections,* Columbia University Press, 1958.

Hampden-Turner, Charles. *Maps of the Mind*. New York: Macmillan Publishing Company, Inc., 1981.

Hall, Edward T. *The Dance of Life: The Other Dimensions of Time*. New York: Anchor Press, Doubleday, 1984.

Hall, Homer Alexander. "The Role of Faith in the Process of Recovery from Alcoholism." D.Min. diss., Drew University, 1984.

Hurston, Zora Neale. *I Love Myself When I am Laughing . . . And Then Again When I Am Looking Mean and Impressive*. Edited by Alice Walker. Introduction by Mary Helen Washington. Old Westbury, New York: The Feminist Press, 1979.

Hyde, Lewis. *Alcohol and Poetry: John Berryman and the Booze Talking*. Dallas, Texas: Dallas Institute Publication, 1986.

Jackson, Charles. *The Lost Weekend*. New York: Farrar & Rinehart, Inc., 1944.

Jackson, Margery Leithliter. "Actualization of Alcoholics Anonymous Members." Ph.D. diss., United States International University, 1980. Ann Arbor, Michigan: University Microfilms International, no. 8019033.

James, William. *The Varieties of Religious Experience*. New York: The New American Library, Inc., 1958.

Jaynes, Julian. "Consciousness and the Voices of the Mind." McMaster-Bauer Symposium on Consciousness. Julian Jaynes with Daniel Dennett, Jonathan Miller and George Ojemann. Edited by S.F. Witelson and A.A. Kristofferson. *Canadian Psychology/ Psychologie Canadienne,* 1986, vol. 27, no. 2: 128-182.

————. *The Origin of Consciousness in the Breakdown of the Bicameral Mind*. Boston: Houghton Mifflin Company, 1976.

————. Conversations with author. Princeton University. December 1987 and January 1988.

Johnson, Vernon E. *I'll Quit Tomorrow*. New York: Harper & Row, Publishers, 1973.

Jung, C.G. *Civilization in Transition*. Translated by R.F.C. Hull. The Collected Works of C.G. Jung, vol. 10, Bollingen Series XX. Edited by Sir Herbert Read, Michael Fordham, Gerhard Adler, William McGuire, Princeton, New Jersey: Princeton University Press, 1970.

————. *Letters,* vol. II, Bollingen Series 95. Princeton, New Jersey: Princeton University Press, 1959.

————. *Memories, Dreams, Reflections*. Recorded and Edited by Aniela Jaffe. Translated from the German by Richard and Clara Winston. New York: Random House, 1965.

_____. _Synchronicity_. The Collected Works of C.G. Jung, vol. 8, Bollingen Series XX. Princeton, New Jersey: Princeton University Press, 1973.

Keen, Sam and James Fowler, _Life Maps: Conversations on the Journey of Faith_. Edited by Jerome Berryman, Dallas, Texas: Word, Inc., Publishers, 1981.

Khan, Hazrat Inayat. _Mastery Through Accomplishment_. New Lebanon, New York: Sufi OrderPublications, 1978.

_____. _The Sufi Message of Hazrat Inayat Khan_. Vol. VII. London: Barrie and Rockliff (Barrie Books Ltd.), 1962. Vol. IX, _The Unity of Religious Ideals_. London: Barrie and Rockliff (Barrie Books Ltd.), 1963; reprinted, London: Barrie and Jenkins, 1974.

Kidder, Rushmore M. Interview of Norman Cousins. _Christian Science Monitor,_ 12 November 1986, 28-29.

_____Interview of Carlos Fuentes, _Christian Science Monitor,_ 28 November 1986, 28-29.

Kinney, Jean and Gwen Leaton. _Loosening the Grip_. St. Louis: The C. V. Mosby Company, 1978.

Kluckhohn, Florence Rockwood, and Fred L. Strodtbeck. _Variations in Value Orientations_. Evanston, Illinois: Row, Peterson and Company, 1961.

Koestler, Arthur. _Roots of Coincidence_. New York: Random House, 1973.

Kohn, George. "Toward a Model for Spirituality and Alcoholism." _Journal of Religion and Health 23, no. 3 (Fall 1984): 250-259._

Kübler-Ross, Elisabeth. _On Death and Dying_. New York: Macmillan Publishing Co., Inc., 1969.

Kurtz, Ernest. _Not-God: A History of Alcoholics Anonymous_. Center City, Minnesota: Hazelden Educational Services, 1979.

_____. "Fiftieth A.A. Anniversary Salute." Lecture. College of St. Thomas, St. Paul, Minnesota. 9 June 1985.

Lifton, Robert Jay. _Boundaries_. New York: Simon and Schuster, 1967.

de Lubac, Henri. _The Religion of Teilhard de Chardin_. Translated by Rene Hague. Garden City, New York: Doubleday & Company, Inc., 1968.

Luke, Helen M. "Letting Go." Interview by Lorraine Kisly. _Parabola_ (February 1985).

Madsen, Richard. Seminar on _Habits of the Heart_. Sponsored by Progressive Roundtable, Minneapolis, Minnesota. 9 November 1985.

Marler, Joan. "A Tribute to Mythologist Joseph Campbell." _Folio: Program Guide for KPFA and KFCF_ (January 1988).

Marshall, Mac. "Social Thought, Cultural Belief and Alcohol." _Journal of Drug Issues_ 15 (Winter 1985): 63-71.

Martin, Greg, pseud. "The Gospel of Christ and the Gospel of Alcoholics Anonymous: Divergent Paths of Human Liberation." Ph.D. diss., San Francisco Theological Seminary, 1983.

May, Gerald G., M.D. _Addiction and Grace_. San Francisco: Harper & Row, Publishers, 1988.

_____. "Spirituality and Addiction." Seminar. Tiburon, California, 22 October 1988. Jointly sponsored by the Pacific School of Religion, the Pacific Center for Spiritual Formation and the San Francisco Theological Seminary.

_____. *Will and Spirit: A Contemplative Psychology*. San Francisco: Harper & Row, Publishers, 1982.

May, Rollo. Lecture. 12 November 1987. First Congregational Church of Berkeley, Berkeley, California.

McLoughlin, William G. *Revivals, Awakenings, and Reform*. Chicago: The University of Chicago Press, 1978.

de Mello, Anthony. *The Song of the Bird*. New York: Doubleday, 1984.

Merton, Thomas. *Zen and the Birds of Appetite*. New York: New Directions, 1968.

Minnesota Multiphasic Personality Inventory. Copyright, University of Minnesota. New York, New York: The Psychological Corporation, 1966.

Moberg, David, ed. *Spiritual Well-Being*. Washington, D.C.: University Press of America, Inc., 1979.

_____. Correspondence with author. 2 March 1987.

Modesto, Ruby, and Guy Mount. "Autobiography of A Cahuilla Pul." *Shaman's Drum* 8 (Spring 1987): 43 48.

Mortimer, R.G., Lyle Filkins, M.W. Kerlan, and B. Mudge. "Mortimer-Filkins Questionnaire." From the report entitled "Court Procedures for Identifying Problem Drinkers," prepared for the United States Department of Transportation, National Highway Traffic Safety Administration; Highway Safety Research Institute, University of Michigan, Ann Arbor, Michigan 48105, Contract FH11-7615, June 1971.

Niebuhr, Reinhold. "A View of Life from the Sidelines." *The Christian Century* (December 19-26 1984): 1195-98.

Noble, David W. Conversation with author. 28 February 1989.

_____. *The End of American History*. Minneapolis, Minnesota: University of Minnesota Press, 1985.

Noble, David W., and Peter N. Carroll. *The Free and the Unfree: A New History of the United States*. New York: Penguin Books, 1977.

Noble, David W., David A. Horowitz and Peter N. Carroll. *Twentieth Century Limited: From World War Two to the Present, vol II*. Boston: Houghton Mifflin Company, 1980.

O'Kane, Walter Collins. *The Hopis: Portrait of a Desert People*. The Civilization of the American Indian Series, vol. 35. Norman, Oklahoma: University of Oklahoma Press, 1953.

Oliphant, Mrs. *Francis of Assisi*. London: Macmillian and Company, 1907.

Ouspensky, P.D. *A New Model of the Universe*. Alfred A. Knopf, Inc., 1931; New York: Random House, 1971.

Pittman, Bill, ed. *Stepping Stones to Recovery*. Seattle: Glen Abbey Books, 1988.

_____. "Alternative Explanations for the Beginnings of Alcoholics Anonymous 1934-39." Summa thesis, University of Minnesota, 1983.

_____. *AA: The Way It Began*. Seattle, Washington: Glen Abbey Books, 1988.

Puligandla, R. *Fundamentals of Indian Philosophy*. Nashville, Tennessee: Abingdon Press, 1975.

Pushpam, Maria. "Peace-Prayer of St. Francis in the Context of Santi-Mantra." *Journal of Dharma,* vol. X, no. 3 (July-September, 1985): 329-340.

Ram Dass. Seminar and videotape. "Blessed are the Peacemakers." Seminar Coordinator, Anthea Francine. Starr King School, Graduate Theological Union, Berkeley, California, 1987.

Roessler, S. James. "The Role of Spiritual Values in the Recovery of Alcoholics." D.Min., diss. Wesley Theological Seminary, 1982.

Rooney, James F., and Joan N. Volpe. "The Role of Androgyny in Alcoholism Recovery." Paper presented at the annual meeting of the Society for the Study of Social Problems, New York, August, 1980.

Roszak, Theodore. *Where The Wasteland Ends.* New York: Doubleday & Company, Inc., 1973.

_____. Lecture. "The Counter-Culture Twenty Years Later." Sonoma State University, Rohnert Park, California, 4 December 1987.

Rychlak, Joseph. *Introduction to Personality and Psychotherapy.* 2d ed. Boston: Houghton Mifflin Company, 1981.

Schaef, Anne Wilson. *When Society Becomes an Addict.* San Francisco: Harper & Row, Publishers, Inc., 1987.

Schnall, Sandra Joy. "An Interpersonal Approach to Alcoholism: The Transformation of Self Through Alcoholics Anonymous." Ph.D. diss., University of Massachusetts, 1980. Ann Arbor: University Microfilms International, no. 8101393.

Schucman, Helen. *A Course in Miracles.* Farmington, New York: Foundation for Inner Peace, 1975.

Sellner, Edward Cletus. "The Event of Self-Revelation in the Reconciliation Process: A Pastoral Theological Comparison of A.A.'s Fifth Step and the Sacrament of Penance." Ph.D. diss., University of Notre Dame, 1981.

Shantanand, Swami. "Science and Spirituality." The Twelfth International Congress: The Union of Science and Spirituality, 19 June 1987. Himalayan International Institute Of Yoga Science and Philosophy of the U.S.A., Honesdale, Pennsylvania.

Singer, June. *Androgyny: Toward a New Theory of Sexuality.* Introduction by Shedlon S. Hendler. 1st Edition. Garden City, New York: Anchor Press, 1976.

Smith, Huston. *The Religions of Man.* New York: Harper & Row, Publishers, 1958.

Smith, John Holland. *Francis of Assisi.* New York: Charles Scribner's Sons, 1972.

Starbuck, Edwin Diller. *The Psychology of Religion.* With a Preface by William James. New York: Charles Scribner's Sons, 1912.

Stein, Howard F. "Alcoholism as Metaphor in American Culture: Ritual Desecration as Social Integration." *Ethos: Journal of the Society for Psychological Anthropology* 13, No. 3 (Fall 1985): 195-235.

Storm, Hyemeyohsts. *Seven Arrows.* New York: Harper & Row, Publishers, 1972.

_____. Song of Heyoehkah. San Francisco: Harper & Row, Publishers, 1981.

Sullivan, Louis. *Kindergarten Chats.* New York: George Wittenborn, Inc., 1947.

_____. *Democracy: A Man Search*. Detroit: Wayne State University Press, 1961.

_____. *The Testament of Stone: Themes of Idealism and Indignation from the Writings of Louis Sullivan*. Edited by Maurice English, Chicago: Northwestern University Press, 1963.

Mother Teresa. Interview by Courtney Tower, *Readers Digest* (December 1987): .175–227.

Thomsen, Robert. *Bill W*. New York: Harper & Row Publishers, Inc., 1975.

Tiebout, Harry M. "The Act of Surrender in the Therapeutic Process with Special Reference to Alcoholism." *Quarterly Journal of Studies on Alcohol* 10, no. 1 (June 1949): 48-58.

_____. "Alcoholics Anonymous—An Experiment of Nature." *Pastoral Psychology* 13 (1962): 45-62.

_____. "Conversion as a Psychological Phenomenon." *Pastoral Psychology* 2, no. 13 (1951): 28-34.

_____. "Crisis and Surrender in Treating Alcoholism." *Quarterly Journal of Studies on Alcohol* 26, no. 3 (September 1965): 496-97.

_____. "The Ego Factors in Surrender in Alcoholism." Hazelden Foundation Pamphlet. Reprinted from *Quarterly Journal of Studies on Alcohol* 15 (1954): 610-621.

_____. "Surrender versus Compliance in Therapy With Special Reference to Alcoholism." Hazelden Educational Materials Pamphlet. Reprinted from *Quarterly Journal of Studies on Alcohol* 14 (1953): 58-68.

_____. "Therapeutic Mechanisms of Alcoholics Anonymous." Paper read at the ninety-ninth annual meeting of The American Psychiatric Association, Detroit, Michigan, May 10-13, 1943. *American Journal of Psychiatry* 100 (1944): 468-473.

Tipton, Steven M. *Getting Saved from the Sixties*. Foreward by Robert N. Bellah. Berkeley, California: University of California Press, 1982.

Tower, Courtney. Interview of Mother Teresa. *Reader's Digest*(Decermber 1987): 175-227.

Underhill, Evelyn. *Mysticism*. New York: E.P. Dutton, 1961.

V., Rachel., comp. *A Woman Like You: Life Stories of Women Recovering from Alcoholism and Addiction*. San Francisco: Harper & Row, Publishers, 1985.

Volpe, Joan N. and James F. Rooney. "The Role of Androgyny in Alcoholism Recovery." A paper presented at the annual meeting of the Society for the Study of Social Problems, August, 1980.

von Franz, Marie-Louise. *On Divination and Synchronicity: The Psychology of Meaningful Chance*. Studies in Jungian Psychology by Jungian Analysts. Toronto: Inner City Books, 1980.

Wagner, Roy. *The Invention of Culture*. Englewood Cliffs, New Jersey: Prentice-Hall, Inc., 1975.

Walker, Alice. *The Color Purple*. New York: Simon & Schuster Inc., 1982.

Wallace, Anthony C. *The Death and Rebirth of the Seneca*. With the assistance of Sheila C. Steen. New York: Random House, 1972.

_____. "Handsome Lake and the Great Revival in the West." *American Quarterly* 4 (Summer 1952): 149-165.

_____. Religion: *An Anthropological View*. New York: Random House, Inc., 1966.

      . "Revitalization Movements." *American Anthropologist* 58 (April 1956): 264-281.

Whitfield, Charles L. *Alcoholism and Spirituality.* Baltimore, Maryland: The Resource Group, 1985.

      . *Healing the Child Within: Discovery and Recovery for Adult Children of Dysfunctional Families.* Baltimore, Maryland: The Resource Group, 1987.

Wilbur, Ken. *The Atman Project.* Wheaton, Illinois: Theosophical Publishing House Quest Book, 1980.

Wilson. Lois. *Lois Remembers: Memoirs of the Co-Founder of Al-Anon and Wife of the Co-Founder of Alcoholics Anonymous.* New York: Al-Anon Family Group Headquarters, Inc., 1979.

      . Conversations with the author. Bedford Hills, New York. 1987, 1988. (Taped interview 1988.)

Wilson, William G. *As Bill Sees It: The A.A. Way of Life . . . selected writings of A.A.'s co-founder.* New York: Alcoholics Anonymous World Services Inc.,1967.

      . *The Language of the Heart: Bill W.'s Grapevine Writings.* New York: The AA Grapevine, Inc., 1988.

      . "The Society of Alcoholics Anonymous." *American Journal of Psychiatry* 106, No. 5 (November 1949): 370-375. Read at the 105th annual meeting of The American Psychiatric Association, Montreal, Quebec, May 23-27, 1949.

Wing, Nell. Interview with the author. New York, New York. December 1987.

Wolf, Christa. *The Quest for Christa T.* Translated by Christopher Middleton. New York: Farrar, Straus & Giroux, 1970.

Woodman, Marion. *The Pregnant Virgin.* Toronto, Canada: Inner City Books, 1985.

      . "Worshipping Illusions." *Parabola* (Summer 1987): 56-67.

Woodruff, C. Roy. *Alcoholism and Christian Experience.* Philadelphia: The Westminster Press, 1968.

Yates, Gayle Graham. *What Women Want: The Ideas of the Movement.* Cambridge, Massachusetts: Harvard University Press, 1975.

      . *Women in Contemporary Religion.* Course Manual for Independent Study. Minneapolis, Minnesota: Produced by Extension Independent Study, University of Minnesota, 1985.

Other Hazelden books that will interest you . . .

Not-God

A History of Alcoholics Anonymous
  by Ernest Kurtz, Ph.D.

The original, unabridged edition of the most complete history of A.A. ever written! This book contains anecdotes and excerpts from the diaries, correspondence, and memoirs of A.A.'s early figures. A fascinating, fast-moving, and authoritative account of the creation and development of the fellowship. 363 pp.
Order No. 1036

Hazelden—A Spiritual Odyssey

  by Damian McElrath, Ph.D.

Through four decades, Hazelden has treated more than 50,000 patients with one predominant concern—restoring human dignity. It is this belief that propels the mission of the foundation, and the spirit that has guided the growth of Hazelden.

This is the definitive history of Hazelden, both the idea and the physical reality. It delivers the far-reaching story of the historic revolution in the treatment of alcoholism, the tensions among founding leaders, and the debates that accompanied development at every turn in Hazelden's growth. A beautiful large hardcover edition, this book contains nearly 50 historic photographs. 174 pp.
Order No. 5004

For price and order information please call one of our Telephone Representatives. Ask for a free catalog describing nearly 1,500 items available through Hazelden Educational Materials.

HAZELDEN EDUCATIONAL MATERIALS

1-800-328-9000	**1-800-257-0070**	**1-612-257-4010**	**1-612-257-2195**
(Toll Free. U.S. Only)	(Toll Free. MN Only)	(AK and Outside U.S.)	(FAX)

Hazeldon Educational Services Int'l
Cork, Ireland
Int'l Code +21+961+269

Pleasant Valley Road • P.O. Box 176 • Center City, MN 55012-0176